Japanese City Pop
1975-1991

by Nicholas Stark

Copyright and Publication Information

Title: Japanese City Pop 1975-1991
Author: Nicholas Stark
Copyright © 2025 by Nicholas Stark
All rights reserved.
First Edition

No part of this publication may be reproduced, distributed, or transmitted in any form or by any means, including photocopying, recording, or other electronic or mechanical methods, without the prior written permission of the author or publisher, except in the case of brief quotations used for review, academic reference, or critical purposes, as permitted by copyright law.

For permission requests or other inquiries, please contact the author at:
starkbooks@outlook.com

This book is a work of non-fiction. While every effort has been made to ensure the accuracy of the information presented, the author does not assume any responsibility for errors, omissions, or differing interpretations of the content. All trademarks, service marks, product names, album covers or other associated imagery appearing in this work are the property of their respective owners and are used for informational or review purposes only. This book is not authorized, sponsored, or endorsed by any of the individuals, artists, record labels, or companies discussed herein.

The author has made a sincere attempt to credit all sources and referenced materials accurately. If you believe that any content in this book infringes on your rights, please contact the author to resolve the issue.

Paperback ISBN: 979-8-9997980-0-8
Hardback ISBN: 979-8-9997980-1-5
Digital ISBN: 979-8-9997980-2-2

Cover design by Fero
https://www.fiverr.com/ferofero_

Dedicated to my three grandmas.

To Eileen AKA Mawmaw, who very generously believes this will sell a million copies.

To Helen AKA Gram, my most avid fan. This book probably wouldn't have gotten finished without your encouragement.

To Elsie, my 'bonus Grandma' who I have been very blessed to have.

Table of Contents

What Is City Pop? 1

1975, Beginnings - Yumi Matsutoya 2
   What Is New Music? 3
   Horo - Sotsugyo Shashin - Band Wagon 4
   Songs 5
   Niagara Moon - First Album - Tropical Dandy 6
   Cobalt Hour 7
   Minako 8
   Caramel Mama 9

1976, The Formative Year - Minako Yoshida 10
   The City Pop Family 11
   Fireball Boy - Sometimes I... - Flapper 12
   Niagara Triangle Vol. 1 13
   Paper Moon - Super Market - Fashionable Lover 14
   Seychelles - Shady - Forgotten Summer 15
   Grey Skies 16
   The 14th Moon 17
   Char - Go! Go! Niagara - Lagoon 18
   Circus Town 19

1977, Refinement - Junko Ohashi 20
   Time - Love Collection - Mari & Red Stripes 21
   Twilight Zone 22
   Rainbow 23
   Our Connection - Takanaka - Deadly Drive 24
   Spacy 25
   Mind Drops - Funny Walkin' - Morning 26
   Sunshower 27
   Flying - Heart To Heart - Tokyo Special 28
   Char II - Have a Wine - City Lights By The Moonlight - Back Mirror 29
   Crystal City 30
   An Insatiable High - Endless Flight - BGM 31

1978, New Faces & New Problems - Taeko Ohnuki 32
   What Is Kayōkyoku? 33
   Caution! - Monsoon Baby - Swingy 34
   Shalom - Beni Suzume - Million Stars 35
   Paraiso - Saravah! - The Memories Are Too Beautiful 36
   It's A Poppin' Time 37
   Pacific 38
   Circus 1 - Stop Motion - Thrill 39
   South of The Border - Moonlight Singing - We Are Just Taking Off 40
   Mignonne 41
   Let's Do It 42
   Streamline '80 - Prismy - New York 43
   Apricot Jam 44
   Beginning 45
   Flush 46
   Go Ahead! 47
   Telescope - Love Heart - Loft Sessions Vol. 1 48

1979, Hitting The Street - Eiichi Ohtaki & Takashi Matsumoto 49
   City Pop and Synth-Pop 50
   Love 51
   White Heat - Pop Lady II - My True Face 52
   University Street - The Aegean Sea - Feelin' 53
   Summer Nerves - Summer-time Love Song - Show Me Your Smile 54
   Late Late Summer 55

Olive - Feel So Cool - American Comics 56
Sudden Wind - Cosmos '51 - Butterfly 57
Moonglow 58
Just My Feeling - My Love For You - Super Percussion Vol. 1 59
The Gallery In My Heart - Fascination - Rotation 60
Toy Box Act 1 - Street Sensation - Feeling Your Love 61
Dream In The Street 62

1980, The New Decade - Miki Matsubara 63
   Manhattan In The Rain - Krishna - Fantastic Love in Wonderland 64
   Pocket Park 65
   Love Songs 66
   Down Town 67
   Chef's Special - Northern Scene - Tasogare 68
   Hotel Without Time - Monday Morning - Made In Japan 69
   Romantique 70
   Song Writer - Magical Liqueur - Summer Wine 71
   Ride On Time 72
   Who Are You? 73
   Monochrome 74
   I'm In Love - Yume Hiko - Le Trottoir D'Après Midi 75
   Natural Road - Goodies - Miss M 76

1981, The Vacation Begins - Toshiki Kadomatsu 77
   The Visuals of City Pop 78
   A Long Vacation 79
   I'm Not In Love - U・TA・GE - Sorry 80
   Reflections 81
   Cupid - Hot Baby - Aventure 82
   Just Call Me Penny - Poker Face - Tea For Tears 83
   Sea Breeze 84
   神経衰弱 (Nervous Breakdown) - City - Joepo~1981Khz 85
   First Light 86
   Portrait 87
   哀しみの孔雀 (Peacock of Sorrow) - Harmotopia - Transit 88
   See You Last Night - Acoustic Moon - Monsters In Town 89
   Coconuts High - Air Kiss - Natural Woman 90

1982, Weekend Beach Trip - Meiko Nakahara 91
   For You 92
   I Love You So - Prophetic Dream - Myself 93
   Niagara Triangle Vol. 2 94
   Weekend Fly To The Sun 95
   The Pressures And The Pleasures - Love Message - Overlap 96
   Someday - Rumor - Pearl Piece 97
   One Night Stand - Awakening - Thru Traffic 98
   Coconuts House - Yoshino Fujimal -246:3AM 99
   色彩感覚 (Sense of Color) - Fly By Sunset - Warm Front 100
   Amore 101
   Light'n Up - Cliché - Seventh Avenue South 102
   Again - Le Plein Soleil - Midnight Cruisin' 103
   Heaven Beach 104
   Love Trip 105
   Moonlight Island - The 20th Anniversary - Shakin' It Up 106
   ~Friday Magic~ - Mata Ashita - 黄昏(Twilight) ~Postcard Fantasy ... 107

1983, City Pop Alive - Anri 108
   AB's - Shylights - Play Room ～ 戯れ 109
   Reincarnation - Next Door - Hold Me Tight 110
   In Motion - Vitamin E.P.O - ひとかけらの夏 (Fragment of Summer) . 111

Summer Breeze 112
On The City Shore - Seaside Lovers - Mistress 113
Fuyū-Kūkan 114
Bi・Ki・Ni 115
Melodies 116
"J" - Quiet Skies - J.I 117
Aqua City 118
Point Zero - Relief 72 Hours - Rosé 119
Can I Sing? - Sexy Robot - Signifie 120
Gentle Breeze - Noriki - Voyager 121
Full Moon - Green Water - Painted Woman 122
Timely!! 123

1984, Making Waves - Tatsuro Yamashita 124
Music Tech of The Times 125
What Can I Do? - Hi·Touch - Hi·Tech - Poison 21 126
Love Me - Gentle A Man - Each Time 127
River's Island - Sahara - Cryptograph 128
After 5 Clash 129
Variety 130
Sunshine Kiz - Visitors - More Relax 131
Big Wave 132
Coool - Gravy - Magical 133
Ocean Side 134
Summer Time Romance~From KIKI - Chocolate Lips - Dream Hunter 135
No Side - Never Ending Summer - Great Texan 136

1985, The Magical Midway - Momoko Kikuchi 137
City Pop's Unsung Heroes 138
Communication - Bitter And Sweet - Aru First 139
Gold Digger ~With True Love~ - This Boy - Just Tonight ... 140
Copine. - Espresso - Wave 141
Another Summer - Twilight Made... - Best Friend 142
Tropic Of Capricorn - Door Of The Heart - Purple Rose 143
Lovers Logic - Da・Di・Da - First Finale 144

1986, End Of The Golden Age - Omega Tribe 145
Ta Ta Ya My Love ~ARU 2nd.~ - Moods - Cologne 146
Pocket Music 147
Love Life - The Season In The Sun - Mystique 148
Touch And Go - Adventure - Summer Breeze 149
Beyond... - This Guy - Urban Blue 150
Navigator 151
Shake It Paradise - It's Friday - Mona Lisa 152
Trouble In Paradise - Crimson - Bells 153

1987, Calm Before The Storm - Mariya Takeuchi 154
Crystal Night - Sunset Hills Hotel - Groovin' 155
Summer Farewells - Escape From Dimension - MiDo 156
Free Drink - Sea Is A Lady - Request 157
A Slice Of Life - Masahito Arai - Steps 158
Quarterback - Kana - Milk 159

1988 & 1989, Goodbye Showa - Tesuji Hayashi 160
Before The Daylight - Catch The Nite - The Actress In The Mirror ... 161
Down Town Mystery - Radio Days - Boogie Woogie Mainland 162
Style - Wink - Aqua 163
僕の中の少年 (The Boy In Me) 164
Thanks Giving 165
Mind Game - Such A Funky Thang! - Delight Slight Light Kiss 166

Candee - Dark Crystal - Shambara 167
Hide'n' Seek - Time The Motion - Love Wars 168

1990 & 1991, The Lost Decade - Haruomi Hosono 169
City Pop's Decline 170
Let's Fall In Love Again - Self Portrait - Pagoda 171
New Moon - Angel Touch - Legacy Of You 172
Natsuko - Silent Moon - Gazer 173
L'arc~en~ciel - Miroir - Fire & Snow 174
Neutral - Moonset - All Is Vanity 175
Artisan 176
Self Jam - State Of Amber - Don't Be Afraid 177
On The Planet - Dawn Purple - Emotional 右側のハートたちへ 178
What Happened After? 179
The Rediscovery 180

References 182-183

Albums A-Z

- "J" - Jake H. Concepcion 117
- 246:3AM - Junichi Inagaki 99
- A Long Vacation - Eiichi Ohtaki 79
- A Slice Of Life - Taeko Ohnuki 158
- AB's - AB's 109
- Acoustic Moon - Rajie 89
- Adventure - Momoko Kikuchi 149
- After 5 Clash - Toshiki Kadomatsu 129
- Again - Kengo Kurozumi 103
- Air Kiss - Amii Ozaki 90
- All Is Vanity - Toshiki Kadomatsu 175
- American Comics - Yuko Sugita 56
- Amore - Alessandra Mussolini 101
- An Insatiable High - Masayoshi Takanaka 31
- Angel Touch - Cindy 172
- Another Summer - S. Kiyotaka & Omega Tribe 142
- Apricot Jam - Anri 44
- Aqua - Hiroshi Sato 163
- Aqua City - S. Kiyotaka & Omega Tribe 118
- Artisan - Tatsuro Yamashita 176
- Aru First - Aru Takamura 139
- Aventure - Taeko Ohnuki 82
- Awakening - Hiroshi Sato 98
- Back Mirror - Tetsuji Hayashi 29
- Band Wagon - Shigeru Suzuki 4
- Before The Daylight 161
- Beginning - Mariya Takeuchi 45
- Bells - Minako Yoshida 153
- Beni Suzume - Yumi Matsutoya 35
- Best Friend - Michiru Kojima 142
- Beyond... - Kiyotaka Sugiyama 150
- BGM - Fujimaru Band 31
- Bi・Ki・Ni - Anri 115
- Big Wave - Tatsuro Yamashita 132
- Bitter And Sweet - Akina Nakamori 139
- Boogie Woogie Mainland - Anri 162
- Butterfly - Kimiko Kasai 57
- Can I Sing? - Masayoshi Takanaka 120
- Candee - Candee 167
- Caramel Mama - Tin Pan Alley 9
- Catch The Nite - Miho Nakayama 161
- Caution! - Shigeru Suzuki 34
- Char - Char 18
- Char II - Have a Wine - Char 29
- Chef's Special - Kaoru Sudo 68
- Chocolate Lips - Chocolate Lips 135
- Cinderella Until 2:00 ~Friday Magic~ - Meiko Nakahara 107
- Circus I - Circus 39
- Circus Town - Tatsuro Yamashita 19
- City - Eri Hayakawa 85
- City Lights By The Moonlight - Tomoko Soryo 29
- Cliché - Taeko Ohnuki 102
- Cobalt Hour - Yumi Arai 7
- Coconuts High - Meiko Nakahara 90
- Coconuts House - Izumi Kobayashi 99
- Cologne - Kaoru Akimoto 146
- Communication - Junko Yagami 139
- Coool - Anri 133
- Copine. - Taeko Ohnuki 141
- Cosmos '51 - Shigeru Suzuki 57
- Crismon - Akina Nakamori 153
- Cryptograph - Asami Kobayashi 128
- Crystal City - Junko Ohashi & Minoya Central Station 30
- Crystal Night - 1986 Omega Tribe 155
- Cupid - Miki Matsubara 82
- Da・Di・Da - Yumi Matsutoya 144
- Dark Crystal - Minako Yoshida 167
- Dawn Purple - Yumi Matsutoya 178
- Deadly Drive - Ginji Ito 24
- Delight Slight Light Kiss - Yumi Matsutoya 166
- Don't Be Afraid - Cindy 177
- Door Of The Heart - Maiko Okamoto 143
- Down Town - EPO 67
- Down Town Mystery ("Night Time" Version) 162
- Dream Hunter - Eddy Yamamoto 135
- Each Time - Eiichi Ohtaki 127
- Emotional - 右側のハートたちへ - Carlos Toshiki 178
- Endless Flight - Masataka Matsutoya 31
- Escape From Dimension - Momoko Kikuchi 156
- Espresso - Rajie 141
- Fantastic Love In Wonderland - Takuya Takahashi 64
- Fascination - Asami Kado 60
- Fashionable Lover - Hi-Fi Set 14
- Feel So Cool - Takuya Takahashi 56
- Feelin' - Anri 53
- Feeling Your Love - Eri Ohno 61
- Fire & Snow - EPO 174
- First Album - Kaze 6
- First Finale - S. Kiyotaka & Omega Tribe 144
- First Light - Makoto Matsushita 86
- Flapper - Minako Yoshida 12
- Flush - Junko Ohashi 46
- Fly By Sunset - Ken Tamura 100
- Flying - Sumiko Yamagata 28
- For You - Tatsuro Yamashita 92
- Forgotten Summer - Yoshitaka Minami 15
- Free Drink - Jadoes 157
- Full Moon - Junko Yagami 122
- Funny Walkin' - Nanako Sato 26
- Fuyü-Kükan - Tomoko Aran 114
- Gazer - Minako Yoshida 173
- Gentle A Man - Hideki Saijo 127
- Gentle Breeze - Piper 121
- Go Ahead! - Tatsuro Yamashita 47
- Go! Go! Niagara - Eiichi Ohtaki 18
- Gold Digger ~With True Love~ - Toshiki Kadomatsu 140
- Goodies - EPO 76
- Gravy - Yasuko Agawa 133
- Great Texan - Terry Funk 136
- Green Water - Kunio Muramatsu 122
- Grey Skies - Taeko Ohnuki 16
- Groovin' - Toshinobu Kubota 155
- Harmotopia - Soap 88
- Heart To Heart - Rajie 28
- Heaven Beach - Anri 104
- Hi-Touch - Hi-Tech - EPO 126

Title - Artist	Page
Grey Skies - Taeko Ohnuki	16
Groovin' - Toshinobu Kubota	155
Harmotopia - Soap	88
Heart To Heart - Rajie	28
Heaven Beach - Anri	104
Hi·Touch - Hi-Tech - EPO	126
Hide'n' Seek - Miho Nakayama	168
Hold Me Tight - Yasuhiro Abe	110
Horo - Chu Kosaka	4
Hot Baby - Amii Ozaki	82
Hotel Without Time - Yumi Matsutoya	69
I Love You So - Tatsuhiko Yamamoto	93
I'm In Love - Fujiro	75
I'm Not In Love - Piper	80
In Motion - Minako Yoshida	111
It's A Poppin' Time - Tatsuro Yamashita	37
It's Friday - Jadoes	152
J.I - Junichi Inagaki	117
Joepo~1981Khz - EPO	85
Just Call Me Penny - Hitomi "Penny" Tohyama	83
Just Tonight - Kyosuke Kusunoki	140
Kana - Kanako Wada	159
Krishna - Yumi Murata	64
L'arc~en~ciel - Keiko Utsumi	174
Lagoon - Shigeru Suzuki	18
Late Late Summer - Bread & Butter	55
Le Plein Soleil - Tatsuhiko Yamamoto	103
Le Trottoir D'Après Midi - Rajie	75
Legacy Of You - Toshiki Kadomatsu	172
Let's Do It - Minako Yoshida	42
Let's Fall In Love Again - Kaoru Aizawa	171
Light'n Up - Minako Yoshida	102
Loft Sessions Vol. 1 - Various	48
Love - So Nice	51
Love Collection - Hi-Fi Set	21
Love Heart - Rajie	48
Love Life - Cindy	148
Love Me - Jackie Chan	127
Love Message - Akiko Mizuhara	96
Love Songs - Mariya Takeuchi	66
Love Trip - Takako Mamiya	105
Love Wars - Yumi Matsutoya	168
Lovers Logic - Piper	144
Made In Japan - Yuuko Shibuya	69
Magical - Junko Ohashi	133
Magical Liqueur - Yuko Iwasaki	71
Manhattan In The Rain - Kingo Hamada	64
Mari & Red Stripes - Masamichi Sugi & Red Stripes	21
Masahito Arai - Masahito Arai	158
Mata Ashita (See You Tomorrow) - Kazuhito Murata	107
Melodies - Tatsuro Yamashita	116
Midnight Cruisin' - Kingo Hamada	103
MiDo - Midori Hara	156
Mignonne - Taeko Ohnuki	41
Milk - Milk	159
Million Stars - Haruko Kuwana	35
Minako - Minako Yoshida	8
Mind Drops - Amii Ozaki	26
Mind Game - Miho Nakayama	166
Miroir - Momoko Kikuchi	174
Miss M - Mariya Takeuchi	76
Mistress - Beers	113
Mona Lisa - Akemi Ishii	152
Monday Morning - Bread & Butter	69
Monochrome - Minako Yoshida	74
Monsoon Baby - Yuko Sugita	34
Monsters In Town - Minako Yoshida	89
Moods - Meiko Nakahara	146
Moonglow - Tatsuro Yamashita	58
Moonlight Island - Haruko Kuwana	106
Moonlight Singing - Issei Okamoto	40
Moonset - Kiyotaka Sugiyama	175
More Relax - Tomoko Aran	131
Morning - Chu Kosaka	26
My Love For You - Jin Kirigaya	59
Myself - Miki Matsubara	93
Mystique - Anri	148
Natsuko - Carlos Toshiki & Omega Tribe	173
Natural Road - Hiroaki Igarashi	76
Natural Woman - Yumi Seino	90
Navigator - 1986 Omega Tribe	151
Neutral - Anri	175
Never Ending Summer - S. Kiyotaka & Omega Tribe	136
New Moon - Taeko Ohnuki	172
New York - Various	43
Next Door - Hitomi "Penny" Tohyama	110
Niagara Moon - Eiichi Ohtaki	6
Niagara Triangle Vol. 1 - Niagara Triangle	13
Niagara Triangle Vol. 2 - Niagara Triangle	94
No Side - Yumi Matsutoya	136
Noriki - Soichi Noriki	121
Northern Scene - Hiroaki Igarashi	68
Ocean Side - Momoko Kikuchi	134
Olive - Yumi Matsutoya	56
On The City Shore - Toshiki Kadomatsu	113
On The Planet - Meiko Nakahara	178
One Night Stand - Naomi Akimoto	98
Our Connection - Ayumi Ishida & Tin Pan Alley	24
Overlap - Masamichi Sugi	96
Pacific - Various	38
Pagoda - Junko Ohashi	171
Painted Woman - Masaki Matsubara	122
Paper Moon - Junko Ohashi	14
Paraiso - The Yellow Magic Band	36
Pearl Piece - Yumi Matsutoya	97
Play Room ～ 戯れ - Nina Atsuko	109
Pocket Music - Tatsuro Yamashita	147
Pocket Park - Miki Matsubara	65
Point Zero - Junko Ohashi	119
Poison 21 - Naomi Akimoto	126
Poker Face - Tatsuhiko Yamamoto	83
Pop Lady II - Yuuko Shibuya	52
Portrait - Mariya Takeuchi	87
Prismy - Amii Ozaki	43
Prophetic Dream - Akira Inoue	93
Purple Rose - Mariko Tone	143

Albums A-Z

Title	Page
Quarterback - Masanori Ikeda	159
Quiet Skies - Makoto Matsushita	117
Radio Days - Masayuki Suzuki	162
Rainbow - Junko Ohashi & Minoya Central Station	23
Reflections - Akira Terao	81
Reincarnation - Yumi Matsutoya	110
Relief 72 Hours - Yurie Kokubu	119
Request - Mariya Takeuchi	157
Ride On Time - Tatsuro Yamashita	72
River's Island - S. Kiyotaka & Omega Tribe	128
Romantique - Taeko Ohnuki	70
Rosé - Mari Iijima	119
Rotation - Shōgun	60
Rumor - EPO	97
Sahara - Rie Murakami	128
Saravah! - Yukihiro Takahashi	36
Sea Breeze - Toshiki Kadomatsu	84
Sea Is A Lady - Toshiki Kadomatsu	157
Seaside Lovers - Various	113
See You Last Night - Yumi Matsutoya	89
Self Jam - Hiroshi Sato	177
Seventh Avenue South - Yoshitaka Minami	102
Sexy Robot - Hitomi "Penny" Tohyama	120
Seychelles - Masayoshi Takanaka	15
Shady - Amii Ozaki	15
Shake It Paradise - Toshinobu Kubota	152
Shakin' It Up - Kaoru Hirose	106
Shalom - Junko Ohashi & Minoya Central Station	35
Shambara - Shambara	167
Show Me Your Smile - Haruko Kuwana	54
Shylights - Junichi Inagaki	109
Signifie - Taeko Ohnuki	120
Silent Moon - Yurie Kokubu	173
Someday - Motoharu Sano	97
Sometimes I... - Seri Ishikawa	12
Song Writer - Masamichi Sugi	71
Songs - Sugar Babe	5
Sorry - Mai Yamane	80
Sotsugyo Shashin - Hi-Fi Set	4
South of The Border - Yoshitaka Minami	40
Spacy - Tatsuro Yamashita	25
State Of Amber - Junko Yagami	177
Steps - Yurie Kokubu	158
Stop Motion - Amii Ozaki	39
Streamline '80 - Yumi Matsutoya	43
Street Sensation - Kinokuniya Band	61
Style - Keiko Kimura	163
Such A Funky Thang! - Toshinobu Kubota	166
Sudden Wind - Tatsuhiko Yamamoto	57
Summer Breeze - Miho Nakayama	149
Summer Breeze - Piper	112
Summer Farewells - Anri	156
Summer Nerves - Ryuichi Sakamoto	54
Summer Time Romance～From KIKI - Toshiki Kadomatsu	135
Summer Wine - Tetsuji Hayashi	71
Summer-time Love Song - The Milky Way	54
Sunset Hills Hotel - Sunset Hills Hotel	155
Sunshine Kiz - Piper	131
Sunshower - Taeko Ohnuki	27
Super Market - Hiroshi Sato	14
Super Percussion Vol. 1 - Tatsuo Hayashi	59
Swingy - Masamichi Sugi & Red Stripes	34
Ta Ta Ya My Love ~ARU 2nd.~ - Aru Takamura	146
Takanaka - Masayoshi Takanaka	24
Tasogare - Mai Yamane	68
Tea For Tears - Junko Ohashi	83
Telescope - Shigeru Suzuki	48
Thanks Giving - RA MU	165
The 14th Moon - Yumi Arai	17
The 20th Anniversary - Naomi Akimoto	106
The Actress In The Mirror - Meiko Nakahara	161
The Aegean Sea - Various	53
The Gallery In My Heart - Yumi Matsutoya	60
The Memories Are Too Beautiful - Junko Yagami	36
The Pressures And The Pleasures - Makoto Matsushita	96
The Season In The Sun - TUBE	148
This Boy - Hiroshi Sato	140
This Guy - Eddy Yamamoto	150
Thrill - Char	39
Thru Traffic - Narumin & Etsu	98
Time - Hiroshi Sato	21
Time The Motion - Kahoru Kohiruimaki	168
Timely!! - Anri	123
Tokyo Special - Kimiko Kasai	28
Toy Box Act 1 - Miharu Koshi	61
Transit - Yasuha	88
Tropif Of Capricorn - Momoko Kikuchi	143
Tropical Dandy - Haruomi Hosono	6
Trouble In Paradise - Anri	153
Twilight Made... - Hideki Saijo	142
Twilight Zone - Minako Yoshida	22
U・TA・GE - Yumi Seino	80
University Street - Anri	53
Urban Blue - Ken Kobayashi	150
Variety - Mariya Takeuchi	130
Visitors - Motoharu Sano	131
Vitamin E.P.O - EPO	111
Voyager - Yumi Matsutoya	121
Warm Front - Masayuki Kishi	100
Wave - Anri	141
We Are Just Taking Off - Sadistics	40
Weekend Fly To The Sun - Toshiki Kadomatsu	95
What Can I Do? - Keiko "Myrah" Tohyama	126
White Heat - Shigeru Suzuki	52
Who Are You? - Miki Matsubara	73
Wink - Miki Matsubara	163
Yoshino Fujimal - Yoshino Fujimaru	99
Yume Hiko - Mioko Yamaguchi	75
ひとかけらの夏 (Fragment of Summer) - Kazuhito Murata	111
僕の中の少年 (The Boy In Me) - Tatsuro Yamashita	164
哀しみの孔雀 (Peacock of Sorrow) - Anri	88
火の玉ボーイ (Fireball Boy) - Keiichi Suzuki & Moonriders	12
神経衰弱 (Nervous Breakdown) - Tomoko Aran	85
色彩感覚 (Sense of Color) - Tomoko Aran	100
黄昏(Twilight) ~Postcard Fantasy~ - Junko Ohashi	107

What Is City Pop?

City Pop is an incredibly unique genre in music history that originated from Japan during the 1970s and became tremendously popular throughout the 1980s. This was a period of prosperity after Japan had finally recovered from the devastation of World War 2 and became the world's third largest economy, only losing out to the USA and Soviet Union, although they would ultimately surpass the latter. In the 1980s the nation flourished under an unprecedented economy with an incredibly strong currency and skyrocketing stock prices. Japanese citizens were now among the wealthiest in the world on average and the dream of living an affluent urban life had never been more thrilling, or more attainable. In retrospect those times were just a little too good, as Japan was actually living in an economic bubble which was in no way sustainable. City Pop was the upbeat soundtrack to these illustrious times, although it's less of a strictly defined style and more like an overarching term used to describe the kind of music that appealed to urbanites. This is most easily understood via City Pop's common themes as the genre often celebrated and glamorized the kinds of activities a consumerist's paradise facilitated. Some of the style's most dependable subjects included summer trips to the beach, tropical vacations, late-night drives, romantic flings, and the crazy nightlife. These themes mirrored the positive outlook (and disposable income) Japanese people had during this period, although not all of City Pop's tunes were so celebratory. Many songs contemplated the unsettling feeling of loneliness that occasionally accompanied city life and tales of love gone awry were quite common. One of the genre's most iconic tracks, Plastic Love, has artist Mariya Takeuchi critiquing this vapid life of partying and meaningless romance by comparing it to plastic, a disposable and unfulfilling commodity. City Pop's actual sound was as exciting as its themes, being akin to a smoothie blended from Western genres which were popular at the time, with some of the most prominent influences being soul, funk, jazz, and adult-oriented rock. Plenty of your eighties favorites like disco and synth-pop were major components in City Pop as well, and as the genre develops you even start to see bits of hip-hop and R&B thrown into the mix. These familiar inspirations gave City Pop an inherently nostalgic appeal which often causes listeners to experience an uncanny sense of Déjà vu, even if they've never heard the music before. It can sometimes feel like City Pop is reawakening stowed away memories of a bustling 1980s Tokyo, but in some cases it illicit an uncomfortable feeling of melancholy, kind of like seeing old family photos you've long since forgotten about. City Pop eventually met its end in the 1990s when Japan's economic bubble inevitably burst, crashing the stock market and sending the populace back to a sobering reality. The style that was once synonymous with fun and luxury eventually fell into obscurity as Japan's citizens moved into The Lost Decade, a stagnant period which was a far cry from the financially blessed 1980s. City Pop's story would have likely ended there if not for a surprising resurgence in interest which began in the 2010s, largely thanks to certain songs like Plastic Love becoming massively popular on YouTube and elsewhere. Listeners from across the world were once again captured by the magic of City Pop, a genre which was paradoxically fresh and oddly familiar. This book hopes to chronicle the story of City Pop from its earliest days until its waning years and explore the style's most popular albums, hidden gems, and the weird bits of history in-between. It also serves as a tribute to the many artists who helped shape this wonderful style of music, especially for those who are no longer with us.

Top: A shot of Tokyo in the 1980s. Japan had a red-hot economy this decade, but Japanese culture and technology were also in a golden age. Cornerstones of Japanese and global commerce like the Nintendo Famicom video game console (released internationally as the Nintendo Entertainment System) were first created during the 1980s, and the Sony Walkman became a must-have device.
Center: Timely!! by Anri is one of City Pop's most cherished records and a perfect introduction to the genre.
Bottom: Mariya Takeuchi was one of City Pop's biggest stars in its prime who released many chart-topping singles and albums. Many decades later her face would become synonymous with City Pop in the west thanks to the surprising attention her song Plastic Love garnered online, a major moment in the genre's revitalization in interest.

1975, Beginnings

Choosing an exact starting point for something as complex as a genre is not an easy task, but 1975 seems to be the year when City Pop starts to crystallize. This is owed to the gradual transformation of Japan's folk influenced New Music scene into something more commercially digestible, as well as the rise of some fresh faces on the block. Established artists such as Haruomi Hosono and Shigeru Suzuki were evolving their sound from its folk inspired roots and lending their support to a marginally younger generation with their band Tin Pan Alley. Meanwhile some new artists were hoping to express themselves through their music, such as the bombastic Minako Yoshida who made her debut in 1973. Future "King of City Pop" Tatsuro Yamashita and genre mainstay Taeko Ohnuki were in the niche band Sugar Babe, and they were in the process of creating their debut album titled Songs with help from Eiichi Ohtaki. Yumi Arai was busy creating Cobalt Hour, an album which may just be City Pop's firstborn child due to its blending of genres and uniquely Western pop sound. Arai was not alone in this effort though, since the members of Tin Pan Alley as well as Tatsuro Yamashita, Taeko Ohnuki and Minako Yoshida all contributed. This set a precedent for the developing style as highly collaborative and familial, with many of the same faces showing up frequently to help each other out. City Pop will prove to be defined by this web of collaborators, as some musicians appear time and time again to slowly shape its identity, and many of the genre's founding figures rose to prominence here.

Yumi Matsutoya

Throughout the history of City Pop one face remains a constant from its creation until the style's twilight years, that being Yumi Matsutoya, also known by her maiden name Yumi Arai. It would be something of a disservice to call her merely a force in Japanese music throughout the late twentieth century, as she was more akin to a hurricane. Matsutoya was responsible for creating dozens of full-length albums, typically releasing one or two per year, with more than twenty of them securing that precious number one spot on the weekly Oricon charts. That's not to mention all her hit singles and songs written for other artists, as well as her many tracks featured in television, movies, and commercials. Her innumerable accomplishments could take up the entire page but like any good origin story Matsutoya had a humble beginning. Her debut single No Need To Reply from 1972 sold a paltry three hundred copies, but she would eventually find success thanks to her fresh approach to pop music heard in albums such as Cobalt Hour and The 14th Moon. Matsutoya was highly influential in evolving Japanese music by incorporating an American and European pop sound to create memorable tunes, which were often complemented by a healthy injection of meaningful lyrics. Whether it was tales of nostalgic school graduations or romance long since past, you could always rely on Matsutoya to deliver a quality song that made a lot of money. In relation to City Pop there's an argument to be made that she did it first, although with something as subjective and nuanced as musical genres there's rarely a definitive beginning. At the very least she was an integral founder of the style who helped set a precedent with some of City Pop's hallmarks such as its Western influence, blending of genres and themes targeting an urban audience. Yumi Matsutoya is a legend whose influence can be felt on decades of Japanese music, and she has more than earned her spot in history.

Top: Yumi Matsutoya as seen on the cover of Yuming Banzai, showing off a totally crazy outfit. Bottom: A picture of her from back when she was still Yumi Arai.

What is New Music?

In order to fully understand the origins of City Pop it's important to take a look at its predecessor, the even more vaguely titled New Music. The genre may have the least helpful descriptor in music history, but it's actually fairly easy to explain from a historical context. During the 1960s Japan took influence from the United States' own renewed interest in the folk genre, although this type of music often carried a certain stigma with it of being anti-establishment, and on the more extreme end it was even thought of as pro-communist. This wasn't helped by the proliferation of the Second Red Scare, a post World War 2 response to the rising threat that the Soviet Union posed to the United States. Throughout the following decades paranoia about theoretical communist infiltrators ran rampant and government action was often taken to try and suppress it. This sometimes included messing with those pesky folk artists, with a prominent example being Pete Seeger of the Weavers. Seeger was accused of being a communist sympathizer and was even brought to testify before Congress over these allegations and was even convicted of being in contempt of court, but these charges were eventually dropped. Due to the atmosphere of the times these folk artists were often relegated to performing at fringe venues such as college campuses or small concerts, environments which gave the music an even bigger counter-culture audience. This feeling carried over well to post-war Japan's youth, who were becoming quite the little rascals themselves. Their approach to folk was similarly free spirited and it was often intentionally designed to contrast music from Japan's prior generations. Japanese music up to this point typically espoused classic themes such as love and rarely dared to challenge national authority directly, something which Japan's next generation were much more willing to do. This sentiment partnered with a blend of folk and rock inspiration, plus a healthy dosage of cool seventies attitude which all came together to make something innovative, New Music. This not very creatively titled New Music was less overtly political in nature compared to the folk it derived from, but it nonetheless evoked a youthful spirit which was more concerned about making music personal to that generation. New Music was often quite urban-centric, as its biggest demographic were those hip, young Tokyo dwellers who were disillusioned with the concrete world of modernity. Many of those themes which appealed to urbanites would eventually carry over into New Music's soon to be born offspring, which we now know as City Pop. It's also worth noting that early on in City Pop's life it was still commonly referred to as New Music, but in recent times the two have been more clearly understood and separated. As with any genre it's difficult to place an exact moment when City Pop had definitively split from New Music, but Yumi Arai's album Cobalt Hour or Songs by Sugar Babe may be good benchmarks. Arai took those more personal themes that Japan's youth were fond of and combined them with a catchy pop sound that ensured she would have some big hits, but New Music isn't City Pop's only parent. The genre was heavily influenced by many Western styles including jazz, pop rock, soul and more, so New Music can't take all of the credit here. While New Music always appealed to a certain small niche the same can't be said about City Pop, which eventually became enormously popular and often topped the charts. Perhaps the greatest irony of all is how the counterculture sounds of folk and New Music slowly gave rise to City Pop, a mainstream genre that actually celebrated the very same modernity those anti-establishment folk artists were skeptical of.

Top: Happy End's 1971 album Windy City Romance is a folk rock masterpiece and may be the poster child for what's considered New Music. The members Haruomi Hosono, Eiichi Ohtaki, Takashi Matsumoto and Shigeru Suzuki were all integral players throughout City Pop's lifespan, appearing on countless albums.
Center: Yumi Arai blurred the line between New Music and what we would now think of as City Pop and has had one of the most prolific careers in Japanese music history.
Bottom: Pete Seeger and The Weavers were prominent folk musicians during America's renewed interest in the genre. Seeger was also a renowned activist who promoted causes such as civil rights and rejection of war.

Horo

Artist: Chu Kosaka
Release: January 25, 1975
Label: Mushroom

Chu Kosaka's Horo has a legacy in the Japanese music world for its innovative soul inspired sound, but for City Pop specifically it's also quite notable for including nearly every one of its founders in the credits. Tin Pan Alley, Tatsuro Yamashita and Minako Yoshida all appear here, with Haruomi Hosono acting as its co-producer and composing many tracks. Kosaka and Hosono actually went way back, as they were both members of the short lived band Apryl Fool, the predecessor to Hosono's band Happy End. The result of all these brilliant minds joining forces was one of the year's best albums, especially for those who enjoy smooth soul music with a cool rock spin. Horo also serves as a prelude to the genre blending that would become so popular in the years yet to come and the significant role collaboration would play for City Pop as a whole.

- A1. Horo
- A2. Kikansha
- A3. Bon Voyage Hatoba
- A4. Hisamezuki No Sketch
- A5. Yugata Love
- B1. Shirakechimauze
- B2. Ryusei Toshi
- B3. Tsurube Ito
- B4. Furaibo

Sotsugyo Shashin

Artist: Hi-Fi Set
Release: February 5, 1975
Label: Express, Alfa

Formed in 1974 with members Shigeru Okawa, Junko Yamamoto and Toshihiko Yamamoto, Hi-Fi Set would go on to become mainstays in City Pop, releasing albums almost annually throughout the years when it was a popular genre. The two Yamamotos are actually a husband and wife pair, giving Hi-Fi Set a unique selling point. Yumi Arai would be a notable contributor to the album and frequently collaborated with the group, writing tracks A3, B2 and B4. Sotsugyou Shashin is a great first album for the newly formed group that shows off the vocal talent the trio would become known for, and includes some memorable, fun and funky songs. A3 or Graduation Photo would end up being used often for graduation ceremonies in Japan around the time, and many graduates from the period likely look back on the song with nostalgia.

- A1. オーバーチャ
- A2. エイジズ・オブ・ロック・アンド・ロール
- A3. 卒業写真
- A4. 胸のぬくもり
- A5. 今日と明日の間に
- A6. 大きな街
- B1. 美術館
- B2. 十円木馬
- B3. フィッシュ・アンド・チップス
- B4. 海を見ていた午後
- B5. 愛の花咲く道

Band Wagon

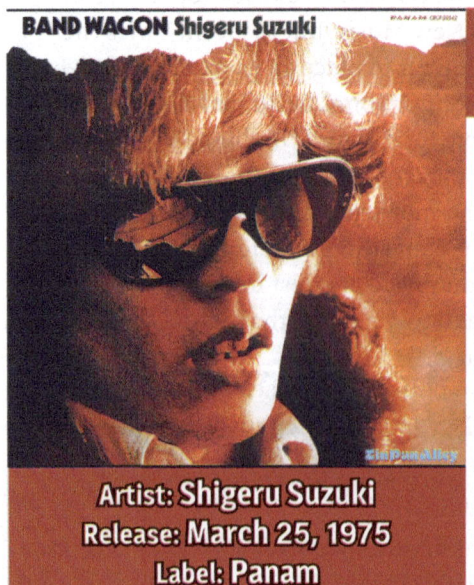

Artist: Shigeru Suzuki
Release: March 25, 1975
Label: Panam

After the band Happy End disbanded in 1972 Shigeru Suzuki decided to take a shot at a solo album, albeit with some help from a former bandmate. Takashi Matsumoto was responsible for writing lyrics for the entire album, and he would go on to become one of the most prolific lyricists of the era with appearances on hundreds of albums. Band Wagon may be slightly too early to the party to really count as City Pop, but it nonetheless features a soundscape that will feel familiar to fans of the genre, and it's especially enjoyable for those who enjoy the soft rock side of things. The album contains a great blend of soft rock with a bit of funk and soul thrown into the mix, making it the perfect addition to a seventies music playlist. Suzuki gets many chances to flaunt his guitar skills here and the album's instrumental tracks have a lot of character.

- A1. 砂の女
- A2. 八月の匂い
- A3. 微熱少年
- A4. スノー・エクスプレス
- B1. 人力飛行機の夜
- B2. 100ワットの恋人
- B3. ウッド・ペッカー
- B4. 夕焼け波止場
- B5. 銀河ラプソディー

Songs

Left: A picture of Sugar Babe all together, a group of aspiring artists who couldn't have guessed how impactful their work would be.
Center: The cover of Songs featuring an illustration of an elderly duo is actually a reproduction of a photo by Nico Jess.
Right: The back of the CD release with pictures of Tatsuro Yamashita, Taeko Ohnuki, Kunio Muramatsu, Kikuo Wanikawa & Akihiko Noguchi.

Artist:
Sugar Babe

Release:
April 25, 1975

Label:
Niagara Records
Elec Records

Track List:

A1. Show

A2. Down Town

A3. 蜃気楼の街 (Mirage City)

A4. 風の世界 (Wind World)

A5. ためいきばかり (Nothing But Sighs)

B1. いつも通り (As Always)

B2. すてきなメロディー (Beautiful Melody)

B3. 今日はなんだか (What Is It Today?)

B4. 雨は手のひらにいっぱい (Rain Fills The Palm Of My Hand)

B5. 過ぎ去りし日々"60's Dream" (Days Gone By "60's Dream")

B6. Sugar

In 1975 the niche band Sugar Babe released their one and only album, the humbly titled Songs. Sugar Babe was formed in 1973 by a group of young musicians whose taste in music was somewhat unorthodox for the time, as they were heavily inspired by Western artists and genres from the 1950s and 1960s. Bandmate Tatsuro Yamashita was a particularly huge fan of American pop artists like The Beach Boys, and he would eventually become known as the "King of City Pop", releasing albums throughout the genre's entire life and influencing Japanese music like few others could. Then there was Taeko Ohnuki, a talented vocalist and songwriter who would fill a similar role as one of City Pop's founders who contributed to dozens of records. Another important figure for Songs was Eiichi Ohtaki, a former member of the New Music band Happy End who had recently launched his own record label, Niagara Records. Songs was chosen to be the label's very first release, although the production wasn't all sunshine and seventies vibes. The studio they recorded in was hot and cramped, while Ohtaki was naturally stressed about this being his label's first album, leading to a lot of arguments between himself and the younger band members. Despite these hurdles Songs turned out quite well, partially thanks to Ohtaki's unique approach to mixing which gave the album an indie sound that felt more like an American record. Songs featured a unique blend of soft rock, folk, soul, and a bit of pop which didn't neatly fall into any preconceived genre, making it one of the first albums which fit the City Pop descriptor. You can also see some of the urban-centric concepts City Pop would become known for in tracks like Down Town, one of Sugar Babe's most popular tunes. Featuring lyrics about a night on the town courtesy of Ginji Ito, it makes for a great singalong choice thanks to its joyous tone and memorable instrumentals. Both Yamashita and Taeko Ohnuki get a chance to show off their vocal talent here, with Wind World being a lovely display of the young artists' skills, but the whole band gives some great performances. Fun and energetic, Songs is the perfect album to play to make a good day even better, or to turn a bad one around. The album's eleven tracks are all classics from these blossoming artists, although Songs wasn't all that popular on release. The album flew under the radar for many consumers at the time, possibly due to how unconventional it was, but more fans eventually gravitated towards this gem. Sugar Babe ultimately disbanded in 1976, and its members split to pursue solo careers, leaving Songs as a true once in a lifetime creation and debatably the first City Pop album ever.

Niagara Moon

Artist: Eiichi Ohtaki
Release: May 30, 1975
Label: Niagara Records, Elec Records

Niagara Moon is the second album by Eiichi Ohtaki, and it's also the second album released under his label Niagara Records. Many of the prominent figures from this very early stage of City Pop's life show up here, such as the members of Sugar Babe who can be heard on track B5. You can also hear Tin Pan Alley in a few songs, as well as mainstays like Ginji Ito and Hiroshi Sato. It'd be a stretch to really call this one City Pop, since it's more so a folk and pop rock album akin to what his fellow Happy End bandmates were making, but it's still worth checking out to enjoy Ohtaki's unique style. He especially gets great use out of some unconventional sounding vocals, and the way he's able to modulate his voice stands out. The cover is also awesome since it advertises that the album is "good at COOL time", which does sound rather appealing.

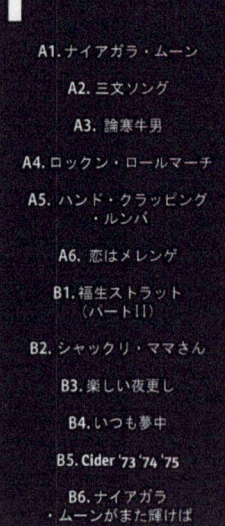

A1. ナイアガラ・ムーン
A2. 三文ソング
A3. 論寒牛男
A4. ロックン・ロールマーチ
A5. ハンド・クラッピング・ルンバ
A6. 恋はメレンゲ
B1. 福生ストラット（パートII）
B2. シャックリ・ママさん
B3. 楽しい夜更し
B4. いつも夢中
B5. Cider '73 '74 '75
B6. ナイアガラ・ムーンがまた輝けば

Artist: Kaze
Release: June 5, 1975
Label: Panam

First Album

Don't be too shocked when I tell you this was the first album by Kaze, a folk duo who were active during the mid-1970s. Within the context of City Pop, the album is interesting for having a lengthy credits filled with the year's starring artists. You can spot most of Tin Pan Alley (minus Shigeru Suzuki), Tatsuro Yamashita, Taeko Ohnuki, Minako Yoshida, and even all the members of Hi-Fi Set. The appearances from all of Hi-Fi Set here are quite notable, as it's rare to see the entire trio present for an album beyond their own. First Album is firmly rooted in a classic folk sound, much like albums such as Songs by Sugar Babe, and others which were inspired by New Music. As such it's a noteworthy snapshot in the genre's development, since you'll almost never see all of these artists working together on a folk album past 1975.

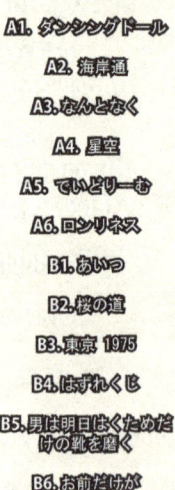

A1. ダンシングドール
A2. 海岸通
A3. なんとなく
A4. 星空
A5. ていどりーむ
A6. ロンリネス
B1. あいつ
B2. 桜の道
B3. 東京 1975
B4. はずれくじ
B5. 男は明日はくためだけの靴を磨く
B6. お前だけが

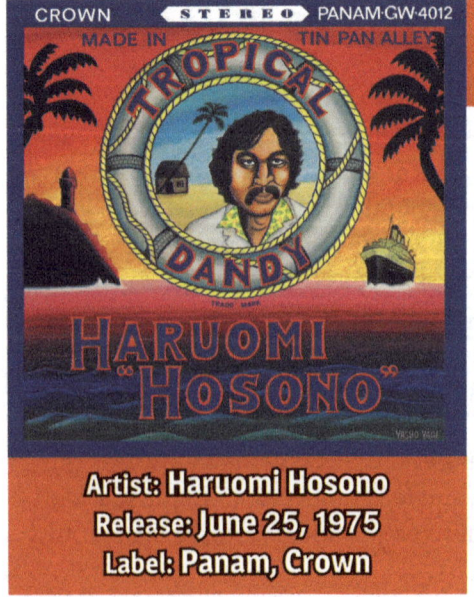

Artist: Haruomi Hosono
Release: June 25, 1975
Label: Panam, Crown

Tropical Dandy

Tropical Dandy doesn't neatly fall into the category of City Pop, as Hosono himself was never really known for creating albums which fit the style. However, his many contributions to the genre are unmistakable, as he can be heard playing on innumerable City Pop records. While it is credited as a Hosono album his latest band Tin Pan Alley played an integral role in its creation, and all the bandmates are accounted for here. Thematically the album does set a notable precedent with its chill pacific sounds and subject matter, both of which will be explored quite often in the following years and become well associated with the genre. Here you can really see one of Japanese music's most varied artists at work crafting incredibly unique tracks, and his influence continues to be felt all throughout not just City Pop, but genres of all kinds, especially electronic music.

A1. チャタヌガ・チュー・チュー
A2. ハリケーン・ドロシー
A3. 絹街道
A4. 熱帯夜
A5. 北京ダック
B1. 漂流記
B2. ハニー・ムーン
B3. 三時の子守唄
B4. 三時の子守唄
B5. 漂流記

Cobalt Hour

Left: The single release for I Want To Return To That Day and A Little Crush.
Center: The cover of Cobalt Hour which depicts Arai as an airline stewardess drawn by Kenkichi Sato, welcoming us on a musical adventure.
Right: The single release for Rouge Message and Don't Ask Me Anything.

Artist:
Yumi Arai

Release:
June 20, 1975

Label:
Express

Track List:

A1. Cobalt Hour

A2. 卒業写真
(Graduation Photo)

A3. 花紀行
(Traveler's Journal)

A4. 何もきかないで
(Don't Ask Me Anything)

A5. ルージュの伝言
(Rouge Message)

B1. 航海日誌
(Ship's Log)

B2. Chinese Soup

B3. 少しだけ片想い
(A Little Crush)

B4. 雨のステイション
(Rainy Staycation)

B5. アフリカへ行きたい
(I Want To Go To Africa)

In June of 1975 Yumi Arai (later known as Yumi Matsutoya) released her third album, Cobalt Hour. Although the style was still in its infancy, Cobalt Hour could be thought of as one of the first albums to really capture the characteristics that City Pop would be associated with. This is most noticeable when comparing it to New Music or even other Kayōkyoku albums from the same period, as it begins to sound more similar to modern pop and emphasize the blending of genres, while its themes of travel and nostalgia became permanent aspects of City Pop. Whether or not it's the first 'true' City Pop album is ultimately a matter of philosophy, but Cobalt Hour nonetheless left behind a massive legacy. The album begins with the titular Cobalt Hour and the pitter patter of a plane's engine midflight to take us on an adventure, setting up travel as a theme which eventually becomes ingrained in City Pop's identity. Many other the songs in Cobalt Hour also revolve around travel to foreign places, such as B1/Ship's Log, Chinese Soup and B5/I Want To Go To Africa. Trips to fun locations such as the beach appear very often in this album and City Pop in general, seemingly as a reflection of the prosperity people in Japan enjoyed at the time, and thus the ease at which they could travel. The highlight song of the album is track A5, Rouge Message, which was originally released as a single that same year. Featuring lyrics about a girl going on trip to meet her boyfriend's mother, only to discover the boyfriend has been cheating, this incredibly catchy song with an unforgettable intro may ironically owe its quality to jealousy. At the time Yumi Arai would utilize different bands depending on if she was touring or recording, with the recording band being considered superior. During one recording session some members of the tour band asked to join in for Rouge Message to strut their skills. However, Masataka Matsutoya, who was in charge of the arrangement, considered the tour band's session to be lackluster and gave them a score of "60 points." That's when he got the idea to add Tatsuro Yamashita to the track, who in turn brought Minako Yoshida, Taeko Ohnuki and Kayoko Ishu to perform alongside him. The result was a memorable chorus which sounded distinctly like an American pop song, making it a huge hit. Rouge Message would later be featured as the opening song for the Studio Ghibli movie Kiki's Delivery Service in 1989, furthering the track's popularity and giving it a permanent pop culture home. Cobalt Hour is still excellent listen 50 years later, and it comes highly recommended for anyone interested in hearing the origins of the genre, or fans of pop music in general. A fantastic 'start' to City Pop, if you'd like to think of it in that way.

Minako

Left: A picture of Yoshida from inside the album, which is tinted pink like the rest of Minako.
Center: The very pink cover of Minako with an illustration by Kenkichi Sato, it certainly stands out among its competition.
Right: The back of Minako featuring Yoshida looking very cool, courtesy of costumer designer Anko Miyasato and stylist Fumiko Miyatani.

After releasing her debut album Door to Winter in 1973 Minako Yoshida would return two years later with her next venture; Minako. As one of the founding figures of City Pop Yoshida had previously contributed backing vocals on Cobalt Hour, and she would go on to become one of the most consistent and prominent figures of the entire genre. Minako is a very early release in City Pop's chronology, and so many of the hallmarks of the genre were still being established, but the album still feels like it fits the classification. This is especially true when considering who was involved in making it, as City Pop staples such as members of Tin Pan Alley, Hiroshi Sato, Ginji Ito, Tatsuro Yamashita and more all participated, giving us another early look at the style's emphasis on tightly knit collaboration. Although definitely leaning more towards being a soul album akin to her earlier Door to Winter, Minako still includes several songs with a distinctly pop sound, and it especially features many jazz elements which would become a staple of the style going forward. The album begins with the very lengthy To Everything That Changes, an over eight-minute-long ballad about the transitory nature of life to set the mood. This song was borrowed from Quincy Jones' 1974 album Body Heat, with an increased runtime and some changes throughout. Yoshida would become very well known for these long running songs, with many of her biggest hits defying convention by being more than twice the length of typical tracks. This then flows directly into the noticeably more uplifting A2/Rainbow Sea Line, a track which feels much more in line with the mood typically associated with City Pop. It's a romantic and incredibly jazzy number with some passionate singing from Yoshida, while A4/Myself was composed by Eiichi Ohtaki and sticks out as one of the album's most fun tracks with its doo-wop inspired backing vocals. Minako also includes a cover of Yumi Arai's song Chinese Soup, which she had previously performed in Cobalt Hour. Yoshida's version includes some noticeable differences compared to the Arai rendition; whereas Arai's begins with a laid-back instrumental session, Yoshida's instead has a more aggressive approach with Yoshida repeating 'CHINESE SOUP!'. You can imagine the Arai version being performed in a piano bar and the more eccentric Yoshida variant accompanying an over-the-top burlesque show, demonstrating the differences in musical philosophies the two have as leading ladies of City Pop. Minako provides a unique look into primordial City Pop and displays Yoshida's blossoming talent and identity very well.

Artist:
Minako Yoshida

Release:
October 25, 1975

Label:
RCA

Track List:

A1. 移りゆくすべてに
(To Everything That Changes)

A2. レインボー・シー・ライン
(Rainbow Sea Line)

A3. 住みなれた部屋で
(In A Familiar Room)

A4. わたし
(Myself)

B1. 夢を追って
(Chasing Dreams)

B2. チャイニーズ・スープ
(Chinese Soup)

B3. パラダイスへ
(To Paradise)

B4. 時の中へ
(Into Time)

B5. ろっかばいまいべいびい
(Rock A Bye My Baby)

Caramel Mama

Left: The four members of the band; Shigeru Suzuki, Haruomi Hosono, Tatsuo Hayashi, Masataka Matsutoya.
Center: The cover of Caramel Mama which depicts a blurry city scene.
Right: The back of Caramel Mama showing off the band's unique painted logo and a floral design.

Artist:
Tin Pan Alley

Release:
November 25, 1975

Label:
Panam

Track List:

A1. Caramel Rag

A2. Chopper's Boogie

A3. はあどぼいるど町
(Hado Island Town)

A4. 月にてらされて
(By The Moonlight)

A5. Choo Choo Gatta Got '75

B1. She is Gone

B2. ソバカスのある少女
(A Girl With Freckles)

B3. Jackson

B4. Yellow Magic Carnival

B5. Ballade Of Aya

After the legendary New Music band Happy End disbanded Haruomi Hosono launched a new musical venture in the form of Caramel Mama alongside Masataka Matsutoya, Shigeru Suzuki and Tatsuo Hayashi in 1973. This original Caramel Mama branding wouldn't last that long since they ultimately changed their name to Tin Pan Alley, a reference to New York City's historical Tin Pan Alley, which housed various music publishing businesses from 1880 until the Great Depression. After reforming as Tin Pan Alley they would release the 1975 album Caramel Mama, a reference to the band's original name. While the album itself doesn't comfortably fall in line with City Pop, the actual members of the band had an undeniable influence on the genre. Shigeru Suzuki would lend his guitar playing, arranging, and songwriting talents to a substantial number of City Pop albums while releasing a few records of his own (including Band Wagon the very same year). Tatsuo Hayashi became one of the most prominent drummers of the era, while Masataka Matsutoya can be viewed as one of the unsung heroes of the genre as he was involved with arranging and producing for many of City Pop's most recognizable artists. Matsutoya becomes especially important for his integral role working on albums with Yumi Arai, who he'd later marry. Finally, there was Haruomi Hosono, who left a permanent mark on Japanese music history and influenced styles far beyond just City Pop, notably as a member of the electronic pioneers in Yellow Magic Orchestra. Caramel Mama is an album which features a little bit of everything ranging from folk, pop, rock, soul, funk and even some country, but it all still manages to work together. The opening song Caramel Rag starts us off with some light piano before getting a little odder with sound effects straight out of Looney Tunes. This includes a man screaming "Aughhh!!!", an explosion and the cooing of a chicken, but this still miraculously makes for an enjoyable song. Chopper's Boogie favors the rock elements and contains some excellent instrumentals, while the bizarrely titled Choo Choo Gatta Got '75 gets wonderful use of its chorus provided by the likes of Taeko Ohnuki and Tatsuro Yamashita. She is Gone is an all-English song which would feel right at home on American radio in the seventies, and there's even a surprise cover of the country song Jackson to show the band's eclectic musical taste. Although maybe not quite City Pop, the album contains a diverse set of songs from these four legends of Japanese music, making Caramel Mama come highly recommended. Get familiar with these four men, City Pop may very well owe its existence to them.

1976, The Formative Year

If 1975 was the year when City Pop was first made manifest, then 1976 was when its identity started to solidify. Throughout the year fresh faced artists such as Char, Junko Ohashi and Amii Ozaki would leave their mark on the genre, and we were also graced with the unique fusion visions of Hiroshi Sato and Masayoshi Takanaka. Perhaps the most impactful event in the long term were the solo debuts of Tatsuro Yamashita and Taeko Ohnuki from Sugar Babe, whose first albums didn't make much of a splash, although they were the beginnings of long and fruitful careers as two of the style's most influential figures. Yamashita kicked things off with Circus Town, an album which was created in both New York and Los Angeles, and this strategy of recording abroad would be utilized by many other City Pop artists who sought a sprinkling of Western magic in their music. Those collaborative efforts only intensified this year with Minako Yoshida putting together one hell of a crew for Flapper, while the trio of Tatsuro Yamashita, Ginji Ito and Eiichi Ohtaki came together for a new band, Niagara Triangle. Many of the themes City Pop would become well known for were deeply explored the year, most notably those relating to the summertime and tropical getaways. Niagara Triangle, Yoshitaka Minami and Shigeru Suzuki all gave us beachside vacations with albums like Lagoon, setting a precedent for this topic which other artists will come back to time and time again. Foundational albums await in 1976, and slowly but surely the concept of City Pop was coming together.

Minako Yoshida

One of the most unique and significant figures in the history of City Pop is Minako Yoshida, although she was there before the genre really started. Yoshida released her debut album Door To Winter in 1973 which was fully composed by her and featured the members of Tin Pan Alley as the band, serving as a prime example of the early City Pop family being formed. She would later find herself working alongside Yumi Matsutoya as a backing vocalist, among other projects, but her most well-known collaborations are likely with Tatsuro Yamashita. Yoshida was the primary lyricist for many of his early albums including Spacy and For You, making them one of the most consistent tag-teams the genre had ever seen. When it came to Yoshida's own projects her style and overall identity is quite different from City Pop's other recognizable female artists, as her music often had a certain edge and mystique to it. This is most easily seen in her album's covers, which sometimes went for a mysterious or even dark look, contrasting the friendly visuals City Pop is well associated with. That's not to say that Yoshida was gloomy all the time, as she often let loose with some incredibly fun and joyous tunes, but they always had that signature Yoshida flair to them. While most artists of the time made their tracks to fit that radio appropriate three-minute runtime, Yoshida bucked this trend by making her songs into lengthy experiences. Many of her most popular tunes are five, six, or even nearing eight minutes long, making them feel like art projects which exist to express herself rather than trying to conform to the industry standard. Whether it was one of her signature lengthy tracks with poetic lyrics, or something lighter and fun, you can always expect Yoshida to deliver memorable songs only she could craft. Yoshida is a foundational part of City Pop with years of fantastic albums to dig into and the genre wouldn't be the same without her innovative vision.

Top: Minako Yoshida was deeply involved with City Pop from the very beginning.
Bottom: Yoshida as seen on the cover of Twilight Zone, a perfect example of the more gritty image she often cultivated.

The City Pop Family

City Pop is a genre that is uniquely defined by a close-knit group of artists which I have adorably dubbed the "City Pop Family". This "family" is made up of an interconnected web of prominent musicians who collaborated very often, forming something akin to a cast of characters who make regular appearances throughout City Pop's history. In the early days many of these relationships blossomed from the members of Haruomi Hosono's bands Happy End and Tin Pan Alley, all of whom left their own marks on City Pop and beyond. Many of the prototypical City Pop albums were influenced by these men, with the likes of Shigeru Suzuki and Masataka Matsutoya being especially important for their constant work as arrangers and performers, while Takashi Matsumoto became a lyrical juggernaut across many different genres. From there a sort of cross pollination began with many more artists being brought into the fold, such as Minako Yoshida, Yumi Arai, as well as the Sugar Babe members Tatsuro Yamashita and Taeko Ohnuki. These individuals would all frequently appear on each other's projects, making the credits list for many City Pop albums look quite similar, but that's far from a bad thing. Since these old reliables showed up all the time there's a consistent quality throughout City Pop, and these masters of their craft always gave a stunning performance. Sometimes these musical endeavors resulted in more than just camaraderie and good music; every now and then two artists fell in love. Yumi Arai and Masataka Matsutoya got married in 1976 and from then on Masataka worked as a producer and arranger on nearly all of her albums. This resulted in a dominant streak for the Matsutoyas with virtually all of Yumi's albums reaching the number one weekly ranking and securing her legacy as one of Japan's most popular artists of all time. Husband and wife duo Ken Sato and Junko Ohashi didn't mingle with the previously mentioned figures much, but they were responsible for creating some of the first albums that are easily recognizable as City Pop. Possibly the most dynamite pairing for this style is Tatsuro Yamashita and Mariya Takeuchi, and if Yamashita is the "King of City Pop" then it's fair to call Takeuchi the queen. The two worked wonders with each other long before they were married though, as Yamashita often created compositions and performed for Takeuchi's earlier albums. 1984's Plastic Love may be the single most well-known City Pop song and both of them were involved with making it, as Takeuchi composed the track and wrote lyrics while Yamashita played various instruments. The power of love helped to make some great albums, but many other platonic team-ups resulted in music making magic. Toshiki Kadomatsu and Anri's composer and artist partnership resulted in Heaven Beach and Timely!!, two of the most celebrated and beloved albums of the genre. Tetsuji Hayashi was another major name in the space who worked with several hugely popular artists, and a lot of our preconceptions about what City Pop sounds like comes from his work. That's not to mention the many dependable session musicians who had close ties to the "family" but don't get enough credit for their impact on the style, some of whom are discussed later as some of City Pop's unsung heroes. The story of City Pop is about so much more than just the actual music, it's also about the artists who made it happen and their relationships with one another. The genre developed the way it did largely thanks to these connections, so when you're jamming out to your favorite City Pop tunes take a moment to check out who was responsible for making it. You might be surprised to see a lot of those same legendary names over and over again.

Top: The members of Tin Pan Alley might be City Pop's most reoccurring characters, especially in its early years, and you can hear them performing on an unreal number of albums.
Center: Some standout artists such as Toshiki Kadomatsu (pictured) and Tetsuji Hayashi served as producers and composers for many albums, and it's likely your favorite City Pop tune was crafted by one of these legends.
Bottom: Sometimes the City Pop family moniker is taken quite literally. Husband and wife duo Tatsuro Yamashita and Mariya Takeuchi (pictured) got married in 1982 and frequently worked together on their music.

火の玉ボーイ (Fireball Boy)

Fireball Boy is an album by Keiichi Suzuki & Moonriders, a band that has experimented with a wide range of styles and are still active now. This early work of theirs managed to have a unique place in the history of City Pop's development, back when those folk influences could still be strongly felt but were steadily being phased out. Like some other albums from the era, it's a large scale collab with contributors including the members of Tin Pan Alley and Akiko Yano. The album is also appropriately divided into a "City Boy Side" and "Harbor Boy Side", which evokes some of the urbanized imagery City Pop would become so associated with. There's a lot of diverse tracks to enjoy such as A1 which is some great uplifting pop rock, and A3 gets pretty funky. It's perhaps somewhat removed from what City Pop would turn into, but still deserving of a listen.

Artist: Keiichi Suzuki & Moonriders
Release: January 1976
Label: Elektra

A1. あの娘のラブレター
A2. スカンピン
A3. 酔いどれダンスミュージック
A4. 火の玉ボーイ
A5. 午後のレディ
B1. 地中海地方の天気予報 ラム亭のMama
B2. ウェディング・ソング
B3. 魅惑の港
B4. 髭と口紅とバルコニー
B5. ラム亭のテーマ ホタルの光

Sometimes I...

The second studio album by Seri Ishikawa was one of the very first to truly fit the bill for City Pop thanks to its mixture of jazz, pop and soul, and it's also one of the first large scale collabs for the style. The impressive credits include Yumi Arai, who wrote quite a few songs for the album, and figures such as Ginji Ito and Masataka Matsutoya were part of the band while the members of Sugar Babe provided backing vocals. Sometimes I... is full of great mellow tracks, passionate ballads and slow mood setters tied together by Ishikawa's lovely singing. A must listen for those interested in the early history of the genre, and to see what these young artists were capable of when working together. Ishikawa's style diverts from City Pop quite a significantly past this album, making her collaborations with this circle something of a one-off.

Artist: Seri Ishikawa
Release: January 25, 1976
Label: Philips

A1. Introduction~朝焼けが消える前に
A2. 霧の掛橋
A3. ときどき私は……
A4. 虹のひと部屋
A5. なんとなく……
A6. さよならの季節
B1. ひとり芝居
B2. Sexy
B3. Tabacoはやめるわ
B4. 優しい関係
B5. フワフワ・Wow・Wow
B6. 遠い海の記憶

Flapper

Minako Yoshida returned in 1976 to make Flapper, which up to this point was possibly the greatest gathering of minds for the developing genre. Just about every one of early City Pop's big names showed up, such as all of Tin Pan Alley's members, and an eclectic mixture of composers including Tatsuro Yamashita and Eiichi Ohtaki. The number of musicians, composers and instruments involved gives the album a somewhat experimental and sometimes 'busy' vibe as there's a lot going on in each song, and it's absolutely loaded with variety. Flapper is a treat of an album which really displays the collaborative strength of these artists, and everyone involved made something truly special here. Of course, the star of the album herself shines brightly, as Yoshida went the extra mile in making Flapper distinct from her previous album.

Artist: Minako Yoshida
Release: March 21, 1976
Label: RCA

A1. 愛は彼方
A2. かたおもい
A3. 朝は君に
A4. ケッペキにいさん
A5. ラムはお好き？
B1. 夢で逢えたら
B2. チョッカイ
B3. 忘れかけてた季節へ
B4. ラスト・ステップ
B5. 永遠に光

Niagara Triangle Vol. 1

Left: A chill photo of the band from inside the album. Curiously they are referred to as 'Tatsuro Kuma (Bear)", "Eiichi Bannai" and "Ginji" here.
Center: The cover of Niagara Triangle Vol. 1 showing a plane in flight over Niagara Falls with the trio; Eiichi Ohtaki, Tatsuro Yamashita and Ginji Ito as stickers.
Right: The cover for the single release of Goodbye To Happiness and Dreaming Day.

Artist:
Niagara Triangle

Release:
March 25, 1976

Label:
Niagara Records

Track List:

A1. ドリーミング・デイ
(Dreaming Day)

A2. パレード
(Parade)

A3. 遅すぎた別れ
(A Farewell Too Late)

A4. 日射病
(Heatstroke)

A5. ココナツ・ホリディ '76
(Coconut Holiday '76)

B1. 幸せにさよなら
(Goodbye To Happiness)

B2. 新無頼横町
(New Burai Yokocho)

B3. フライング・キッド
(Flying Kid)

B4. Fussa Strut Part I

B5. 夜明け前の浜辺
(The Beach Before Dawn)

B6. ナイアガラ音頭
(Niagara Ondo)

Three of City Pop's founding fathers who were involved with the creation of Sugar Babe's album Songs are back with a new band; Niagara Triangle. The band consisted of Tatsuro Yamashita, Ginji Ito and Eiichi Ohtaki, a trio who split up their compositional duties in roughly equal measure. The three wrote a couple of tracks each, but every song is a great demonstration of the individual artist's musical sensibilities. Yamashita's tracks are chill and joyful like the music he'd eventually become famous for, while Ohtaki's tracks heavily utilize interesting sound effects. Ito's pop rock tunes suit the album's tone perfectly and foreshadows the music he'd be making in his debut album Deadly Drive next year. Niagara Triangle Vol. 1 is an interesting snapshot in the style's history because it's one of the very first to be centrally themed around tropical escapes. Many of the songs here involve some familiar City Pop themes such as summer vacations, trips to the beach, and general celebrations of prosperous living. City Pop would eventually be largely defined by these concepts, so the members of Niagara Triangle were really onto something here. The opening song Dreaming Day was composed by Yamashita and immediately sets the tone for the album as fun and uplifting, a feeling which carries into his next song Parade. This track was composed when Yamashita was at home one night enjoying a cheap bottle of wine, an elixir which has been reliable creative fuel for many geniuses. You can play the album and easily visualize it being the soundtrack to a 1970s beach trip, especially while listening to track A5, Coconut Holiday '76. A fascinating and very fun little song, Coconut Holiday '76 was composed by Ginji Ito and is over 7 minutes long, but its lyrics consist only of a single repeated word; coconuts. The album isn't all sunshine and coconuts though, as Goodbye to Happiness features some genuinely heartbreaking lyrics about the pain of lost love. It was inspired by Ginji Ito's own experience breaking up with a past girlfriend over a bad miscommunication, but the song ends on a positive note by wishing the other person happiness. New Burai Yokocho has somewhat of an unconventional country flavor to it, plus the lady yelling afterwards is actually lyricist Minako Yoshida making a cameo. One of Ohtaki's tracks that seemed to just work out nice and easy was The Beach Before Dawn, since Ohtaki wrote the lyrics in just a few minutes and nailed the recording after just two takes, making for quite an efficient turnaround. Niagara Triangle Vol. 1 is another great album from this trio and highly recommended to those looking for some early City Pop hits. The "Volume 1" in the name implies there were plans for more, but those wouldn't materialize for another few years.

Paper Moon

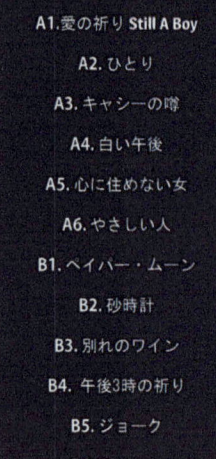

Artist: Junko Ohashi
Release: May 1976
Label: Philips

In 1976 Junko Ohashi released Paper Moon, an album which contrasted her debut record, Feeling Now. Whereas Feeling Now consisted of covers of Western songs, Paper Moon had twelve original tracks composed by various musicians, including her future husband, Ken Sato. The prolific songwriter Tetsuji Hayashi was also involved, and his music can be heard on albums for many of City Pop's greatest. This team of composers were unified by Ohashi's singing to create a spectacular album for the developing genre which contains many of the traits City Pop would become known for, including the blending of various musical styles like pop, funk and soul to create a sound which felt original. Ohashi was just getting started though, as next year she'd join forces with the band Minoya Central Station to make some of the genre's most beloved records.

A1. 愛の祈り Still A Boy
A2. ひとり
A3. キャシーの噂
A4. 白い午後
A5. 心に住めない女
A6. やさしい人
B1. ペイパー・ムーン
B2. 砂時計
B3. 別れのワイン
B4. 午後3時の祈り
B5. ジョーク
B6. ひきしお

Super Market

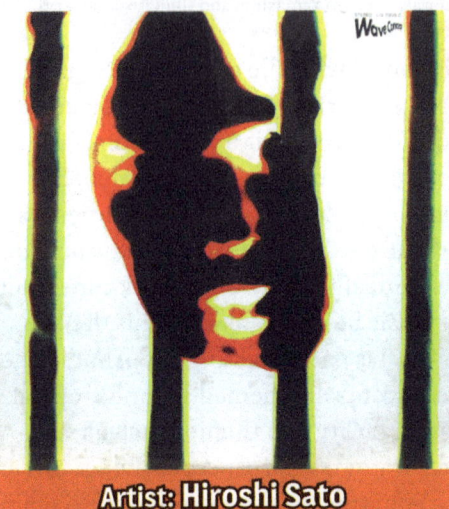

Artist: Hiroshi Sato
Release: May 25, 1976
Label: Wave Concept

The debut album from Hiroshi Sato, one of City Pop's most acclaimed keyboard players and a master of genre fusion. Sato can be heard performing on many of the genre's greatest records, notably for Tatsuro Yamashita's For You and Mariya Takeuchi's Variety. He also has some solo albums under his belt, all of which provide very special experiences. Sato takes influence from electronic music and soul to craft songs which illicit a wide range of feelings. The opening A1 is a fun and funky introduction, while A2 blurs the line between cool and hypnotic. You're always going to be wondering what happens next with Super Market, as once the B-side rolls around, you're sucked in to the eight minute long High Times. This track takes you on a real stylistic adventure, although the same could be said about the album as a whole.

A1. 私の彼氏は200歳
A2. レインボー・シーライン
A3. F.W.Y.
A4. 用意はいいかな
A5. Night In L.A.
B1. High Times
B2. いとしのマリー
B3. スーパー・マーケット
B4. パラダイス
B5. For Jun

Fashionable Lover

Artist: Hi-Fi Set
Release: June 5, 1976
Label: Express

The second album by Hi-Fi Set, Fashionable Lover, may actually be an undercover Yumi Arai project. This is because a staggering nine of the ten songs include her lyrics or compositions, giving fans of Arai's music something to sink their teeth into. The credits also contain a stacked roster including the members of Tin Pan Alley with Masataka Matsutoya as the arranger, and many other iconic musicians of the genre can be spotted throughout. A1 provides a fun and uplifting introduction, and individual members of the trio are given a chance to shine on A2 and Je M'Ennuie. It's easy to get lost in the rhythmic singing in Farewell Party, and finally Grand Canyon appropriately brings to mind visions of a chaotic family vacation, complete with all those hurdles that make the journey worth it.

A1. 星のストレンジャー
A2. 朝陽の中で微笑んで
A3. Je M'ennuie
A4. Farewell Party
A5. 冷たい雨
B1. Fashionable Lover
B2. 荒涼
B3. 真夜中の面影
B4. 月にてらされて
B5. Grand Canyon

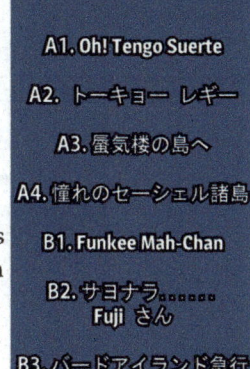

Seychelles

Seychelles is the highly beloved solo debut album for Masayoshi Takanaka, one of the most recognizable names for the fusion genre which City Pop was closely associated with. The album takes inspiration from an array of styles to make its signature tropical sound, with jazz and funk being two of the most prominent, but you can hear all sorts of influences throughout. It's light on the lyrics and instead focuses on being an instrumental delight which warps you to the islands the album is named after, and as such it fits in quite well with other similarly themed albums from the time. The opening Oh! Tengo Suerte is among Takanaka's most popular songs, a timeless track which perfectly exhibits his talent as a composer and performer. Seychelles is a fantastic time all around, standing out as one of 1976's best albums and the first of many gems from Takanaka.

Artist: Masayoshi Takanaka
Release: July 1, 1976
Label: Kitty Records

- A1. Oh! Tengo Suerte
- A2. トーキョー レギー
- A3. 蜃気楼の島へ
- A4. 憧れのセーシェル諸島
- B1. Funkee Mah-Chan
- B2. サヨナラ……Fuji さん
- B3. バードアイランド急行
- B4. Tropic Birds

Shady

Releasing her debut album Shady in the summer of 1976 was a new star, one who would have a prolific career in the City Pop era and beyond; Amii Ozaki. At only 19 years old Ozaki hit the scene with the smooth sounds of Shady, an album which she composed nearly every track for. Shady is another album from the era which is debatably City Pop, as it falls more in line with Kayōkyoku, but is nonetheless a quality record. The album begins with the Prologue, an instrumental track which is both enticing and unnerving as you're surrounded by the sounds of tranquil rain turning into roaring thunder. This then fades as the weather clears up and Shady reveals its true colors as a mellow and pleasant easy listening experience, the perfect companion piece to a quiet night. A solid origin point for Ozaki, whose lengthy artistic journey had only just begun.

Artist: Amii Ozaki
Release: August 5, 1976
Label: Express

- A1. プロローグ
- A2. 影絵の街
- A3. 冬のポスター
- A4. 私は何色
- A5. 届かない春
- A6. とまり木
- B1. 瞑想
- B2. 風の中
- B3. 私を呼んで
- B4. 追いかけてきたけれど
- B5. 遠くの光が……

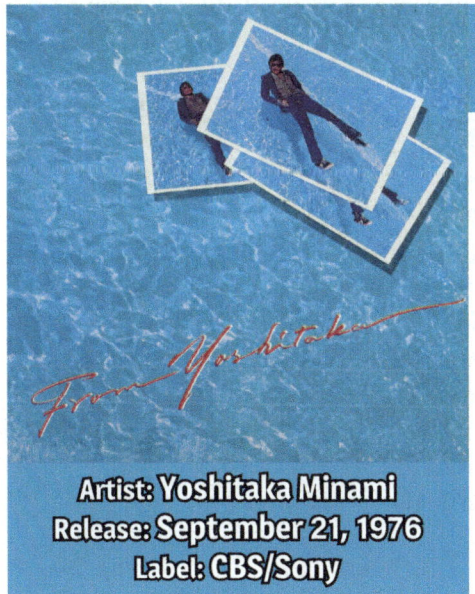

Forgotten Summer

In the latter half of 1976 Yoshitaka Minami released Forgotten Summer, beginning his journey into the still developing world of City Pop. Forgotten Summer falls firmly into the tropical and/or summer themed approach to City Pop, which maintains relevance as one of the genre's most well-known subjects for its entirety. This theming can notably be heard in albums like Niagara Triangle Vol. 1 and Lagoon from this year, and it will only continue to grow in popularity as the Japanese economy develops throughout the eighties. Minami was one of the first to make a City Pop album truly dedicated to this approach, and it fittingly captures the feeling of being on the beach with a cold drink in hand. The album has all of those chill tunes you'd expect, as well as jazzy mood setters and tracks to put some pep in your step.

Artist: Yoshitaka Minami
Release: September 21, 1976
Label: CBS/Sony

- A1. これで準備OK
- A2. ジャングル・ジム・ランド
- A3. ブルースでも歌って
- A4. 眠りの島
- A5. 忘れられた夏
- B1. 月夜の晩には
- B2. ヤシの木の下で
- B3. 静かな昼下り
- B4. ひとつの別れ
- B5. これで準備OK (Inst.)

Grey Skies

Left: The back of Grey Skies featuring a big picture of Ohnuki, happy as can be.
Center: The cover of Grey Skies by Taeko Ohnuki. A minimalist design with a heavy emphasis on white color featuring a smiling Ohnuki after a meal.
Right: The single release of Love is an Illusion and One's Love.

Taeko Ohnuki finally decided it was time to pursue a solo career after a few years as a member of Sugar Babe, although she was understandably anxious about such a big change. This was made worse by her lack of confidence in her artistic skills compared to former bandmate Tatsuro Yamashita, but there were many who saw her latent potential. One such individual was Ryuichi Sakamoto, who played instruments and arranged many songs on Grey Skies, and he would later become a pioneer of electronic music in the band Yellow Magic Orchestra. In time this electronic scene would have a major influence on Ohnuki, and her style gravitates more towards it as the years progress. Grey Skies naturally feels quite derivative of her time spent with Sugar Babe and quite a few of the songs were composed during or before the band's lifespan, such as Afternoon Rest. This makes it slightly harder to feel like it really 'fits in' with that preconceived idea of what City Pop is, but it does take influence from genres that are pivotal to City Pop's own unique design. You can most prominently hear a lot of jazz stylings throughout, with One's Love and Wander Lust both utilizing it well. The album begins with the incredibly comforting Beginning of Time, an uplifting introduction with lyrics that express Ohnuki's support for the listener through tough times. One notable aspect of Ohnuki's music are her beautiful lyrics which she writes herself more often than not. Whether she is singing about love, loss or lament her words always manage to leave an impression which sticks thanks to her gentle singing. A great showcase of this can be found in Afternoon Rest, a tranquil song about a moment of peace in a rocking chair as the summer sun beams down. The song is written and performed in such a way that it's easy to visualize the exact scene and feeling being described, the getaway from our busy lives we've all been needing. Street is a song about a classic subject in City Pop, the ironic loneliness of city living. It was inspired by Ohnuki's own experiences as a fresh faced 20 year old living on her own for the first time, making it quite personal and relatable. The album ends with the entirely instrumental Breakin' Blue, a track which shows off the wide range of instruments used in the album, most of which were played by Ryuichi Sakamoto. Its electronic soundscape is a prelude for what was soon to come for Ohnuki and beyond since the electronic genre was about to really kick off. Grey Skies is a wonderful debut album for Ohnuki and firmly established her approach to the genre, providing a sort of musical comfort food to the listener.

Artist:
Taeko Ohnuki

Release:
September 25, 1976

Label:
Panam

Track List:

A1. 時の始まり (Beginning of Time)

A2. 約束 (Promise)

A3. One's Love

A4. 午后の休息 (Afternoon Rest)

A5. 愛は幻 (Love Is An Illusion)

B1. Wander Lust

B2. 街 (Street)

B3. いつでも そばに (Always By My Side.)

B4. When I Met The Grey Sky

B5. Breakin' Blue

The 14th Moon

Left: The single release for Fading Room and Velvet Easter with Arai in a particularly striking outfit.
Center: The cover of The 14th Moon, a beautifully wrapped present from Yuming herself.
Right: The cover of Yuming Brand, a Yumi Arai compilation album which included actual 3D glasses and pictures.

Artist:
Yumi Arai

Release:
November 20, 1976

Label:
Express

Track List:

A1. さざ波
(Ripples)

A2. 14番目の月
(The 14th Moon)

A3. さみしさのゆくえ
(Where Does The Loneliness Go)

A4. 朝陽の中で微笑んで
(In The Morning Light)

A5. 中央フリーウェイ
(Central Freeway)

B1. 何もなかったように
(Like Nothing Ever Happened)

B2. 天気雨 (Sunshower)

B3. 避暑地の出来事
(A Summer Place)

B4. Good Luck And Good-By

B5. 晩夏 (ひとりの季節)
(Late Summer
(The Lonely Season)

Yumi Arai returned following the release of the iconic Cobalt Hour with another smash hit, The 14th Moon, her first al-bum to achieve the number 1 ranking. The album once again featured a track list entirely composed and written by Arai and included an array of the era's other stars as contributors such as the incredibly impressive group of backing vocalists. Heavy hitters such as Tatsuro Yamashita, Amii Ozaki, Minako Yoshida and Taeko Ohnuki lent their voices, as well as the jazz ensemble Time Five who are featured on some other City Pop albums throughout the years. Members of Tin Pan Alley are also credited, like Haruomi Hosono who deviates from his typical bass playing and is instead on the steel drums for this release. Masataka Matsutoya played keyboard and produced the album and also happened to marry Arai the same year. The 14th Moon is an especially powerful showcase of Arai's lyrical talent, as the album features some of her most beautiful writing. The opening song Ripples starts off with upbeat instrumentals which belies the songs true meaning, as she sings about nostalgia for romantic days gone by. Arai paints a picture of herself drifting alone in a boat reflecting on a book of memories which quickly reaches its epilogue. The titular 14th Moon is another classic Arai romantic pop hit about the uncertainty of romance, while In The Morning Light is a poetic track that begins with soft guitar playing and includes some powerful lyrics. The most popular song from the album is Central Freeway, a definitive early City Pop track which features all the staples of the genre. Arai sings about a night time drive with a lover, describing the duo as a pair of meteors racing down the freeway with a hand on the steering wheel and another wrapped around a shoulder. It's a song which exemplifies the youthful spirit that's often throughout City Pop, and many a romantic drive must've been had while listening to this classic. One song with a saddening inspiration is Like Nothing Ever Happened, which was written to express grief over the loss of her dog named Shepherd. A Summer Place features some of the prominent instruments of the entire album, then Good Luck And Good-Bye plays just in time to break your heart before the experience is over. Finally Late Summer (The Lonely Season) closes the album out with its haunting and descriptive lyrics about the end of the summer, a very genre-appropriate finale. The 14th Moon is another spectacular record from Arai, and a perfect end to the Yumi Arai era, as from here she goes by Yumi Matsutoya after marrying fellow musician Masataka Matsutoya.

Char

Artist: Char
Release: September 25, 1976
Label: See・Saw

Making his solo debut in 1976 was another figure who would become a legend in City Pop and beyond, Char. A veritable rock star, Char would deliver some of the first albums which could easily fit into the modern idea of City Pop, and he did so largely removed from many of the genre's founding figures. Char was a phenomenal release, creating a perfect blend of Western rock and soul music with a Japanese flair. An incredibly accomplished guitar player, Char lets loose playing on several tracks such as Kagerou and Smoky, and his singing skills are top notch too. Shinin' You, Shinin' Day is a great example of a prototypical City Pop hit with its memorable chorus and liberal use of English, and tracks like Navy Blue and Smoky are also awesome. Char was truly ahead of the game for his first album, and it still hits just right fifty years later.

A1. Shinin' You, Shinin' Day
A2. かげろう
A3. It's Up To You
A4. 視線
A5. Navy Blue
B1. Smoky
B2. I've Tried
B3. 空模様のかげんが悪くなる前に
B4. 朝

Go! Go! Niagara

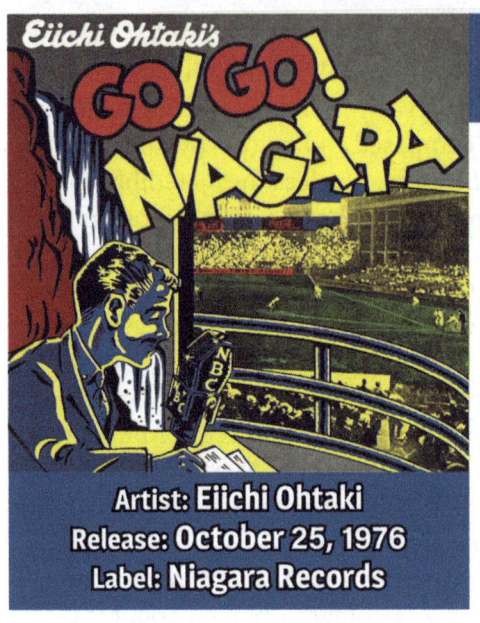

Artist: Eiichi Ohtaki
Release: October 25, 1976
Label: Niagara Records

The latest Niagara themed release from Eiichi Ohtaki continues to differ quite a lot from the music his peers were releasing. Go! Go! Niagara was made to be reminiscent of a radio broadcast, and as such has a very showman-like quality to it. Intermissions are baked into the track list, which includes charming segments like an announcement during a baseball game. Between songs you can also hear Ohtaki singing "Niagara" in several ways, like you're listening to a commercial break or radio jingle. Ohtaki's penchant for creative tracks that skirt the line between pop, rock, and something else entirely shines brightly here. While probably not in line with what fans of City Pop are looking for, Ohtaki's unique musical sensibilities provide a lot of listening material for those willing to explore a little.

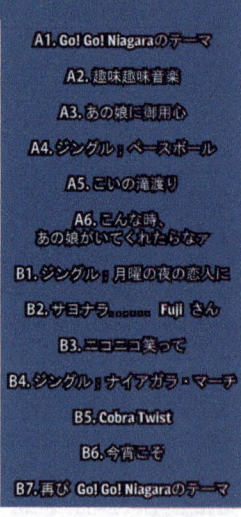

A1. Go! Go! Niagaraのテーマ
A2. 趣味趣味音楽
A3. あの娘に御用心
A4. ジングル：ベースボール
A5. こいの滝渡り
A6. こんな時、あの娘がいてくれたらなア
B1. ジングル：月曜の夜の恋人に
B2. サヨナラ Fuji さん
B3. ニコニコ笑って
B4. ジングル：ナイアガラ・マーチ
B5. Cobra Twist
B6. 今宵こそ
B7. 再び Go! Go! Niagaraのテーマ

Lagoon

Artist: Shigeru Suzuki
Release: December 5, 1976
Label: Panam

Shigeru Suzuki's next release, Lagoon, was made to be an unmistakably tropical, chill, and hip early City Pop experience. It was one of the first within this niche to be dedicated to this summer vacation theming, something which will be forever linked with City Pop in due time. Adding to the album's tropical identity are some of the more uncommon instruments he plays, the marimba and ukulele. This is alongside all the other work he did on the album such as producing and composing for it, all of which serve to make Lagoon feel like it's a true Suzuki project. Lagoon is an innovative release from Suzuki featuring memorable tunes like Lady Pink Panther and a selection of pleasant instrumental tracks. It also sets a precedent for one of City Pop's most common themes; music which brings to mind the joys of summer.

A1. Lady Pink Panther
A2. デビル・ゲーム
A3. Brandy Wine
A4. Tokyo・ハーバー・ライン
A5. Hawaiian
B1. 走れラビット
B2. コルドバの夜
B3. Almeria
B4. 8分音符の詩

Circus Town

Left: A picture of Yamashita from the album about to do his thing in New York.
Center: The cover of Circus Town by Tatsuro Yamashita. The blurry image isn't your eyes deceiving you, the album just looks like that.
Right: A picture of Yamashita alongside the credits for the album, showing off that adorable smile of his.

Artist:
Tatsuro Yamashita

Release:
December 25, 1976

Label:
RCA

Track List:

A1. Circus Town

A2. Windy Lady

A3. Minnie

A4. 永遠に
(Forever.)

B1. Last Step

B2. City Way

B3. 迷い込んだ街と
(The City I Wandered Into)

B4. 夏の陽
(Summer Sun)

After his work in bands such as Sugar Babe and Niagara Triangle, alongside many other musical collaborations, Tatsuro Yamashita finally made his solo debut in 1976 with the album Circus Town. Technically that's only half true though, since Yamashita's first solo album dated back to 1972 with the self-published Add Some Music To Your Day, which mostly included covers of Western songs. This was an extremely limited release with only 100 copies made, but it would later get another run after Yamashita was more famous. The breakup of Sugar Babe was quite the blow to Yamashita's morale since he was rather reluctant to pursue a solo career, partially because the 60s inspired style he was fond of wasn't all that popular in Japan. Rather than giving up on the approach Yamashita doubled down and sought to make Circus Town in New York City to replicate that American sound he was so attached to, with the idea being to perfect his already existing approach rather than starting over. However, some budgetary concerns got in the way of this idea, and so to save costs half of the album was recorded in Los Angeles while the other half would be done in New York. This was then reflected in the design of the product itself, having a New York Side functioning as Side A, and a Los Angeles Side as Side B. The young Yamashita wasn't exactly prepared for the inner workings of New York's music scene though. He witnessed cut-throat talks about money and even experienced racism, while he described producer Charlie Calello as not being very friendly. On the flip side of the continent people in Los Angeles were nicer, but less skilled. Yamashita considered the first bassist and guitarist they tried out to be incompetent and he was so frustrated he thought about just giving up before more talented help arrived. In the end things worked out though, and the international trip provided Yamashita with some much-desired insight and experience. In the place of Sugar Babe's folk roots there are more jazz and soul inspiration, and naturally there's a Western flair throughout. You can also see the creative partnership between Minako Yoshida and Yamashita blooming here, with Yoshida providing the lyrics for more than half of the album, and the song Forever from the album Minako makes a reappearance here. The album holds loads of memorable tracks such as Circus Town, which really does feel like a circus in your headphones, and it ends with Summer Sun, an enthusiastic farewell song about Yamashita's surroundings and inner struggles on a sweltering summer day. Circus Town is a noteworthy first solo album for Yamashita and serves well as a launching point for the future 'King of City Pop.'

1977, Refinement

With 1977 rolling around many of the common themes for what would become City Pop were getting established and the genre's artists were all keeping busy. The year is home to some of early City Pop's most classic records, as well as a handful of underrated hidden gems. Minako Yoshida shifted from the fun and sometimes wacky sounds of Flapper to Twilight Zone, a moody, more 'adult' album with some deep lyrics and exceptionally long tracks. Others were also in the process of discovering themselves and experimenting with their music like Taeko Ohnuki, who became influenced by the growing popularity of the fusion genre, leading to the creation of Sunshower. Tatsuro Yamashita returned from the United States with many lessons learned and crafted Spacy with a hand-selected band consisting of Japan's finest. Meanwhile Junko Ohashi and her band Minoya Central Station released two stunning albums in Rainbow and Crystal City, being some of the first to nail the vibe we now associate with City Pop. This was partially thanks to some compositions by Tetsuji Hayashi, a soon-to-be legendary composer who also released his album Back Mirror this year. Slowly but surely Hayashi would become one of the most influential songwriters for the genre, and the typical image of a City Pop song likely stems from his many creations. Others would make their debut albums this year like Rajie, Ginji Ito and Masamichi Sugi, and the catalog of artists was only growing. For now it seemed like everything was moving in the right direction for these young creatives, but sadly nothing goes according to the plan forever, as they'd eventually discover in 1978.

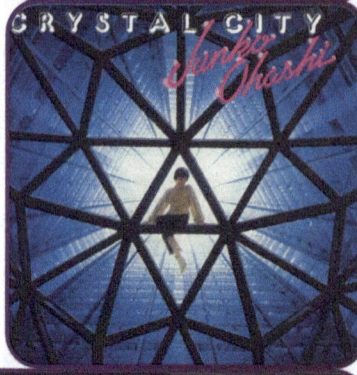

Junko Ohashi

In the mid to late seventies one artist was making music which fit the City Pop moniker perfectly, and she did so independently from the core groups like Tin Pan Alley and Sugar Babe. Junko Ohashi's debut album Feeling Now from 1974 mostly featured covers of Western songs, but she would soon develop into her signature style with her band Minoya Central Station and their excellent records like Crystal City. Influences such as disco, soul, jazz, funk and pop all converged to give Ohashi and Minoya Central Station a fresh sound which was bombastic and fun. The group was also quite varied, and you could expect everything from exciting tracks made to light up the dance floor, smooth love songs, or just whatever creative musical experiment they came up with. They also stood out because of Ohashi's powerful singing voice and the fusion of genres their music employed, which benefitted from some very catchy songwriting. This was owed to Ohashi's main composer and husband Ken Sato, who was the genius behind many of her biggest hits like Simple Love and the beloved City Pop gem Telephone Number, and he also later wrote tracks for Miki Matsubara, among others. Although Minoya Central Station disbanded around 1980 Ohashi continued her career as a solo artist and eventually ended up moving to New York City. For those looking to get into her music the compilation album Magical from 1984 is a great sampler with many of her most renowned songs, while Crystal City, Shalom and Point Zero are also stunning, but you really can't go wrong with any of her creations. Sadly in 2018 Ohashi was diagnosed with esophageal cancer, as well as breast cancer later in 2019, which necessitated a brief hiatus. Afterwards she continued performing for several more years until she eventually passed away in November of 2023 at the age of 73. Ohashi leaves behind a legacy as one of City Pop's pioneers, as well as all the decades of fantastic music she gifted us with.

Top: Ohashi as seen on the cover of her album Terra 2 from 2009 with a striking red hair color.
Bottom: Ohashi always carried herself with a cool elegance, and a short haircut.

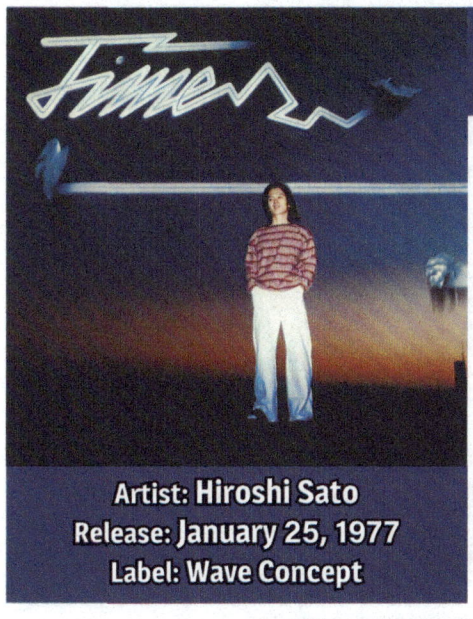

Time

Hiroshi Sato followed up on his debut record Super Market with Time, an album which he crafted with a fascinating fusion of rock, jazz, blues, electronic and more. Time stands out amongst its peers for how unique it is, since you never know exactly what sort of weird mixture of genres or electronic sound Sato will surprise you with next. Sato can be heard putting his skills on synthesizer and electric piano to great use with almost every song, such as the funky Choit, the spellbinding Yamate Hotel or the trippy Akanegumo-No Machi. The result is a well-rounded release with great variety, and it's stacked with content considering there's 13 songs here. Time is a psychedelic trip that transports you to a digital world of Sato's creation and comes as highly recommended listening for those interested in early electronic music.

Artist: Hiroshi Sato
Release: January 25, 1977
Label: Wave Concept

- A1. Time
- A2. Joint
- A3. Minami Kaikisen
- A4. Choit
- A5. Yamate Hotel
- A6. Bad Janky Blues
- B1. Mezame
- B2. Akanegumo-No Machi
- B3. Black Coffee
- B4. Island Fantasy
- B5. Kage-Ni Mukatte
- B6. Saigo-No Tejina
- B7. Merry-Go-Round

Love Collection

Love Collection once against showcases Hi-Fi Set's strongest trait and selling point in the realm of City Pop, their unique vocal style as a trio. This is backed by the variety of composers and lyricists on board for this project who gave each of the songs a unique style, which are then unified by Hi-Fi Set's lovely singing. The album also features two tracks courtesy of Yumi Arai who wrote Rainy Station and Central Freeway, which had previously been sung by Arai on her albums Cobalt Hour and The 14th Moon. Hi-Fi Set puts a fun new spin on these songs, with Rainy Station being especially memorable by having Junko Yamamoto as the lead singer giving a heartfelt performance. Central Freeway likewise puts a jazzy spin on a classic song, and the addition of male voices gives a nice contrast to the Arai original.

Artist: Hi-Fi Set
Release: February 5, 1977
Label: Express

- A1. オン・エニィ・サンデイ
- A2. 雨のステイション
- A3. 眠い朝
- A4. まぶしい貴方
- A5. 夜の傷
- B1. クリスタル・ナイト
- B2. フィーリング
- B3. カントリー・ボーイ
- B4. 夢に見たジャマイカ
- B5. 中央フリーウェイ

Mari & Red Stripes

The very first album released by Masamichi Sugi, a future member of Niagara Triangle and the mind behind quite a number of albums and City Pop songs. Mari & Red Stripes is one of only two releases by the short lived band Masamichi Sugi & Red Stripes, but is still an interesting window into that early intersection of rock and City Pop. Despite being called a band Red Stripes was more akin to a rotating group of performers who played alongside Sugi, who was the real star of the show. While Sugi jams out on tracks like Fickle Mother and On The Main Street the album leans more towards the soft rock side, which makes for great listening if you're looking for something with energy but won't explode your brain. A solid first album, but many of Sugi's later endeavors vastly overshadow it.

Artist: Masamichi Sugi & Red Stripes
Release: March 25, 1977
Label: Victor

- A1. ムーンライト・ベイビー
- A2. 気まぐれママ
- A3. 思い出の為
- A4. トゥナイト
- A5. 表通りで
- A6. はやく君を抱きたい
- B1. バイ・バイ・ウサギ君
- B2. 君は一人かい
- B3. ファニー・ダンサー
- B4. ドライブ・オン・ザ・ハイウェイ
- B5. ベイビー
- B6. エピローグ～気まぐれママ・パートⅡ

Twilight Zone

Left: The back of Twilight Zone, showcasing either an innocent or sultry scene, depending on your perspective. Center: The cover of Twilight Zone by Minako Yoshida. An alluring and dim shot of Yoshida, cigarette in hand, which contrasts the friendly look of her previous album. Right: The cover of the live album Minako II - Live At Sun Plaza Hall which released the same year as Twilight Zone.

After releasing Flapper in the previous year Minako Yoshida would shake things up with Twilight Zone, an album that features a noticeably different vibe compared to its predecessor. Flapper was made with many different composers all coming together to create its tracks, which made it quite varied but also somewhat eclectic. This time Yoshida wanted to make something that was totally hers and write the whole album by herself, like she did with her debut album Door To Winter. It was also made to be quite thematically different from Flapper, which was generally fun or even zany with its unique songs and instrumentals, but Twilight Zone has a more distinct and often times downbeat philosophy that it's adhering to. Whereas Flapper featured inviting pictures of Yoshida, Twilight Zone instead shows her in a dim corner which gives it a dark allure. Most of the songs are solemn and slow, and they tell stories about loneliness in the city at night and saying goodbye to former lovers, all of which perfectly suit the album's visual design. These were quite personal and introspective songs, something which the album's co-producer Tatsuro Yamashita was supportive of. He believed that it was ultimately good for one's mental wellbeing to let those feelings out, even if it meant the music wouldn't sell as well. One notable trait about Twilight Zone is the length of its songs, as more than half of the tracks clock in at over six minutes long, with the longest being Love at eight minutes. This would become something of a trademark for Yoshida, as many of her future albums would focus heavily on lengthy tracks. Twilight Zone isn't totally bereft of shorter songs though, with Uptown and Raspberry Slope both being under four minutes, but most of the album is designed with lengthy listening in mind. As such it feels like Yoshida wasn't concerned with making the next bunch of radio hits and instead wanted to put into music some ongoing thoughts she had about topics like the paradoxical loneliness of city living, all while giving these tracks the breathing room they needed. That's not to say the album is a total mood killer, as there's a handful on the brighter side which still hold true to Twilight Zone's tone. Raspberry Slope is a particularly provocative song that has some steamy lyrics, and Uptown has a more lively sound more in line with Flapper. You can also enjoy one of her most popular tunes here in Love is a Meteor, an engaging track which transforms into an instrumental adventure halfway through. Although maybe not conforming with modern preconceptions about the joyful nature of City Pop, Twilight Zone is still a beautiful and incredibly worthwhile album for Minako Yoshida's discography which influenced her music for years to come.

Artist:
Minako Yoshida

Release:
March 25, 1977

Label:
RCA

Track List:

A1. Twilight Zone (Overture)

A2. 恋 (Love)

A3. 駆けてきたたそがれ (Quack Who Ran For The Hills)

A4. メロディー (Melody)

A5. 恋は流星 (Love is a Meteor)

B1. Uptown

B2. 天気雨 (Sun Shower)

B3. Raspberry Slope

B4. さよなら (Goodbye)

B5. Twilight Zone

Rainbow

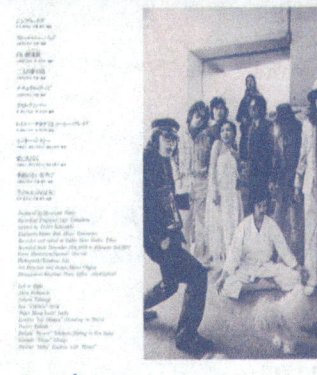  

Left: A photo of the band's members from Rainbow seemingly from a costume party. Some of the unique outfits on display include a karate gi and a cowboy. Center: The cover of Rainbow shows off a subtle and colorful illustration of Ohashi. Photos by Yasukuni Iida. Right: A bright purple picture of Ohashi alongside the tracklist for Rainbow.

Artist:
Junko Ohashi & Minoya Central Station

Release:
April 1977

Label:
Philips

Track List:

A1. Simple Love

A2. Feel So Bad

A3. 白い鎮魂歌 (White Requiem)

A4. 二人の夢の島 (The Island of Two Dreams)

A5. Natural Foods

A6. The Last Number

B1. Rainy Saturday & Coffee Break

B2. Lucky Day

B3. 愛にさよなら (Goodbye To Love)

B4. 季節のない街角で (On A Street Corner With No Season)

B5. 今シルエットのように (Like the silhouette now.)

Junko Ohashi followed up her previous release Paper Moon with an album starring a newly formed band; Minoya Central Station. Full of creative vigor, Ohashi and the gang released two jam packed albums throughout 1977, starting with Rainbow in April. City Pop mainstay and longtime Ohashi collaborator Ken Sato composed three of the album's songs while several others were composed by Tetsuji Hayashi, a man who would become inseparable from the identity of City Pop during the eighties. Since Hayashi was the mind behind some of the genre's most famous songs, like the renowned Midnight Door/Stay With Me by Miki Matsubara, many will associate his approach with the genre as a whole. You can also catch former Happy End bandmate Takashi Matsumoto as one of its lyricists, another big name in the space who worked on an astronomical number of albums. The involvement of these icons makes Rainbow feel like it's ahead of the game when it comes to City Pop's stylistic development, so those who are familiar with City Pop tunes from the 80s will feel quite comfortable here. Rainbow starts up with an Ohashi classic, Simple Love, one of her most popular songs. Ohashi's stunning singing found a perfect companion with the performances from Minoya Central Station and it's a track which feels right at home with Ohashi's bombastic musical sensibilities, making it easy to visualize like a concert right in your head. Likewise, Feel So Bad has some criminally groovy bass provided by Ikujirō Fukuda, and the song gets some great synthesizer usage in. We start to slow down with White Requiem's soulful singing until The Island of Two Dreams brings to mind visions of summer with its castanets and marimba. You would expect a track named Natural Foods to be somewhat passive, but its instead a frantic rock session with lots of Ohashi shouting. The Last Number features some beautiful piano and saxophone performances to elevate Ohashi's voice, while Rainy Saturday and Coffee Break is bubbly fun with a memorable English chorus you may find yourself singing the next time you have a nice, caffeinated cup. The fun atmosphere keeps up with Lucky Day and the charming "da dum dum dum" Ohashi sings midway through, while On A Street Corner With No Season is heavy on the jazz. We close out on the captivating Like The Silhouette Now, which ends with another jam-packed instrumental session. Rainbow is an innovative album from Junko Ohashi & Minoya Central Station, and the beginning of a beautiful ensemble which will provide splendid tracks for many years yet to come. The very same year they also released Crystal City, another early City Pop masterpiece.

Our Connection

Artist: Ayumi Ishida & Tin Pan Alley
Release: April 25, 1977
Label: Columbia

Our Connection is a collaboration between the members of Tin Pan Alley and Ayumi Ishida, who had been a successful singer and actress since 1969. Ishida is most well-known for performing the very popular song Blue Light Yokohama and had been consistently releasing albums throughout the seventies. The two musical forces joining up created one of their most memorable albums to date, perfectly utilizing Ishida's vocal talents and Tin Pan Alley's ever wonderful playing. The songs were all either composed by Haruomi Hosono or Mitsuo Hagita, a very prolific songwriter who mostly made songs for female artists. As you might expect from the diverse Hosono there's great variety here, and styles ranging from pop to soul and even Latin are experimented with. Our Connection would be Ishida's second to last album, although she did continue to work regularly as an actress.

- A1. 私自身
- A2. ひとり旅
- A3. 六本木ララバイ
- A4. ダンシング
- A5. バレンタイン・デー
- A6. 黄昏どき
- B1. 真夜中のアマン
- B2. 哀愁の部屋
- B3. ウィンター・コンサート
- B4. そしてベルが鳴る
- B5. ムーン・ライト
- B6. バイ・バイ・ジェット

Takanaka

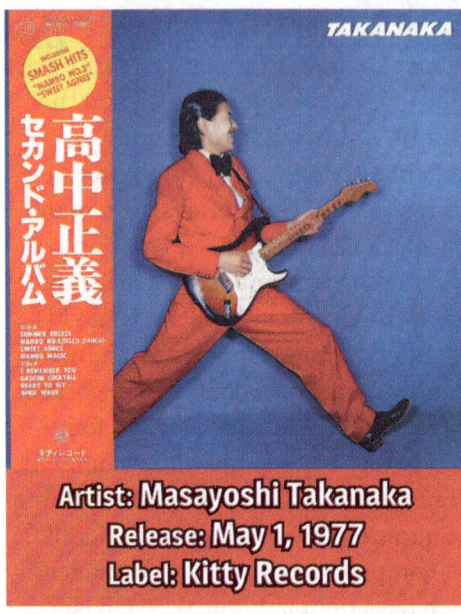

Artist: Masayoshi Takanaka
Release: May 1, 1977
Label: Kitty Records

Masayoshi Takanaka is back with Takanaka, a worthy sequel to 1976's iconic album Seychelles. The album is conceptually similar to his previous work with its emphasis on genre fusion, but the vocals are more prominent this time around. The opening track Summer Breeze lures you in with the charming cliche of thunderstorms giving way to serenity, but your expectations get subverted a bit with electronic beeps and bops which flow into the song proper. Latin influence gets some love in A2 and A4, and their blend of mambo, funk and jazz will really have you moving, while Sweet Agnes is another impressive showcase of Takanaka's skills. The B-side is all instrumental and has some great offerings too, including the soothing I Remember You and exciting Ready To Fly. Takanaka is a stellar album that feels rather appropriately named.

- A1. Summer Breeze
- A2. Mambo No. 5 (Disco Dango)
- A3. Sweet Agnes
- A4. Mambo Magic
- B1. I Remember You
- B2. Gascon Cocktail
- B3. Ready To Fly
- B4. April Wave

Deadly Drive

Artist: Ginji Ito
Release: May 25, 1977
Label: Asylum Records

Despite his numerous appearances in music throughout the seventies it wasn't until 1977 when Ginji Ito released his first album, Deadly Drive. Akin to his previous work on Niagara Triangle Vol. 1, Deadly Drive is a blend of pop and soft rock with some early City Pop vibes mixed in, making for an album that's fun, smooth, and at times rather experimental, with many songs including liberal usage of sound effects. One track which leans more on the creative side is King Kong which leads us in with a journey through the jungle with the sounds of birds and monkeys intact. The song Deadly Drive is an instrumental soft rock joyride, with some high-speed vehicles and car crashes thrown in to keep you on your toes. This impressive release from Ginji Ito is a testament to his creativity, as it has the soft rock you'd expect and elements that will throw you for a loop.

- A1. 風になれるなら
- A2. I'm Telling You Now
- A3. Deadly Drive
- A4. こぬか雨
- B1. King Kong
- B2. あの時はどしゃぶり
- B3. Sweet Daddy
- B4. Hobo's Lullaby

Spacy

Left: The back of Spacy, which includes art of a child shooting down a plane with his laser eyes. Striking.
Center: The cover of Spacy by Tatsuro Yamashita features a colorful and eyecatching design which was made with acrylic blocks.
Right: The very pink interior of Spacy with a picture of Yamashita and the credits for the album.

Artist:
Tatsuro Yamashita

Release:
June 25, 1977

Label:
RCA

Track List:

A1. Love Space

A2. 翼に乗せて
(On Wings)

A3. 素敵な午後は
(Lovely Afternoon)

A4. Candy

A5. Dancer

B1. アンブレラ
(Umbrella)

B2. 言えなかった言葉を
(Words I Couldn't Say)

B3. 朝の様な夕暮れ
(Dusk Like Morning)

B4. きぬずれ
(Rustling of Clothes)

B5. Solid Slider

Yamashita returned to the land of the rising sun after his successful romp in the United States, now with a revitalized creative spirit. This was partially thanks to Circus Town co-producer Charlie Calello giving Yamashita the scores from the album, who studied their unconventional but still practical structure. This newfound curiosity and desire for innovation would carry over into his next album Spacy, which Yamashita sought to make with a hand-selected group of musicians, possibly to avoid some of the issues he faced while working with random musicians of varying skill in New York. Some of these conscripts included Haruomi Hosono, Hiroshi Sato, Ryuichi Sakamoto and many other talented musicians who played on albums all throughout City Pop's history. Spacy marks another gradual shift for Yamashita's musical style and feels a lot more unified compared to Circus Town, which had a very eclectic mixture of sounds due to its cross-continental creation process. Although his music would obviously change and develop throughout the coming years, Spacy is where you can see Yamashita's sensibilities really solidified, and this is the general style he would become known for. Fitting in with its name Spacy begins with the cosmic themed Love Space, a track dedicated to a love so strong it feels like you're soaring through the stars. Yamashita lets out some passionate verses in this song especially, and those same celebratory themes of love are present throughout the entire album. A lesson was learned with Lovely Afternoon, a song which had a highly detailed score with intricate movements, although these were largely ignored by the musicians. The song turned out excellently either way, leading to Yamashita realizing that kind of micromanagement isn't needed when working with such talented people. Candy is a smooth Yamashita classic with some nice and sensual instrumentals, and Dancer is loaded with that ever-cool seventies funk. Dusk Like Morning is an acapella piece which traces its origins back to a week-long stay at Eiichi Ohtaki's house, since he was stranded there due to an ongoing train station worker strike. It was inspired by a sensation Yamashita experienced after staying up all night, then waking up late into the evening and being confused about what time it was, which is a pretty relatable origin story honestly. The final track Solid Slider was made to appeal to the growing adult-oriented rock scene, which would often intersect with City Pop as the two had a similar audience, and its lengthy runtime gives Yamashita a lot of time to express himself. Spacy is another excellent showing from Yamashita which sets the tone for his career going forward.

Mind Drops

Artist: Amii Ozaki
Release: June 5, 1977
Label: Express

In the summer of 1977 Amii Ozaki released her second album, Mind Drops, which feels akin to her previous Shady thanks to its emphasis on soul and mellow sound, but the album is far from a retread. It shakes things up by introducing more pop elements to create some tracks that emphasize catchy lyrics and instrumentals provided by an impressive band, including most of Tin Pan Alley. A2 is a classic slow Ozaki track with some soft but passionate singing, then Bye-Bye Mr. Random lightens the mood especially thanks to its memorable line "Mr. Random, sayonara, bye bye!" sprinkled throughout. To Say Goodbye's wonderful piano playing is fantastic alongside the serenading sounds of Ozaki's voice. Mind Drops is another great early album from the developing Ozaki and a nice piece of early City Pop's history.

- A1. 太陽のひとりごと
- A2. 涙の雨
- A3. Bye-Bye Mr. Random
- A4. うわさの男
- A5. 夢子とかげろう
- B1. Booming Cracker
- B2. 旅
- B3. 偶然
- B4. 初恋の通り雨
- B5. さよならを言うために

Funny Walkin'

Artist: Nanako Sato
Release: June 25, 1977
Label: Blow Up

1977 would see the debut of another artist who would put her own spin on City Pop; Nanako Sato. Funny Walkin' stands as an excellent debut album packed full of twelve unique songs, most of which were composed by Motoharu Sano, whom Sato met in college. Sano's role in City Pop doesn't end there either, as he would later become a member of Niagara Triangle for their second album in 1982, among other projects. The album places a heavy emphasis on both jazz and soul, giving it a retro and classy vibe, but there's many unexpected stylistic choices to be heard here. Sato's stint in City Pop ended before the style was really rolling, as she stopped making music throughout the eighties to pursue other ventures such as photography. She eventually did return many years later in 1995 and has come out with albums as recently as 2022.

- A1. サブタレニアン三人ぼっち
- A2. トワイライト
- A3. 真夜中のロックンロール・ダンス
- A4. 綱渡り
- A5. 赤いドレスでファニー・ウォーキン
- A6. ラグタイム・フォーエヴァー
- B1. ストリート・コーナー・ベティ
- B2. 土曜の夜から日曜の朝へ
- B3. スターダスト・ドライヴ
- B4. ピアニストの恋人
- B5. 恋にゆれて
- B6. 夜のイサドラ

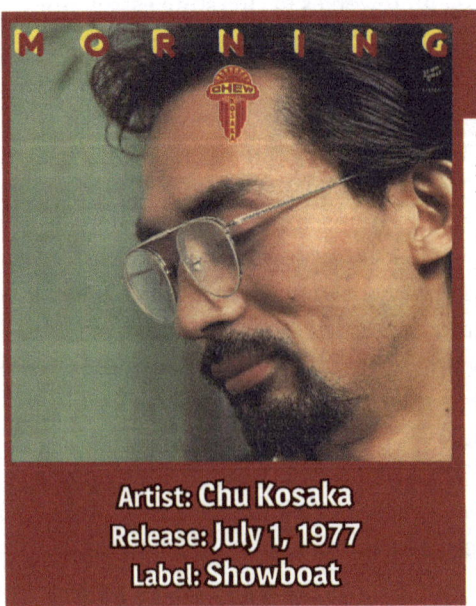

Morning

Artist: Chu Kosaka
Release: July 1, 1977
Label: Showboat

Chu Kosaka's Morning gives us another fantastic album made in conjunction with members of Tin Pan Alley, sans Masataka Matsutoya, as well as Hiroshi Sato who composed a few songs. The album works wonderfully in creating a chill atmosphere with its great combination of soul and pop influences, making this a stellar choice for some late-night relaxation. Some of the album's most popular tracks include A1 which expresses Morning's mood very well, while A4 is a cute and fun tune. Past this point Kosaka became deeply involved with the Christian faith in Japan and even became a pastor. Most of his albums past this point focused on Gospel music, which he released somewhat infrequently for the next few decades. Kosaka sadly passed away in 2022 due to complications with cancer, but his career in music is widely celebrated.

- A1. ボンボヤージ波止場
- A2. 港に架かる橋
- A3. Flying Saucer
- A4. Ice Cream Shop Girl
- A5. 朝は好きかい
- B1. 早起きの青い街
- B2. Silk Rendez-Vous
- B3. Focus Love
- B4. 一人じゃないよ
- B5. 上を向いて歩こう

Sunshower

Left: A great set of photos of the band from Sunshower, including folks like Haruomi Hosono and Nobu Saito.
Center: The cover of Sunshower. Similarly to her previous album it includes a mostly white and grey color scheme, which is subdued but inviting.
Right: Another photo of Ohnuki included with the album which displays her near a microphone ready to work her magic.

Artist:
Taeko Ohnuki

Release:
July 25, 1977

Label:
Panam

Track List:

A1. Summer Connection

A2. くすりをたくさん
(Lots of Medicine)

A3. 何もいらない
(I Don't Want Anything)

A4. 都会 (City)

A5. からっぽの椅子
(Empty Chair)

B1. Law of Nature

B2. 誰のために
(For Whom)

B3. Silent Screamer

B4. Sargasso Sea

B5. 振子の山羊
(Pendulum Goat)

After creating Grey Skies, the previous year Taeko Ohnuki became more influenced by the developing fusion genre, which combined assorted styles like jazz and soul into something new. This was also when Ohnuki was gradually losing interest in the American pop and rock which Sugar Babe was so inspired by and instead started focusing on trying novel approaches for her next album; Sunshower. Ryuichi Sakamoto returned to help out Ohnuki after his work on Grey Skies, and in Sunshower's case he acted as its music director and arranger. The pair were mostly left to their own devices for this production, since Ohnuki's agency disbanded around this time, and the label Panam seemingly didn't care much about micromanaging the record either. This gave Ohnuki and Sakamoto the opportunity to experiment with their newfound passion more freely for genre fusion, which Ohnuki chose to prioritize above the album's vocals. Sunshower begins with the appropriately pleasant Summer Connection, a track about one of City Pop's most classic subjects, the delightful season of summer. Featuring buoyant instrumentation and lyrics that bring to mind a nostalgic beach trip, it's a fun way to start the album and includes a righteous guitar solo. Lots of Medicine has possibly the strangest subject matter seen in the fledgling genre yet, that of course being prescription drugs. Considering the fun and upbeat instrumentals you'd never guess that, but the lyrics speak for themselves as Ohnuki takes a jab at medical institutions being a little too willing to prescribe meds as a cure all. One of her most iconic songs in City can be found here, a track would end up becoming a staple of City Pop playlists everywhere. Appropriate to the name of the genre, City is a poetic track about the discomforts of life in the city and a desire to return to home, away from all the chaos. One song that feels almost out of place in the album is Sargasso Sea, mostly due to the constant synthesizer sounds throughout which replicate the feeling of being underwater. This song actually serves as a prelude to the electronic music Ohnuki would eventually become very well-known for in the mid-1980s in albums like Signifie, but that won't be for several years. Despite being looked back on as a standout album in the history of City Pop and one of Ohnuki's best, Sunshower didn't perform well upon its release. Fortunately, in later years the album got the recognition it deserved for its interesting mixture of styles, memorable songs, and of course Ohnuki's ever beautiful singing throughout. Sunshower would end up becoming one of the most iconic early City Pop records, although it'd take a while for people to genuinely appreciate this work.

Flying

Artist: Sumiko Yamagata
Release: July 25, 1977
Label: Blow Up

Sumiko Yamagata's Flying from 1977 feels very aligned with the constantly developing City Pop, thanks to its familiar credits list. Flying was directed by foundational artist Shigeru Suzuki, who also composed and arranged quite a few tracks. The highly recognizable names don't stop there though, as Takashi Matsumoto was the lyricist for nearly every song. You can also catch Haruomi Hosono, Ginji Ito and Hiroshi Sato here, making this something of a surprise mega collab. With names like those attached it's no surprise that Flying turned out to be fantastic, as you get to hear creations from some of the best combined with Yamagata's perfected singing. Sadly, this seemed to be a lightning in a bottle moment, as none of them returned for her final solo album, which would release next year.

- A1. Flying
- A2. ペーパーミント・モーニング
- A3. あなたにテレポート
- A4. Today
- A5. 黄昏遊泳
- A6. 私春記
- B1. ムーンライト・ジルバ
- B2. 夢色グライダー
- B3. Good-bye・グラフィティ
- B4. 夜を渡って
- B5. クリスタル・ホテル

Heart To Heart

Artist: Rajie
Release: September 21, 1977
Label: CBS/Sony

Heart to Heart is an album which feels almost ahead of its time since it fits the bill for City Pop so well. It perfectly combines pop and soul with just a hint of jazz and soft rock, giving us a glimpse into what the genre was shaping into. The opening song Hold Me Tight is an example of a track that feels in line with the modern idea of City Pop, and its frequent use of English lyrics guarantee that it stays stuck in your head. Airport is a quick but powerful song which alludes to a meeting that never happened, as Rajie says goodbye while up in the sky. We end on the album's namesake Heart To Heart, an optimistic tune with short verses about singing songs and shining smiles. Heart to Heart is a fantastic solo debut album for Rajie, and a must listen for those interested in early City Pop, since she may be an artist who slipped under your radar.

- A1. Hold Me Tight
- A2. 静かな瞳
- A3. It's Me...It's You
- A4. さらさらの町
- A5. 愛はたぶん
- B1. The Tokyo Taste
- B2. 素敵なフィーリング
- B3. 気分を出してもう一度
- B4. エアポート
- B5. Heart To Heart

Tokyo Special

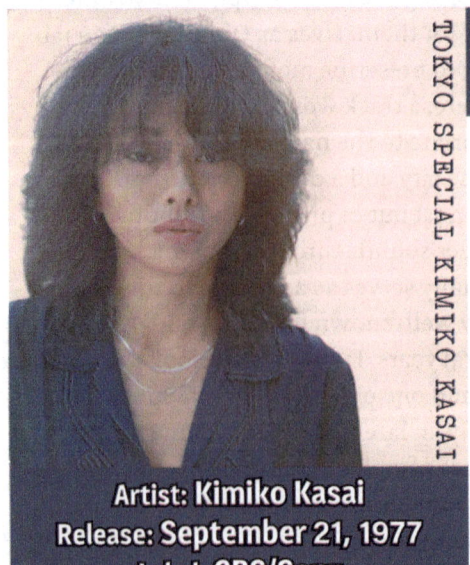

Artist: Kimiko Kasai
Release: September 21, 1977
Label: CBS/Sony

Kimiko Kasai's Tokyo Special may be her most well-known album, at least within the City Pop sphere. This is partially due to the involvement of a certain Tatsuro Yamashita, who composed the song Love Celebration. The funky track feels perfectly suited to Kasai's soft but confident singing and finds itself in a comfortable spot between a slower soul song and frantic disco tune. Those who do enjoy those slow jams will love track A2, an over six minute long treat which has Kasai serenading you throughout. Fast paced fun awaits in track A4, and the jazz performance leaves an impression. The same can be said for the song Tokyo Special, which will shift from a creeping sort of cool to rapid fire at a moment's notice. Tokyo Special is one of Kasai's very best and especially appealing to City Pop fans.

- A1. Love Celebration
- A2. やりかけの人生
- A3. 夏の初めのイメージ
- A4. ベリー・スペシャル・モーメント
- A5. Just Another Love Song
- B1. Tokyo Special
- B2. Sequoia Forest
- B3. テイク・ミー
- B4. Laid Back Mad Or Mellow

Char II - Have a Wine

Following up on the debut album Char was its sequel, naturally titled Char II: Have a Wine, and despite it only being his second album it's marked by a noticeable change in his musical style. Whereas the original Char album had a large emphasis on rock blended with soul and pop music, Have a Wine tones the rock elements down in favor of pop and even disco. Char still belts out some fantastic guitar playing throughout this album, and although it's much more reserved you can still catch glimpses of Char's love for rock and roll in songs like Tokyo Night and Rainy Day. Have a Wine is another standout release from Char which feels like a worthy sequel to its predecessor and contrasts his previous album quite well. You can very strongly feel that infectious 1970s DNA at work here, so fans of that sort of vibe should check this one out.

Artist: Char
Release: October 1977
Label: SeeSaw

A1. 過ぎゆく時に
A2. Sunday Night To Monday Morning
A3. 秋風
A4. 気絶するほど悩ましい
A5. Tokyo Night
B1. Ice Cream
B2. Rainy Day
B3. ふるえて眠れ
B4. 夜
B5. Fraulein

City Lights By The Moonlight

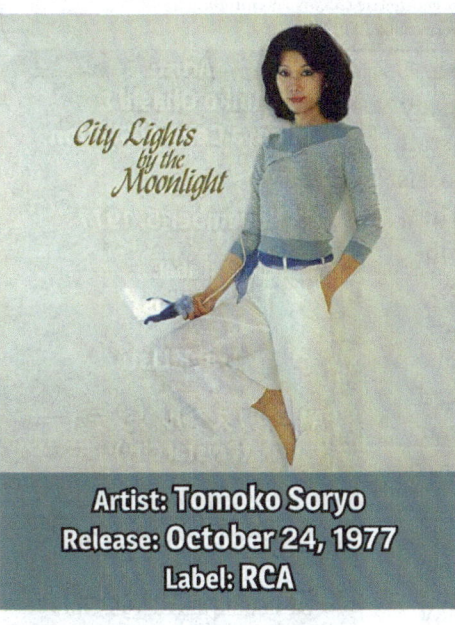

Tomoko Soryo's second album is historically interesting for being one of the first to promote itself with the term 'City Pop.' You can spot it on the album's obi, a paper strip included on some records which helped to advertise it and provide more information. The album's emphasis on jazz and funk gives its tracks some groove, and while it certainly feels like City Pop it still maintains some of that Kayōkyoku identity. The titular City Lights By The Moonlight is a classic about love in the city, the exact kind of song that feels synonymous with the genre. I Say Who which will have you moving and shaking to its fast-paced lyrics, and the rest of the B-side is also fun. Soryo wouldn't release another solo album until 1981, as she would spend the next few years in the duo Tinna alongside Mariko Takahashi.

Artist: Tomoko Soryo
Release: October 24, 1977
Label: RCA

A1. City Lights By The Moonlight
A2. 信号機
A3. きらめいた日々
A4. 愛の世界
A5. あじさいの花
B1. めざまし時計
B2. ふたりの朝
B3. ウイスキー・ララバイ
B4. I Say Who
B5. ほほえみを見せた

Back Mirror

Back Mirror is the second album by Tetsuji Hayashi, although it is his first which feels right to call City Pop, as his first album Bruges came out in 1973. Hayashi would have a genre defining career as a composer, crafting songs such as Stay With Me for Miki Matsubara, and his own albums are splendid too. Fans of Junko Ohashi may recognize the song Rainy Saturday & Coffee Break, which Hayashi originally composed, and he provides a great self-cover of it for this album. Track A3 is another must listen thanks to its smoking hot guitar played by Kenji Omura, although most of the album leans towards lighter tracks. These all give Hayashi a chance to show off his singing chops accompanied by smooth instrumentals, and it's interesting to take an earlier look at Hayashi before he became the songwriting titan we know.

Artist: Tetsuji Hayashi
Release: 1977
Label: Kitty Records

A1. Marci (I)
A2. Rainy Saturday & Coffee Break
A3. 夜のおわり
A4. 彼女の長い一日
A5. 燃えつきる日まで
B1. 追憶
B2. レター
B3. 年老いた水夫のバラード
B4. 金色のライオン
B5. 鳥の背に飛びのれたら
B6. Marci (II)

Crystal City

Left: Photos of Ohashi and the members of Minoya Central Station included with the album.
Center: The unique and mesmerizing cover of Crystal City showing Ohashi skybound amidst geometric shapes and buildings.
Right: The single release for Crystal City and funky Little Queenie which was released in 1978.

Junko Ohashi and the newly formed Minoya Central Station managed to release a second album in 1977; however, the structure and chemistry of the band had already gone through a shift since Rainbow. While many of the lyricists and production staff stayed the same some of the performers left in favor of other ventures, such as bassist Ikujirō Fukuda who was graduating from college. Ohashi would later reflect on the state of the band for Crystal City on her official website, mentioning that the atmosphere was quite different due to the shake up. The differing musical sensibilities, personalities and lack of experience between the members all proved to be obstacles in creating the album, and Ohashi ultimately came to realize how a feeling of harmony and trust is necessary for a band to keep going. The album gets us started with the eponymous Crystal City, a track which perfectly reflects the unique visual design of the album's cover. Leading us in with mesmerizing violin play from Hiroki Tamaki, the song gives a fantastical depiction of the city at daybreak. Describing it like a brilliantly cut diamond where there's always something new to see, it's easy to get lost in the song and imagine yourself in the idealized cityscape Ohashi describes. Embraced by Mist slows down the pace a bit before the absolutely explosive Funky Little Queenie shakes things up. This frantic and unique song has heavy electric piano usage alongside a 'DJ' to provide some added vocals, and to introduce the funky little queenie the song is named after. It's sure to be a hit at your next impromptu seventies disco dance party. The lovebirds Ohashi and Ken Sato perform another duet for the album in Pavement With Men and Women, and fans of the trombone will enjoy Eiji Arai's playing in Sunset Scene. Despite its name Arabian Nights more so brings to mind visions of a tropical getaway thanks to the marimba and saxophone, while the very cool Highway at Night would have made for a fitting music choice for a late-night drive with a special somebody. The standout feature of Heroine of Fire is its chorus from Jun Fukamachi, Ken Sato and Ohashi, while Silhouette of Wind has a cameo appearance from the King of Sax himself, Jake H. Concepcion, City Pop's most prevalent saxophone star. Finally, we end on the moving Like A Sea Gull, which starts off quite slowly but gradually reveals powerful instruments and vocals to leave a lasting impact before the album ends. Despite the troubles the band faced Crystal City would prove to be another successful effort for Ohashi & Minoya Central Station, and a definitive early City Pop album.

Artist:
Junko Ohashi & Minoya Central Station

Release:
November 5, 1977

Label:
Philips

Track List:

A1. クリスタル・シティー
(Crystal City)

A2. 霧に抱かれて
(Embraced By Mist)

A3. Funky Little Queenie

A4. 男と女のいる舗道
(Pavement With Men and Women)

A5. 落日風景 (Sunset Scene)

B1. アラビアン・ナイト
(Arabian Nights)

B2. 夜のハイウェイ
(Highway at Night)

B3. 炎のヒロイン
(Heroine of Fire)

B4. 風のシルエット
(Silhouette of Wind)

B5. Like A Sea Gull

An Insatiable High

Artist: Masayoshi Takanaka
Release: December 1, 1977
Label: Kitty Records

Masayoshi Takanaka's second album for 1977 gave us more of his irresistible jazz fusion, now made in conjunction with a renowned American band. The members of Tower of Power were brought on to perform for An Insatiable High, and they can be heard on tracks A1, B1 and B2. Those three tracks are expectedly some of the album's best, but every song has that exceptional Takanaka quality. The quite lengthy A3 clocks in at over ten minutes and feels like a marathon akin to the one seen on the album's cover. The song maintains a frantic energy throughout its first half, then cools down and becomes quite mesmerizing as we enter the B-side. B1 feels like it's straight from an American R&B album, and Takanaka really gets to rock on B2 and B3. The album finishes up with B4, a bittersweet tune that might have you reflecting on the past for a while.

- A1. Sexy Dance
- A2. Malibu
- A3. An Insatiable High
- B1. E.S.P.
- B2. M5
- B3. Sundrops
- B4. Good (Bad?) Old Days

Endless Flight

Artist: Masataka Matsutoya
Release: December 25, 1977
Label: Panam

The first solo album from Tin Pan Alley member Masataka Matsutoya would be one of the only solo releases credited to him. This is rather surprising considering how impactful he was on City Pop, not to mention his crucial contributions to Yumi Arai's career. Although it was a Matsutoya project all of his Tin Pan Alley bandmates took part, along with other genre defining figures like Taeko Ohnuki. Endless Flight is most similar to a folk rock album with a bit of jazz sprinkled in and is full of those songs that'll make you feel right at home, no matter where that may be. Possibly the cutest detail about the album is the cover's artist, as it was drawn by pop sensation Yumi Arai, who would soon become Masataka's wife. Loaded with feel-good tracks, Endless Flight is certainly one to check out, especially for fans of Tin Pan Alley.

- A1. 沈黙の時間
- A2. 荒涼
- A3. 煙草を消して
- A4. 霜の降りた朝
- B1. もう二度と
- B2. 気づいたときは遅いもの
- B3. 乗り遅れた男
- B4. Hong Kong Night Sight
- B5. 夜の旅人

BGM

Artist: Fujimaru Band
Release: 1977
Label: King Records

The sole album by Fujimaru Band, named after its leading member Yoshino Fujimaru, who would later become a part of groups such as Shogun and AB's while also having a successful solo career. Fujimaru's first venture was akin to the style of music he'd be making going forward, as it mostly involves a mix of pop and folk rock. Despite being his first record BGM feels quite sophisticated, and it's a real treat for those who enjoy digging into some of City Pop's lesser known albums. The album is filled with 11 great songs, but some favorites are A2 with its slick instrumental work, and B1 has some moving singing from Fujimaru. Paper Machine is an all instrumental standout from BGM due to its memorable mix of funk and electronic, and B3 is another welcome addition to the album. An awesome launching point for Fujimaru, who was just getting started.

- A1. ハイウェイ
- A2. 雑踏の中で
- A3. 哀しみの舗道
- A4. 避暑地の出来事
- A5. 雨の昼下がり
- A6. 陽のあたる道
- B1. Can't We Start It All Over Again
- B2. Paper Machine
- B3. Don't Ever Say Good-Bye To The Sun
- B4. I Know It's Gonna Last
- B5. Theme

1978, New Faces & New Problems

Lots of new blood was entering the music world now that many of the conventions of City Pop were established, including quite a few female artists who would become some of the genre's star players. Instantly recognizable names such as Anri and Mariya Takeuchi both got started here, and within just a few years they would be creating some of City Pop's most iconic songs and albums. Junko Yagami also arrived on the scene to serenade us with her beautiful voice and the four-person group Circus delivered their own unique vision of a chorus. A new era began for Yumi Arai, who started making music under her newlywed name of Yumi Matsutoya and gradually began dominating the charts. While things were looking up overall, trouble was brewing for many artists who were still finding their footing. Taeko Ohnuki was under scrutiny for her previous album's lackluster sales, leading to a controlling atmosphere and heavy expectations from her new label. Tatsuro Yamashita was going through a similar struggle with his unique music not reaching a wider audience, which was compounded by growing concerns that the industry was evolving at a pace he couldn't keep up with. Junko Ohashi landed a homerun with the song Twilight My Love, although her label's executives wanted more than just a one-off hit and became more controlling over her band's activities. Finally, Minako Yoshida got wrapped up in some business politics and was 'strongly encouraged' to fly over to the United States and record Let's Do It. New dreams were born this year, while several others came dangerously close to ending.

Taeko Ohnuki

Few City Pop artists can claim they were involved in the genre from the very start, but Taeko Ohnuki certainly can. Ohnuki got her start as a member of the band Sugar Babe alongside Tatsuro Yamashita, but she would eventually pursue a solo career and undergo one of the most interesting evolutions among her peers. Initially her music was very derivative of the folk that Sugar Babe was known for, but after her debut album Grey Skies she would experiment heavily with new sound techniques and the developing fusion genre, which looked to incorporate a range of styles into something new. Ohnuki's first three albums unfortunately didn't sell well back in the 1970s, but nowadays these albums are highly regarded as some of early City Pop's treasures thanks to Ohnuki's beautiful singing and lyrics, the blending of genres that they employ, as well as all the creative usage of sound throughout. These albums were also rich with themes that were both uplifting and worrying to the adolescents of 1970s, and they're loaded with Ohnuki's youthful desire to innovate. Grey Skies, Sunshower and Mignonne all exemplify some of City Pop's major draws and what made the genre such a memorable snapshot in music history, even if they didn't get the love they deserved back then. In the 1980s she stood out thanks to her European trilogy, a series of unique albums which had synth-pop on the forefront and took inspiration from the music of Europe. Throughout the rest of the decade, she continued to improve her craft with electronic music, often aided by Ryuichi Sakamoto and other members of Yellow Magic Orchestra, who were some of synth-pop's pioneers in Japan. Her musical journey has continued ever since, and she's proven her skills with a wide variety of styles, as well as authoring several books. Ohnuki's contributions to City Pop are many, and it'd be difficult to imagine the genre without her creativity and the depth of her skillset.

Top: Ohnuki in her younger days, although she really hasn't aged much since then.
Bottom: A more recent photo of Ohnuki, who always exudes a joyful energy.

What is Kayōkyoku?

While looking into Japanese music from days gone by you might encounter another term used alongside City Pop, that being Kayōkyoku. Translating to "popular song", the term is a very broad descriptor of pop music that was prevalent throughout Japan from the 1960s until the 1990s. Owing to its somewhat nebulous meaning of "popular song" it can sometimes be difficult to determine what exactly counts or doesn't count as Kayōkyoku. Some general trends include familiar lyrics about topics the average person could relate to such as romance, and their ease of singing, with mass appeal usually being its selling point. Kayōkyoku songs could be enjoyed by everyone from teenage girls to forty something salarymen, and this was especially helped by the massive popularity that karaoke saw throughout the latter half of the century. Karaoke was, and still very much is, a massive industry in Japan, and taking some time off to sing a catchy tune has been an old reliable pastime for generations now. As a bonus fact for anybody wondering what karaoke even means, its from the Japanese word "kara" which means empty, and "oke" from the Japanese pronunciation of orchestra, ōkesutora. In relation to City Pop, Kayōkyoku often ran parallel to it, especially in the 1970s when City Pop was just getting started. The two aren't mutually exclusive, a song can be (and often is) both Kayōkyoku and City Pop, as City Pop is more so a sub-genre and lovechild of various different types of sound. Many City Pop artists also got their start with songs that were more akin to Kayōkyoku, such as Junko Yagami and Anri, who both gravitated more towards the City Pop approach as their careers progressed. Sometimes you might listen to music that is listed as only being Kayōkyoku, but it still feels like City Pop. At which point it's ultimately up to your better judgement to decide if the music 'counts' as one or the other, just don't let the intricacies of genre and labeling the subjective drive you too crazy. Kayōkyoku itself is an offspring of the even earlier Ryūkōka (also translates to popular song, just spelled with different characters) which was at the forefront of the music scene from the 1910s until the 60s. Ryūkōka could be viewed as the first modern fusion of Japanese and Western music, as Japan was isolationist during its Edo period which lasted from 1603 to 1868. Foreign culture, and by extension music were not allowed to enter the island nation for most of those years, but during the Meiji and Taishō periods (1868-1926) these Western influences were finally able to blend with Japan's existing musical stylings. Japanese artists at the time took inspiration from jazz, blues, and classical music and combined it with already existing forms of music such as folk songs or Min'yō gave birth to Ryūkōka. It would remain popular throughout the first half of the 20th century until Kayōkyoku rose to prominence thanks to its greater youth appeal, which largely stemmed from introducing elements of contemporary Western pop and rock. This made Kayōkyoku feel even more removed from the traditional elements found in Ryūkōka, but those who enjoyed these 'old school' inspirations would find comfort in another one of its stylistic offsprings; Enka. This type of music had a heavy emphasis on vocal performances and a more traditional approach to songwriting, but it wasn't entirely removed from those modern influences, thus striking a balance between old and new. Ultimately Kayōkyoku would meet the same fate as its father-genre Ryūkōka when new styles with more modern appeal took over, mostly notably J-Pop, which is still going strong today. Although not the standard for music in Japan anymore Kayōkyoku lives on through its decades of hit songs, its musical descendants like J-Pop, and in our hearts.

Top: Sumako Matsui performed Katyusha's Song, composed by Shinpei Nakayama. Sometimes considered the first Ryūkōka song, it found a middle-ground between Eastern and Western musical philosophies.
Center: Kayōkyoku singer Kyu Sakamoto performed the only Japanese song that ever reached #1 in the USA. His hit song Ue o Muite Arukō from 1963 was renamed Sukiyaki overseas and has sold over 13 million copies worldwide.
Bottom: The idol group Candies are an example of prominent Kayōkyoku performers. Formed in 1973, the trio of Ran Ito, Yoshiko 'Sue' Tanaka and Miki Fujimura were highly successful during their five year tenure. They were also some of the first commercially successful 'idols', a type of female entertainer which would only grow more popular.

Caution!

Artist: Shigeru Suzuki
Release: January 25, 1978
Label: Panam

Shigeru Suzuki managed to stay busy throughout 1978 and released two full albums, kicking the year off with Caution! Despite the name there's nothing to be cautious about, as the album is full of soft rock mood setters with a tropical flavor, somewhat akin to Lagoon. The members of Tin Pan Alley are all accounted for playing on tracks like Rainy Station and Hyacinth, and rising talent Rajie is on the backing vocals for Satin-doll and Tsupparing Blues. Songs like Summer Wine provide a much-needed momentary escape to the beach, while Juliet is reminiscent of a hit from the 60s pop rock era. The introductory Rainy Station is a jazz delight with some awesome saxophone playing and Tsupparing Blues adds a splash of funk to the album. Caution! is another well rounded release from Suzuki with a lot to love.

- A1. Rainy Station
- A2. Summer Wine
- A3. Hyacinth
- A4. Juliet
- A5. Satin-doll
- B1. はるかぜを待つ人
- B2. はじめは他人…
- B3. Tsupparing Blues
- B4. Moon Baby
- B5. クリスタル・ホテル

Monsoon Baby

Artist: Yuko Sugita
Release: January 25, 1978
Label: Invitation

Monsoon Baby is the highly underrated debut album by Yuko Sugita, an artist who had a short but sweet run in the music game. Sugita herself was responsible for composing and writing lyrics for the entire album except for track B4, and she was accompanied by a powerful lineup including most of Tin Pan Alley and Ryuichi Sakamoto. Akin to some other albums from the time period, Monsoon Baby skirts the line between pop and rock, resulting in a record with a youthful energy appropriate to the times. Tracks such as A1 and B3 lean more on the soft rock side, but the album has you covered with its many pop songs and slower jams as well. As expected from Tin Pan Alley, the instrumentals are consistently on point, making this a treat for fans of their playing, and a nice City Pop hidden gem overall.

- A1. 演奏旅行
- A2. キラキラ
- A3. 終電車
- A4. 秋から冬へ
- A5. あてのない一日
- B1. 旋律
- B2. カリフォルニアの空
- B3. モンスーン・ベイビー
- B4. YOUのテーマ
- B5. パステル・ラブ

Swingy

Artist: Masamichi Sugi & Red Stripes
Release: February 25, 1978
Label: Victor

Masamichi Sugi's second album, and the last one created alongside the Red Stripes band. Swingy is arguably a more refined album compared to his previous work and the songs featured are noticeably more diverse, ranging from the fast paced pop rock Sugi is known for to more somber tunes. Sadly, the Red Stripes crew would disband after this album, although to be fair they were more so a rotating ensemble designed to play alongside Sugi, rather than having permanent members. The dissolution of Red Stripes wasn't due to the typical 'creative differences', but rather it was because Sugi came down with acute meningitis after a concert. Being unable to perform left him with time to compose for artists like Mariya Takeuchi and Miki Matsubara, thus shaping City Pop history forever, so it wasn't all bad.

- A1. スインギー
- A2. 僕のレディー
- A3. 青梅街道
- A4. インスピレーション
- A5. あこがれの中南米
- A6. 帰り道
- B1. ロックン・ロール・ウーマン
- B2. 雨の日のバースデー
- B3. ジョージアの月の下
- B4. マドンナ
- B5. ハニー

Shalom

Artist: Junko Ohashi & Minoya Central Station
Release: 1978 Label: Philips

Shalom was the third album created by Junko Ohashi alongside the Minoya Central Station band, and it came out only six months after Crystal City. While Shalom has many songs with that classic City Pop blend of soul and jazz, it's also noteworthy for experimenting with styles the band had never really tried before. Many unique instruments like the Kalimba and Timpani drum are used here, offering a foreign sound which is emblematic of City Pop's quest to blend genres. The opening A1 is a fantastic showcase of their innovation, providing an almost psychedelic first half before swapping from smooth jazz to rock as the song ends. Other highlights include A3 which is cool and crazy, and Spanish Wind which feels like five different songs all in one. Shalom is an excellent album jam packed with some truly splendid tracks from this talented group.

- A1. Journey To The Mind
- A2. 季節風便り
- A3. Soul Trainまっしぐら
- A4. China Dream
- A5. Spanish Wind
- B1. サンバ・デ・カランコ〜アラ・パナマ
- B2. Summer Dreamin'
- B3. Star-Light Train
- B4. (I'm) Just Fallin' In Love
- B5. 愛のメッセージ

Beni Suzume

Artist: Yumi Matsutoya
Release: March 5, 1978
Label: Express

The first album released by Yumi Arai after getting married to Masataka Matsutoya, which came out over a year after The 14th Moon. Beni Suzume is a fairly subdued album, with songs like A2 and A5 reading like poetry that can be enjoyed totally removed from the music that accompanies them. One of the most memorable songs is B1 which has a lovely bit of Latin influence sprinkled in, while B4 has a groovy instrumental segment that really stands out. Beni Suzume is a solid album, but those looking for a more typical pop experience might not find what they're looking for. The album initially received harsh criticism for this, which Matsutoya attributed to Beni Suzume's heavy Latin influence and lack of bright sounds. Despite this her lyrics are strong as ever, and she would only continue to improve from here on.

- A1. 9月には帰らない
- A2. ハルジョオン・ヒメジョオン
- A3. 私なしでも
- A4. 地中海の感傷
- A5. 紅雀
- B1. 罪と罰
- B2. 出さない手紙
- B3. 白い朝まで
- B4. ランドリーゲイトの想い出
- B5. 残されたもの

Million Stars

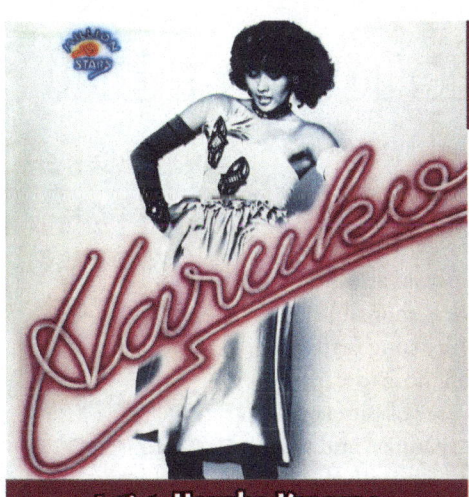

Artist: Haruko Kuwana
Release: April 1978
Label: Philips

The debut album of Haruko Kuwana, a lesser-known figure in the realm of City Pop who released some standout records. Many of the songs were written by Kuwana herself, although some were made with assistance from her brother Masahiro Kuwana. Bill Payne of Little Feat was the producer for Side B, and as such that side features many American musicians which gave Million Stars a global feeling. The album is a must-listen for those who enjoy the City Pop cocktail of jazz, soul, pop and all those genres you associate with the cool seventies. Synthesizers and other electronic instruments are used well here, which shows how City Pop and synth-pop were mingling early on. While the A-side is full of great songs, the B-side absolutely crushes it, and it's clear that everyone from the Kuwana siblings to the band gave it their all for this one.

- A1. あこがれSundown
- A2. さりげなく過ぎゆく時に
- A3. I Rememeber You
- A4. You're Young
- A5. よそうよ
- A6. Million Stars
- B1. Give A Little
- B2. 待ち合わせ
- B3. 風の中に
- B4. Sure Thing
- B5. Set Me Free

Paraiso

Artist: The Yellow Magic Band
Release: April 25, 1978
Label: Alfa

Paraiso is an album made by Haruomi Hosono and the Yellow Magic Band, the predecessor to the synth-pop group Yellow Magic Orchestra who released their first album later in 1978. Although Paraiso does include YMO members Ryuichi Sakamoto and Yukihiro Takahashi, this record is much more akin to some of Hosono's previous albums like Tropical Dandy. This is due to its wide range of City Pop adjacent influences, as you can spot everything from soft rock to country to soul here, but you can still enjoy some electronic stylings here and there. Paraiso has a very global approach, and it really does feel like a musical world tour as you move from the fast-paced Tokio Rush to the exotic sounds of Fujiyama Mama, then to the playful Femme Fatale. It's another incredibly creative piece of work from Hosono and crew which foreshadows their prolific careers in electronic music.

A1. Tokio Rush
A2. Shimendoka
A3. Japanese Rhumba
A4. Asatoya Yunta
A5. Fujiyama Mama
B1. Femme Fatale
B2. Shambala Signal
B3. Worry Beads
B4. Paraiso

Saravah!

Artist: Yukihiro Takahashi
Release: June 21, 1978
Label: Seven Seas

The incredibly star-studded first solo album by Yukihiro Takahashi, one of the members of Yellow Magic Orchestra and a recurrent face in City Pop albums. Takahashi brought the heat for Saravah!, and you can catch the likes of Haruomi Hosono, Rajie, Tatsuro Yamashita and many more as vocalists and performers here. Saravah! is quite different from the electronic music Takahashi would eventually become renowned for, instead emphasizing genres like soul and disco with a Latin infusion. It's an intriguing look into his musical sensibilities before fully embracing the digital revolution of the late seventies and early eighties, but it's still excellent regardless. Many of the tracks create a dandy and cool atmosphere, such as the opening track Volare while Elastic Dummy and Back Street Midnight Queen ups the disco sound for a lively time.

A1. Volare (Nel Blu Dipinto Di Blu)
A2. Saravah!
A3. C'Est Si Bon
A4. La Rosa
A5. Mood Indigo
B1. Elastic Dummy
B2. Sunset
B3. Back Street Midnight Queen
B4. Present

The Memories Are Too Beautiful

Artist: Junko Yagami
Release: June 25, 1978
Label: Discomate

Although this was her first proper album Junko Yagami had been working as an artist releasing singles for years, many of which appear here. Her debut song Alone on a Rainy Day was made back in 1974 when Yagami was only 16 years old, thus beginning a long and successful career from an early age. A prodigious talent, Yagami herself was responsible for composing and writing lyrics for almost every song featured in this album. The tracks here generally lean more towards Kayōkyoku ballads, but you can catch glimpses of City Pop's genre blending here and there. A2 gets pretty funky, and the smooth soft rock instrumentals of A4 pair nicely with Yagami's singing. Her stunning voice always leaves an impact, with tracks A4, B4 and B5 being especially gorgeous, but the whole album is a lovely listen.

A1. 雨の日のひとりごと
A2. 時の流れに
A3. 思い出の部屋より
A4. 思い出は美しすぎて
A5. 追慕
B1. 気まぐれでいいのに
B2. せいたかあわだち草
B3. 窓辺
B4. もう忘れましょう
B5. さよならの言葉

It's A Poppin' Time

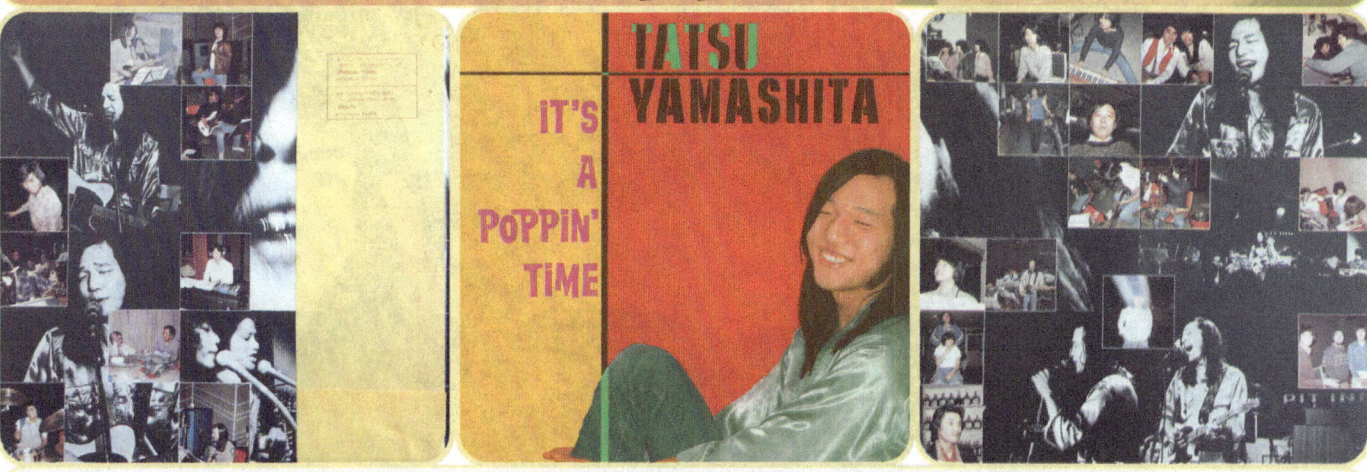

Left: A collage of pictures featuring Yamashita during some of his live performances, among other subjects.
Center: The cover for It's A Poppin' Time features a real happy looking Yamashita. It's a very delightful picture.
Right: More pictures of Yamashita and crew.

Artist:
Tatsuro Yamashita

Release:
May 25, 1978

Label:
RCA

Track List:

A1. Space Crush

A2. Rain Queen

A3. Pink Shadow

A4. 時よ (Time)

A5. Silhouette

B1. Windy Lady

B2. 素敵な午後は (A Lovely Afternoon)

B3. Paper Doll

B4. Candy

C1. Escape

C2. Hey There Lonely Girl

D1. Solid Slider

D2. Circus Town

D3. Marie

It's A Poppin' Time is a live album from Tatsuro Yamashita which was born from less than ideal circumstances, something which ends up being a reoccurring trend all throughout 1978. At this point Yamashita was a solo artist who already released two albums, but he was failing to gather mainstream attention, much to the chagrin of his label RCA. Another issue was that Yamashita's recording sessions gave him much less time to perform live, something which he really enjoyed doing and helped boost his income a little. While the live shows were somewhat sparse, they were undeniably good, so much so that they caught the attention of Ryuzo Kosugi, the man who initially signed Yamashita to the RCA label after Sugar Babe broke up. Ever the shrewd businessman, Kosugi suggested Yamashita create a live album, since it'd be much cheaper than making another studio recorded album and Yamashita would get to jam out live some more. However, Yamashita didn't want this to be just some slapdash record made to turn a quick profit, and he went all the way including new and previously unheard songs in its track list. It's A Poppin' Time was then recorded at The Pit Inn over in Tokyo's Roppongi district, which happened to be directly connected to a studio in the same building, making the recording process quite easy. Although it was a live album the first song Space Crush was recorded in an actual studio, and the reasoning for this was quite simple; Yamashita just felt like doing it that way. You can also spot a cover of the Bread & Butter song Pink Shadow, although Yamashita's version has a much faster tempo which suited his style, and he borrowed Time from Minako Yoshida, a song which would soon appear on her album Let's Do It. Another new track was Silhouette, a song which was made to be rather difficult for the band to play since it switches from slow to fast unexpectedly. Paper Doll was originally planned to be a single, but the record company didn't have confidence in it and rejected the song, so Yamashita just included it here. The astonishingly big Escape is 13 minutes long, meaning side C was only able to fit in and Hey There Lonely Girl, but it was probably worth the inclusion considering it's delightful. Yamashita may have actually gone overboard with this album and absolutely stuffed it with music, requiring it to be released in a more expensive double record set. This naturally made it harder to sell for the still somewhat niche Yamashita, so the money-making plan may have initially backfired for RCA. It's A Poppin' Time is so much more than your typical live album and really shows the effort Yamashita puts into every idea.

Pacific

Left: The back of Pacific showing off some neon signs, bringing back visions of the seventies.
Center: The cover of Pacific, a classic island view that perfectly shows what to expect with the album.
Right: The single release for Shigeru Suzuki's Rainy Station and Juliet which released the same year as Pacific.

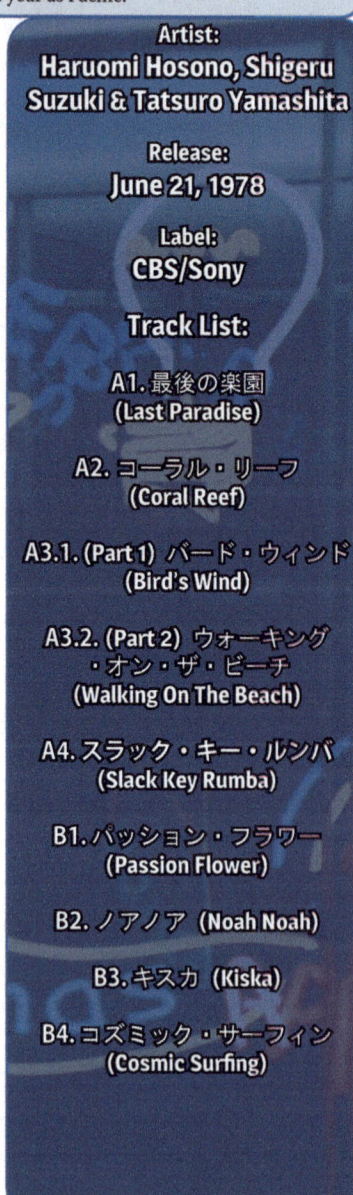

Artist:
Haruomi Hosono, Shigeru Suzuki & Tatsuro Yamashita

Release:
June 21, 1978

Label:
CBS/Sony

Track List:

A1. 最後の楽園 (Last Paradise)

A2. コーラル・リーフ (Coral Reef)

A3.1. (Part 1) バード・ウィンド (Bird's Wind)

A3.2. (Part 2) ウォーキング・オン・ザ・ビーチ (Walking On The Beach)

A4. スラック・キー・ルンバ (Slack Key Rumba)

B1. パッション・フラワー (Passion Flower)

B2. ノアノア (Noah Noah)

B3. キスカ (Kiska)

B4. コズミック・サーフィン (Cosmic Surfing)

Joining forces for a new project were three artists who were already well acquainted at this point: Haruomi Hosono, Shigeru Suzuki and Tatsuro Yamashita. Although this time around they opted not to form a new band as Hosono is so prone to doing (Hosono has been involved in over twenty bands, he's kind of a band maniac) and instead just credit this release with all three of the main contributors' names. This was the genesis of the Sound Image Series, a collection of compilation records that highlighted some of City Pop's best songs and artists and would later include the likes of Memories In Beach House and The Aegean Sea. Some may be disappointed to find that the album doesn't actually feature any songs including both or even all three of the artists, as in you won't hear Hosono and Yamashita together on the same song. The album was instead made in a piecemeal style across various studios, with each member writing and arranging their own tracks, before finally combining them into Pacific. There is some overlap in terms of the musicians playing like Tatsuo Hayashi who lends his drumming talent, alongside other mainstays like Ken Sato, Motoya Hamaguchi, Jake H. Concepcion and more, forming an all-star cast. The trio all wrote and arranged tracks for the album in roughly equal measure, but they're all united by the tropical theme and its emphasis on instrumentals. Vocals are heard very rarely, as the album was made with a certain style and idea in mind, letting you escape into the soundscape the three created. Hosono's Last Paradise is equally relaxing and haunting, capturing the calmness and possible paranoia one might feel alone on an island. Suzuki's Coral Reef captures those vacation vibes perfectly, while Yamashita's lengthy two-parter Bird's Wind/Walking On The Beach may leave you entranced, and it's wonderful for those needing that ten minute long mental getaway. Passion Flower is another Suzuki track which turns up the energy with its backing vocals provided by Kayoko Ishu Group, and it continues the albums recurring trend of having Suzuki's songs include a lot of instruments. Yamashita's song Kiska really delivers on the jazz right before the album nears its conclusion, but Cosmic Surfing stands out as the album's oddball. Hosono really gets usage out of the sequencer used to create its electronic sound, giving us a preview of his prolific future in electronic music as a member of Yellow Magic Orchestra. While some may miss the vocal performances these artists are known for, fans of instrumental and especially tropical music may find a favorite in the tropical creation that is Pacific.

Circus 1

Artist: Circus
Release: July 5, 1978
Label: Alfa

Originally formed in 1977, Circus was a new chorus group akin to Hi-Fi Set who released their debut album in 1978, although they would stand out by being a quartet as opposed to a trio. Family ties run deep in the roster of Circus as its very first ensemble consisted of three sisters and a male cousin, and for the past forty years there's always been at least one member of the original family taking part. The first track Mr. Summertime was originally released as a single and proved to be one of Circus' biggest hits, selling over a million copies. It serves as a perfect showcase of the groups talent and ability to function as a chorus, with the male and female voices complimenting each other perfectly. The rest of the album is also excellent and did an excellent job launching this group, which has continued their activities for decades.

A1. Mr. サマータイム
A2. 夢で逢えたら
A3. 二人だけ
A4. ケッペキにいさん
A5. 僕のエモーション
B1. 経験
B2. 恋はマジック
B3. 愛で殺したい
B4. 赤いレイ
B5. 火の鳥

Stop Motion

Artist: Amii Ozaki
Release: July 5, 1978
Label: Express

Stop Motion marks a shift in Amii Ozaki's music, as it's even closer to resembling what we now think of as City Pop. This is owed in part to her increased responsibilities while crafting the album, as she found herself in the producer role for the first time, giving her even more creative control. Ozaki worked hard to create an album that perfectly integrates pop, soul, funk and more alongside Ozaki's quality compositions to create some of her best yet. Tracks like A1 offer a soft pop with a jazzy twist, while A4 and B4 distinguish themselves with some gnarly guitar work. Ozaki's singing is also excellent, with her performance in B1 being especially noteworthy. Stop Motion might be Ozaki's best work to date, and it highlights a bold new direction for her music and a producer, a role she'd stick to for many of her albums going forward.

A1. センセイション
A2. ジョーイの舟出
A3. 嵐を起こして
A4. ドランクダウン
A5. 来夢来人
B1. ストップモーション
B2. 春の予感
B3. 悪魔がささやく
B4. もどかしい夢
B5. ラストキッス

Thrill

Artist: Char
Release: July 10, 1978
Label: SeeSaw

Char continued his yearly releases with his third album Thrill, although this one would be a dividing point for his musical career. Char, Have a Wine, and Thrill can be thought of as a City Pop trilogy with a general unifying sound, even if some had more or less elements of boogie or rock. Past this release Char's music becomes noticeably more rock centric, a trend which continued throughout the eighties when City Pop was ironically at its most prominent. You can look forward to many more songs with that signature Char style here, including the titular Thrill which is subversively a song about avoiding the temptation of momentary thrills. Thrill is a strong conclusion to Char's City Pop trilogy, but far from his last album, as he's continued to make killer music for the past 40 years.

A1. You Got The Music
A2. 闘牛士
A3. 波
A4. Thrill
A5. My Friend
B1. あいつのBoogie
B2. Tomorrow is Coming For Me
B3. 表参道
B4. Wondering Again

South of The Border

Artist: Yoshitaka Minami
Release: July 21, 1978
Label: CBS/Sony

While Yoshitaka Minami's previous album Forgotten Summer brought to mind visions of the beach and pacific, South of The Border would instead take us on a journey to a Latin soundscape. All the pieces seemed to fall into place for this record, as Minami's singing and songwriting worked wonders alongside an A-list band which included members of Tin Pan Alley. You'll find yourself lost in the consistent experience it provides, as the Latin inspiration is present throughout its entire runtime instead of being a gimmick applied to a handful of songs. The whole album deserves to be thoroughly enjoyed, but A4 comes recommended thanks to Taeko Ohnuki's appearance. Minami himself would reflect quite fondly on the album in 2013's All Time Best ~Cuarenta~ compilation, referring to it as "a highly polished work", a sentiment you're likely to agree with.

- A1. 夏の女優
- A2. プールサイド
- A3. 朝焼けにダンス
- A4. 日付変更線
- A5. 常夜灯
- B1. 夜間飛行
- B2. ワンナイト・ヒーロー
- B3. ブルー・メロディ
- B4. 早くあいつに逢いたい
- B5. スフィンクスの夢
- B6. 終末のサンバ

Moonlight Singing

Artist: Issei Okamoto
Release: July 25, 1978
Label: Discomate

Issei Okamoto's debut album Moonlight Singing was made with a remarkable band including many of City Pop's brightest. Haruomi Hosono, Shigeru Suzuki, Tatsuro Yamashita, Chuei Yoshikawa and Hiroshi Sato can all be heard performing here, along with a few other of the style's all-stars. Okamoto himself makes a very strong first impression here, as the whole album was composed by him and features a wide array of influences. You can hear an awesome blend of jazz, adult-oriented rock and soul which makes Moonlight Singing feel right at home with other City Pop releases from the period. Okamoto's deep singing voice pairs with the music wonderfully while giving the album a cool and mature vibe. Okamoto released albums in 1980 and 1982 but then changed his name to Akira Okamoto and continued working as a composer.

- A1. アトリエ
- A2. 逃げ道
- A3. ムーライト・シンギング
- A4. 想いつめた冬
- A5. 酔いしれて
- B1. ムーン・マジック
- B2. 街の生活
- B3. どしゃぶりの街角
- B4. このままで
- B5. ナイトスタンド

We Are Just Taking Off

Artist: Sadistics
Release: August 25, 1978
Label: Invitation

The second album released by the band Sadistics, a group which consisted of some big City Pop names including Masayoshi Takanaka and Yukihiro Takahashi. Among their three albums this one is most likely to appeal to fans of City Pop due to its tropical theming and emphasis on genre fusion, but the eponymous record Sadistics and The Live Show are also worth listening to. Appropriate to its name We Are Just Taking Off does feel like something of a journey, as the opening track enthusiastically welcomes us into this mini vacation. Blue Curacao is a constantly shifting track that really shows what this talented ensemble is capable of, as does the lively Close Your Eyes. The B-side's main attraction is definitely the track On The Seashore where you can hear Haruko Kuwana's fabulous singing, and the combination of rock and jazz throughout is bound to impress.

- A1. We Are Just Taking Off
- A2. Blue Curaçaò
- A3. Adios
- A4. Close Your Eyes
- B1. Nao
- B2. Game
- B3. On The Seashore
- B4. Floating On The Waves

Mignonne

Left: A picture of Ohnuki from the album, continuing her trend of enjoying sleek black and white imagery in her releases.
Center: The cover of Mignonne with Ohnuki covering her face is mysterious and playful.
Right: Another shot of Ohnuki alongside the track list from a CD release of the album.

Artist:
Taeko Ohnuki

Release:
September 21, 1978

Label:
RCA

Track List:

A1. じゃじゃ馬娘 (Unmanageable Girl)

A2. 横顔 (Profile)

A3. 黄昏れ (Twilight)

A4. 空をとべたら (If One Could Fly)

A5. 風のオルガン (Wind Organ)

B1. 言いだせなくて (I Couldn't Bring Myself To Tell You.)

B2. 4:00 A.M.

B3. 突然の贈りもの (Sudden Gift)

B4. 海と少年 (The Sea and The Boy)

B5. あこがれ (Yearning)

Mignonne (which translates to "cute" in French) released in 1978 following Sunshower, an album which unfortunately ended up being somewhat of a commercial letdown despite how creative it was. After Sunshower's lackluster performance Taeko Ohnuki switched labels from Panam to the much larger RCA, a shakeup which came with a few positives, but many more negatives. RCA was quite intent on producing a hit album and making Mignonne sell, which was more feasible thanks to their larger size and outreach. While this may have helped Ohnuki get her music out there, it came at a cost. This greater emphasis on profit created a totally different environment from what Ohnuki was used to, as RCA was more controlling over the creative process, something Ohnuki wasn't fond of. She was also assigned a producer, Eji Ogura, who had been critical of her music in the past. Ogura wanted to inject more pop elements into her music to give it a wider appeal, which must have added to her frustration considering she began gravitating away from that style with Sunshower. Despite all of their efforts Mignonne would tragically meet the same fate as Sunshower and sold poorly. Whereas previously Ohnuki could write off these failures as a learning experience, the added pressure and lack of creative freedom for this project drove her to consider quitting the industry altogether. It would be another two years before she released her next album. Although Mignonne's origin story may not be the happiest, as a piece of art it managed to win in the end since Mignonne is now viewed as one of early City Pop's absolute best. Many of the songs here feel quite personal, such as the opening track Unmanageable Girl which paints a picture of a bolder Ohnuki who doesn't care about the approval of others, possibly influenced by the unpleasant environment she found herself in. While the album is consistently great there's one track that fans of City Pop will immediately recognize: 4:00 AM. With its mysterious introduction, lyrics about a romance on the verge of collapse and absolutely stunning chorus of "Lord give me one more chance!", it's a song you'll never forget. Sudden Gift is a great track to let your mind melt into and relax with, while The Sea and The Boy gives us another boost of energy right before the album ends. The final song Yearning can be rather haunting with its subject matter of getting older, and the realization that adulthood isn't all that fun, a track that might hit remarkably close to home for some. Mignonne may have been a slow seller at first, but it stood the test of time and is now beloved as one of Ohnuki's greatest achievements, and a must-listen for fans of City Pop.

Let's Do It

Left: A fold-out poster of Yoshida included with the album. Her bright smile contrasts the picture used for the cover quite a lot.
Center: The pretty serious looking cover of Let's Do It. Despite the impression it may give the album is a lot of fun.
Right: The back of Let's Do It with another picture of Yoshida.

The year 1978 would see quite a shakeup for Minako Yoshida, who was already on her sixth studio album. Let's Do It would end up echoing Tatsuro Yamashita's previous record Circus Town, as it too was recorded in Los Angeles with an almost entirely American band, the big difference being that it wasn't even Yoshida's idea to begin with. The situation began when Yoshida had swapped record labels from RCA to Alfa, a change which had an unexpected side effect. The co-founder of Alfa and future Yellow Magic Orchestra producer Kunihiko Murai had already signed a contract to make a yet-unspecified album with Gene Page, a renowned composer in the United States. Murai ultimately drafted newly signed Alfa talent Minako Yoshida to the task, although it wasn't an idea she was keen on. Yoshida thought to herself that Murai must've "gotten confused" trying to figure this whole situation out, and even though she didn't particularly want to make it the contract had already been signed. Rather than kicking up a fuss about this inconvenient state of affairs she decided to take a trip to Los Angeles and begin work on Let's Do It. About half of the tracks for this album were composed by Yoshida herself, but she did bring some firepower to fill in the gaps. Tatsuro Yamashita assisted by composing three songs for the album; I'll Teach You All About Love, Flames of Love and Clouds, all of which he'd later perform on his own albums. Ryuichi Sakamoto then composed B4, and A5 was done by the duo of Carol Bayer-Sager and Peter Allen. Let's Do It contrasts the dark and moody Twilight Zone by being more lighthearted overall with its emphasis on funk and a splash of disco, a sound which reflects its American birthplace. There are still some real heartbreakers included though, and Yoshida's commonly used themes of love and passion are present throughout. The introductory song Let's Do It brings to mind the carefree enjoyment expressed while dancing, while I'll Teach You All About Love is a slower track about the fleeting beauty of romance. Flames of Love has some playful and provocative lyrics, while Cat has Yoshida describing herself as a feline doing as she pleases throughout the night. The album closes us out with another romantic track, I Wanna Be Your Shadow, which expresses a desire to always by a partner's side like a shadow, thus completing our journey through Let's Do It and Yoshida's ode to love. Even though the album wasn't a child of Yoshida's own imagining like with Twilight Zone, it still turned out very well, and it's an extremely welcome addition to her constantly growing discography.

Artist:
Minako Yoshida

Release:
October 25, 1978

Label:
Alfa

Track List:

A1. 愛は思うまま
(Let's Do It)

A2. 恋の手ほどき
(I'll Teach You All About Love)

A3. 時よ
(Time)

A4. 海
(The Sea)

A5. アイド・ラーザー・リーヴ・ホワイル・アイム・イン・ラヴ
(I'd Rather Leave While I'm In Love)

B1. 愛の炎
(Flames Of Love)

B2. 猫
(Cat)

B3. 雲のゆくえに
(Clouds)

B4. 影になりたい
(I Wanna Be Your Shadow)

Streamline '80

Artist: Yumi Matsutoya
Release: November 5, 1978
Label: Express

Yumi Matsutoya's second album for 1978 has a greater emphasis on those catchy pop tunes compared to Beni Suzume, a record which favored the slower tracks. Matsutoya continues to perfect her greatest export here, romantic pop hits with beautiful lyrics. A2 is a fitting example of this, as it takes you through a dramatic journey detailing love on the brink. Songs which involve the winter in some way are also quite prominent, serving as a prelude for Matsutoya's frequent exploration of Christmas romance in later albums. One such song is A3, which describes a girl enthusiastically watching a guy surf during the winter, even if it seems like he kind of sucks at it. Tatsuro Yamashita also shows up as the backing vocalist for this song, alongside his work playing electric guitar. Streamline '80 and Beni Suzume both have a lot to offer listeners, just in separate ways.

- A1. ロッチで待つクリスマス
- A2. 埠頭を渡る風
- A3. 真冬のサーファー
- A4. 静かなまぼろし
- A5. 魔法のくすり
- B1. キャサリン
- B2. Corvett 1954
- B3. 入江の午後3時
- B4. かんらん車
- B5. 12階のこいびと

Prismy

Artist: Amii Ozaki
Release: November 20, 1978
Label: Express

It seemed that Amii Ozaki enjoyed the greater control that came alongside her responsibilities as producer for Stop Motion, since her next album Prismy saw her being even more involved. Alongside her work composing, singing, and producing the album, Ozaki also played an impressive number of instruments such as the marimba, piano, organ, synthesizer and more. This makes Prismy feel like even more of an Ozaki pet project, maintaining the energy of songs from Stop Motion while introducing more experimentation with the instruments on display. The greater emphasis on using a synthesizer serves as foreshadowing for her later work, as Ozaki would lean heavily towards making synth-pop in the years to come. Both of her albums from this year are worth checking out, and both laid the groundwork for her future in music.

- A1. Shocking Shine
- A2. 気分を変えて
- A3. Perfect Game
- A4. 気まぐれ予報
- A5. Tender Rain
- B1. Cosmic Blue
- B2. 少年の日のメリーゴーランド
- B3. 白夜
- B4. Temptation
- B5. I Never Sing A Love Again

New York

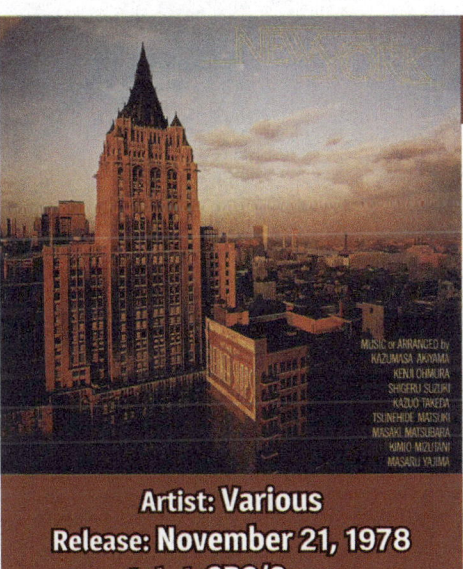

Artist: Various
Release: November 21, 1978
Label: CBS/Sony

New York is another compilation album within the Sound Image Series, which also included Pacific from the same year, and it too was made with some recognizable contributors. These include Shigeru Suzuki, Masaki Matsubara, and Tsunehide Matsuki, who all composed and performed their own tracks. New York is a mostly instrumental experience designed to conjure the feeling of being in the big apple with fitting names like Central Park and Manhattan Sunrise. It's fun to hear each artist's take on the concept, although some of the songs are covers from Westerners like Boz Scaggs. A few highlights are New York Subway which adds to the realism by including English chatter in the background, and Masaki Matsubara really struts his stuff on his cover of Hard Times, but the whole album is slick.

- A1. Kennedy Airport
- A2. Hard Times
- A3. New York Subway
- A4. Hymn To Stuff
- B1. Central Park
- B2. My One And Only Love
- B3. Manhattan Sunrise
- B4. New York Woman Serenade

Apricot Jam

Left: The single release for Listening To Olivia and So Long with a closeup of a young Anri.
Center: The cover for Apricot Jam features a neutral Anri, a look which was applied to all of her releases from 1978.
Right: Another picture of Anri included with the Listening To Olivia single.

1978 would prove to be a significant year for the history of City Pop with many monumental debuts, especially since this is when the world was introduced to Anri. Anri (real name Kawashima Eiko) hit the scene at only 16 years old and would go on to release some of City Pop's most popular songs and albums, establishing a career that continues even today. Her first single Listening To Olivia was written by fellow City Pop prodigy Amii Ozaki, who would craft several more songs for Anri's then upcoming album. The name "Olivia" in the song's title actually comes from a specific source which was brought up when Anri and Ozaki met to discuss the music they would be making together. Anri mentioned liking the late singer and actress Olivia Newton-John, whose music was quite popular in Japan at the time, and she would also star in the film Grease that same year. Ozaki then designed a song revolving around Olivia, although not as its actual subject. The song involves a heartbroken woman dealing with a breakup and finds comfort in the music by Olivia, but the connections to Newton-John don't end there. The phrase "Making a good thing better" is repeated often, and it's a reference to Newton-John's 1977 song Making A Good Thing Better. While Listening To Olivia wasn't a runaway success at first, throughout the years it steadily gained in popularity, and it's still one of her most recognized songs. It has also been covered by many artists, and even Anri herself has done renewed versions of it. Apricot Jam features quite a number of composers and lyricists on board, with the most notable being Amii Ozaki who was responsible for Listening To Olivia, Flying Departure at 10 a.m. and Chinese Doll, with Anri herself only doing the composition for So Long. While Listening To Olivia is the most popular song on the album the other tracks on offer leave an impression, such as the poetic Feeling Chilly. So Long dives into the sorrow felt after a breakup, while ultimately expressing that love is beautiful, despite the pain that may accompany it. We tap into one of the primal City Pop subjects in Flying Departure at 10 a.m., that of course being plane travel, for a song that feels somewhat more in line with some of Anri's later releases. Chinese Doll's thought-provoking lyrics give the song weight which will have you thinking back on it, while Blue City strikes a nice blend between pop and soft rock. Apricot Jam is a decent first album for the fresh talent, even if it's quite different from the summertime City Pop jams she'd become associated with. From here on Anri will only continue to refine her craft and end up becoming one of City Pop's all-time greatest.

Artist:
Anri

Release:
November 21, 1978

Label:
For Life Records

Track List:

A1. オリビアを聴きながら (Listening To Olivia)

A2. ラプソディー (Rhapsody)

A3. そぞろ寒 (Feeling Chilly)

A4. 西日うすれて (Waning Twilight)

A5. So Long

B1. Flying午前10時発 (Flying Departure at 10 a.m.)

B2. 中国人形 (Chinese Doll)

B3. キーワードを探せ (Keyword Search)

B4. Blue City

B5. フェイド・アウト (Fade-out)

Beginning

Left: The single release for Come Back, My Time and Just Friend.
Center: The cover of Beginning's picture of Takeuchi in a hat is quite innocuous, as all great beginnings are.
Right: A single release featuring Hollywood Cafe, a collaborative song which Takeuchi composed and Taeko Ohnuki wrote lyrics for.

Artist:
Mariya Takeuchi

Release:
November 25, 1978

Label:
RCA

Track List:

A1. Good Bye Summer Breeze

A2. 戻っておいで・私の時間
(Come Back, My Time)

A3. 夏の恋人
(Summer Lover)

A4. 輝くスターリー・ナイト
(Shining Starry Night)

A5. 目覚め
(Waking Up Alone)

B1. Just Friend

B2. 突然の贈りもの
(Sudden Gift)

B3. おかしな二人
(Funny Couple)

B4. ムーンライト・ホールド・ミー・タイト
(Moonlight Hold Me Tight)

B5. サンタモニカ・ハイウェイ
(Santa Monica Highway)

B6. すてきなヒットソング
(My Hit Songs)

The final big debut for 1978 was for a young talent whose face would become synonymous with City Pop in the west, although it'd take about 35 years for that to happen. Mariya Takeuchi hit the scene with the appropriately titled Beginning, an album which seemed primed for success as it includes several songs composed by proven artists. Some of these include Tetsuji Hayashi, Masamichi Sugi and even Haruomi Hosono, giving the young Takeuchi some very solid material to work with. Perhaps the most fated encounter for this album was with Tatsuro Yamashita, who composed the track Summer Lover, a title which may have served as some real-world foreshadowing. Takeuchi and Yamashita would later get married in 1982, establishing one of City Pop's ultimate power couples who helped each other throughout their whole careers. Takeuchi's own songwriting was fairly limited for this first release, as the only tracks she composed on her own were Santa Monica Highway and My Hit Songs. Throughout her career she would become more experienced with songwriting until eventually albums like Variety and Request contain songs exclusively written by her. Thanks to this mishmash of renowned contributors Beginning is an album that feels right at home with its City Pop siblings from the time. Having so many different composers means you're highly likely to find at least a few songs you love, especially due to all of the relevant themes throughout. Classics like love in the summer, and its opposing concept of quiet loneliness are both plentiful here. The downside is that the album isn't as consistent as some of her later work, but it's nonetheless an impressive start to her career. We open with Goodbye Summer Breeze, a song which paints a nostalgic picture of a time gone by, with the summer itself being a metaphor for a lost love. Come Back, My Time gets great usage out of its occasional English lyrics, and Tatsuro Yamashita's song Summer Lover almost directly contrasts Good Bye Summer Breeze, instead detailing a beautiful romance in the sunshine. For a killer combo of soft rock instrumentals and moving lyrics look no further than Sudden Gift, and Funny Couple includes a stacked band with Shigeru Suzuki and Jun Sato playing. The final track My Hit Songs then provides a glimpse into Takeuchi's own writing talent. It's fittingly an ode to the power of music and the idea that while things may change for the worse, those hit songs and the joy they bring will always remain. While Beginning isn't one of Takeuchi's most beloved albums it's still a great first effort backed by City Pop's icons, a group that she'll soon join.

Flush

Left: The single release for Twilight My Love and Love Machine, which proved to be one of Ohashi's biggest hits.
Center: The cover of Flush feels very dynamic, which is appropriate for the fast paced and exciting songs within.
Right: The track list and credits for Flush is a little more risque compared to its cover.

Both Junko Ohashi and her band Minoya Central Station stayed busy throughout the year and released two albums, although one could say they were actually suffering from success. Earlier in 1978 they released the excellent and highly creative album Shalom, then in August Ohashi had struck gold with the single Twilight My Love. On the week of its release the single peaked at number 2 on Japan's Oricon charts, and number 40 for its yearly ranking, making it one of her biggest hits to date. Just a few weeks later it was used as the theme song for the primetime TV drama Like a Lion, which further boosted its popularity. To try and capitalize on their rising stardom the record company quickly put together a best-of album which naturally included Twilight My Love, although this was something that Ohashi herself had mixed feelings on. The scary thing about success is that you're constantly being pushed to surpass your previous results, which is especially true in the cutthroat world of music. Their next album Flush was therefore expected to do even better than Twilight My Love, which was quite a tall order, especially considering how the band was going through some creative burnout after making so many albums. The solution the label came up with was to assign Kyohei Tsutsumi, the composer for Twilight My Love, to write all of the tracks for the album's B-side, while Takashi Matsumoto of Happy End wrote the lyrics. Therefore, only the A-side actually features songs composed by band members, but their relationship with Tsutsumi seemed to work out as he let the band do the arrangement on the songs, thus letting them have a degree of control over their music. While things were fine with Tsutsumi the same couldn't be said about the label at large, as Ohashi would later state that it felt like the band wasn't being left to their own devices anymore. Despite the production shakeup Flush turned out well and fits right in with Ohashi's other work. Hold On, Hold Tight and Swaying Midnight deliver that late-seventies sound you'd expect, and would've been a lot of fun at discos back in the day. Fans of slower songs will enjoy Winter Sleep and Rouge Et Noir alongside its other offerings, as while the album is energetic it's a little less explosive compared to Crystal City or Rainbow. All of the songs on offer in Flush are high quality, but you may find it's less creative than their other work, which is likely owed to the burnout the band was experiencing. Flush is a good album from Ohashi and crew, but it probably feels like their the most 'standard' since being formed, especially when compared to Shalom from the same year.

Artist:
Junko Ohashi

Release:
December 16, 1978

Label:
Philips

Track List:

A1. サファリ・ナイト (Safari Night)

A2. 傷心飛行 (Emotional Flight)

A3. マイ・ソング (My Song)

A4. Hold On, Hold Tight

A5. 冬の眠り (Winter Sleep)

B1. 揺れながらミッドナイト (Swaying Midnight)

B2. メビウスの輪 (Möbius Strip)

B3. Rouge Et Noir

B4. ディープ・ソウル (Deep Soul)

B5. 火のように水のように (Like Fire, Like Water.)

Go Ahead!

Left: The single release for Let's Dance Baby and Bomber, released a year later after Go Ahead! when Bomber proved to be a surprise hit.
Center: The cover for Go Ahead! mirrors It's A Poppin' Time with a caricature of Yamashita, although the artstyle received some flak in Japan upon release.
Right: The back of Go Ahead! gets great usage out of its colors and geometric patterns.

Artist:
Tatsuro Yamashita

Release:
December 20, 1978

Label:
RCA

Track List:

A1. Overture

A2. Love Celebration

A3. Let's Dance Baby

A4. Monday Blue

A5. ついておいで
(Follow Me Along)

B1. Bomber

B2. 潮騒
(The Whispering Sea)

B3. Paper Doll

B4. This Could Be The Night

B5. 2000トンの雨
(2000 Tons of Rain)

1978 was a year defined by obstacles for many of City Pop's artists who weren't quite new, but not quite industry veterans either. Minako Yoshida and Taeko Ohnuki both faced problems with their respective record labels this year, and it seemed like it was now Tatsuro Yamashita's turn. Although the sales figures on Yamashita's records were decent up to this point they still weren't quite up to his label's expectations. This was especially true after It's A Poppin' Time underperformed due to its high price, leaving Yamashita's future in music uncertain. On a more personal and artistic note Yamashita began to think that the musical landscape he had grown accustomed to was changing. It seemed possible that he would get left in the dust if things didn't improve, and so he decided to make Go Ahead! as if it were to be his very final album. This urgency resulted in Yamashita giving it his all and writing some of his best tracks possible to create something of a musical bucket list. Due to this quality over quantity approach Yamashita eventually realized that he wouldn't be able to create a full-length album because he was putting so much time into each song. Therefore, the rest of the album was essentially sourced from 'wherever', such as a few unused compositions he had sitting around, as well as covers of other songs. This unique and somewhat contradictory approach led to Go Ahead! being criticized for its disparate songs, but in later years listeners would come to appreciate this aspect. Love Celebration was reclaimed from an ill-fated album by singer Linda Carriere which Yamashita wrote songs for, and since the production was cancelled the track was up for grabs. A classic disco-inspired Yamashita tune appears via Let's Dance Baby, although it was originally written for a totally different album and repurposed for this one. The seven-minute-long Monday Blue was styled after R&B and must have been quite the taxing production, as the blurb about the song from the album recounts the production team sighing after the successful take. One song which turned out to be a surprising success was Bomber, which stood out as one of the album's best thanks to its funky instrumentals. It proved to be especially popular at a disco in Osaka, leading to it getting a single release the following year. This Could Be The Night was another cover, albeit one where Yamashita was playing almost every instrument. Yamashita can be heard as the guitarist, pianist, drummer, and bassist here, showing how incredibly versatile of a musician he really is. Go Ahead! was a make-or-break moment for Yamashita's career, and even though the philosophy behind its creation was rather unorthodox there's a lot of beauty to be found in its idiosyncrasies.

Telescope

Artist: Shigeru Suzuki
Release: November 25, 1978
Label: Panam

Suzuki's second album for 1978 provides more of those classic summertime jams with a delightful mix of pop, rock, funk, and jazz. The mood is set well by the fun and lighthearted Tuesday Queen, and the sleeper hit A2/Image Change has exciting instrumentals with backing vocals that make its chorus hit hard every time you listen to it. Another memorable song is A3, which details a short lived romance with a local woman from the Hawaiian island of Lahaina who only speaks one word of Japanese, although the singer promises to come back and visit someday. Telescope is a highly underrated album by Suzuki loaded with some of his best tracks, and you may find a few of your new favorites here. The 2020 special edition release is also rich with content such as backing tracks and unused takes, giving us a deeper look at this great record.

- A1. Tuesday Queen
- A2. イメージ・チェンジ
- A3. ラハイナ・ガール
- A4. ストリップ・ティーズ
- A5. マドモアゼル
- B1. スパニッシュ・フライ (媚薬)
- B2. ハヴァナ・シガレット
- B3. 10セントの魂
- B4. スウィート・インスピレーション
- B5. テレスコープ

Love Heart

Artist: Rajie
Release: December 21, 1978
Label: CBS/Sony

Love Heart follows up on Rajie's previous album by providing more of those pop tracks to sink your teeth into, and it features a stellar band including the likes of Haruomi Hosono and guitarist Chuei Yoshikawa, while Yukihiro Takahashi and Ryuichi Sakamoto worked as co-producers. Hosono and the other members of Yellow Magic Orchestra would have a huge influence on Rajie, and she'd become one of the first City Pop artists to heavily incorporate synth-pop into her music. Some of the standout tracks include the introductory Tea For One which features pop with a rock twist, and Winter Portrait which immediately lures you in with its synthesizer. Yoshitaka Minami also appears for a duet in Cool Down, and Tatsuro Yamashita can be heard on the chorus for Just In The Rain, making the song a real treat.

- A1. Tea For One
- A2. 風によせて
- A3. Cool Down
- A4. Love Heart
- A5. 冬の肖像
- B1. たびだち
- B2. 優しい関係
- B3. Last Chance
- B4. Just In The Rain

Loft Sessions Vol. 1

Artist: Various
Release: 1978
Label: Victor

Loft Sessions Vol. 1 is a unique compilation album which features songs by female artists, many of whom fall under the City Pop umbrella. Loft Sessions wasn't exactly an all-star production though, as many of these artists were still amateurs or had yet to make a proper debut. The album is most historically significant for being the debut of Mariya Takeuchi, months before her album Beginning was out. She provided two songs, A5 and B2, giving us a chance to hear some very early examples of Takeuchi at work. Sadly, not all of the participants reached the level of fame that Takeuchi did, but you can still find Masako Takasaki as a member of Kinokuniya Band, and Kaoru Uemura released the album Just My Feeling in 1979. Loft Sessions provides an interesting look into the origin point for one of City Pop's most beloved icons, and many more songs to enjoy.

- A1. 星くず
- A2. ブラック・コーヒー
- A3. こぬか雨
- A4. 雨はいつか
- A5. ハリウッド・カフェ
- B1. 気楽にいくわ
- B2. 8分音符の詩
- B3. きょうから…
- B4. Motif-M

1979, Hitting The Street

1978 was a year that could easily be described as hectic with its plentiful debuts and the sheer number of scuffles with record labels. As a result of the chaos two of City Pop's leading ladies, Taeko Ohnuki and Minako Yoshida, took breaks from releasing albums this year, and their absences can certainly be felt. On the bright side Tatsuro Yamashita found solace in Air Records, a smaller label which offered more creative freedom that allowed him to create Moonglow. Mariya Takeuchi also released University Street, an album rich with the youthful themes associated with City Pop. The brotherly duo of Bread & Butter totally reinvented themselves for this year with Late, Late Summer, a perfect addition to the summer obsessed genre featuring an unreal band. Many newcomers like Tatsuhiko Yamamoto, Asami Kado and Jin Kirigaya all strutted their stuff for the first time, while some artists dematerialized as quickly as they appeared. Noriyo Ikeda gave us Dream In The Street, an excellent record for the developing genre, then went quiet. Meanwhile a group of college kids inspired by the likes of Sugar Babe worked on their only album, Love, and self-published it with a meager 200 copies. In doing so they unknowingly gave the world a musical time capsule which would be rediscovered decades later. This year could be viewed as the unofficial end for 'early' City Pop, as the trend seemed fairly solidified at this point. Common traits including the blending of Western genres, a general audience of urban listeners, and a group of reoccurring artists were all codified by now. The 1980s are upon us, but the 1970s are about to receive a fitting finale with some great records.

Eiichi Ohtaki & Takashi Matsumoto

Top: Eiichi Ohtaki hard at work, or maybe just enjoying some music on his downtime.
Bottom: You don't see Takashi Matsumoto's face very often, but he's one of Japan's greatest lyricists of all time.

Eiichi Ohtaki and Takashi Matsumoto are two of Japan's most renowned artists who were deeply involved with City Pop's predecessor genre New Music. As members of the inventive folk band Happy End, they helped pave the way for what eventually became City Pop, and they significantly affected the genre for its whole lifespan. Throughout the seventies Ohtaki released several solo albums, produced for Tatsuro Yamashita's band Sugar Babe, and formed Niagara Triangle with Yamashita and Ginji Ito. Takashi Matsumoto likewise found enormous success working as a lyricist, but his reach extended far beyond just City Pop. Since the 1970s he's been the lyricist behind thousands of songs and has become a legend as Japan's third best-selling lyricist of all time. Matsumoto was especially known for his work with various idols in the seventies and eighties, but in the City Pop niche he has worked with Mariya Takeuchi and Miki Matsubara, among many others. Despite their close ties it was rare for Ohtaki and Matsumoto to collaborate after Happy End disbanded in 1972, but that all changed with A Long Vacation in 1981. The duo worked together to craft a gem of an album which quickly became Ohtaki's most successful to date, selling over a million copies and cementing itself as a City Pop staple. Their team-up for 1984 in Each Time was another winner, and it became Ohtaki's only album to hit number one. Each Time would also end up being the final solo album Ohtaki released during his lifespan, as he shifted his focus towards composing and producing for others afterwards. Ohtaki sadly passed away in 2013 at the age of 65 due to an aneurysm, but in the following years some of his music was released posthumously. Debut Again from 2016 holds many songs discovered after his passing, most of which date back to the 1980s, giving us access to some musical treasures which could have been lost to history.

City Pop and Synth-pop

Alongside the rise of City Pop there was another developing genre which was rapidly growing in popularity called synth-pop, and the two quite often crossed paths. Electronic music and its various subgenres have an incredibly rich and deep history, but the story of synth-pop functionally begins in the 1970s thanks to advancements in technologies like drum machines and the synthesizer, which is where the genre's name comes from. In the early 1970s European groups such as Kraftwerk were among the first to popularize heavy usage of synthesizers to create their music, a trend which soon went global and especially took off in Japan. Many artists in Japan began utilizing these devices to make music, but few were as prolific as the members of Yellow Magic Orchestra. Consisting of Haruomi Hosono, Ryuichi Sakamoto and Yukihiro Takahashi, these three men were godfathers of the Japanese electronic scene thanks to their innovative work with cutting-edge technology and techniques. Yellow Magic Orchestra had a major influence on synth-pop's popularity, as their albums regularly reached number one on Japan's Oricon chart, but their most well-known venture is their album Solid State Survivor from 1979 which sold over two million copies and even made waves internationally. Yellow Magic Orchestra went dormant after 1984, but by this point the digital revolution was already in full effect. This fascinating with the potential of electronic music also hit the still forming world of City Pop, especially since Hosono and Sakamoto were already deeply involved with the genre. Sakamoto performed on many of City Pop's greatest albums and worked closely with Taeko Ohnuki since the beginning of her career, and in Hosono's case City Pop partially descended from his past work in New Music. Since the two genres were connected via these men this there was bound to be overlap, and towards the end of the seventies there was a noticeable uptick in City Pop artists using synthesizers. Rajie, Hiroshi Sato and Amii Ozaki were among the first in the niche to heavily use electronic sound, but in time just about everybody was realizing the value these gadgets could bring to their music. The close relationship between the two genres stayed strong in the eighties, and some of City Pop's most popular albums were synth-pop adjacent. Toshiki Kadomatsu frequently used synthesizers in his music to add some cybernetic cool, which can easily be heard both in his own albums and his collaborations with Anri such as Timely. Another beloved example is Tomoko Aran's Fuyü-Kükan, which had synth-pop at the forefront, but it also used funk, rock and more to excellent effect. This made it one of the best albums for demonstrating what made City Pop and synth-pop such good partners, but some artists were so taken with electronic music they slowly gravitated towards making synth-pop their primary style. Taeko Ohnuki went through a fascinating journey as she changed from being inspired by American folk and rock to designing her music with a European approach, and then in the mid-eighties she became renowned for her synth-pop. Another interesting example of this happening is Miharu Koshi, who originally had an image and style similar to other idols of the era. She started to shake up this perception with 1983's Tutu, an electronic album produced by Haruomi Hosono which altered the course of her career forever. Since then, she has continued to make electronic music shaped by global genres of all sorts, including classical and French chanson. City Pop and synth-pop are like friends who grew up together, and a significant part of City Pop's charm can be attributed to strides made with electronic music throughout the seventies and eighties.

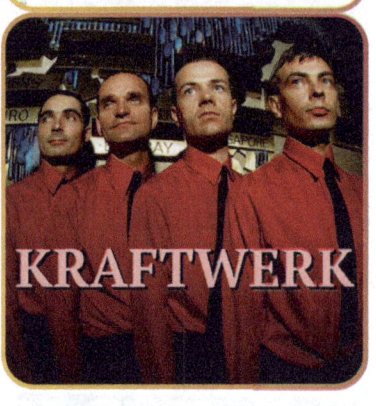

Top: Yellow Magic Orchestra's album Solid State Survivor is one of synth-pop's most influential albums, especially from Japan. Michael Jackson planned to cover Behind The Mask from this album for Thriller, but it ultimately wasn't included. This version finally found a home in the posthumous album Michael along with other unreleased songs.
Center: Taeko Ohnuki had always experimented with synthesizers in her past work, but Signifie from 1983 marked a big shift in her style. It also happened to be her most commercially successful album to date, which must have been encouraging.
Bottom: The German group Kraftwerk were some of electronic music's pioneers, and they heavily influenced Yellow Magic Orchestra along with innumerable other artists.

Love

Left: The members of So Nice, all of whom were students at the Nihon University College of Arts.
Center: The colorful cover of Love emulates 60s American art, and reflects the style of the music perfectly.
Right: A 2021 single release for Tight Night and Love Sick, over 40 years after the original album.

Artist: So Nice

Release: 1979

Label: Self Released

Track List:

A1. So Nice

A2. 光速道路 (Faster-Than-Light Highway)

A3. Last Kiss

A4. 陽だまり (Sunny Spot)

A5. Tight Night

B1. Love Sick

B2. かけぬける風 (Breeze Blowing Through)

B3. Earth Mover

B4. 別離 〈わかれ〉 (Separation)

B5. Dancing All Night Long

1979 was a momentous year for a group of students at the Nihon University College of Arts, as they were graduating. Their band, So Nice, were all members of the school's folk music club who met in 1976, and like many college artists they mostly played covers from some of their favorites. In So Nice's case they were big fans of Sugar Babe and Tatsuro Yamashita, who would serve as major inspirations for them. After their time in school together ended the band decided on a proper sendoff, crafting an original album of their own. From February 26th to April 28th of 1979 So Nice recorded Love, their one and only album, and self-released it with an extremely limited 200 copies. Afterwards the members all went their separate ways, and Love was left as just another blip in musical history. Due to its very small production run it wouldn't be enjoyed by any except the original band and those few who got the opportunity to listen to it. At least that was the case for about 30 years, until the album was rediscovered and gained quite a lot of popularity. Its influences were very clear to see as it almost felt like a long lost Sugar Babe album, perfectly blending soft rock, pop and even some good old folk to give listeners a real blast from the past. Songs like Faster-Than-Light Highway and Tight Night felt like little time capsules to an era that had long since passed, and it was full of that delightful optimism about the present and the possibilities of the future. Perhaps most impressively of all it was made by a bunch of fresh college graduates who were just making an album for themselves, leaving it free from any corporate interference. Thanks to So Nice's newfound audience it was published on CD for the first time ever in 2011, meaning you no longer had to track down one of the original, mythical 200 copies. This new wave of recognition even inspired the original members of So Nice to reunite, and they have since performed live and even made some new songs together. Some versions of Love even include covers of Sugar Babe songs, live performances and recording sessions from all the way back in 1977, letting you dive even deeper into this band's short but sweet history. Love is a wonderful album which is very symbolic of City Pop as a whole, reflecting an era of music that feels nostalgic even for those who never lived in it. It's also a testament to the immortality of music and the idea that art can exist forever as long as somebody is there to appreciate it. It may have taken a few decades but eventually Love and So Nice got the recognition they deserved. There may yet be more albums with untold stories just like Love's waiting to be found and hopefully appreciated forever.

White Heat

Artist: Shigeru Suzuki
Release: February 25, 1979
Label: Invitation

Shigeru Suzuki was quite fond of including instrumental songs in his earlier albums, with the most notable example being Lagoon. His later releases gradually included less and less of them, but perhaps he was saving them for the almost exclusively instrumental White Heat. Suzuki performs some of his best compositions to date for this album, with the only other composer being fellow City Pop mainstay Motoya Hamaguchi. Hamaguchi can also be heard in one of his only vocal appearances on the album's lone track with lyrics; On The Coast. White Heat is a real journey through Suzuki's musical mind as he performs songs that incorporate bits of rock, jazz and a fair amount of Latin inspiration, showing his mastery of fusion. From the funky sounds of Wild Fire to the moving Da Doo Love For You, White Heat is as hot as its name suggests.

A1. Hot Blooded
A2. Wild Fire
A3. City Streets
A4. Moonstruck
B1. On The Coast
B2. Los Enamorados
B3. Starlite Melody
B4. Da Doo Love For You

Pop Lady II

Artist: Yuuko Shibuya
Release: March 21, 1979
Label: King Records

Pop Lady II is unsurprisingly the sequel to Yuuko Shibuya's Pop Lady and follows in the footsteps of its predecessor by offering a diverse array of tracks. Many of the same influences from Pop Lady are found here, especially with the likes of disco and soft rock. The record features a great band with some of City Pop's lesser known, but still incredibly talented session musicians such as Tsugutoshi Goto and Chuei Yoshikawa. Shibuya's voice is as bright as ever, but the band deserves a lot of praise for making her compositions feel complete. You'll get lost in the slow and mesmerizing play found in Blue City, and Rain Waltz & Loving You's guitar just feels cool to listen to. Track B3 is another high point from an album that's filled with hidden gems, making Pop Lady II a memorable time.

A1. For You
A2. Little Fantasy
A3. Blue City
A4. Hong Kong Paper Doll
A5. Rain Waltz & Loving You
B1. Jesse
B2. Slow Dancing
B3. 少年の炎を消さないで
B4. Make Up
B5. 午前五時の旋律

素顔の私 (My True Face)

Artist: Junko Yagami
Release: April 5, 1979
Label: Discomate

My True Face was Junko Yagami's second album, and her first to reach number 1 on Japan's Oricon Charts. This is largely thanks to the inclusion of track A4, Light Pink Rain, which was a massive hit for Yagami. It sold over 600,000 copies and maintained a spot on Japan's This Week's Spotlight show, staying in the top ten for nine weeks. The fun pop song was inspired by a walk Yagami took in Tokyo's Harajuku district and was completed with lyrics by Yoshiko Miura. Miura would accumulate quite a few successful songs during her career, most notably Miki Matsubara's Stay With Me. While Light Pink Rain was the album's big mover it has a lot of other great songs to enjoy. A2 is an especially memorable one thanks to its chorus, and Yagami's Kayōkyoku influences can really be heard in the lengthy track A5.

A1. バースデイ・ソング
A2. 明日に向かって行け
A3. 揺れる気持ち
A4. みずいろの雨
A5. 夜間飛行
B1. アダムとイブ
B2. そっと後から
B3. ハロー・アンド・グッドバイ
B4. 渚
B5. Dawn

University Street

An all-star roster of City Pop legends came together to craft University Street, an album rich with genre-appropriate themes. Tales of romance are plentiful here, while songs like A1/On The University Street describes a scenario which will feel very nostalgic to graduates who miss those more innocent school days. For an example of this album's stacked contributors you can check out B2/Blue Horizon, which was composed by Tatsuro Yamashita, features lyrics by Taeko Ohnuki and has Minako Yoshida on backing vocals. It's a real treat to hear all of these icons on the track, especially considering Yoshida and Ohnuki didn't release an album for 1979. The album ends right where we began in the entirely english song Good-bye University, a fitting farewell to those youthful days full of friends, love, and time that went by way too fast.

Artist: Mariya Takeuchi
Release: May 21, 1979
Label: RCA

A1. オン・ザ・ユニヴァーシティ・ストリート
A2. 涙のワンサイデッド・ラヴ
A3. 想い出のサマーデイズ
A4. イズント・イット・オールウェイズ
A5. ホールド・オン
B1. J-Boy
B2. ブルー・ホライズン
B3. ドリーム・オブ・ユー〜レモンライムの青い風
B4. かえらぬ面影
B5. グッドバイ・ユニヴァーシティ

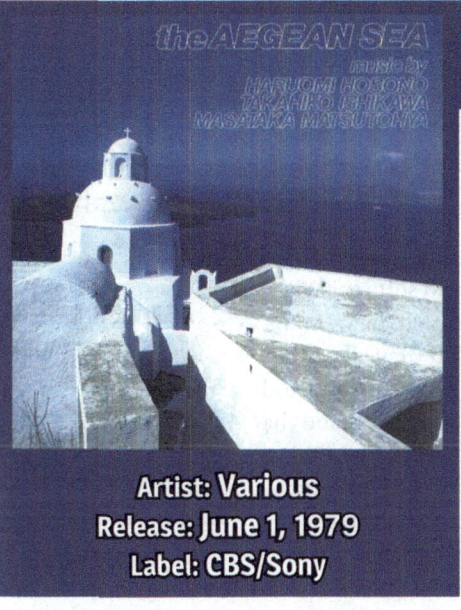

The Aegean Sea

The Aegean Sea is a collaborative album between Haruomi Hosono, Masataka Matsutoya and Takahiko Ishikawa, a guitarist and arranger who had been active all throughout the seventies. While Ishikawa had appeared quite sparingly in City Pop albums during this time, his skills were put to incredible use for this album. Akin to the somewhat conceptually similar Pacific, it's an all instrumental, experimental fusion experience with each artist contributing a song. Electronic sound is found in abundance thanks to Hosono, making this a must listen for fans of Yellow Magic Orchestra. The album is kept balanced thanks to Ishikawa's songs which go for a more natural sound in comparison, and Matsutoya's meet somewhere in the middle. It's quite easy to drift away to the sounds of The Aegean Sea that these three crafted.

Artist: Various
Release: June 1, 1979
Label: CBS/Sony

A1. キャトル
A2. ときどき魔法
A3. コンサート
A4. わたしはすてき
A5. 風の道
B1. 星に乗って
B2. クリスマス
B3. 月の光
B4. 一枚のフォトグラフ
B5. キリンのいる風景

Feelin'

Feelin' is Anri's second album, released about half a year after her debut record Apricot Jam. Amii Ozaki continued to be quite involved as she has five songs to her name here, including The Dancers of Cordoba and Blue Moon among others. You can also enjoy Shigeru Suzuki's guitar playing and arrangement skills, and many of City Pop's other star performers like Ryuichi Sakamoto are present. The Dancers of Cordoba starts the album off with an exciting Spanish vacation right at home and continues to ebb and flow between fun pop tunes and slow mood setters. Feelin' is another solid release for the rising talent, but it's often overlooked since it's still quite removed from the summertime jams she eventually became known for. Anri would skip out on creating an album for 1980, but the rest of the decade is hers to claim.

Artist: Anri
Release: June 21, 1979
Label: For Life Records

A1. コルドバの踊り子
A2. 九月の砂
A3. ブルー・ムーン
A4. スリップアウェイ
A5. マホガニータウン
B1. 地中海ドリーム
B2. モーニング・フライト
B3. 悲しみは窓の向こう
B4. ときめき
B5. めぐり来る季節のように
B6. 海辺から

53

Summer Nerves

Artist: Ryuichi Sakamoto
Release: June 21, 1979
Label: CBS/Sony

Synth-pop and summer collide in Ryuichi Sakamoto's Summer Nerves! This album by the Yellow Magic Orchestra member was also made alongside The Kakutougi Session, a group that is only really credited on this album, but it included the incredibly talented Yukihiro Takahashi, Akiko Yano and Kenji Omura. The group actually has their own theme song here in track A4, a diverse tune that incorporates elements of disco and rock, but all of Summer Nerves thrives on variety. The electronic techniques used in A1 fit the song's cool tropical vibe well, and the voice distortion effects in A2 are very charming. You can also enjoy hearing Akiko Yano on A3, and B1 and B2 both feel like quick voyages to some alien dimensions. Summer Nerves ends with the totally far-out Neuronian Network, a fitting end to this digital summer.

- A1. Summer Nerves
- A2. You're Friend To Me
- A3. Sleep On My Baby
- A4. Theme For "Kakutougi"
- B1. Gonna Go To I Colony
- B2. Time Trip
- B3. Sweet Illusion
- B4. Neuronian Network

Summer-time Love Song

Artist: The Milky Way
Release: 1979
Label: Seven Seas

Summertime Love Song is the sole album from The Milky Way, a band which notably included future City Pop titan Makoto Matsushita. Despite being an early work, the album is beyond what you'd expect and is a genuine stunner of a record. The band delivers a relaxing journey into a summertime soundscape with a fantastic blend of jazz and soft rock with some Latin inspiration that just makes you melt away. Many of the songs are covers of American jams, but they all end up feeling so united thanks to the work done by Matsushita and Kazuo Nobuta on the arrangement. The album is so good that every single song feels like a highlight, and it's impossible to pick favorites, but their renditions of Harbor Lights and White Wave are especially lovely. A tragically underrated album, Summertime Love Song is one to remember.

- A1. Theme From "A Summer Place"
- A2. Wave
- A3. Surfin' Summer "La Costa"
- A4. Harbor Lights
- B1. White Wave
- B2. Under The Jamaica Moon
- B3. Memories In The Sand
- B4. Summer-Time Love Song
- B5. Endless Summer

Show Me Your Smile

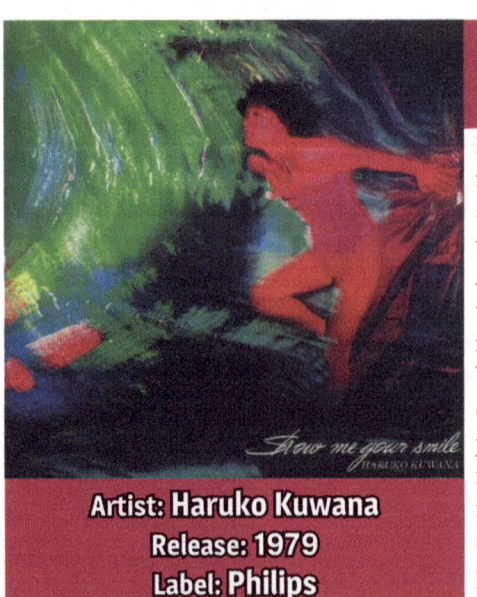

Artist: Haruko Kuwana
Release: 1979
Label: Philips

Haruko Kuwana returned with Show Me Your Smile to deliver more of that great blend of soul, pop and funk, this time with an electronic edge. Almost every song except for gets great usage out of their synthesizers and electric pianos, such as And The Phone Rings which starts the album off with fantastically frantic instrumentals and Kuwana's enthusiastic singing. Weather Forecast gets really funky with its synthesized bass and Azure Wind has a splendid array of instruments on display, making headphones a must for this album. Chance just feels cool to listen to and the addition of male vocalists for the chorus adds a lot to Kuwana's already excellent performance. It ends with the slow and captivating Solo Show, closing out this release from Kuwana which features some perfect electronic sound, and is possibly her best album.

- A1. そして電話のベルは
- A2. Show Me Your Smile
- A3. 天気予報
- A4. 蒼い風
- B1. Chance
- B2. On The Seashore
- B3. もっとイマジネーション
- B4. Few
- B5. 一人芝居

Late Late Summer

Left: The single release for As It Was Then and Let's Go To The Beach with the duo looking quite fancy.
Center: The cover of Late Late Summer is monochrome except for its colorful logo, the pink and light green indicate the eighties are approaching.
Right: The back of the album features the duo alongside some canine companions.

Artist:
Bread & Butter

Release:
June 25, 1979

Label:
Alfa

Track List:

A1. あの頃のまま
(As It Was Then)

A2. タバコロード 20
(Tobacco Road 20)

A3. 別れのあとの憩い
(Rest After Parting)

A4. The Last Letter

A5. 渚に行こう
(Let's Go To The Beach)

B1. ゆううつ
(Gloom)

B2. 忘れ得ぬ貴女
(The Unforgettable Girl)

B3. Summer Blue

B4. 青い地平線
(Blue Horizon)

B5. Julianne

In 1979 Bread & Butter released Late Late Summer, although it was far from their first album. The group consists of two brothers, Fuyumi Iwasawa and Satsuya Iwasawa, who had been releasing music as far back as 1969. Their first album Images came out in 1973, although for the majority of the decade their style was most similar to folk rock, with 1974's Barbecue being their highlight album from that era and is loaded with fun homestyle tracks. After not releasing an album for 77 or 78 the pair unleashed Late Late Summer, a record that would totally change up their style and set them down a path to becoming City Pop icons. The duo enlisted the best of the best for this creation, including Tin Pan Alley, who they had previously worked with on Barbecue. Haruomi Hosono went all out for this album playing a variety of instruments, as did his fellow Tin Pan Alley members, while other titans of the style such as Motoya Hamaguchi, Ray Ohara and Eiji Arai all appear as well. The album begins with As It Was Then, a fantastic showcase for one of the group's most defining features, their harmonious duets. The brothers often appear side by side for their songs, giving them a unique selling point amongst their peers. A vocal and instrumental treat, As It Was Then begs to be listened to multiple times. Tobacco Road 20 likewise offers a delightful pop rock experience before Rest After Parting appears to slow things down, although it manages to surprise you with some expert guitar playing throughout. The Last Letter immediately feels like a Hosono song, which isn't too surprising because he actually wrote it, and has a cameo as a background voice. For a few moments of classic summertime fare Let's Go To The Beach is a classic, and the rhythmic 'dun dun dun' midway through will have you singing along every time. Gloom actually shares something with As It Was Then and Tobacco Road 20, they were all composed by Karuho Kureta. This was no mere blossoming songwriter, it was actually an alias used by Yumi Matsutoya, giving the album even more star power. The most popular song from the album ended up being Summer Blue, which is no surprise considering how it feels like a perfect slice of the style. Its funky instrumentals with a healthy amount of synth sound work wonders alongside bittersweet lyrics about memories of better times, all the hallmarks are here. The energy keeps up with Blue Horizon, a track full of English lyrics, before the beautiful Julianne closes us out with its delicate instrumentals before turning up the groove before it ends. Late Late Summer is a spectacular change in direction for Bread & Butter, and one of the year's very best.

Olive

Artist: Yumi Matsutoya
Release: July 20, 1979
Label: Express

Yumi Matsutoya's first album for 1979 was another 'all hands on deck' effort, with her husband Masataka Matsutoya getting especially involved in his producer role. Other familiar contributors include titanic vocalists Tatsuro Yamashita and Minako Yoshida on the chorus. Olive delves into some beautiful and tragic subject matter, like The Future is in The Fog which reflects her nostalgia for the 1960s and events such as the moon landing. Like A Swallow is a genuinely heartbreaking song about a girl who took her own life, and its poetic lyrics are some of her saddest yet. Homecoming and Cold Rain both delve into feelings of unexpressed love and betrayal, but the album has its share of fun songs like She's A Lightning Bolt. Olive once again displays Matsutoya's talent as one of the best songwriters in the industry.

- A1. 未来は霧の中に
- A2. 青いエアメイル
- A3. ツバメのように
- A4. 最後の春休み
- A5. 甘い予感
- B1. 帰愁
- B2. 冷たい雨
- B3. 風の中の栗毛
- B4. 稲妻の少女
- B5. りんごのにおいと風の国

Feel So Cool

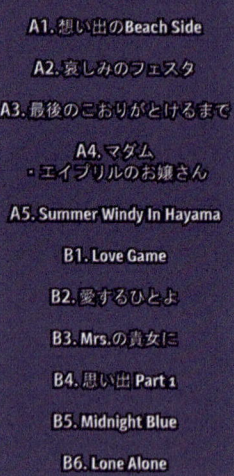

Artist: Takuya Takahashi
Release: July 21, 1979
Label: F-Label

Feel So Cool is the first of only two albums by Takuya Takahashi, who was previously a member of the rock band Lou. Although their first (and only) album came out in 1976, many of its members followed along to perform on Takahashi's record. Despite being a relatively unknown figure in City Pop's history, Feel So Cool is an exceptional record which fits right in with others of the period. It especially leans quite heavy on the rock elements with songs like Memories of Beach Side and Fiesta of Sorrow, but other styles get a chance to shine too. Summer Windy in Hayama is definitive pop with a jazzy twist, while Love Game ups the funk. The album has you covered with slow tracks like My Dearest One and Lone Alone, creating a very well-rounded record which sadly never got a reissue past its initial vinyl and cassette offerings.

- A1. 想い出のBeach Side
- A2. 哀しみのフェスタ
- A3. 最後のこおりがとけるまで
- A4. マダム・エイプリルのお嬢さん
- A5. Summer Windy In Hayama
- B1. Love Game
- B2. 愛するひとよ
- B3. Mrs.の貴女に
- B4. 思い出 Part 1
- B5. Midnight Blue
- B6. Lone Alone

American Comics

Artist: Yuko Sugita
Release: July 25, 1979
Label: Invitation

American Comics was Yuko Sugita's second album, and also her last. Sugita once again composed and wrote lyrics for the entire album, which really makes it feel like a product that was crafted by just her. The band featured here is almost an exact recreation of the one found in Monsoon Baby, with Shigeru Suzuki and other Tin Pan Alley members returning to lend their always phenomenal talents. For better or worse this makes the album feel very similar to Monsoon Baby, including its leaning towards a pop rock sound. A2 is a great example of this with its frequent instrumental sessions, and B1 is also a treat for the ears, especially when Suzuki gets a chance to work his magic on guitar. Sugita ceased her activities after this release, leaving us with just those two albums to enjoy.

- A1. ハイ・ウェイ101
- A2. サーフィン娘
- A3. テレフォン・ラブ・ボックス
- A4. タイム・アラウンド
- A5. 風見鶏
- B1. 魔力
- B2. 恋のタップ・ダンス
- B3. マイ・スイート・スマイル・ボーイ
- B4. ハイヤイヤ
- B5. フルムーン・ナイト

Sudden Wind

Artist: Tatsuhiko Yamamoto
Release: 1979
Label: Philips

The debut album from Tatsuhiko Yamamoto, a fresh face who would become a consistent contributor to City Pop all throughout its prime years. Impressively the entire album was composed by Yamamoto himself, with lyrics by Ayumi Date who would later work alongside Kaoru Sudo. As the cover would suggest Yamamoto also plays piano on quite a number of songs, and the instrument is quite prominent throughout the album. Most of the songs consist of slow mood setters like the titular Sudden Wind and The Sea After The Rain which are greatly complemented by Yamamoto's smooth singing voice. Even songs with more of a pop style to them like Dreamy December stay subdued thanks to his mellow voice. This makes the album feel quite consistent, although perhaps slightly lacking in variety, but is still a strong debut showing.

A1. 突風 サドゥン・ウィンド
A2. 雨上がりの海
A3. カフェテラス
A4. 名画館
A5. スブニール
B1. 最上階
B2. Just Fallin' In Love
B3. Dreamy December
B4. 麗夢
B5. 風のソネット

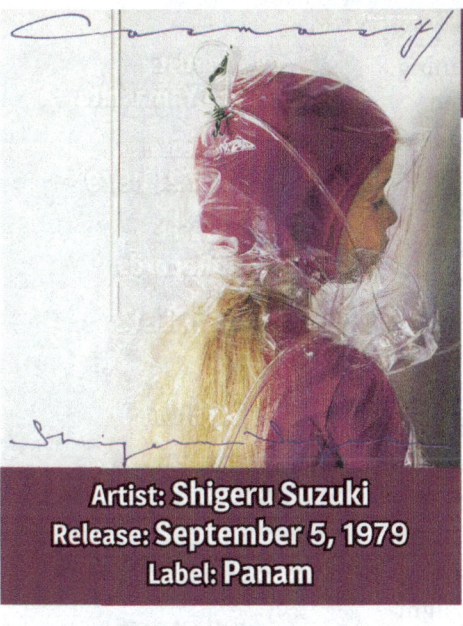

Cosmos '51

Artist: Shigeru Suzuki
Release: September 5, 1979
Label: Panam

Suzuki's second album for 1979 was back to having vocals on many of the tracks, although it is noticeably lighter on the rock elements. Cosmos '51 instead put greater emphasis on a pop rock sound, which isn't totally out of left field for Suzuki, but still feels somewhat unlike his usual fare. The album was partially recorded in the United States and includes a number of American musicians on board, most notably famed saxophone player Buddy Collette. Backing vocals are put to great use throughout quite a number of songs such as Galaxy Girl and Hey! Woman, which help to accentuate Suzuki's already great singing. Sadly, this would end up being Suzuki's last album for half a decade. Past this point he still lent his incredible talent as a musician to innumerable records, including some of City Pop's greatest.

A1. You Are A Bad Liar
A2. Five Steps
A3. Illusion
A4. Galaxy Girl
A5. Viva California
B1. Hey! Woman
B2. Bad Dream
B3. Santa Monica Rally
B4. Cold Blood
B5. Phoenix

Butterfly

Artist: Kimiko Kasai
Release: September 21, 1979
Label: CBS/Sony

Kimiko Kasai's latest musical venture was a collaboration which heavily featured Herbie Hancock, an American jazz pianist and composer who has dozens of albums and innumerable contributions to other projects. It's almost easier to describe what Herbie didn't do for this album, as he acted as a producer, contributed backing vocals, played a variety of instruments including electric piano, synthesizer and many more. Herbie's involvement gives this record a unique sound amongst Kasai's discography, creating a sound that blends just about everything from jazz to blues to pop to electronic. These unique instrumentals work wonders with Kasai's own soft singing, giving rise to an album that feels like a real journey. Butterfly is one of Kasai's best and most creative yet, and absolutely one to experience for yourself.

A1. I Thought It Was You
A2. Tell Me A Bedtime Story
A3. Head In The Clouds
A4. Maiden Voyage
B1. Harvest Time
B2. Sunlight
B3. Butterfly
B4. As

Moonglow

  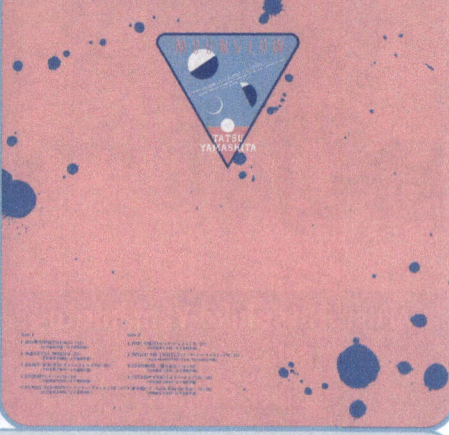

Left: The back of Moonglow displays a scrumptious meal consisting of the Moon and a little wine.
Center: The cover of Moonglow shows off Yamashita holding a beautifully shining globe which immediately draws your attention.
Right: The interior track list has a great aesthetic with its bright pink color and blue splotches, two of City Pop's signature colors.

Things managed to stabilize for Tatsuro Yamashita after having a career determining scare with Go Ahead! possibly being his last album, though this fortunately ended up not being the case. It seemed that Yamashita's corporate woes would soon be past him as he joined the newly formed Air Records, a sublabel within RCA by Ryuzo Kosugi, who was the director for Go Ahead. Air Records offered more creative freedom compared to the main RCA label, and Moonglow would go on to be its very first release. While Yamashita's lessened restrictions encouraged more experimentation, we also have to thank a concert in Osaka for broadening his perspective. Yamashita had previously performed in Osaka while he was still a member of Sugar Babe five years ago, but he felt that their shows weren't as well received due to what he called an "anti-Tokyo" atmosphere, which is where his music was most popular. Much to his surprise the concert was full of people quite unlike his usual crowd who were supportive of his work, which left him feeling appreciative that his music was reaching a wider demographic. This trip to Osaka motivated Yamashita to design his next album to be well suited to the live performances he loved doing, and more palatable for a modern audience. Akin to Go Ahead! the album begins with some a cappella in Nightwing which lures you in with its doo-wop style singing that flows right into Eternal Full Moon, a groovy track with backing vocals by Minako Yoshida. Yoshida's involvement for this record was quite significant, as she was the lyricist for eight of its ten tracks. Rainy Walk is described as a "Chicago style soul number" and would've been the perfect song to play with that new Walkman of yours while out on a stroll. Storm likewise took influence from Chicago's soul scene but is quite a lot slower than Rainy Walk, while Funky Flushin' looked to emulate the surprise hit Bomber from his last album. It's easy to envision disco crowds from the era really getting down to this one and clapping along. Some rock and roll edge is added to the album with Hot Shot, plus it gave Yamashita a chance to strut his stuff on guitar. Touch Me Lightly is an all-English song you can partake in a romantic dance to, while Sunshine -The Golden Age of Love- is pure feel-good pop. One song with a rather strange origin story is Yellow Cab, as it was inspired by a car accident Yamashita got into while riding in a New York City taxi. The track appropriately features zany English lyrics which do a good job emulating what a foreigner must experience in a big American city. Moonglow is another spectacular record from Yamashita, whose popularity would grow exponentially in the 1980s.

Artist:
Tatsuro Yamashita

Release:
October 21, 1979

Label:
Air Records

Track List:

A1. 夜の翼 (Nightwing)

A2. 永遠のFull Moon (Eternal Full Moon)

A3. Rainy Walk

A4. Storm

A5. Funky Flushin'

B1. Hot Shot

B2. Touch Me Lightly

B3. Sunshine -愛の金色- (Sunshine -The Golden Age of Love-)

B4. Yellow Cab

B5. 愛を描いて -Let's Kiss The Sun- (Drawing Love -Let's Kiss The Sun-)

Just My Feeling

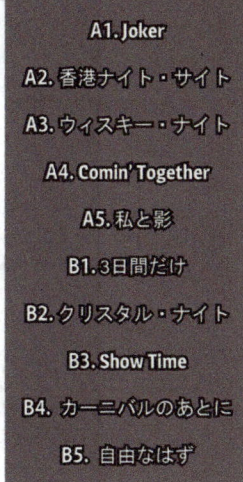

Artist: Kaoru Uemura
Release: November 21, 1979
Label: CBS/Sony

Just My Feeling is the only album by Kaoru Uemura, an artist who first appeared alongside Mariya Takeuchi on Loft Sessions. Although she is a niche artist in City Pop's history, her sole release stands out as a real hidden gem. Joker provides an ultra-jazzy and fun introduction, and the guitar work on A3 hits quite nicely. Another tragically underrated song is Comin' Together which has an instrumental segment that'll knock your socks off, while B1 will have you swinging your hips to the cool groove it provides. B2 likewise has entrancing instrumentals, and Uemura's singing is great throughout the whole album. Just My Feeling is an awesome time from start to finish, so it's a shame Uemura never made another album. However, she has regularly done live shows for decades now and is still rocking out all these years later.

- A1. Joker
- A2. 香港ナイト・サイト
- A3. ウィスキー・ナイト
- A4. Comin' Together
- A5. 私と影
- B1. 3日間だけ
- B2. クリスタル・ナイト
- B3. Show Time
- B4. カーニバルのあとに
- B5. 自由なはず

My Love For You

Artist: Jin Kirigaya
Release: November 25, 1979
Label: Alfa

Jin Kirigaya's debut album set up a niche for him as a male singer with an incredibly soft and smooth voice, well equipped for delivering moving ballads. This was helped by the phenomenal band assembled for the album, with the likes of Haruomi Hosono, Shigeru Suzuki and Masataka Matsutoya appearing. The album is a real treat for those who enjoy delicate vocals combined with fittingly moving instrumentals, and both parts of the musical equation are equally enjoyable. A1 provides a very strong introduction with its diverse instruments played by some of Japan's absolute best, and Unhappy Day's overlapping vocals result in a strong effect. A5 comes with some electronic sound sprinkled in and Return To The Sky is another memorable tune. My Love For You is a real sleeper hit from 1979 and certainly worth checking out.

- A1. しおさい
- A2. Unhappy Day
- A3. 冷たいままでベイビー
- A4. 海へ帰ろう
- A5. 四谷ゆうまぐれ
- B1. 帰郷
- B2. あさがやの街
- B3. あなたがいる人生
- B4. Return To The Sky
- B5. 愛はそのまま

Super Percussion Vol. 1

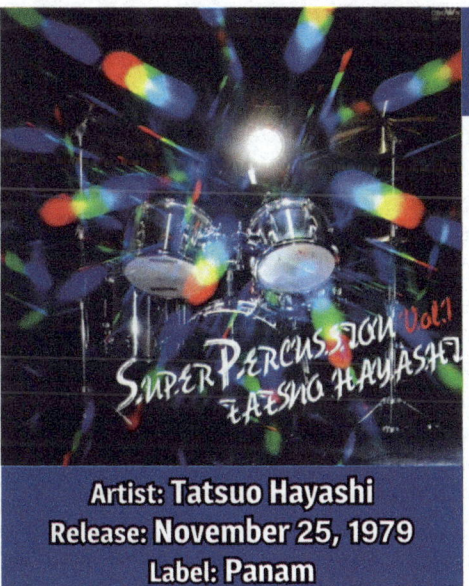

Artist: Tatsuo Hayashi
Release: November 25, 1979
Label: Panam

Despite being one of the most acclaimed drummers in Japan throughout the seventies, Tatsuo Hayashi never seemed like much of a solo album guy. Super Percussion Vol. 1 ended up being the Tin Pan Alley member's one and only solo album, although it's unlike what you'd expect. The B-side is your usual collection of songs by Hayashi, while the A-side consists of extracted rhythm sections for drums and percussion. As the album itself states this is to help people who don't have a drummer available or aren't able to play them because of how loud they are. The songs are labeled to match their style such as Latin Rock, Fast Disco and more, and Japanese DJs got quite a lot of mileage from the beats included. The B-side meanwhile is a treat for fans of Hayashi's drumming and compositional skills, making this a unique album which certainly helped many.

- A1. Fast Disco
- A2. Straight Rock
- A3. Slow Disco
- A4. Latin Rock
- A5. Ballad
- B1. Sucha-Roca
- B2. Metalcharm
- B3. Hi-G
- B4. El Paso
- B5. Castin' Blue

The Gallery In My Heart

Artist: Yumi Matsutoya
Release: December 1, 1979
Label: Express

The Gallery In My Heart closed out the year for Matsutoya with ten more high quality tracks. Quite a number of the songs from this album were big hits, and many of them gained recognition from appearances on television. Destiny in particular proved very popular and gained a second wind after being featured in the eighties drama Tales From an Unseasonable Coast. Dancing in a Green Town is a song about a vacation to Morioka, a city in northern Japan. It seems the residents of Iwate prefecture where Morioka is located really like this one, as it's the theme song for their Hanamaki Airport. 78 is a unique track with some funky instrumentals which was inspired by Matsutoya's interest in mysticism. The title '78' is a reference to the cards in a Tarot deck, and features lyrics that seem like she's calling forth an arcane invader.

- A1. The Story Of Giacobini's Comet
- A2. We're All Free
- A3. Ode of Morioka
- A4. Destiny
- A5. Silhouettes
- B1. The Gallery In My Heart
- B2. As I'm Alone
- B3. Horizon & Grenadine
- B4. 78
- B5. The Ocean and I

Fascination

Artist: Asami Kado
Release: December 5, 1979
Label: Union Records

The appropriately fascinating debut album by Asami Kado, who would stay as a consistent figure in City Pop until her final album released in 1988. Kado makes a strong showing as the composer or lyricist for nearly every song except for Osamu Totsuka's South Shore, which is a tropical instrumental track. All of the songs here reveal her musical talent, which is further accentuated by the ever reliable Shigeru Suzuki on the arrangement, and even Masataka Matsutoya shows up to arrange Good Luck. Fascination has an excellent mixture of influences ranging from Kayōkyoku fashioned ballads to the funky songs City Pop is largely known for. The album stays fresh throughout its entire run, and it never feels like Kado is relying too heavily on one style, making for a lovely listening experience.

- A1. Portrait Woman
- A2. Lion Under The Moonlight
- A3. Sleeping Lady
- A4. 渚にて
- A5. Marie, Come Back
- B1. Monroe Walk
- B2. Route 88
- B3. Dear Mr. Sharlock
- B4. Vision In The Rain
- B5. Manhattan Gigolo
- B6. Simple Song

Rotation

Artist: Shōgun
Release: December 5, 1979
Label: CBS/Sony

Fujimaru Yoshino was the frontman for another group after his brief time in the eponymous Fujimaru Band, this time with the much longer lasting Shōgun. The band released music from 1979 until 1997, and many of their albums benefited greatly from the involvement of Casey Rankin. Rankin was an American artist who moved to Japan in the 1970s and found success with Shōgun, among other ventures, notably by composing the band's first hit single Otokotachi-no-melody. He also wrote lyrics for the entire album and composed many of its tracks, writing even more than Yoshino did. This gave Rotation a very American sound, and all of the album's lyrics are in English, and it is heavily influenced by Western genres like jazz and funk. It's easy to forget that this is actually a Japanese album, but that global feeling is a big part of City Pop's appeal.

- A1. As Easy As You Make It
- A2. Imagination
- A3. Sailor-Sailor
- A4. Yesterday, Today And Tomorrow
- B1. Margarita
- B2. Bad City
- B3. The Tourist
- B4. I Should Have Know Better
- B5. Lonely Man

Toy Box Act 1

Toy Box Act one is the first album by Miharu Koshi, a figure who would begin her career like some of the period's other idols but ultimately ended up on a different path. Every song on the album includes compositions and lyrics from Koshi, alongside her own piano playing. You can also spot Minako Yoshida and Tatsuro Yamashita on the chorus for a few songs like Love is A Funny Feeling. The album stands out amongst its peers thanks to Koshi's unique approach to music which made for some incredibly fun songs, and it's especially impressive considering she was only nineteen when it was made. Also notable is the frequent use of electronic sound throughout, as she would gravitate more towards it throughout her career and abandon her former idol image, largely thanks to the influence of Yellow Magic Orchestra.

Artist: Miharu Koshi
Release: 1979
Label: RCA

A1. Whimsical Highway
A2. Let Me Dream
A3. Last Drive
A4. Snoopy
A5. Love Is A Funny Feeling
B1. Love Step
B2. Seashore
B3. Don't Go
B4. May Winds
B5. Mysterious Girl

Street Sensation

Street Sensation is the only album ever released by Kinokuniya Band, although it is a very good one. It features vocals by Masako Takasaki, who made her debut alongside Mariya Takeuchi on Loft Sessions Vol. 1, but sadly she never made another album. Street Sensation is loaded with great tracks such as Crystal Magic which has some exhilarating instrumentals, while Goodbye Again really shows off Takasaki's vocal skills. A wonderful cover of Taeko Ohnuki's 4:00 AM can also be heard, and the band put a unique spin on the song which really ups the rock elements. Other notable songs include Jump with its crazy keyboard play, and Opening Theme which is so explosive it may as well be the opening theme for the apocalypse. A real gem of an album, one has to wonder what could've been if these talented artists made more.

Artist: Kinokuniya Band
Release: 1979
Label: Polydor

A1. Crystal Magic
A2. Goodbye Again
A3. 4:00 AM
A4. Usou (Thought in the Rain)
A5. Jump
B1. Opening Theme
B2. You Send Me
B3. Hangin' Around
B4. I Go Carelessly
B5. One Night Affair

Feeling Your Love

Feeling Your Love is the debut album for Eri Ohno, an artist who brought some especially jazzy and distinctly Western feeling music with her. Despite being Japanese Ohno sings the album's many songs in English, so it'd be quite easy to mistake this for an American record, especially considering Stevie Wonder wrote tracks A3 and B3. Some other genres such as soul are mixed in as well, with songs like Moonraker and Autumn in New York being slow and passionate experiences which are well suited to Ohno's singing voice. You're likely to get hooked with the very first song Living Inside Your Love, a real smooth track with some incredible instrumentals which work well in showing off what Eri Ohno is all about. An excellent first release from Ohno, and a must listen for fans of jazz.

Artist: Eri Ohno
Release: 1979
Label: Better Days

A1. Living Inside Your Love
A2. Good Morning Heartache
A3. Tell Me Something Good
A4. Walz For Debby
A5. Moonraker
B1. Rock The Boat
B2. Deja Vu
B3. Don't You Worry About A Thing
B4. Autumn In New York

Dream in The Street

Left: This smiling picture of Ikeda amidst nature is one of the few available pictures we have of her.
Center: The cover of Dream In The Street features a subdued but cool picture of Ikeda. One oddity about this image is that she seemingly has six fingers, but that's probably caused by an optical illusion. Right: A rare promotional version of the album which has some songs the retail release lacks.

Dream in The Street is the one and only album by Noriyo Ikeda, and it's as mysterious as it is good. Even one of the most basic aspects of the album's existence, its release date, is strangely contentious. Most sources say that it came out in 1979, whereas others say it was 1980, and its exact release day or even month seems completely unknown. The artist behind it is also quite enigmatic and we know virtually nothing about Noriyo Ikeda's life before or after Dream In The Street, including why she left the music industry. Ikeda just about vanished from the public and stopped making music after this album, with some very niche exceptions. In 1982 she shows up as a vocalist for the album Information by Wonder City Orchestra, and in that same year she can be heard on The Greeting Song, which was made for the children's show Hirake! Ponkikki. These two obscure items seem to be the last time she was credited on anything that wasn't a compilation or re-release. While the person responsible for the album may be quite befuddling, there's no denying its quality. Like many of its City Pop brethren Dream In The Street finds that sweet spot with pop, disco, and jazz to form a coherent but still quite varied album. It was also made alongside some of City Pop's brightest, such as Shigeru Suzuki and Jake H. Concepcion all playing their instruments of choice. The man responsible for the album's most popular track was none other than Tatsuro Yamashita, who composed the titular Dream In the Street. You'll quickly realize that this acclaimed song came from Yamashita, as it'd feel right at home on one of his albums, and you can even hear him in the chorus. Another hit from the album was the funky Freezing Rain which has one of the finest instrumental performances of the whole record and would have really lit up the dance floor at discos. While the final version of the album turned out amazingly, the mystique of Dream in The Street doesn't end there. Rare promotional copies of the album were manufactured which feature a different track order, an unused Prologue and Epilogue for Side B, and two songs which can't be found on the album. Little Child and Rainbow Glass were excluded from the final version, but the curious thing is that they were never released as singles either. This meant you had to track down those extremely uncommon promo records to listen to them, or just find the songs online somewhere. Luckily in 2020 both of these tracks were published on a 7" vinyl, making them much more accessible. Dream In The Street is a fascinating piece of City Pop's history, and hopefully Noriyo Ikeda found success and happiness doing whatever she chose to pursue in life.

Artist:
Noriyo Ikeda

Release:
1979

Label:
Orange House Records

Track List:

A1. アディオス
(Adios)

A2. Dream In The Street

A3. サマーオレンヂの恋
(Summer Orange Love)

A4. 冷たい雨
(Freezing Rain)

A5. Love Is Like A Party

B1. My Prayer

B2. 愛のかけら
(Fragment of Love)

B3. 恋のジャイロ
(Gyro of Love)

B4. Sunday Morning

B5. たたずんだ街角
(Tucked Away On A Street Corner)

1980, The New Decade

The 1980s are officially on, and while the 1970s certainly laid the groundwork and had some splendid albums, this is when City Pop really came to life. Most of the style's iconic songs and albums were made in this decade, but the year 1980 in particular had an unprecedented influence on City Pop's perception. Artists such as Miki Matsubara had an explosive start with the incredibly beloved Midnight Door/Stay With Me, a track which was quite popular upon its debut and greatly contributed to City Pop's new wave of interest in the 2010s. Another one of City Pop's other leading ladies Mariya Takeuchi released two stellar albums, both of which solidified her position as a musical icon. A handful of new players also emerged like EPO, Hiroaki Igarashi, Kaoru Sudo and many more, all of whom brought their own twists to the style. Fortune was finally shining on Taeko Ohnuki, who had been there since the very first days of City Pop, but always struggled to find that sweet spot between creativity and commercial success. Her album Romantique was the beginning of her European Trilogy, a fresh start which shaped her identity for years to come. The same could also been said about Tatsuro Yamashita, who still had a somewhat niche audience, but he was about to absolutely explode with the slam dunk single Ride On Time and the album of the same name. In many ways 1980 feels like the start of next chapter in the genre's history. City Pop previously had a handful of chart topping tracks, but the style firmly entered into the mainstream after this year, and that momentum would continue throughout the 1980s.

Miki Matsubara

Top: One of the most common pictures of Matsubara, which is used as the cover for her Best Collection. Bottom: Another picture of Matsubara, whose beautful smile was taken from us too soon.

If you asked anyone familiar with City Pop to name just one of its artists, chances are they'll mention the legendary Miki Matsubara. As a child Matsubara was seemingly destined to be a musician, as she learned piano at the young age of three and joined various bands throughout her adolescence. She then made her professional debut in 1979 with her ultra popular song Midnight Door/Stay With Me, one of the tracks responsible for City Pop's wave of renewed interest in the 2010s, but it was also quite successful back in the 1980s. The song is a masterpiece discussed in detail later, but its unmistakable opening, addictive chorus, and uplifting instrumentals which hide a heartbreaking story all turned out perfectly. Matsubara was set up for success from then on, but aside from that mythical track she created many more hits, including Hello Today and Jazzy Night, among many others which are emblematic of the style's unique charm. Matsubara released records from 1980 until 1988, but she retired from recording music in 1988, just a few years before City Pop had largely fallen out of favor. In the years after Matsubara mostly stayed out of the spotlight, and not much is known about her activities during this period. Tragically in the year 2000 she was diagnosed with cervical cancer, a revelation that caused Matsubara to isolate from the people closest to her and cease any work with music. She reportedly began to look back on her career with regret, and she even ended up destroying sheet music and other items associated with her time as an artist. Matsubara sadly passed away from her cancer in 2004 at just 44 years old. The circumstances surrounding her passing are heartbreaking, especially considering how Matsubara never lived to see the massive resurgence in her music's popularity. Miki Matsubara is one of City Pop's most beloved icons, as well as one of its most tragic, but she is now immortalized through her amazing music.

Manhattan In The Rain

Artist: Kingo Hamada
Release: January 21, 1980
Label: Air Records

The debut album from Kingo Hamada, an artist whose music is quite popular among fans of pop rock, a style which has remarkably close ties to City Pop. Appropriate to its title the album was partially recorded in Manhattan, giving it some of that New York musical sensibility. The album carries out its mission as an introduction for what Hamada was capable of, showing off a wide compositional range. May Sick is a fun pop rock start to the album, and Midnight Boxer's instrumentals make it an audio delight. Hamada also has you covered with the slower tracks like Modern Times and Lonely Wind, both of which highlight his sensual singing. Fans of jazz will also find a lot to love here, especially in songs such as Holiday and Game is Over, both of which benefit greatly from the saxophone play from Dave Tofani.

- A1. May Sick
- A2. Hotel Surf-rider
- A3. Midnight Boxer
- A4. Modern Times
- B1. Game is Over
- B2. Lonely Wind
- B3. Rainyday Cowboy
- B4. Holiday
- B5. Sunrise-Sunset

Krishna

Artist: Yumi Murata
Release: 1980
Label: Blow Up

The second album by Yumi Murata, an underrated artist who released a number of City Pop adjacent records in the 1980s. Krishna is an especially splendid album that combines various styles, but you'll mostly see classic City Pop ingredients like disco and soul. Let It Blow is a spirited opening which exposes you to Murata's powerful singing, and the electronic infusion later in the song gives it a lot of character. Another great one is Midnight Communication with its kicking bass, and Mischief uniquely feels like it transports you from a party to a surreal realm. The album and song Krishna are both named after the Hindu deity of protection, and the titular track's cool groove feels quite worthy of its godly title. We then end on Love Survival, a perfect fusion of a ballad and rock concert to wrap up this memorable record.

- A1. Let It Blow
- A2. Red High Heel
- A3. Morning Telephone
- A4. Midnight Communication
- A5. Mischief
- B1. Glenn Miller Medley
- B2. クリシュナ
- B3. 街角で
- B4. Love Survival

Fantastic Love in Wonderland

Artist: Takuya Takahashi
Release: 1980
Label: Canyon

Fantastic Love in Wonderland is the whimsically titled second album by Takuya Takahashi, and also his last. Takahashi went out with a bang though, as Fantastic Love in Wonderland is in fact a fantastic City Pop album. A lovely mix of soft rock, jazz and pop awaits in songs like the super groovy Coast-Line which would fit right in with sixties surf music. The album doesn't shy away from rocking out in songs like Natural Life, while Shadow on The Wall is wonderfully funky. The B-side is no slouch either, containing the quirky Lettuce Salad and Onenight Stand which really shows off Takahashi's singing chops and features some killer sax. Sadly, after this Takahashi more or less disappeared from the music scene, only having confirmed credits on two releases following this album, and little information on his activities exist past that point.

- A1. Coast-Line
- A2. Natural Life
- A3. 2度目のSummer Story
- A4. Shadow On The Wall
- A5. Akiya-Sunset
- B1. My Benny
- B2. Fantastic Love In Wonderland
- B3. 君はLettuce Salad
- B4. Onenight Stand
- B5. 愛の歴史

Pocket Park

Left: The cover of Miki Matsubara's debut single Stay With Me, possibly the best first song in City Pop history.
Center: The very understated cover of Pocket Park has little more than a small picture of Matsubara, her name, and the album title.
Right: Matsubara looking adorable on the back of Pocket Park.

Artist:
Miki Matsubara

Release:
January 25, 1980

Label:
SeeSaw

Track List:

A1. 真夜中のドア/
Stay With Me
(Midnight Door/Stay With Me)

A2. It's So Creamy

A3. Cryin'

A4. That's All

A5. His Woman

B1. Manhattan Wind

B2. 愛はエネルギー
(Love is Energy)

B3. そうして私が
(And So I Did)

B4. Trouble Maker

B5. Mind Game

B6. 偽りのない日々
(Days Without Pretense)

The 1980s kicked off with the debut album for the late Miki Matsubara, a figure who would end up becoming synonymous with City Pop, although her story actually begins back in 1979 with her debut song Midnight Door/Stay With Me. The track might just be the greatest debut single in City Pop history, a pop song masterpiece composed by Tetsuji Hayashi with lyrics by Miura Yoshiko, it's now one of the style's most recognizable. The song lures you in with its groovy and jazzy instrumentals combined with Matsubara's beautiful singing, but its upbeat sound betrays its true meaning. The song is actually a tale of heartbreak and loneliness as Matsubara begs another person to "stay with me" and languishes over once happy memories. Despite its dark subject matter, the song lends itself very well to karaoke, and it's almost impossible to resist singing its legendary chorus. The single was a huge hit upon release and sold over 100,000 copies, reaching number 28 on the Oricon Singles Chart, but ironically it would hit its peak popularity 40 years later. Midnight Door/Stay With Me gradually became one of the most viral songs during the City Pop revival period when people across the globe rediscovered the genre, especially during the Covid years. In 2020 the song accumulated millions upon millions of hits on various platforms and was even the number one song on Spotify for two weeks. It was also the subject of a TikTok trend where the song was played to Japanese people who grew up in the eighties, eliciting a nostalgic and often dance filled response from them. It's not often when an artist's very first song ends up as their most popular, but Matsubara was truly gifted, and the song is now beloved by people all over the world. While Midnight Door/Stay With Me may have been the album's standout, Pocket Park was far from a one trick pony. The album is full of Matsubara hits, such as the feelgood It's So Creamy which counterbalances the unexpectedly sad lyrics of Stay With Me. That's All is a heartbreaker of a song which really shows off Matsubara's singing talent and voice which was mature far beyond her years, as she was only 19 when the album was recorded. Another all-time classic from Matsubara can be enjoyed here with B2 or Love Is Energy, which is Pocket Park's second most popular song, likely owed to its memorable chorus provided by Tatsushi Umegaki and Michiko Ogata. The album closes on Mind Game, which has lyrics that are sweet as candy and describe a perfect Saturday with omelets cooking and kittens playing, then B6 closes things out with another underrated song. Pocket Park is a stellar debut for Matsubara with some truly incredible songs, and it marks a defining moment in City Pop's history.

Love Songs

Left: The single release for Mysterious Peach Pie and Goodbye Dawn. Pink was the name of the game for this cover. Center: The cover of Love Songs is sleek and monochrome, except for the bright pink of its logo. Art Direction by Minoru Ogawa. Photos by Takuhiro Sugihara. Right: The single release for September and One Sided Love in Tears.

Mariya Takeuchi's latest venture Love Songs delivered some of her biggest hits to date, boosting her star power even further. A pair of songs that were first released as singles are especially noteworthy for topping the charts way back when, those being September and Mysterious Peach Pie. September was composed by songwriting mastermind Tetsuji Hayashi with lyrics by Takashi Matsumoto of Happy End, a true musical dream team made of two City Pop titans. The song details a bittersweet day in September with some feelgood instrumentals, and its description of a changing Autumn season is quite unique for City Pop, considering the style's fixation on the summertime. September also marks one of the very first appearances for EPO, a fellow City Pop icon who was about to leave her own mark on its history. EPO can be heard as a backing vocalist during the chorus and is credited as being responsible for its arrangement, but this was actually a shrewd marketing trick. About forty years later Shigeki Miyata, a producer for the album, admitted that he handled the arrangement, but he just gave EPO the credit to help bolster her perception in the industry right before debuting. While September was a great success and sold over 100,000 copies, it was nothing compared to Mysterious Peach Pie. This catchy pop song was composed by Kazuhiko Kato with lyrics by Kazumi Yasui, and would be Takeuchi's first top ten hit, peaking at number 3 and selling nearly 400,000 copies. The lyrics for Mysterious Peach Pie are especially fun, with Takeuchi describing herself as feeling "like a peach pie", whatever that means, but it's great lighthearted fun either way. The song was also used in commercials for Shiseido Cosmetics and was originally just called Peach Pie before a more alluring name was suggested. The 'Mysterious' part was an idea from Shigesato Itoi, a name video game fans may recognize as being the creator of the Mother/Earthbound series, but he actually shows up pretty often as a lyricist in Japanese music. The success of this song helped Takeuchi establish herself in the industry, and it's still fondly remembered today as one of her classic tracks. Love Songs also featured the Tatsuro Yamashita composition Goodbye Dawn with some beautiful lyrics by Takeuchi herself, another great collaboration from this duo. Music Paper is simple but effective and its only instrument is a guitar, with the rest of its sound just coming from snapping and backing vocals which gives it a doo-wop like sound. Love Songs is another memorable album from Takeuchi which helped to propel her into the mainstream, but she kept this momentum going just a few months later with Miss M.

Artist: Mariya Takeuchi

Release: March 5, 1980

Label: RCA

Track List:

A1. Fly Away
A2. さよならの夜明け (Goodbye Dawn)
A3. 磁気嵐 (Magnetic Storm)
A4. 象牙海岸 (Ivory Coast)
A5. 五線紙 (Music Paper)
B1. Lonely Wind
B2. 恋の終わりに (At The End of Love)
B3. 待っているわ (I'll Be Waiting)
B4. September
B5. 不思議なピーチパイ (Mysterious Peach Pie)
B6. Little Lullaby

Down Town

  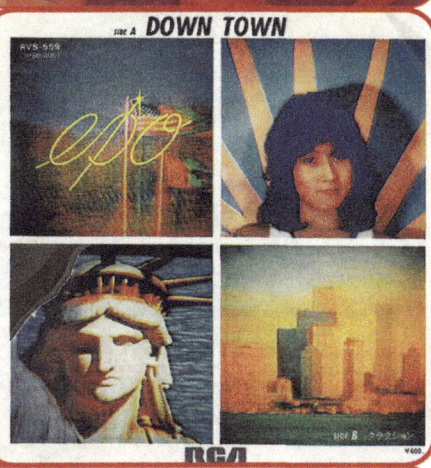

Left: A 1982 single release for Down Town which prominently shows off EPO.
Center: The artsy cover of Down Town includes pictures of New York City and EPO herself, among other subjects.
Right: The single release for Down Town mirrors its full album counterpart.

Artist:
EPO

Release:
March 21, 1980

Label:
RCA

Track List:

A1. Down Town

A2. 約束は雨の中
(Promises in The Rain)

A3. クラクション
(Klaxon)

A4. 日曜はベルが鳴る前に
(Sunday Before The Bell Rings)

A5. 語愛 (Love Language)

B1. ポップ・ミュージック〜
Down Town
(Pop Music Down Town)

B2. アスファルト・ひとり…
(Asphalt Alone...)

B3. 言い訳はしないけど
(I'm Not Making Excuses)

B4. 水平線追いかけて
(Chasing The Horizon)

B5. 珈琲タイム
(Coffee Time)

EPO hit the scene in 1980 with her debut album Down Town, which was named after and prominently features a cover from one of her biggest inspirations. Like many rising stars of the era EPO was a fan of Tatsuro Yamashita, as well as his former band Sugar Babe, and she wanted to cover their song Down Town as her first single. Fate seemed to favor this idea, since one day when EPO was recording a demo tape at the RVC studio she happened to spot Yamashita. She then boldly asked if it was okay to cover his song, to which he said yes, and the rest is history. EPO's cover of Down Town maintains the song's fun and youthful spirit, with the most noticeable shake-up being its usage of a synthesizer to give it a subtle electronic sound, providing a version that feels both familiar and fresh. She elaborated almost two decades later in her compilation album 'epocha 1980-1986' that she felt uncomfortable entering the music industry and had doubts about her skills, although these were alleviated after Down Town was well received. While its headlining song turned out pretty well, the rest of the album's creation proved to be quite the task for EPO, who was still a young college student at the time. She somehow managed to handle the workload from being a college student during the day while recording music in the evening, sometimes all the way into the morning hours. Although such a hectic schedule may be grueling for most, EPO actually found it to be rather exciting and even fun. While the titular Down Town is the album's most well-known number, the rest of its offerings are also great listens. Almost every track features compositions and lyrics by EPO herself, and some of them even come from her high school days. EPO described this style of music as "yellow pop", sort of an in-between of pop and rock. While nowadays we would most likely refer to this kind of music as City Pop, it's always interesting to see what kinds of terminology was used back in the day to describe something which didn't really have a unified name. Many of the album's songs were made to reflect EPO's own life experiences and naturally feature relatable lyrics which would've been appealing to the urban audience she was targeting. Some standout songs include the uplifting Promises in The Rain and Sunday Before The Bell Rings, a track which perfectly displays the mix of pop and rock EPO was going for. I'm Not Making Excuses really shows off EPO's singing chops, plus it features a cameo from Mariya Takeuchi on the backing vocals, mirroring her album Love Songs which similarly EPO working as a backing vocalist. Down Town is a solid first venture for EPO, whose craft will only continue to improve from here.

Chef's Special

Chef's Special is the debut album for Kaoru Sudo, another City Pop mainstay who was active all the way until 1991 when the style's popularity faded. The album had some major players working on it, such as Yumi Matsutoya, Eiichi Ohtaki, Masamichi Sugi and Masataka Matsutoya, which gives it a quality edge some other debut albums may lack. The delightfully 60s Americana style cover is reflective of the music within, making it feel like a portal to a time even further past us. Many of the songs have a pop rock sound, such as Foolish which starts the album off right thanks to its memorable chorus. The standout track may be the Ohtaki composition A5 'Only I Love You', which has a very memorable chorus with a very pronounced clacking sound. A fantastic start to Sudo's career, Chef's Special still holds up decades later.

Artist: Kaoru Sudo
Release: April 17, 1980
Label: CBS/Sony

- A1. Foolish
- A2. Love Again
- A3. 恋に落ちよう
- A4. なにげなく二人
- A5. あなただけI Love You
- B1. Wow Wow トレイン
- B2. やさしい嘘つき
- B3. 涙のメモワール
- B4. Hello Sadness
- B5. Summer Dream

Northern Scene

The debut album for Hiroaki Igarashi, an artist who showed up right when City Pop was really heating up and managed to secure quite a few hits throughout his career. Igarashi takes inspiration from quite a few different styles including pop, rock, and some folk, with songs like Only Today really leaning in on the rock side. This may be owed to the involvement of Shigeru Suzuki who was responsible for the arrangement on the entire album, giving it some of that Tin Pan magic. As a result, the instrumentals shine here, but Igarashi's singing is also a great asset. His debut single Love is Left To The Wind is also featured on this album, a solid choice to kick off a career with, as it really shows off Igarashi's vocal skills with a delicate song which swings towards soft rock at the very end with a nice guitar solo.

Artist: Hiroaki Igarashi
Release: May 21, 1980
Label: CBS/Sony

- A1. 今日かぎり
- A2. 夢泥棒
- A3. ディープ・パープル
- A4. 愛は風まかせ
- A5. バイ・バイ
- B1. デ・ジャ・ヴー (De-Ja-Vu)
- B2. ミルク・レディ
- B3. 冬子の朝
- B4. だきしめたい
- B5. 今はひとりで

Tasogare

1980 was a huge year for City Pop debuts, with Mai Yamane's Tasogare being a particular highlight. Yamane's incredibly powerful voice made her a mainstay during the City Pop years, but she is perhaps most well known for her vocal work on the Cowboy Bebop soundtrack alongside The Seatbelts. Makoto Matsushita was a major contributor to this one, as he was responsible for the arrangement and guitar play on most of the album. The album's mixture of jazz, funk and rock makes for an incredibly cool experience, especially in its titular opening song. The nearly seven minute long song is a masterpiece with instrumentals that rival and compliment the power of Yamane's singing. Tasogare is an extremely high quality work from Yamane and crew, and every one of its eight tracks more than satisfy.

Artist: Mai Yamane
Release: May 25, 1980
Label: Continental

- A1. たそがれ
- A2. ハート・フォー・セール
- A3. Get Away
- A4. インタールード/よれよれボーイ
- B1. シティー・ドライブ
- B2. ウエイヴ
- B3. フーリン・マイセルフ
- B4. 光と風と波と

Hotel Without Time

Artist: Yumi Matsutoya
Release: June 21, 1980
Label: Express

Yumi Matsutoya continued her two album per year streak in 1980, starting off with Hotel Without Time in June. The cover photo was taken at the Brown's Hotel in London, a historic building which has been around since 1837 and was also the site of Europe's first successful telephone call. Akin to her previous work Hotel Without Time includes songs with some heavy subject matter, such as Miss Lonely which describes a woman still waiting for her lover to return from war, even though fifty years have passed. The album's namesake track is also very heavily inspired by the Cold War, with Matsutoya's vocals sometimes having a static effect to emulate radio broadcasts. In one very striking live performance she even sang the song in a trench coat and gas mask, really showing off what makes Matsutoya a brilliant artist.

A1. セシルの週末
A2. 時のないホテル
A3. Miss Lonely
A4. 雨に消えたジョガー
A5. ためらい
B1. よそゆき顔で
B2. 5cmの向う岸
B3. コンパートメント
B4. 水の影

Monday Morning

Artist: Bread & Butter
Release: June 21, 1980
Label: Alfa

Monday Morning continues to evolve Bread & Butter's newly adopted City Pop style with more of those smooth audio offerings. While not as popular as their previous Late Late Summer the album still has a couple of hits and underappreciated jams. One of its highlights is Japanese Woman, a real cool song which compares a Japanese girl to Princess Kaguya, a character from a thousand year old story who originated from the moon. Another big hit from the album is Cruising On, a totally perfect summer song about sailing with friends and enjoying the beauty of living. Its unique mixture of jazz rock and funk with the memorable English chorus makes it a fun listen. While those two were the albums big movers it has much more to enjoy, such as Paradoxical Love's super funky instrumentals and the moving vocals shown off in Marie.

A1. Hold On
A2. Monday Morning
A3. クルージング・オン
A4. マティーニを飲みながら
A5. Thanks My Lady
B1. Japanese Woman
B2. マリエ
B3. Paradoxical Love
B4. 惑星 1999
B5. Let Us Love

Made In Japan

Artist: Yuuko Shibuya
Release: July 21, 1980
Label: King Records

Made In Japan would end up being Yuuko Shibuya's final album, but she managed to close out her brief run in music with a bang. The album appropriately feels like the culmination of Shibuya's musical wisdom, taking her stylistic alchemy to a new level. Expect a blend of rock, soul, funk, and pop which all come together to make an album that just feels like a cool experience. Speaking of cool, the album's cover didn't need to be this awesome, and it definitely drew a lot of eyes towards it back in the eighties. A particular favorite is track B2 which has a killer combo of a highly singable chorus and memorable instrumentals, especially from the bass played by Tsugutoshi Goto, but the whole album is great. Shibuya retired from making music after this release, but it was quite a way to close things out.

A1. Made In Japan
A2. もしも
A3. 悪魔街のロンド
A4. 5AMはバイオレット・ピンクで
A5. Sail Away
B1. シノワズリー・パーティ
B2. 都会の絵本
B3. Memorize
B4. ムーンライト・ラプソディ
B5. Silent Shadow

Romantique

Left: A somewhat haunting picture of Ohnuki from inside the album.
Center: The cover of Romantique maintains Ohnuki's love for monochrome but is more solemn compared to her earlier albums.
Right: The single release for Carnaval used the same picture as the album, just with text swapped around.

1978 and 1979 were both challenging years for Taeko Ohnuki, who was still struggling to find her place in the music world. Her previous album Mignonne was a commercial letdown, but she wasn't willing to change up her style just to pursue financial success. While she stayed active as a songwriter and backing vocalist in 1979, she didn't release an album of her own and had even considered giving up as a solo artist. That is until Kenichi Makimura, who had worked on Grey Skies, suggested she give European style music a shot since some of her earlier work had a dash of a European sound already. Romantique was therefore designed with inspiration from various European countries, with France being most prominent, but there are Italian and Russian influences as well. Ohnuki wanted to achieve a sound which allowed the listener to visualize a song's intended setting even without lyrics and thus put special attention towards Romantique's compositions. She also decided to adjust her singing style, as she felt her "wild" voice just wouldn't fit the album's subdued flavor. Kenichi Makimura secured the producer role for this record and was genuinely invested in fulfilling Ohnuki's vision. Makimura and Ohnuki spent many months working on Romantique, and Makimura would later state that the album was a huge challenge to create, but that he wanted to give Ohnuki the push she needed to make her talents more recognized. Romantique is an album which feels like a fresh start for Ohnuki, and it seems the European influence worked wonders for her. The album also serves as a meeting point for Ohnuki and the rapidly developing Electronic music scene, as Haruomi Hosono's band Yellow Magic Orchestra can be heard on songs like Carnaval and Decayed Night. Many of its tracks also feature some deep subject matter and meanings, for example Watchtower of Youth is meant to evoke nostalgia, but maybe not in a good way. It was made to reflect good times that will never come again and the blind optimism of youth, while Bohemian describes a drifter moving from town to town in pursuit of success, both of which may have been personally applicable to Ohnuki. The past is also represented here in a much more tangible way, as the album's final song is a fresh recording of Mirage City, a track she originally created as a member of Sugar Babe. The song was included as a treat for fans of her old work and as a way to show how she had developed as an artist. Romantique was a truly pivotal moment in Ohnuki's career, and it would go on to influence her approach to music forever as the start of her European trilogy.

Artist:
Taeko Ohnuki

Release:
July 21, 1980

Label:
RCA

Track List:

A1. Carnaval

A2. ディケイド・ナイト (Decayed Night)

A3. 雨の夜明け (Rainy Dawn)

A4. 若き日の望楼 (Watchtower of Youth)

A5. Bohemian

B1. 果てなき旅情 (Endless Journey)

B2. ふたり (Two People)

B3. 軽蔑 (Scorn)

B4. 新しいシャツ (New Shirt)

B5. 蜃気楼の街 (Mirage City)

Song Writer

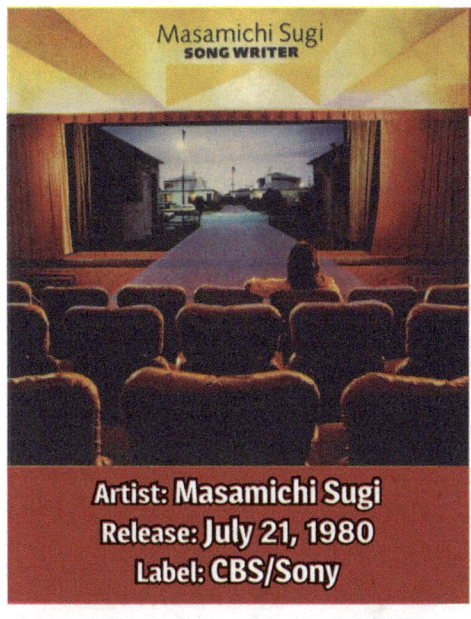

Artist: Masamichi Sugi
Release: July 21, 1980
Label: CBS/Sony

Song Writer marks Masamichi Sugi's return to recording music, this time ditching the Red Stripes band and going at it solo. The style of his music hasn't changed too drastically since his last release, but it does feel far more polished. Also accompanying him includes a stellar lineup of musicians like Shigeru Suzuki and Masataka Matsutoya, and you can spot Mariya Takeuchi and Rajie on the chorus. Those who enjoyed the pop rock sound of his previous work will enjoy Don't Stop The Music and Klaxon, and Missin' Angel's unique instrumentals make it stand out. Hold On delivers a moving number that's sure to have you swaying along thanks to Sugi's singing which is completed by its chorus. Song Writer has many more tracks to enjoy and displays Sugi's artistic evolution quite well.

A1. Don't Stop The Music
A2. Missin' Angel
A3. Hold On
A4. Klaxon
A5. Send Her Back To Me
B1. Something's Gonna Change
B2. Catherine
B3. Sunshine Love
B4. My Baby's Back
B5. Dreamin'

Magical Liqueur

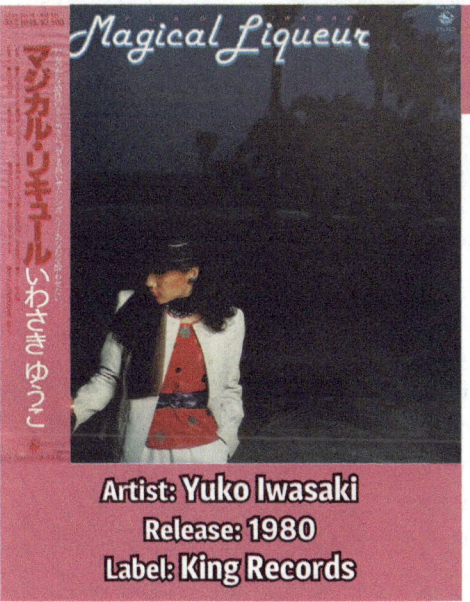

Artist: Yuko Iwasaki
Release: 1980
Label: King Records

Magical Liqueur is the lone album by Yuko Iwasaki, who has a somewhat different story compared to other 'one album wonders'. As the title suggests, the record is quite magical, a real hidden gem from 1980 which exemplifies Iwasaki's skills as an artist. Magical Liqueur is at sort of an intersection between seventies Kayōkyoku and City Pop, as her singing style is clearly influenced by the former. Songs like the opening Leave Everything To Us and When The Southern Wind Blows show off her ability to seamlessly swap between and combine styles, the exact kind of fusion that City Pop is all about. As it turns out Yuko Iwasaki was just a pseudonym used for this album and a few others. During the eighties she found success as a lyricist using her real name, Yuho Iwasato, and would go on to have a very prolific career which is still going strong today.

A1. すべておまかせ
A2. 幾千万の夜をこえて
A3. 南風の吹く頃
A4. Endless Summer
A5. ルイーザの夢
B1. 52階の窓
B2. 恋愛休暇
B3. One Night
B4. ふたりのイエスさま
B5. My Lonesome Boy

Summer Wine

Artist: Tetsuji Hayashi
Release: 1980
Label: Invitation

It had been a few years since Tetsuji Hayashi released an album, with his last being Back Mirror in 1977. After the massive success of his compositions such as September and Stay With Me it seemed the time was right for another Hayashi album, and Summer Wine certainly delivers. Hayashi composed and performed all of the album's catchy tunes himself, showing off more of what this City Pop titan was capable of. Goodbye Tokyo is an especially memorable one owed to Hayashi's somber singing, and the Rock edge it adopts towards the end. We also have appearances from Mariya Takeuchi and EPO on the chorus for a handful of songs. You can hear them on tracks like Silly Girl, another example of Hayashi getting a lot of mileage out of a repeated English phrase that really gets stuck in your head.

A1. Stand By, All Right
A2. Good-bye Tokyo
A3. Running Man
A4. Feeling Blue
A5. After Five Years
B1. Silly Girl
B2. We Sail From Love To Love
B3. Proposal
B4. Bye Bye, Love Dream
B5. Summer Wine

Ride On Time

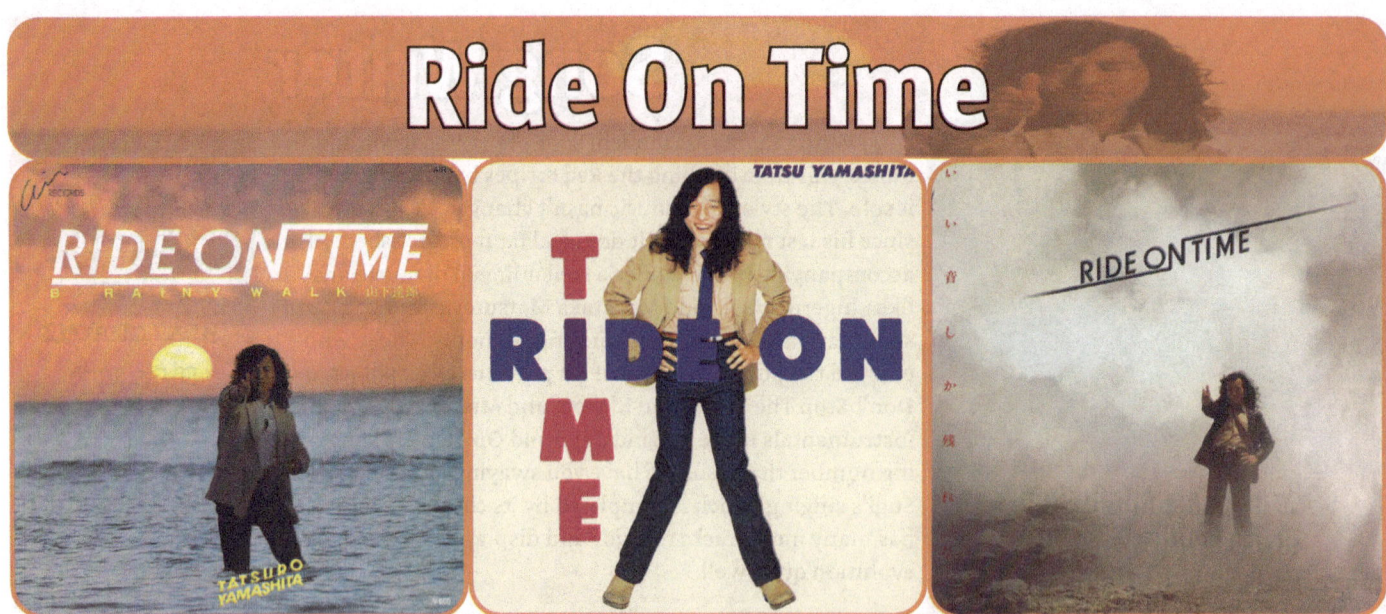

Left: The single release for Ride On Time. This song wasn't just a big deal, it was genre defining.
Center: The more common cover for Ride On Time which features Yamashita in a quirky little pose.
Right: The original, quite smoky cover for Ride on Time came from a photoshoot for the song's commercial tie-in.

1980 would be a year of monumental importance for Tatsuro Yamashita and City Pop as a whole, as one of the styles most recognizable songs was about to be born. Ride on Time was made for a commercial advertising Maxell cassette tapes, which Yamashita himself starred in. The ad actually has very little to do with the tapes considering they only show up in the last three seconds, and the rest of its runtime is made up of footage featuring Yamashita delivering a mighty finger bang. The song itself was unbelievably catchy, and Japanese TV viewers back in 1980 probably looked forward to the commercial running just to hear it again. The bright lyrics, fun instrumentals and chorus which gets stuck in your head then absolutely refuses to leave all contributed to its quality. While it was certainly a good tune, the response from consumers was far beyond expectations. Ride on Time was a stunning success, giving Yamashita his first chart topper with an incredibly impressive 3rd place for the week and over 400,000 copies sold. This marked a turning point in his career, as it seemed like the sales troubles he was facing just two years ago were going to be a thing of the past. Logically his studio album for 1980 was going to capitalize off the success of Ride on Time, and thus it was chosen as the record's namesake. Thanks to Yamashita's newfound success he was able to craft the album with a healthy budget and without fear of this album being his last production. While Yamashita himself was on the compositions, Minako Yoshida was in charge of writing lyrics for every song except Ride On Time and Kissing Goodnight, making this a true collaborative effort from this stellar duo. Daydream happens to be a personal favorite of Yamashita's, and he's stated it's the best song Yoshida has ever written for him. The song feels like a painting put into words as Yamashita rapidly lists off unique colors and is a real testament to Yoshida's songwriting. Silent Screamer was made as something of a spiritual success to Bomber from Go Ahead! and has an 'old fashioned' sound by design. Of course, Ride On Time itself is included, but the album version is actually different from its single release and is just slightly slower. It seemed that Yamashita was feeling nostalgic for more innocent times, as My Sugar Babe is an ode to his former band Sugar Babe. The song can be enjoyed without knowing the context, but the lyrics about time flying by leave a much greater impact when you know the full story. One could argue that City Pop as we know it really begins here with the groundbreaking release of Ride On Time, but at the very least this is when Tatsuro Yamashita became a household name.

Artist:
Tatsuro Yamashita

Release:
September 19, 1980

Label:
Air Records

Track List:

A1. いつか (Someday)

A2. Daydream

A3. Silent Screamer

A4. Ride On Time

B1. 夏への扉 (The Door Into Summer)

B2. My Sugar Babe

B3. Rainy Day

B4. 雲のゆくえに (Clouds)

B5. おやすみ (Kissing Goodnight)

Who Are You?

Left: A cool picture of Matsubara from the album. The colors are super eighties and very City Pop appropriate.
Center: The cover of Who Are You? features some unique visuals with a flashy pyramid in the background.
Art Direction by Teruhisa Tajima. Right: The single release for Hello Today and It's Always A Party In Town.

Artist:
Miki Matsubara

Release:
September 21, 1980

Label:
RCA

Track List:

A1. あいつのブラウンシューズ
(His Brown Shoes)

A2. 気まぐれうさぎ
(Run Rabbit Run)

A3. Rainy Day Woman

A4. Hello Walls

A5. Jazzy Night

B1. Marshia

B2. 宇宙ネコの古さわり
(Howa Howa Shuwa Shuwa)

B3. 夕焼けの時間です
(It's Sunset Time)

B4. Who Are You?

B5. 三日月形の犬をもとめて
(Twinkle Twinkle Starlight)

Miki Matsubara maintained her momentum from the release of Pocket Park with Who Are You? later in the same year. While Pocket Park certainly had some talented people working on it, such as Tetsuji Hayashi and Ken Sato, it was time to bring out the big guns for this next project. Shigeru Suzuki was brought on to play electric guitar and arrange a number of tracks, and he even composed Howa Howa Shuwa Shuwa. Masataka Matsutoya composed and arranged a few songs and Tatsuo Hayashi returned as the drummer, making this album one step removed from being a Tin Pan Alley reunion. We also have contributions from Masamichi Sugi who composed the first two songs, and Tetsuji Hayashi crafted Jazzy Night, which unsurprisingly ended up being the album's most popular. With such a killer lineup Who Are You? was destined for greatness, making it a worthy follow up to her previous album Pocket Park. While the album may lack a ferociously viral hit like Stay With Me, it does feature quite a number of Matsubara's other iconic songs. His Brown Shoes is one such song and was even chosen as the leading track for her 2008 Best Collection. It feels rather reminiscent of an older song, perhaps something from the sixties, but still has those modern pop sensibilities which work together to make it naturally nostalgic. Run Rabbit Run shows off the vocal talent for the album's dedicated chorus members, the jazz ensemble Time Five. They also appear on Rainy Day Woman which has some beyond funky instrumentals that are completed with its lyrics about a dejected woman. For a particularly sad narrative look no further than Hello Walls, a track which tells of a woman left all alone, with her only companionship being from the walls that surround her. Jazzy Night would prove to be the album's biggest hit and a beloved staple of the genre, and in many ways feels like a counterpart to Stay With Me. Both were made by the same duo of Tetsuji Hayashi and Miura Yoshiko, feature a memorable chorus designed around an English phrase, and both have quite sad subject matter despite seeming like bubbly pop songs. One rather underappreciated song from the album is Marsha, which has a great performance from Matsubara, and while Howa Howa Shuwa Shuwa has a really funny name it's also a great song that takes you on a nearly 7-minute-long journey. The smooth sounds of It's Sunset Time begin to wind the album down before Who Are You and Twinkle Twinkle Starlight close us out. Who Are You is an extraordinary sequel to Pocket Park, and it's incredibly impressive that Matsubara released two exceptional albums in the same year.

Monochrome

Left: The back of Monochrome shows off a quite artsy looking microphone amidst shadow.
Center: The cover of Monochrome is bold and sexy, a new direction for Yoshida who was taking control of her career.
Right: Credits from inside the album which are all handwritten.

1979 ended up being somewhat of a sabbatical year for Minako Yoshida, and in many ways it mirrored the struggles that fellow icon Taeko Ohnuki was going through. Yoshida eventually grew tired of the complications involved with the music industry, such as the issues involved with making Let's Do It, and instead spent the year working on songs for other artists. Despite the issues she had faced it seemed that karma was about to work in her favor. While her swap to Alfa initially came with some hurdles, the bright side was that there was less pressure to sell records compared to her previous label RCA, and it afforded artists more time to craft their albums. Those in charge at Alfa had a lot of confidence in Yoshida, as she was told to "not be lazy and make an album for eight million yen". At the time this was about 50,000 US dollars, but when adjusted for inflation this would've been a nearly $200,000 budget. Yoshida wasn't exactly keen on the idea of producing the album, but she was ultimately up to the challenge. As producer she was responsible for the entire project, ranging from the cover design to the music direction, and of course keeping the entire thing within the budget. By the end of it Yoshida was left with far greater knowledge of the entire album making process, a skillset which would serve her for the rest of her lengthy career. Monochrome could be viewed as Yoshida's true passion project, and her first where just about everything was made according to her liking. As such, it's an album that feels like the truest reflection of her talent and philosophy and feels incredibly consistent as a result. The opening track Tornado has Yoshida comparing herself to a tornado that's going to take everything in, and its funky instrumentals beg to be enjoyed with headphones. Rainy Day is borrowed from Tatsuro Yamashita's Ride on Time, and while both versions are great the Yoshida iteration really captures the feeling of loneliness the song describes. Black Moon has Yoshida rhythmically singing the first three syllables of each verse, creating a song that's fun to sing along with, and the funky instrumentals are killer. Like with some of her earlier albums many of Monochrome's tracks are quite lengthy, such as the almost eight-minute-long Sunset and Midnight Driver, the record's most popular song. The track is a journey into an ethereal dimension, just be prepared to hear "sliding through the night, splashing sense of sight" in a sort of endurance marathon throughout its second half. Monochrome was a huge moment in Minako Yoshida's career, as she would go on to produce all of her own albums from this point forward.

Artist:
Minako Yoshida

Release:
October 21, 1980

Label:
Alfa

Track List:

A1. トルネード
(Tornado)

A2. レイニー・デイ
(Rainy Day)

A3. ブラック・ムーン
(Black Moon)

A4. サンセット
(Sunset)

B1. エアポート
(Airport)

B2. ミラージュ
(Mirage)

B3. ミッドナイト・ドライバー
(Midnight Driver)

B4. 午後
(Afternoon)

I'm In Love

Artist: Fujiro
Release: October 25, 1980
Label: Continental

The sole album by Fujiro, a unique figure in City Pop who disappeared as quickly as he arrived. I'm In Love is a fantastic album from Fujiro which feels so much more refined than a typical first release. Fujiro's manly voice is often complemented by Mai Yamane on the chorus, and that's not to mention the variety of songs on display. Whether its pop rock or slow jams, the tracks in I'm In Love are all audio delights. So, what exactly happened to this promising artist? Fujiro had a rough performance on a TV show which was quite a traumatic experience for him, leading to his early retirement from music. For the next decades Fujiro focused on his local business but made a surprise return in 2009 with a few songs in conjunction with a Buddhist sacred sites tour. Fujiro sadly passed away in 2018, leaving behind this lone masterpiece.

- A1. 愛の行方 (Did You Find It)
- A2. 俺のハピネス
- A3. I've Been Loving You
- A4. 三番目の女
- A5. Walking In The Rain
- B1. 電話
- B2. 愛の唄など歌えない
- B3. マリア
- B4. 見果てぬ夢
- B5. 自由への旅

Yume Hiko

Artist: Mioko Yamaguchi
Release: November 1980
Label: F-Label

The debut album by Mioko Yamaguchi, an artist who released three unique albums in the early 1980s before shifting her focus towards composing. Yume Hiko fits in with other City Pop records which had a heavy focus on synth-pop, but other dependable genres including rock and disco are fused in here as well. When City Pop started its resurgence in popularity during the 2010s many new fans discovered Yamaguchi's music, but surprisingly none of her albums were ever put on CD. The influx of people asking for a modern release encouraged Yamaguchi to contact the rights holders for her old albums, which finally got put on CD in 2017. Later in 2019 Yamaguchi returned to making music after a decade long hiatus, and since then she has made three full length records and a mini album.

- A1. Arabian Rhapsody
- A2. Tokyo Lover
- A3. Hidamari No Naka De
- A4. Dream Of Eμ
- A5. Omatsuri
- A6. Itsuka Yurarete Toi Kuni
- B1. A Dream Of Mio
- B2. Yume Hiko
- B3. Aru Yo No Dekigoto
- B4. Koi No Air Play
- B5. Waltz
- B6. Paradise

Le Trottoir D'Après Midi

Artist: Rajie
Release: November 1, 1980
Label: CBS/Sony

1980's Le Trottoir D'Après Midi (The Sidewalk After Noon) was the next step in Rajie's musical journey and had her falling further down the electronic rabbit hole, while still embracing her pop roots. All of the members of Yellow Magic Orchestra appear once again, providing a level of quality that only these pioneers of electronic music could offer. Some other familiar contributors include Masamichi Sugi, Yoshitaka Minami and Taeko Ohnuki, who all lent their own excellent compositions. The album finds a good middle ground between the slowly fading seventies pop sound and the blossoming Electronic scene, with some songs leaning much more heavily on one element or the other. It's an interesting piece of early synth-pop history and another welcome addition to Rajie's repertoire.

- A1. ラスト・シーン
- A2. 真昼の舗道
- A3. 霧の部屋
- A4. 偽りの瞳
- A5. アパルトマン
- B1. ラジオと二人
- B2. ヨジレアン・ツイスト
- B3. みどりの声
- B4. 秋の嵐
- B5. 忘却

Natural Road

Artist: Hiroaki Igarashi
Release: November 21, 1980
Label: CBS/Sony

Hiroaki Igarashi's second album was released about half a year after Northern Road and includes his first major hit. The song Pegasus Road was first released as a single earlier in the month and garnered a lot of attention throughout 1981. Its great mixture of pop and soft rock styles with Igarashi's smooth voice made it a fun listen, and it managed to sell well over 500,000 copies. It was also used in a commercial advertising Meiji chocolate which shows off a sweaty white dude on a jog, drying off and then sensually eating a delicious candy bar. While Pegasus Road may be the album's main attraction it has a lot of lesser-known tracks to appreciate. Breezy Night is a lovely and soft song where Igarashi sings quietly, almost in a whisper, and it's accompanied by some smooth and jazzy instrumentals as the song wraps up.

- A1. ペガサスの朝
- A2. フォギー・ナイト
- A3. 小さな明日
- A4. 雪が降る前に
- A5. ナチュラル・ロード
- B1. ブリージー・ナイト
- B2. 流星群
- B3. イノセント
- B4. いつまでも
- B5. 幸せいろのなみだ

Goodies

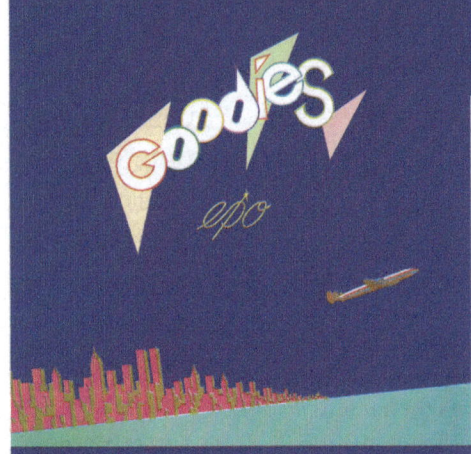

Artist: EPO
Release: November 21, 1980
Label: RCA

EPO's second album Goodies ended up being an international production that was recorded in the trifecta of Tokyo, New York and Los Angeles. The name Goodies was designed to evoke feelings of excitement, a concept that carries over quite well into the album's joyous music. The ever skilled Tatsuro Yamashita played a large role in this album's creation, as he composed track A4, arranged a few tracks, played guitar and also contributed backing vocals. Park Ave. 1981 was also released as a single and is a standout from a year with ferocious competition. The delightfully happy song sings of a busy avenue with kids skating around and love in the air, and has backing vocals courtesy of Taeko Ohnuki, who you can also spot on tracks throughout the album. Goodies certainly lives up to its namesake as quite the delightful treat.

- A1. Goodies
- A2. 雨のケンネル通り
- A3. 週末は"Week-End"で
- A4. パレード
- A5. チアーガール
- A6. 異国行き
- B1. Park Ave. 1981
- B2. ドライブ・ソング
- B3. 足のないベッド
- B4. 分別ざかり
- B5. Goodies

Miss M

Artist: Mariya Takeuchi
Release: December 5, 1980
Label: RCA

Mariya Takeuchi wrapped up the year with Miss M, an album featuring an international recording process, with its A-side being known as the 'L.A. Side' and the B-side as the 'Tokyo Side'. The album begins with one of Takeuchi's most iconic songs, Sweetest Music. This track features entirely English lyrics and energetic instrumentals which skirt the line between pop and rock, creating a consistently fun listening experience. While the L.A. Side had songs composed by other artists, the Tokyo side was where Takeuchi got to strut her stuff. Every track on that side had lyrics by her, and the albums final three songs were also her compositions. While Miss M wasn't quite the smashing commercial success that Love Songs was, it does mark a huge shift in Takeuchi's own composing and lyrical skills, both of which would serve her well in years to come.

- A1. Sweetest Music
- A2. Every Night
- A3. Morning Glory
- A4. Secret Love
- A5. Heart To Heart
- B1. 二人のバカンス
- B2. 遠く離れて (When You're So Far Away)
- B3. 雨のドライヴ
- B5. Farewell Call

1981, The Vacation Begins

The affluent themes and mesmerizing sounds of City Pop were quickly finding a mainstream audience thanks to some hugely successful songs from 1980 like Ride on Time and Midnight Door/Stay With Me, as well as that year's many popular albums. Unsurprisingly this also meant that many new artists were adopting the style and putting their own spin on it. Makoto Matsushita had been working in the industry for a few years, but he was about to blow everyone away with the stunningly smooth debut album First Light. Synth-pop savant Tomoko Aran got her start this year, as did Hitomi "Penny" Tohyama, an unconventional City Pop artist who grew up speaking English as the child of American and Japanese parents. Possibly the most impactful event from this year was the emergence of Toshiki Kadomatsu, a man who was going to tie City Pop to vacations and summer forever. The emergence of these rookies was certainly exciting, but the old guard were ready to show these kids how it's really done. Former Happy End members Eiichi Ohtaki and Takashi Matsumoto joined up for A Long Vacation, an album that ended up fraught with hardship due to the tragic passing of Takashi Matsumoto's sister, but it ultimately came together as Ohtaki's magnum opus. The actor Akira Terao made his return to music after spending a decade as an actor, but the music world was shocked when his album song Ruby Ring unexpectedly became a record-shattering success. Get ready for a much-needed vacation here in 1981, a year full of exciting City Pop innovations and memorable music from newcomers and old-timers alike.

Toshiki Kadomatsu

When thinking about the stereotypical image of what City Pop is about, a few concepts probably come to mind such as summer, the city hustle, and travel. Toshiki Kadomatsu's music embodied these concepts, and a lot of our modern preconceptions about the genre came about because of his work. Like many of City Pop's other titans he was inspired by the New Music scene of the early seventies, being especially fond of Shigeru Suzuki's guitar skills, and he admired Tatsuro Yamashita. His debut album Sea Breeze was a quality addition to the style which further codified its easygoing tropes, but some within his label thought he was too similar to Tatsuro Yamashita. Both artists were signed to the overarching RVC company, just in different sections, but the department Yamashita was attached to considered Kadomatsu a knock-off designed to imitate their success. Kadomatsu did manage to distinguish himself with his albums which beautifully mixed several genres, notably disco, soul and funk, and they were quite specific in their theming. His music usually revolved around beachside bashes, adorable expressions of love, and other topics adolescents of the time enjoyed. This carried over to his work producing for Anri, and together they made some of City Pop's most cherished albums, notably Timely!! in 1983. Midway through the eighties Kadomatsu really put the "City" in City Pop with music focusing on urban ideas of night-time escapades and passionate romance, which is best experienced in his fantastic album After 5 Clash. Kadomatsu stayed as a reliable artist for City Pop's entire lifespan, typically releasing an album per year, but like virtually everybody else he drifted away from the style over time. Few artists managed to nail the City Pop vibe as well as Kadomatsu, and his albums are a perfect way to introduce others to the style. His career is still ongoing today and he still regularly performs and creates albums, some of which are remakes of his 1980s classics.

Toshiki Kadomatsu is one of City Pop's coolest cats, and one of its most influential artists. While he may not have invented City Pop's cliches he absolutely helped to popularize them.

The Visuals of City Pop

Beyond just the incredible music and brilliant artists of City Pop there's another aspect which is deeply intertwined with its identity, the visuals. During City Pop's relevant years there were hundreds of albums and singles released, many of which featured surprisingly consistent imagery that evolved along with the style. These album covers often captured many of the genre's core themes and subjects, and their now retro aesthetic is totally evocative of the seventies and eighties period they originated from. Summer is probably the most revisited concept in City Pop, so naturally a large number of album covers show off some fun in the sun. Iconic albums like Summer Breeze by Piper, Timely!! by Anri, and A Long Vacation by Eiichi Ohtaki all have eye catching covers taken at or depicting the beach, letting potential consumers know what kind of leisurely vibe awaited them. These summertime albums also indirectly took some cultural snapshots of the absolutely booming economy of 1980s Japan. The financial freedom afforded to Japanese citizens back then meant these album covers weren't just pop song propaganda, a nice beachside vacation with the family was actually very attainable. Of course, it wouldn't be called City Pop if there wasn't some city imagery, and the mystique of the concrete jungle was always a reliable subject. You can see this in the flashy cover for After 5 Clash by Toshiki Kadomatsu, but cityscapes also appear in more subtle forms such as the serene cover of Aqua City by S. Kiyotaka and Omega Tribe. City Pop artists surprisingly showed a lot of restraint when it came to city-centric covers, as they're much rarer than the genre's name might imply, so perhaps they thought it was cliche even back then. Water also tends to appear very often, likely as another extension of City Pop's summer fixation, but the natural calm of water pairs nicely with the chill atmosphere many of the genre's musicians sought. City Pop covers were typically very colorful, but pink and blue both stand out as being the genre's de-facto signature colors. The recurring trendsetter that was Yumi Arai's Cobalt Hour prominently featured pink and blue, and many later albums followed suit. Albums such as Big Wave by Tatsuro Yamashita, Tomoko Aran's Fuyū-Kūkan and Adventure by Momoko Kikuchi all put vibrant blues and popping pinks to good use. Strangely enough there's also a large amount of art inspired by fifties and sixties Americana. This makes sense when you consider how many of City Pop's main players were influenced by American rock and folk from those decades, and their own attachment to the era's music seems to have carried over to its imagery too. Perhaps the most well-known of these retro-inspired covers is Eizin Suzuki's iconic artwork on For You by Tatsuro Yamashita, a beautiful piece which pairs perfectly with one of City Pop's best albums ever. Another artist with a similar style is Hiroshi Nagai, whose art has become synonymous with City Pop's modern revival thanks to his work on the Pacific Breeze series of compilation records. Nagai's album covers are colorful, peaceful, and even radiate a mysterious feeling, as their scenery devoid of people might make you feel a little lonely or even uncomfortable. While these may be some of the more common trends for City Pop's albums the genre had a ton of variance and unique looks that broke the mold. The monochrome looks on Mariya Takeuchi's Variety and Taeko Ohnuki's Mignonne come to mind, but there's an entire world of interesting covers to sift through. The unforgettable covers of these albums are nostalgic masterpieces, but they're also fascinating as visualizations of the optimism the Japanese people had during this period.

> Top: The cover of For You features art by the legendary Eizin Suzuki. This Americana style is one of City Pop's hallmarks, with Hiroshi Nagai being another very prominent artist with a similar approach. Just like how we're nostalgic for the 1980s, City Pop's artists were very nostalgic for the 1960s while making their music.
> Center: After 5 Clash by Toshiki Kadomatsu takes City Pop quite directly, showcasing the lights and luster of the city. This is oddly not as common as you'd perhaps expect for a genre called City Pop.
> Bottom: Summer and aquatic imagery is depicted far more often than views of the city. Many of the genre's most recognizable covers like Summer Breeze by Piper feature bodies of water and beaches.

A Long Vacation

Left: The single release for Karen In Love and Rainy Wednesday has that classic Americana look Ohtaki loved.
Center: The cover of A Long Vacation. Hiroshi Nagai's artstyle is linked to City Pop forever.
Right: The single release for Farewell Trans-Siberian Railway and the Niagara Triangle song Fall In Love On The A-side.

Artist:
Eiichi Ohtaki

Release:
March 21, 1981

Label:
Niagara Records

Track List:

A1. 君は天然色
(You Are A Natural Color)

A2. Velvet Motel

A3. カナリア諸島にて
(In The Canary Islands)

A4. Pap-Pi-Doo-Bi-Doo-Ba Story

A5. 我が心のピンボール
(Pinball In My Heart)

B1. 雨のウェンズデイ
(Rainy Wednesday)

B2. スピーチ・バルーン
(Speech Balloon)

B3. 恋するカレン
(Karen In Love)

B4. FUN×4
(Afternoon)

B5. さらばシベリア鉄道
(Farewell Trans-Siberian Railway)

Despite Eiichi Ohtaki being an established artist for nearly ten years, and even having his own record label, the sales for his albums were always behind his peers. In the blossoming age of City Pop many of his contemporaries such as Tatsuro Yamashita were making names for themselves with successful albums like Ride On Time, but it seemed that Ohtaki wanted to secure a smash hit of his own. To help accomplish this he enlisted his former Happy End bandmate Takashi Matsumoto to be the album's lyricist, and A Long Vacation was expected to be done by July of 1980. However, tragedy struck when Matsumoto's sister unexpectedly passed away, which left him in no state to write lyrics. Ohtaki received a call from Matsumoto, who explained his situation, and suggested that he find a new lyricist for the project. Ohtaki didn't change his plans however, as he was committed to having his friend on board and stated that he'd delay the album's release until Matsumoto was ready to write again. Although it ended up a little behind schedule, A Long Vacation did finally release in March of 1981 with Matsumoto as its lyricist. Despite the hardship that the duo went through during its lengthy production, A Long Vacation proved to be well worth the wait and was a massive success for Ohtaki. It especially gained traction in 1982 on that fancy new CD thing, selling over a million units. A Long Vacation felt like a beautiful evolution for Ohtaki's style, keeping those pop and rock influences from his previous work while making it more appealing to a general audience. The popular song You Are A Natural Color drew from Matsumoto's experience dealing with loss, as he recounts the color being gone from his life during that time. In The Canary Islands perfectly fits the vacation theming of the album, and Matsumoto recalls that Ohtaki particularly liked the lyrics for this one. Pap-Pi-Doo-Bi-Doo-Ba Story has a real goofy sounding name and an origin story defined by problems. Ohtaki had quite a few issues with the synthesizer used to achieve the songs electronic sound and couldn't get the exact effect he was hoping for. He ultimately decided that the disjointed sound worked in its own way and just left it in, a feeling of capitulation many creative types can certainly relate to. You can also hear Shigeru Suzuki playing guitar on this track, and Haruomi Hosono also shows up in some songs playing bass. FunX4 is as fun as you'd expect with its bit of doo-wop influence, and fans of The Beach Boys will enjoy the reference to their song Fun, Fun, Fun. A Long Vacation is still remembered and beloved as Ohtaki's masterpiece and a City Pop gem, but it wouldn't have been possible without Takashi Matsumoto's contributions.

Artist: Piper
Release: 1981
Label: Yupiteru Records

I'm Not In Love

I'm Not In Love is the debut album by Piper, a surprisingly rare example of a fully fledged band in City Pop. Their style leans heavily in the adult-oriented/soft rock approach which is very fitting to the eighties, and is consistently cool. With three different vocalists on board there's quite a lot of audible variety, and listening to the contrast between the singers adds a lot. The album starts off with a subdued energy in I'm Not In Love to get you going before kicking it up with Lavender Trips and Far Away, and the rest of the A-side is dedicated to chill pop rock tunes. The B-side carries its weight as well with an emphasis on rock, including memorable songs like B3, and the very unique B4 with its totally radical guitar play. An awesome first release for Piper and one of 1981's most under-rated albums, although their next release would have a very different design philosophy.

A1. I'm Not In Love
A2. Lavender Trips
A3. Far Away
A4. Funny Face
A5. Love Song
A6. Dance
B1. Zenny, I Love You
B2. Lovely Night
B3. 9月の空
B4. 翔べない鳥
B5. 冬のおくりもの

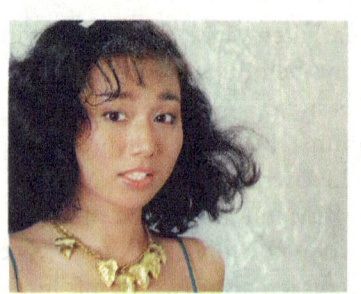

Artist: Yumi Seino
Release: March 1981
Label: Blow Up

U・TA・GE

U・TA・GE is the debut album for Yumi Seino, a lesser known artist who had a fairly brief career in music and released a total of three records. The album had quite a few composers behind it, but the most frequent one was Akira Inoue who also worked as U・TA・GE's arranger. With five composers on board the album ended up being quite diverse, and each song has a different flavor. Dream Song is a jazzy and soulful slow track, while Rio No Maho Tsukai is more akin to the kind of songs you'd expect from the genre. The Inoue composed Hasta Manana has some Latin influence and a soft rock edge, and the guitar play in Tu es malin gets real nice. U・TA・GE is a good first album from Yumi Seino and its multitude of composers but has a hard time standing out amidst all of 1981's great records.

A1. Hasta Manana
A2. Dream Song
A3. Tu es malin
A4. Nineteen-Eighty-One
A5. SEXY Claws
B1. Marvel Shadow
B2. U・TA・GE
B3. Rio No Maho Tsukai
B4. Gin No Yubiwa
B5. Beautiful Romancers

Artist: Mai Yamane
Release: March 25, 1981
Label: Continental

Sorry

Mai Yamane's second album Sorry has nothing to apologize for considering how good it is. This time Yamane came equipped with a beyond stellar lineup of talent working on the record, including Shigeru Suzuki and Makoto Matsushita who shared arrangement duty. You can also hear Tatsuo Hayashi, Jun Sato and many more delivering a soulful and jazzy experience as Yamane continues to perfect her beautiful singing. Her voice shines on tracks such as My Saturday Man and In Love, providing performances that are guaranteed to move you. The instrumentals are also expectedly excellent, with Out Of The Night having an awesome jazz-rock session midway through, while Turn On Street just radiates a funky swagger. Sorry is another big winner from Yamane and crew and absolutely deserving of a listen.

A1. My Saturday Man
A2. Sorry (Kawaisoh Da To Iwanaide)
A3. Emi
A4. Ima Mo Hitomi Sa
B1. Out Of The Night
B2. Turn On Street
B3. Yoake Wa Show Time
B4. In Love

Reflections

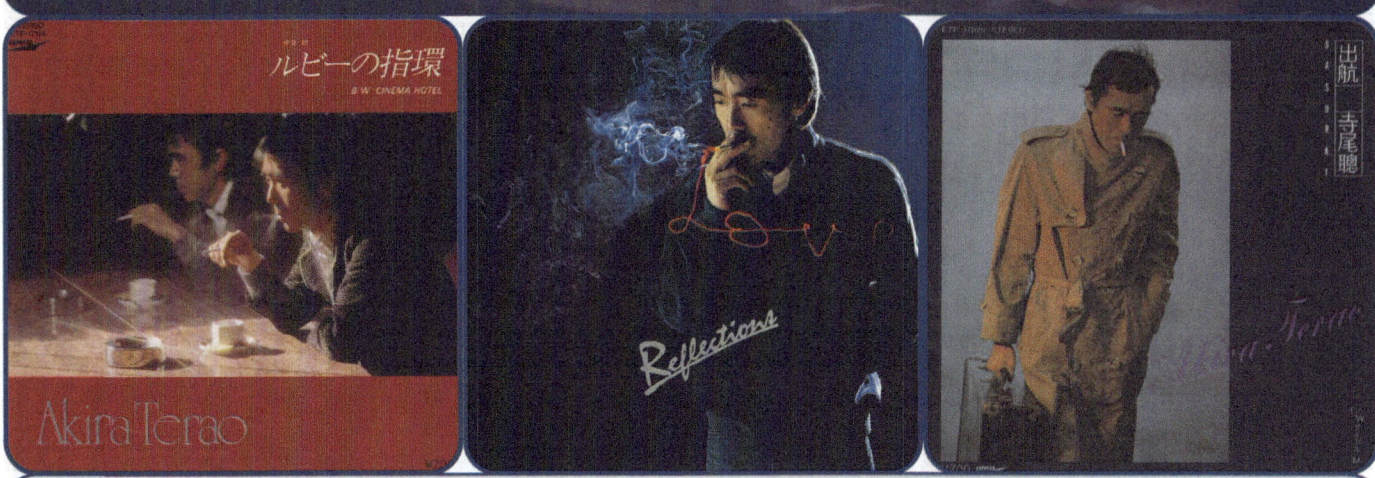

Left: The single release of Ruby Ring and Cinema Hotel, depicting a real cool scene of Terao having a smoke.
Center: The cover of Reflections is a stoic icon of Japanese music from the eighties.
Right: The single release for Departure Sarusai and Dial M. Terao sure likes his cigarettes.

Artist:
Akira Terao

Release:
April 5, 1981

Label:
Express

Track List:

A1. Habana Express

A2. 渚のカンパリ・ソーダ
(Campari Soda on The Beach)

A3. 喜望峰
(Cape of Good Hope)

A4. 二季物語
(Tale of Two Seasons)

A5. ルビーの指環
(Ruby Ring)

B1. Shadow City

B2. 予期せぬ出来事
(Unforeseen Event)

B3. ダイヤルM (Dial M)

B4. 北ウィング
(North Wing)

B5. 出航 Sasurai
(Departure Sasurai)

Akira Terao released Reflections as his second album in 1981, although it could be thought of as a reset for his musical career considering his debut record came out way back in 1970. Terao had instead spent the past decade working as an actor in various TV shows and movies, so few probably expected his return to music to make that much of a splash. This initially proved to be true with the single releases for a few of his tracks throughout 1980, such as Shadow City and Departure Sasurai, neither of which gained much traction at first. The single release for Ruby Ring in February of 1981 seemed to be following the same trajectory until March rolled around and it mysteriously gained a new wave of interest thanks to word of mouth. This was no mere jump in sales however, it was a totally unprecedented level of popularity. Not only did it hit number one on Japan's Oricon Charts, it maintained its top position for months and sold over a million copies by the end of the year. When you listen to the song you immediately understand why, as it features an incredibly captivating composition by Terao and lyrics by Takashi Matsumoto, who just helped make A Long Vacation a smash success with his lyrical brilliance. The song's funky instrumentals, Terao's deep voice and lyrics which manage to blend heartbreak with a certain stoic coolness to create a perfect song, one which seemingly appealed to everyone. It also cleaned house at that year's Japan Record Awards, winning best composition, best lyrics and best arrangement thanks to Akira Inoue's work. This success then retroactively carried over to his earlier singles, all of which skyrocketed in terms of sales and popularity. Naturally, the album itself was destined for commercial greatness, and it likewise sold over a million copies while holding total dominance over the Oricon Charts, keeping its grip on that number one spot for twelve weeks. It's easy to understand why Reflections did so well in the early 1980s, as it combines various different styles in a way that feels unique while still being commercially viable (extremely so, in fact). The album finds itself at a sort of midway point between the catchy pop which appealed to a younger audience and the more mature adult-oriented rock that an older crowd would jam out to. It's also the exact kind of music that those hip urban folk would've found cool, thus fitting the City Pop billing quite well. Reflections did pretty alright for itself, ending up as the bestselling album in Japan throughout the entirety of the 1980s. Never let a slow start discourage you, it's always possible you have another Reflections situation going on.

Cupid

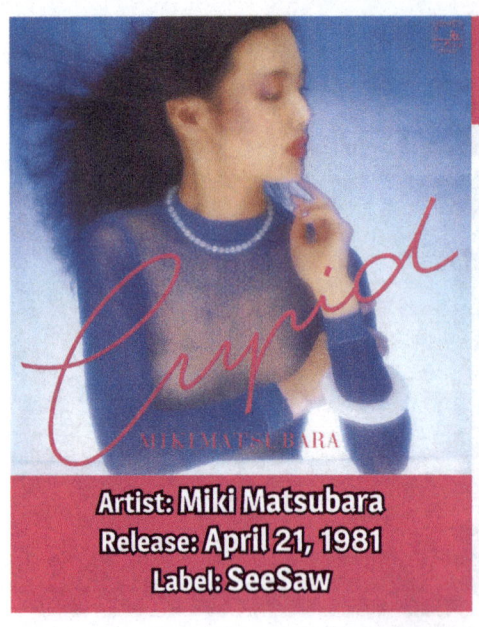

Artist: Miki Matsubara
Release: April 21, 1981
Label: SeeSaw

Miki Matsubara's album Cupid had fewer smash hits compared to her previous two ventures but still offered some premium City Pop. This time Miura Yoshiko, the genius behind the lyrics for Stay With Me, was given the lyricist role for every single song. This naturally gave Cupid some of Matsubara's most lyrically strong songs yet, such as B2 or Neat na Gogo 3 Ji, which is just fun to say. The track has a disco edge which would've lit up clubs in the eighties, and its addictive energy keeps going throughout its entire length. The titular Cupid would end up being the album's most popular, and its smooth combination of playful and sexy skirts the line between pop and jazz. Cupid has a few other lesser-known songs, like One Summer Night which has a fantastic electronic flourish to it, or the mighty smooth track B3.

- A1. 10カラット・ラブ
- A2. One Way Street
- A3. 青いボールペン
- A4. 私はもどれない
- A5. オアシス
- B1. Cupid
- B2. ニートな午後3時
- B3. スーヴェニール
- B4. One Summer Night
- B5. Dream In The Screen

Hot Baby

Artist: Amii Ozaki
Release: May 5, 1981
Label: F-Label

The first of Amii Ozaki's two albums for 1981 came with a unique (and highly collectible) gimmick. The album had three assorted color variations with purple, blue and green being available, although the actual contents within were obviously the same. Akin to Mariya Takeuchi's Miss M various members of the band TOTO appeared, giving the album an American infusion, and the musical genius David Foster was put in charge of the arrangement. Much of the electronic influence Ozaki experimented with in prior years has left in favor of an emphasis on jazz and soul which is best displayed in Love is Easy and Wanderer in Love. The band does get a chance to rock out on Prism Train and track B4, but the album generally leans towards lighter pop tunes. Hot Baby feels both fresh and familiar, making it a great addition to Ozaki's musical history.

- A1. Love is Easy
- A2. 身体に残るワイン
- A3. キャッツアイ
- A4. 限りない憎しみの果てに〜花が咲いたよ〜
- B1. Angela
- B2. Prism Train
- B3. Wanderer in Love
- B4. 蒼夜曲 セレナーデ

Aventure

Artist: Taeko Ohnuki
Release: May 21, 1981
Label: RCA

Taeko Ohnuki continued her journey into a world of European inspired music with 1981's Aventure, an album which features quite the shakeup for her. Aventure marks a new direction for Ohnuki as it has a noticeable focus on an electronic pop sound which reflects her own bright self. Yellow Magic Orchestra lent a hand as she was accompanied by Japanese electronic music's greatest with Yukihiro Takahashi and Ryuichi Sakamoto, and Haruomi Hosono even shows up for a song. The album is all Ohnuki though, and she composed and wrote lyrics for every song, and they range from somber ballads to bombastic pop tunes. That European influence from Romantique can still be felt here, but its synth-pop style gives it a totally unique flavor from its sibling, making Aventure quite the album.

- A1. 恋人達の明日
- A2. Samba De Mar
- A3. 愛の行方
- A4. アヴァンチュリエール
- A5. テルミネ
- B1. チャンス
- B2. グランプリ
- B3. La Mer, Le Ciel
- B4. ブリーカー・ストリートの青春
- B5. 最後の日付

Just Call Me Penny

Artist: Hitomi "Penny" Tohyama
Release: May 25, 1981
Label: Columbia

Just Call Me Penny is the first album by Hitomi "Penny" Tohyama, a unique talent and mainstay for City Pop. Born in Okinawa to a Japanese mother and American father, Penny primarily spoke English throughout her life but was encouraged to try singing in Japanese by producer Hikaru Kanematsu. Despite her unconventional origin story Penny delivered a stellar first album, to the point where you probably wouldn't even guess that Japanese wasn't her native language. The jazzy So Many Dreams fittingly starts with a blend of English and Japanese singing, although as you'd expect from City Pop the stylistic fusion doesn't stop there. Look forward to a mixture of those classic Kayōkyoku vocals, funk and more which all come together to make a delightful record, and the first of many from her.

- A1. So Many Times
- A2. My Guy (Café Sign)
- A3. Image Change
- A4. Rainy Driver
- B1. Station
- B2. Baby, Baby, Baby
- B3. Midnight Express
- B4. SFO-Oakland
- B5. Instant Polaroid

Poker Face

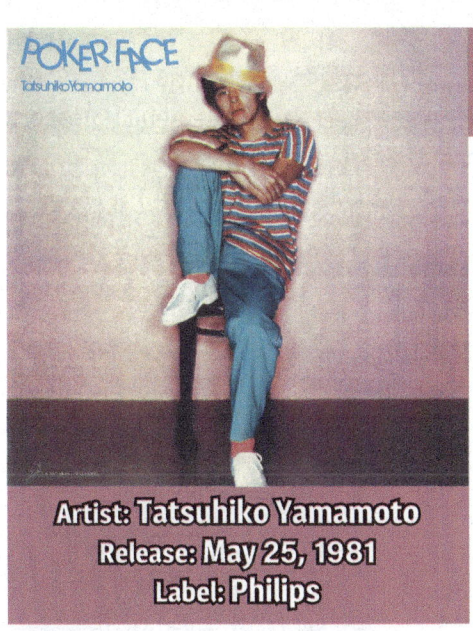

Artist: Tatsuhiko Yamamoto
Release: May 25, 1981
Label: Philips

Poker Face is Tatsuhiko Yamamoto's third album, and it feels even closer to the City Pop standard thanks to its greater emphasis on funk. This time around he is accompanied by a stellar band including some City Pop icons like Tatsuo Hayashi, Jake H. Concepcion and Masaki Matsubara, with Yamamoto himself continuing to flaunt his skills on piano. Track A5 AKA Sunrise Highway secures its place as the album's most popular song likely due to its slick instrumentals, and the backing vocals which work well to give Yamamoto's own vocals a greater impact. 1974 is a sleeper hit of a song which reflects on days since past and has some of the album's best instrumentals. Poker Face is another release from Yamamoto worth looking into, and you may find some new additions to your City Pop playlist here.

- A1. 恋のマッド・ゲーム
- A2. シャイニング・ルーム
- A3. さまよえる時間旅行者
- A4. ラブレター・オン・サイドシート
- A5. サンライズ・ハイウェイ
- B1. Fly To Me
- B2. 星を着た魔女
- B3. Return To 1974
- B4. ロンリー・トゥナイト
- B5. 夜のピアノ

Tea For Tears

Artist: Junko Ohashi
Release: May 1981
Label: Philips

Tea For Tears was Junko Ohashi's first album released after Minoya Central Station broke up, and she would continue as a solo artist from here on. Despite the change her music stayed pretty similar to how it was with the band, largely owed to Ken Sato remaining to compose most of the album's tracks. Expect more of that signature Ohashi blend of funk, soul and just the right amount of disco infusion to help give the songs a danceable edge. Tea For Tears is also home to one of Ohashi's most beloved songs, track A5, also known as Telephone Number. Its jazzy instrumentals and iconic chorus will have the numbers 5-6-7-0-9 ingrained into your memory, and it's no surprise the song became so popular during City Pop's revival in the late 2010s. A great start to Ohashi's now solo career with some real jams.

- A1. Another Day, Another Love
- A2. 恋のアドリブ
- A3. サイレーン (海の精の物語)
- A4. ラ・ローザ
- A5. テレフォン・ナンバー
- B1. Maroon Person
- B2. シジフォスの朝
- B3. ブックエンド
- B4. 名前のない馬
- B5. Tea For Tears

Sea Breeze

Left: This picture of a beach chair propped up next to the ocean is simple, but very alluring. Center: The cover of Sea Breeze captures the delight felt in a beachside condo perfectly. The photos for the album were actually taken on the balcony of a pastry shop, but the illusion works pretty well. Right: The back of Sea Breeze has Kadomatsu a bit away from view on the balcony, drink in hand. I'd join him!

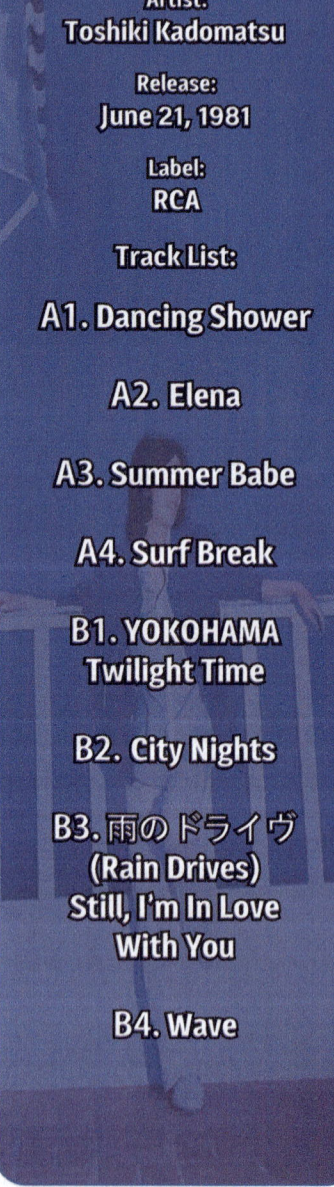

Artist: Toshiki Kadomatsu
Release: June 21, 1981
Label: RCA
Track List:
A1. Dancing Shower
A2. Elena
A3. Summer Babe
A4. Surf Break
B1. YOKOHAMA Twilight Time
B2. City Nights
B3. 雨のドライヴ (Rain Drives)
Still, I'm In Love With You
B4. Wave

Making his debut in 1981 was Toshiki Kadomatsu, a new talent who would become one of City Pop's greatest artists and producers. Kadomatsu is especially noteworthy for encapsulating many of City Pop's most common themes in his music, such as summertime fun and the thrills of adventurous urban life. This all comes complete with the inherently cool, but still chill way Kadomatsu presents himself, making him a real poster child for what City Pop is all about. Sea Breeze includes eight tracks which Kadomatsu composed and wrote the lyrics for, a very impressive feat considering many new artists outsource those elements from others. Also impressive is the band that was assembled for the production, a real A-list cast including Shuichi 'Ponta' Murakami and Tatsuo Hayashi on drums, Masaki Matsubara and Shigeru Suzuki playing guitar, and many more recognizable names. Some of the greats were brought along for the chorus as well, notably EPO and Makoto Matsushita, who was soon to release his own solo debut. The album immediately gets the groove going with Dancing Shower, an uplifting track which captures the essence of Kadomatsu's approach to music well. Its frequent English lyrics and super funky instrumentals make it a perfect party starter, just exciting enough to get down to, but just lowkey enough to keep the atmosphere cool. Meanwhile Elena in unsurprisingly a tune dedicated to a woman named Elena, but like with many of these kinds of romantic songs the Elena in question could be whoever you want it to be about. The track's chorus is well designed to get stuck in your head, and you're treated to some mighty fine guitar play towards the end. The album wouldn't be complete without a track like Summer Babe, which details a day at the beach with a girl, and all the fun that entails. The summer vibes keep going with the slower Surf Break, a more somber approach to the tale of a scorching romance. YOKOHAMA Twilight Time was released as Kadomatsu's first single, and its lyrics about two lovers on a nighttime drive through the city are classic as can be. The metropolitan magic keeps going with City Nights which perfectly captures the paradox of city loneliness, and Still, I'm In Love With You winds us down with a heartbreaking tale of lingering love. The album ends with Wave, a moving goodbye to the summer with a powerful theme of time's infinite flow. Even when it's time to say farewell those waves will still roll up to the shore, as if nothing ever changed. Sea Breeze is a beautiful start to Kadomatsu's career, and still a City Pop delight that will be enjoyed forever.

神経衰弱 (Nervous Breakdown)

Artist: Tomoko Aran
Release: July 25, 1981
Label: Warner Bros. Records

Tomoko Aran's debut album has kind of a scary sounding name, but it's probably unlikely to cause any major freak-outs. Aran would become well associated with the Synth-pop and New Wave side of City Pop music, and you can see the genesis of her personal style here. Nervous Breakdown finds itself at a unique intersection between old and new with her Kayōkyoku influenced vocals and the album's very unique instrumentals which took full advantage of what synthesizers were capable of. The instrumentals often slightly overpower Aran's own voice, creating a hypnotic effect best experienced in tracks A3 and A5, but songs such as B1 are more 'standard' while still being enjoyable listens. B3 is especially heavy on the synth sound, which may not be to everyone's taste, but those who do like the style or are willing to try something different will enjoy this one.

- A1. Secret Desire
- A2. 悲しきボードビリアン
- A3. So Get Up
- A4. 乱れたベッド
- A5. 狂った歯車
- B1. 完全犯罪
- B2. 雨のかわりに毒薬を
- B3. 神経衰弱
- B4. ノアの箱舟
- B5. Meditation

City

Artist: Eri Hayakawa
Release: August 25, 1981
Label: Continental

City is a very genre-appropriate name for this album by Eri Hayakawa which was made with some of City Pop's best. A few of the composers on board included the legend Tetsuji Hayashi, who made tracks A1 and B2, as well as Ken Sato and Daisuke Inoue. City generally leans towards a soul influenced approach reminiscent of some of her seventies predecessors, but with that bit of pop sprinkled in. Hayakawa's deeper singing voice pairs well with the album's slow jams like Sorry and track A5, and track A3 is a great mood setter with a mysterious vibe. While this was the only album made by 'Eri Hayakawa', the very same artist would go by a new name in 1983, Nina Atsuko. As Atsuko, she continued to make albums until 1987, providing us with quite a lot of listening material throughout the 1980s.

- A1. メタモル シティ
- A2. Sorry
- A3. プラスティック レディ
- A4. Play
- A5. 罪な雨〜So Sad Rain
- B1. 酔わせて！ダンディ
- B2. ドラマティック グッドナイト
- B3. You Move Me!
- B4. ラスト タイフーン
- B5. メロディ

Joepo~1981Khz

Artist: EPO
Release: September 21, 1981
Label: RCA

JOEPO~1981KHz is EPO's latest album with a fun to say name, and an even more fun concept behind it. The entire record is designed to be reminiscent of a fictional radio broadcast called JOEPO, complete with all the jingles, intermissions and over the top intros you would expect from such a show. It's also technically considered a mini-album due to the sparse number of full-length songs, with a lot of the runtime taken up by those radio flourishes. Despite this, every song available is excellent, such as the Tatsuro Yamashita composed track A4. B1 is another memorable song, with EPO serving as her own backing vocalist to make a song reminiscent of Doo-wop. JOEPO~1981KHz is a great creative showing from EPO and comes especially recommended to those who love that radio show style.

- A1. Joepo
- A2. National Album Count Down ~This Week No.1!
- A3. 身代りのバディー
- A4. 真夜中にベルが2度鳴って
- A5. See You Next Side Again
- B1. ポップ・ミュージック 2nd.
- B2. Joepo- 安易テクノポップの巻
- B3. エスケイプ
- B4. 逆さ時計が欲しい
- B5. Doo Wak Doo

First Light

Left: The original cover of First Light presents a typical street at twilight, which is both serene and nostalgic.
Center: The re-release version of First Light, its bright colors are gloriously eighties.
Right: The single release for One Hot Love and September Rain.

After working as a session musician on a few projects and being a member of the band The Milky Way (who released the absurdly underrated album Summer-Time Love Song) it was finally time for Makoto Matsushita to release a solo album. This was no mere first record however, as he may have made the greatest debut album in City Pop history with the incredibly beloved First Light. The album features a selection of everything from jazz, rock, pop, electronic and any other fusion of those descriptors you could think of to make something that feels totally unique. It's just experimental enough to be interesting but has enough mass appeal to fit in with the average Tokyo urbanite's musical sensibilities, which might just be what City Pop is all about. Matsushita put in major work for this record and composed every single song, alongside being the album's only guitarist. He also acted as its producer and arranger, giving him essentially total control over how First Light turned out, and it really shows. The opening First Light lures you in with its funky instrumentals and lyrics about one of City Pop's mainstay topics, that being travel. Matsushita describes departing from the airport to an unknown destination, and befitting any City Pop classic it includes very frequent English lyrics, but the whole album is heavy on English. One Hot Love is another killer track which describes a desire to escape from the tedium of city living and take a well-deserved trip to the beach. Songs involving the summer are especially prominent throughout City Pop, making this one fit right in with its fellow uplifting jams. The brief Resort For Blue is a soft instrumental session which perfectly sets up the melancholy sounds of September Rain. This all English tune adds some heartbreak to the album as Matsushita sings of a summer and love that have both left, leaving only the September rain to wash away his sorrows. The somber mood keeps going with Lazy Night, a tale of a man alone at night who is trying to erase lingering feelings of love with a cocktail of lime and gin, a method which usually doesn't end well. This Is All I Have For You creates a moody and sexy atmosphere as Matsushita describes a romantic Saturday evening visit, but the only thing he has to offer is himself. I Know… serves a similar function to Resort For Blue as a brief song before the mega-hit Love Was Really Gone. This all-English song has it all; beyond cool instrumentals, a story about heartbreak and phenomenal backing vocals that draw you in and don't let go until the song ends. The album finishes with the lengthy Sunset, a thematically appropriate end to our journey with First Light, one of City Pop's greatest ever and a must listen for fans of the style.

Artist:
Makoto Matsushita

Release:
September 21, 1981

Label:
Air Records

Track List:

A1. First Light
A2. One Hot Love
A3. Resort For Blue
A4. September Rain
A5. Lazy Night
B1. This Is All I Have For You
B2. I Know…
B3. Love Was Really Gone
B4. Sunset

Portrait

Left: The single release for Strawberry Temptation and Sad Night & Day has a cute and appropriately strawberry themed design.
Center: Portrait's cover shows off Takeuchi front and center, wearing a hat just like she did in her debut album.
Right: The single release for Natalie and Apple Papple Princess, a song which didn't make it to the album.

Artist:
Mariya Takeuchi

Release:
October 21, 1981

Label:
RCA

Track List:

A1. ラスト・トレイン (Last Train)
A2. Crying All Night Long
A3. ブラックボード先生 (Mr. Blackboard)
A4. 悲しきNight & Day (Sad Night & Day)
A5. 僕の街へ (To My Town)
A6. 雨に消えたさよなら (Goodbye Lost In The Rain)
B1. リンダ (Linda)
B2. イチゴの誘惑 (Strawberry Temptation)
B3. Natalie
B4. ウエイトレス (Waitress)
B5. Special Delivery ~特別航空便~ (Special Delivery~Special Air Mail~)
B6. ポートレイト ~ローレンスパークの想い出~ (Portraits~Memories of Laurence Park~)

Mariya Takeuchi was already on her fifth album by 1981, although Portrait was no ordinary release, largely owed to the change her life was about to undergo. Takeuchi and fellow City Pop superstar Tatsuro Yamashita had already been dating for a while at this point, and the two were already living together with the intention of getting married when the time was right. Portrait was therefore designed to serve as the closing for one chapter of Takeuchi's story and the start of another, as she planned to take a break and enjoy her newfound married life with Yamashita afterwards. To help accomplish this one of the most unbelievable musical rosters ever was assembled to compose Portrait's various tracks. Major names like Taeko Ohnuki, Ginji Ito, Tatsuro Yamashita, Yasuhiro Abe and Tetsuji Hayashi all lent to the album's lengthy list of twelve tracks, and Takeuchi herself composed four of them. Some other recognizable faces include EPO as a backing vocalist, Makoto Matsushita on guitar, and for a real throwback you can even spot former Sugar Babe members Kunio Muramatsu and Yutaka Uehara on a few songs. With such a dynamite roster of artists involved it was inevitable that Portrait would turn out so well, and it features twelve of Takeuchi's best songs to date. The A-side of the album is especially full of heartbreakers such as Last Train and Crying All Night Long, which start the album off with showing of Takeuchi's signature melancholy. Some of these songs' most prominent themes are those of romantic loss, betrayal, and yearning, which all give the side a consistent feeling. The B-side keeps things much lighter and includes more of those pop hits you'd expect from Takeuchi, such as Strawberry Temptation, her latest 'fruit themed' song following in the footsteps of her popular track Mysterious Peach Pie. Takeuchi composed and wrote lyrics for the songs Natalie and Linda, tracks that mirror each other with their English lyrics and female protagonists. Linda is an uplifting song with reassuring lyrics about love and the reliable support of your partner, whereas its counterpart in Natalie tells a sadder story. The song serves as a cautionary tale about the corruption of fame as Takeuchi describes a woman who found success in L.A, but has since lost her smile. Following Portrait's release Takeuchi took time to rest and focus on other things in life, namely getting married to Tatsuro Yamashita. She wouldn't create another album until 1984, the same year their daughter Minako Yamashita was born. Takeuchi considered Portrait to be a new beginning for her, and for the next three years she enjoyed her time as a new wife and mother.

哀しみの孔雀 (Peacock of Sorrow)

Artist: Anri
Release: September 21, 1981
Label: For Life Records

It had been over two years since Anri released her last album Feelin', but Peacock of Sorrow has quite a different flavor compared to it. This is owed to the involvement of Moonriders lead by Keiichi Suzuki who produced it along with composing and arranging a few tracks. Suzuki's unique approach to music permeates the album's identity, and although you can still hear many of those pop tunes Anri was known for, it's more common to hear songs that feel somewhat closer to experimental eighties New Age. This is best shown in tracks such as A1, A5 and A6, which all have an unconventionally surreal atmosphere, the kind of music that's just weird enough to be interesting but not difficult to digest. The album is loaded with twelve tracks, so there's definitely something here for everybody, but Peacock of Sorrow does feel like an oddity in Anri's discography.

- A1. 異国の出来事
- A2. エスプレッソで眠れない
- A3. Face Face Face
- A4. 白いヨット
- A5. セシルカット
- A6. リビエラからの手紙
- B1. ヘッドライト
- B2. シルエット オブ ロマンス
- B3. Am I Afraid?
- B4. いつの日か Happy End
- B5. さよならは夜明けの夢に
- B6. 哀しみの孔雀

Harmotopia

Artist: Soap
Release: 1981
Label: Epic

The sole album by short lived band Soap, a group which consisted of Hideki Matsubara, Hisae Hasegawa, Takanori Arisawa (who composed the Sailor Moon soundtrack) and his wife Keiko Arisawa. Harmotopia is most similar to some albums from groups like Circus or Hi-Fi Set which all have multiple vocalists working together to provide a rich listening experience. It also features a very well-rounded set of tracks, all of which incorporate various styles. You'll be jumping from the bombastic A1 to A3, which feels like a slightly older styled pop track, and then a moving ballad in A5. The B-side holds its own as well with the distinct Latin sounds of B2, the subtly cool B3 and B4 with its rapid-fire singing. You'll be wishing this group made more as the album closes out with "Welcome to the Harmotopia."

- A1. 新宿トランスファー
- A2. ルームメイト
- A3. Bye Bye プロフェッサー
- A4. ポパイの朝・アリスの空
- A5. 水平線の見える場所で
- B1. Kiss Again
- B2. バルコニー・パーティー
- B3. 星空の時代
- B4. さよならホームタウン
- B5. ハーモトピア

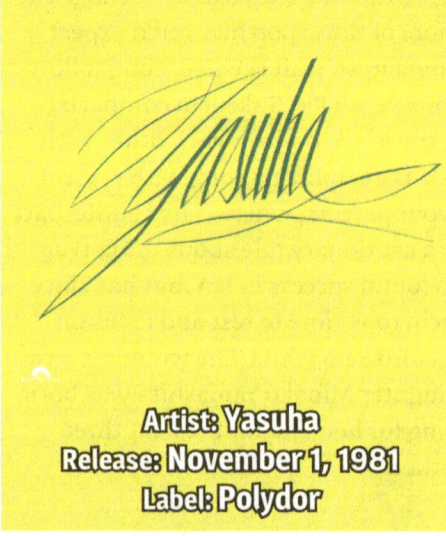

Transit

Artist: Yasuha
Release: November 1, 1981
Label: Polydor

Transit is the very yellow first album by Yasuha, an artist who is mostly known for one extraordinarily popular track. Similarly to Miki Matsubara, Yasuha's debut song would end up becoming her most popular, and especially beloved many years after its creation. The track Fly-day Chinatown was composed by Yasuha herself and found enormous popularity during City Pop's revival period in the 2010s, becoming a staple of the genre with millions of fans. Its groovy instrumentals and catchy English chorus made it a great sample for what the genre is all about, but the album has a lot of lesser-known songs to enjoy. The instrumentals are especially strong for tracks A1 and B3 as well as Love Magic which all incorporate genres such as disco and pop rock to create a diverse product. An incredible first album for Yasuha, Transit has a legendary City Pop song and many more to enjoy.

- A1. 恋 1/2
- A2. モーニング・デート
- A3. ありきたりな筋書き
- A4. Bye-Bye Lover
- A5. 空中ブランコ
- B1. Love Magic
- B2. Fly-Day Chinatown
- B3. ミッドナイト・トレイン
- B4. アリスのレストラン
- B5. Remember Summertime

See You Last Night

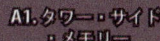

See You Last Night is the latest from songwriting super genius Yumi Matsutoya, and it also happens to include one of her biggest songs ever. Track A5 or I Want To Protect You was a major hit thanks to its elegant but still simple presentation and an alluring chorus comprised of several vocalists. This chorus can be heard throughout the whole song, which gives it a dynamic feeling, and its occasional English lyrics fits right in with other pop tracks from the era. While A5 was the album's big winner, there's lots of other tracks to love as well. B1 combines her beautiful lyrics with energetic instrumentals to make a memorable song. A4 is another classic jam from her, getting great usage out of her romantic lyrical sensibilities to make a song that's smooth and moving, while still maintaining a fun identity.

Artist: Yumi Matsutoya
Release: November 1, 1981
Label: Express

- A1. タワー・サイド・メモリー
- A2. 街角のペシミスト
- A3. ビュッフェにて
- A4. 夕闇をひとり
- A5. 守ってあげたい
- B1. カンナ8号線
- B2. 手のひらの東京タワー
- B3. グレイス・スリックの肖像
- B4. グループ
- B5. A Happy New Year

Acoustic Moon

Seemingly ever intent on changing up her style, Rajie's Acoustic Moon once again moves the needle for her. This time she took heavy inspiration from Latin sounds such as Bossa Nova, as well as the usual City Pop suspects like soul and jazz. She of course came equipped with composers such as Masamichi Sugi and Yoshitaka Minami, as well as the heavy hitters Tatsuo Hayashi and Shigeru Suzuki in the band. Acoustic Moon is an especially great release from Rajie, with tracks such as Rosy Blue showing off her approach to Latin inspired pop. Track A4 is mighty cool and funky, and Tsuyoshi Kon has a great guitar segment midway through. Do You Wanna Dance brings to mind her earlier work, and B2 has some of the finest instrumental work of the whole album. Acoustic Moon is well worth the listen, as it's a real highlight from Rajie's catalogue.

Artist: Rajie
Release: November 21, 1981
Label: CBS/Sony

- A1. Rosy Blue
- A2. 紫苑（シオン）
- A3. アコースティック・ムーン
- A4. ストーミー・ナイト
- A5. ブラック・ムーン
- A6. 薔薇のグラス
- B1. Do You Wanna Dance
- B2. パラダイス・ワイン
- B3. メモリー・スルー（追想）
- B4. パズル・ヌーン
- B5. リラの日曜日

Monsters In Town

Monsters in Town was the logical next step in Yoshida's evolution as an artist and producer, and while it has a lot in common with Monochrome it's far from being a rehash. The album was designed to contrast its sibling Monochrome by having an emphasis on elaborate arrangements and backing tracks. The idea was to make the album have a true unison between Yoshida's vocals and the instrumentals, a philosophy which paid off quite well. The opening song Town is a perfect showcase for what gives City Pop its unique identity, as Yoshida poetically describes the concrete monoliths and floods of people you'd encounter in an urban area. Monsters in Town is another great success for Yoshida, who seemed to be excelling with producing her own albums, and it's very tough to pick a favorite between this record and Monochrome.

Artist: Minako Yoshida
Release: November 21, 1981
Label: Alfa

- A1. Town
- A2. Lovin' You
- A3. Nights In Her Eyes
- A4. Black Eye Lady
- B1. Monster Stomp
- B2. Knock, Knock
- B3. Moment Of Twilight
- B4. Back In Town

Coconuts High

Are you ready to get funky? Izumi Kobayashi's Coconuts High sees Japanese and American musical sensibilities collide for an album that's totally stuffed with style. Genres like Latin, disco, soul, jazz and more of City Pop's biggest inspirations fuse together magically here, and you never quite know what Kobayashi is going to hit you with next. The opening Palm St. gives all of these talented musicians some time to flex, many of whom are from the USA. The groove really gets going in the synth-heavy Penaten and Small Dynamite, but you'll soon end up totally entranced by the hypnotic Crazy Love. Another instrumental delight awaits in The 4th Dimension Butterfly, and those who liked the trippy sound of Crazy Love will also enjoy the final two tracks Lazy Love and Mr. Cool. Coconuts High is a killer release from Kobayashi with a lot to offer fans of the genre fusion City Pop is known for.

Artist: Izumi Kobayashi
Release: December 1, 1981
Label: Kitty Records

A1. Palm St.
A2. Small Dynamite
A3. Penaten
A4. Crazy Love
B1. The 4th Dimension Butterfly
B2. Coconuts High
B3. Lazy Love
B4. Mr. Cool

Air Kiss

Amii Ozaki's second album for the year shared a lot of DNA with its sibling album Hot Baby, most notably the continued involvement of David Foster. Foster returned as the arranger alongside playing keyboards, and aside from him the album was made with a very tiny core band of Mike Baird on drums and Michael Landau playing guitar and bass. This crew was small but mighty, and delivered some amazing songs alongside Ozaki, such as the moving track A2 and Foggy Night, where her voice sounds especially cool. Air Kiss also delivered track B1, Junjou, which would become one of her most popular songs. Its opening is instantly recognizable, and the song's addictive rhythm will have you tapping along to it every time. Air Kiss finished 1981 for Ozaki on a high note with big hits and some less appreciated songs to be enjoyed.

Artist: Amii Ozaki
Release: December 5, 1981
Label: F-Label

A1. Deep
A2. グラスのルージュ
A3. Foggy Night
A4. 銀幕の恋人
B1. 純情
B2. Flash Back
B3. ハートの色は海の色
B4. Just Once Again

Natural Woman

Yumi Seino released a second album in 1981 with Natural Woman, which followed many of the same principles as U・TA・GE. Once again, a large number of composers were on board such as the returning Akira Inoue, as well as Yoichi Takizawa who wrote for Hi-Fi Set and Bread & Butter. You can also catch a song by Tatsuhiko Yamamoto with track B2, a slow and moving number which Seino performs well. The standout song is the introductory You & I which manages to blend jazz, electronic flourishes and effective backing vocals to make a memorable jam. Akira Inoue's Midnight Blue is a real hidden gem of a song, and its ultra funky instrumentals would pair well with a really late night out, when the unscrupulous side of town comes out to play. Natural Woman has a lot of slick songs just waiting to be discovered and enjoyed.

Artist: Yumi Seino
Release: December 25, 1981
Label: Blow Up

A1. You & I
A2. Caledonia Love Day
A3. Airport 4:30 P.M
A4. サマーホテル
A5. 海辺の December
B1. スカイレストラン
B2. ディナーが終わるまで
B3. ムーンライト マジック
B4. Tokyo City Nights
B5. Midnight Blue

1982, Weekend Beach Trip

Are you ready for the summer? City Pop continues to enjoy its time in the sun here in 1982, a year which is certainly in contention for being the style's greatest of all time with many exciting developments. Tatsuro Yamashita returning from a nationwide tour to create For You, one of his most beloved records of all time. The long dormant Niagara Triangle was revived by Eiichi Ohtaki for a final venture with two new members, while Anri teamed up with Toshiki Kadomatsu to create Heaven Beach. This album characterized her style for most of the eighties and pushed her towards becoming one of City Pop's leading female artists. The year was also stacked with debuts including Meiko Nakahara, Kazuhito Murata, Junichi Inagaki and many more, showing more evidence of how hot the style really was now. Not everyone managed to become an overnight sensation unfortunately, as evidenced by Takako Mamiya who released her only album Love Trip to very poor sales and then seemingly left the industry forever, but decades later it'd become a highly cherished record. Possibly the single strangest event in City Pop history happened this year, namely an amateur Italian singer who didn't speak Japanese somehow releasing an album. If that wasn't odd enough for you her name is Alessandra Mussolini, and she's actually Benito Mussolini's granddaughter. On the technological side of things, the CD was made available, making these early eighties artists some of the very first to release music on the revolutionary format. 1982 is a year of smash hits, deep cuts, reinventions and hot getaways, not to mention it's home to many of the best City Pop albums.

Meiko Nakahara

Top: A picture of Meiko Nakahara, who always managed to look cool in any outfit.
Bottom: Another photo of Nakahara, who has hopefully enjoyed a peaceful life these past decades.

Mysterious entities are quite common in the music world, as many artists prefer to stay anonymous or let their music speak for itself. This is also quite true for City Pop, but Meiko Nakahara might be the artist people are most curious about, as she hasn't made a public appearance in thirty years. Nakahara made her debut in 1982 when City Pop was continuously soaring in popularity, and she made a strong impression with the albums Coconuts House and Cinderella Until 2:00 Friday Magic. She was even promoted by her record label as being "The Second Yumi (Matsutoya)", a moniker and comparison Nakahara was understandably opposed to, as she thought her work was distinct from Matsutoya's. From 1982 onwards Nakahara lead a very successful career, releasing albums annually while City Pop was in its prime. Nakahara continued as one of the style's premier artists until 1991, at which point she abruptly vanished. There's not much conclusive information about where she went, and the extent of her activities in the industry after 1991 are spotty at best. It is believed Nakahara wrote for the group Checkicco and singer Vivian Hsu in the 90s, but little else has been attributed to her. The band Lotos are known for covering many of Nakahara's songs, and their lead singer Megu has provided tidbits of information, albeit coming from some unconfirmed sources. In the past she has shared accounts of Nakahara's relatives confirming that she is alive, and others saying she now lives in her hometown of Chiba in Japan. There is no real proof backing these claims, so their validity is questionable and should be taken with a grain of salt. It is likely that Nakahara simply chose to settle down after a hectic life in show business and has been enjoying her time away from the spotlight. While her presence has certainly been missed by many, it's also fair to say that she deserves her privacy after blessing us with a decade of hard work and great music.

For You

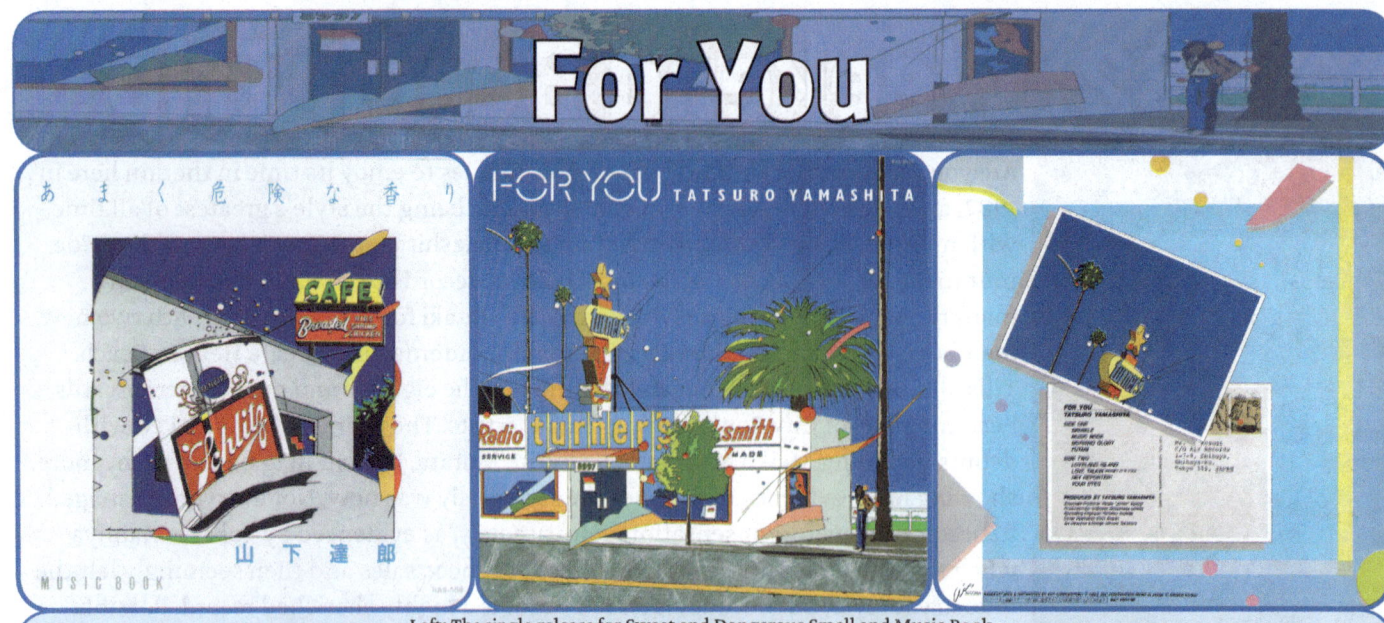

Left: The single release for Sweet and Dangerous Smell and Music Book.
Center: The cover of For You goes for an Americana look which harkens back to the aesthetic and music Tatsuro Yamashita grew up with.
Right: The back of For You keeps up that playful and colorful vibe.

The release of 1980's album Ride on Time was a career defining moment for Tatsuro Yamashita, as it secured his first number one album and held on to that spot for an impressive 19 weeks. Despite this newfound commercial momentum Yamashita didn't release a new album back in 1981, as he was preoccupied with a national tour across Japan. Although he had very little time to work on his next album, the nonstop live shows offered great practice for Yamashita and his band, an experience which certainly paid off when recording time on For You finally came along. Thanks to Ride on Time's success Yamashita was able to pour his heart into the album's tracks without any timing or budgetary restrictions. He was able to craft an absurd 27 songs, the vast majority of which didn't even make it to the final product. The album was also blessed by a lack of issues during the recording process, which Yamashita described as being "unusually trouble free," and everything from the band to the equipment to the audio engineers just seemed to work out. This perfect storm of factors lead to For You being one of Yamashita's most consistent and highest quality releases to date, and it also happened to benefit nicely from technological advancements of the time. The advent of the Walkman allowed listeners to take their For You cassette tapes wherever they wanted, which helped to bolster City Pop's reputation as feelgood music that appealed to an active young audience. For You was naturally another killer album from Yamashita which felt like the true perfection of his unique style which incorporated so many different genres. Minako Yoshida returned as a lyricist for many songs such as the groovy Sparkle, a track which Yamashita considers a masterpiece. The song magnificently combines his compositional skills with Yoshida's knack for powerful lyrics to create an entrancing opening. Yamashita reclaimed his composition Morning Glory from Mariya Takeuchi's last album for his own purposes, as he didn't really like the way the arrangement on her version turned out. Another Takeuchi adjacent song is Hey Reporter, a track with a noticeably harder sound compared to Yamashita's other music which was inspired by his experiences being hounded by the paparazzi while dating her. Speaking of Takeuchi, this was also the year when the pair got married, thereby establishing City Pop's greatest power couple who would work together on many albums yet to come. Between his wedding and For You holding the number 1 spot for a staggering 38 weeks it seemed to be a rather good year for Yamashita. For You is another all-time great from the king of City Pop, and it's often considered his best album ever.

Artist:
Tatsuro Yamashita

Release:
January 21, 1982

Label:
Air Records

Track List:

A1. Sparkle

A2. Music Book

A3. Interlude A Part I

A4. Morning Glory

A5. Interlude A Part II

A6. Futari

B1. Loveland, Island

B2. Interlude B Part I

B3. Love Talkin' (Honey It's You)

B4. Sunset

B5. Interlude B Part II

B6. Your Eyes

I Love You So

I love you too, Tatsuhiko! I Love You So is the first of Tatsuhiko Yamamoto's two albums for 1982, and it was made in conjunction with the band Nobody who acted as producers. Their own style, which leans heavily towards rock, is very apparent throughout the album and gives I Love You a rock and roll spin which is quite fresh for Yamamoto. Midnight Harbor starts things off right with a perfect mixture of pop, rock, and funk, while Last Show has a unique identity as a kind of doo-wop song, kind of all out rock session. Many songs throughout have impressive instrumental segments such as Sunset Blue and Mrs. Show, and 24-2689 is an interesting one where Yamamoto's voice is distorted throughout. I Love You So is one of his best albums yet, especially for those who like their City Pop with a fair amount of rock injected in.

Artist: Tatsuhiko Yamamoto
Release: February 21, 1982
Label: Eastworld

- A1. Midnight Harbor
- A2. Last Show
- A3. Magic
- A4. Mrs. Show
- A5. Sunset Blue
- B1. I Love You So
- B2. 24-2689
- B3. Marianne
- B4. Man+Woman=100%
- B5. 摩天楼ブルース
- B6. Good Night Sweetheart

Prophetic Dream

Akira Inoue's Prophetic Dream is another incredibly welcome addition to City Pop's library of synth-pop focused music. Inoue himself is a very underappreciated figure in City Pop's history who was involved with albums like Takako Mamiya's Love Trip and Toshiki Kadomatsu's Sea Breeze, and his own work doesn't disappoint. Prophetic Dream is a refined fusion album which integrates many of City Pop's most trusted companion genres, naturally including electronic and jazz, but there's also some adult-oriented rock thrown in. A1 makes a strong first impression with its very memorable chorus while A3 has a serene and unbelievably cool feeling to it. It's easy to melt away to Lost Passengers and Cosmonaut while Gravitations has some moving singing from Inoue, but every track here has a certain flavor that's sure to appeal to somebody's taste.

Artist: Akira Inoue
Release: March 1, 1982
Label: Express

- A1. バルトークの影
- A2. Subway-Hero
- A3. レティシア
- A4. Double Crossing
- A5. Lost Passengers
- B1. リンドバーグ物語
- B2. ヒンデンブルグ号へようこそ
- B3. Cosmonaut
- B4. Gravitations
- B5. ユヴェスキューレ

Myself

Miki Matsubara released two albums throughout 1982, starting off with Myself. The album has a distinctly American flavor thanks to the involvement of the band Dr. Strut, whose members served as the backing band and arrangers for the album. They served a similar role in her last album Cupid, so fans of that album are likely to enjoy this one too. The album starts with A1 or Ballerina, an energetic start with a fun and frantic middle. A5 is another high point for the album due to its oh so cool sounding instrumentals and memorable English chorus. It ended up being See-Saw Love which took the prize as Myself's big hit, lending credence to the idea that including semi-random English phrases in a City Pop song makes it better. Myself has some wonderful songs to enjoy, including a few of Matsubara's lesser known ones.

Artist: Miki Matsubara
Release: March 1982
Label: SeeSaw

- A1. バレリーナ
- A2. 二人で踊らない
- A3. 微熱が平熱
- A4. Somewhere
- A5. カランドリエ
- B1. 流星スウィング
- B2. See-Saw Love
- B3. 5つ数える間に
- B4. ハレーション
- B5. Myself
- B6. Three Candles

Niagara Triangle Vol. 2

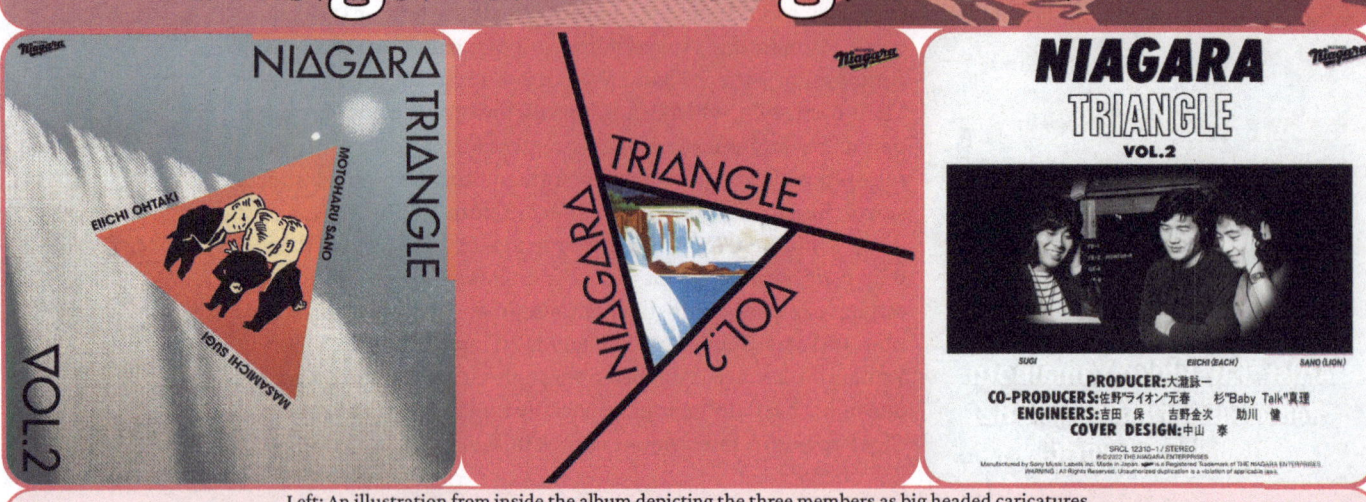

Left: An illustration from inside the album depicting the three members as big headed caricatures.
Center: The cover of Niagara Triangle Vol 2 is pretty simple, but that City Pop appropriate pink really pops!
Right: The new Niagara Triangle with its members Masamichi Sugi, Eiichi Ohtaki and Motoharu Sano.

Half a decade ago the trio of Eiichi Ohtaki, Tatsuro Yamashita and Ginji Ito came together as the band Niagara Triangle and released one album, but the name had been dormant since then. Years later in 1981 Ohtaki attended JAPACON, an event designed to showcase rising musical talent, including the likes of Masamichi Sugi, Kingo Hamada and Motoharu Sano. After Sugi's performance he invited Ohtaki on stage, who had a surprise announcement to make. He was considering reviving Niagara Triangle but was looking for some fresh blood to join him, so he abruptly asked Sugi and Sano to join as a members. In a rather serendipitous moment Sugi and Sano both happily agreed, thus the new Niagara Triangle was born. Ohtaki's years of experience proved to be a great influence on the two less experienced artists, as Sano would later reflect that Ohtaki was both very knowledgeable and wise, but also quite willing to share lessons learned throughout his career. Akin to its predecessor Volume 2 was made with the same shared responsibility between the three members, and each provided a roughly equal number of songs. Although Tatsuro Yamashita didn't return for this record, you can catch Niagara Triangle alumnus Ginji Ito playing guitar and working as a supervisor for Sano's tracks, a very appreciated appearance from one of the group's founders. Despite the new lineup the album feels fairly similar to Volume 1 and is a fantastic showcase of the three members talents for creating some of the best pop rock in the business. The opening Fall In Love On The A-side was the first of Ohtaki's songs and was first released as a single to test how much demand existed for this team up, and since it sold well the rest of the album was greenlit. Sano's track She is Delicate originally had more of a rock vibe, since Sano was fond of that style, but Ohtaki suggested lightening it with some percussion and acoustic guitar, thus making it fit in better with the pop rock flavor that permeates the album. Girlfriend is a slow acoustic track that Sugi derived from Awakening (Waking Up Alone) which he wrote for Mariya Takeuchi, this time with some fresh lyrics. Ohtaki thought of Dreaming Shore as being the "most Sugi-like song" he had presented, a sentiment which took a while for Sugi to understand, but he ultimately agreed with what his fellow artist meant. Weekend Lovers is dedicated to people in their 20s still seeking a meaning in life and who were uncertain about their futures, a feeling the still young Sano and Sugi likely found relatable. Volume 2 would be the final release from Niagara Triangle, thus closing the books on this unique trifecta of artists which took on two totally different forms during its lifespan.

Artist:
Niagara Triangle

Release:
March 21, 1982

Label:
Niagara Records

Track List:

A1. A面で恋をして (Fall In Love On The A-side)
A2. 彼女はデリケート (She's Delicate)
A3. Bye Bye C-Boy
A4. マンハッタン ブリッヂにたたずんで (Standing on Manhattan Bridges)
A5. Nobody
A6. 夢みる渚 (Girlfriend)
A7. ガールフレンド (Dreamy Shore)
B1. Love Her
B2. 週末の恋人たち (Weekend Lovers)
B3. オリーブの午后 (Olive Afternoon)
B4. 白い港 (White Harbor)
B5. Water Color
B6. ♡じかけのオレンジ (♡ Fresh Orange)

Weekend Fly To The Sun

Left: The single release for Friday To Sunday and I'll Call You. Look at that water!
Center: The cover of Weekend Fly To The Sun. While one boat washes ashore, another more distant ship is free to sail.
Right: Kadomatsu in a picture from the album, who looks particularly playful here.

Artist:
Toshiki Kadomatsu

Release:
April 5, 1982

Label:
RCA

Track List:

A1. Office Lady

A2. Rush Hour

A3. Brunch

A4. Space Scraper

B1. Friday To Sunday

B2. Crescent Aventure

B3. I'll Never Let You Go

B4. 4 A.M.

After the success of his debut album Sea Breeze Toshiki Kadomatsu came back next year with Weekend Fly To The Sun, although in order to record it he took a flight over to another continent. The album was recorded in various studios across California, with its roster of musicians being comprised of mostly Americans. Some big names were involved with this project, such as Al McKay who was previously a member of Earth, Wind & Fire, as well as Nathan East who has played alongside Michael Jackson and Phil Collins. Another prominent figure was Tom Tom 84 who arranged the entire album, and he can be spotted working on the arrangement for hundreds of soul albums. Despite the change of scenery that accompanied the album's creation, Weekend Fly To The Sun still maintains a similar style to Sea Breeze and was meticulously crafted with Kadomatsu's target audience of young urbanites in mind. The first five tracks of the album were designed to evoke imagery of a particular time of day, which each subsequent track moving up a bit through the clock. The opening song Office Lady is meant to reflect the early morning, and the song even begins with the sound of an alarm clock ringing. The bass at the beginning has an energetic coolness and its upbeat instrumentals do a fantastic job carrying the feeling that a day full of possibilities has just started, and it would've been a great listen on your brand-new Walkman for that daily business commute. Rush Hour was then made to evoke that ever so hectic time of day late in the morning, once it's really time to get to business. It's a delightfully energetic song that will have you tapping your feet for its entire duration, and the addition of female backing vocalists gives it that classic disco feel. The middle of the day is brunch time's territory, now that things have calmed down somewhat it's time for a relaxing tune to take the stress off. Once the late afternoon rolls around and you're free from the shackles of work Space Scraper comes along. As expected from the creative melting pot that is City Pop you can hear rock and disco blending together perfectly here. Finally, there's Friday To Sunday, a classic Kadomatsu song which is designed with the weekend in mind, providing you with that much needed musical vacation. The rest of the B-side is then comprised of slower ballads which highlight Kadomatsu's delicate singing. Before you know it night has returned again with 4 A.M as a new day dawns, ending things in a cyclical way similarly to how his last album Sea Breeze was designed. Weekend Fly To The Sun is another excellent work from Kadomatsu which feels tailor-made for City Pop's primary audience, the hustling young city-dwellers of 1980s Japan.

The Pressures And The Pleasures

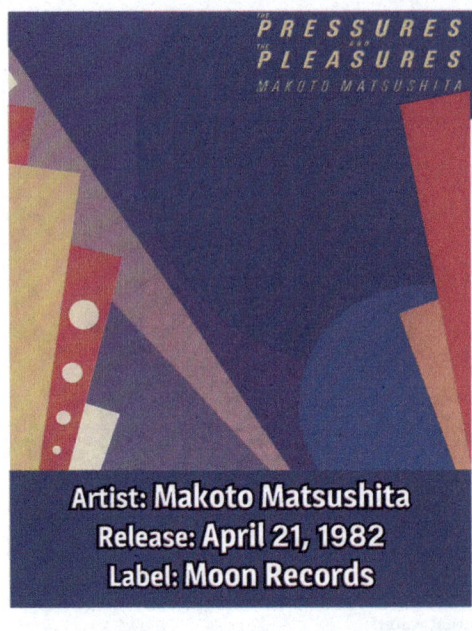

Artist: Makoto Matsushita
Release: April 21, 1982
Label: Moon Records

Makoto Matsushita unleashed The Pressures And The Pleasures in 1982, an album with an ambitious concept behind it. While the album has a total of eight tracks they were more so designed to be thought of as four long songs, just cut up into more digestible pieces. The various songs are all designed to tell a sort of story about an average businessman in Japan, although the story told is anything but ordinary. Despite his life's repetitive nature, he yearns for love and happiness, and he continues to do his best at work to carry out this dream. During his tale we experience dreamlike interruptions as his mind wanders, the joyful release after a long day's work, and many other elements which are up to the listener's interpretation. This makes the album quite fun to discuss with others, and it's another excellent addition to Matsushita's catalogue.

- A1. The Pressures And The Pleasures
- A2. Business Man (Part 1)
- A3. The Bridge
- A4. Business Man (Part 2)
- B1. The Garden Of Walls
- B2. Carnaval
- B3. The Quiet Storm
- B4. Morning Blue

Love Message

Artist: Akiko Mizuhara
Release: May 21, 1982
Label: Electric Bird

Love Message is technically the debut album for Akiko Mizuhara, but this is actually a pseudonym for the Korean artist Ji Sook. Sook had been releasing music in Korea since the early 1970s as a child, but this was her first production made as an adult. To make this an even more international experience most of the songs are covers of songs by Western artists. These include tracks from Carole King and Stevie Wonder, as well as many Brazilian composers like Antonio Carlos Jobim. The final product is a really stunning album which takes fuses genres and styles from all over. There's a heavy focus on soul, Latin, and funk, but you can hear traces of all kinds of music. Summertime and You Are The Sunshine of My Life's sleek instrumentals are fabulous, and What's Going On's funky factor is off the charts. Love Message is a stylistic collision deserving of your time.

- A1. It's Too Late
- A2. Love Duet
- A3. Summertime
- A4. It's Never Too Late
- B1. Boassanova Medley
- B2. You Are The Sunshine Of My Life
- B3. What's Going On
- B4. All In Love Is Fair

Overlap

Artist: Masamichi Sugi
Release: May 21, 1982
Label: CBS/Sony

Masamichi Sugi's second solo album released right after Niagara Triangle Vol. 2 and includes twelve tracks, all of which feature lyrics and compositions from Sugi himself. He was a busy guy in 1982! Overlap follows in the footsteps of his prior work as it primarily has a pop rock sound, with the occasional smooth ballad thrown in for good measure. Lonely Girl is classic Sugi to start the album off right, while Catch Your Way ended up as the album's most popular likely owed to its fun chorus. Goodbye City Lights feels very appropriate to the urban-centric genre, that is City Pop, and the instrumentals found in Selena give it a classic feel. With a name like Teardrops Are Falling you'd assume it's kind of depressing, but it actually has a nice uplifting flow to it, which could be said about Overlap as a whole.

- A1. Lonely Girl
- A2. Last Night
- A3. Little Girl
- A4. Don't Cry Francis
- A5. Simulation Game
- A6. Catch Your Way
- B1. Goodbye City Light
- B2. Selena
- B3. Young One
- B4. Downsloped Way
- B5. Teardrops Are Falling
- B6. Glass-Made Lovers

Someday

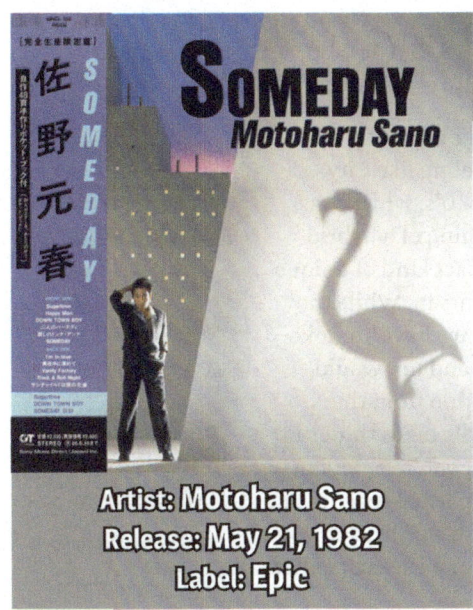

Artist: Motoharu Sano
Release: May 21, 1982
Label: Epic

Motoharu Sano's first album after his stint in Niagara Triangle alongside Eiichi Ohtaki and Masamichi Sugi delivers more of the pop rock he was becoming recognized for. Surprisingly, Sano considered this album to be a dire make-or-break situation, as he may have given up on his music career if the album did badly. Luckily for us Someday did prove to be successful and is now looked back on as a highlight for the intersection between City Pop and pop rock. Of particular note is the titular track Someday, one of Sano's most popular songs which was frequently used in commercials across the decades. Surprisingly, the track didn't even make the top one hundred when released as a single in 1981, but it garnered more attention with the accompanying album. Those who enjoyed Niagara Triangle Vol. 2 should absolutely consider giving Someday a listen.

- A1. Sugartime
- A2. Happy Man
- A3. Down Town Boy
- A4. 二人のバースディ
- A5. 麗しのドンナ・アンナ
- A6. Someday
- B1. I'm In Blue
- B2. 真夜中に清めて
- B3. Vanity Factory
- B4. Rock & Roll Night
- B5. サンチャイルドは僕の友達

Rumor

Artist: EPO
Release: May 21, 1982
Label: RCA

EPO's third full length album came with more of those delightful City Pop jams she was becoming well known for, with almost the entire album being composed by her. One exception was the song Girl in Me, which was composed by Ray Parker Jr., who you may know from creating the Ghostbusters theme song, and it's as fun as you'd expect. Some other hits include B1 which has Taeko Ohnuki as a backing vocalist, and there's never a dull moment when On Sundays is playing. Joepo~Down Town then fuses the radio show aesthetic of her previous mini album JOEPO~1981KHz with an enjoyable new cover of Down Town to give us an incredibly cool finale. Rumor was also made after EPO made the final decision to drop out of university to pursue music as a career, a choice which seems to have paid off in the end.

- A1. Girl in Me
- A2. 真夏の青写真
- A3. ある日の貴方へ
- A4. Secret Agent
- A5. 雨のめぐり逢い
- B1. うわさになりたい
- B2. 夜の寝息
- B3. On Sundays
- B4. ワンダー・ランド
- B5. 安眠妨害
- B6. Joepo-Down Town

Pearl Piece

Artist: Yumi Matsutoya
Release: June 21, 1982
Label: Express

Pearl Piece is Yumi Matsutoya's 13th album (does she ever take breaks?) and was specifically designed to appeal to the rapidly growing demographic of urban office workers. This is best shown off with track A3 which centers around a busy office employee on her lunch break, watching the hustle and bustle of the city pass by before she's drawn back into work. Track A1 is your classic Matsutoya heartbreaker, and it actually takes inspiration from a story which was told in a real fan letter that she got. Dang Dang has an extremely catchy chorus with Matsutoya repeating the songs title, but as you may expect from Matsutoya by now the lyrics are anything but cheerful. B3 is another tearjerker as she fantasizes about reliving precious memories with a past boyfriend and how she'd do things differently this time around.

- A1. ようこそ輝く時間へ
- A2. 真珠のピアス
- A3. ランチタイムが終わる頃
- A4. フォーカス
- A5. 夕涼み
- B1. 私のロンサム・タウン
- B2. Dang Dang
- B3. 昔の彼に会うのなら
- B4. 消息
- B5. 忘れないでね

Artist: Naomi Akimoto
Release: June 21, 1982
Label: Invitation

One Night Stand

One Night Stand is the second of Naomi Akimoto's three albums for 1982, and it's much closer to feeling like City Pop compared to her debut record Rolling 80's, which was primarily centered around jazz. It's something of a hybrid between synth-pop and classic jazz, the exact kind of unique genre experimentation that City Pop delights in. While the songs were largely written by Westerners, we have Tomoko Aran on as a lyricist, and later on Akimoto and her would together for 1984's Poison 21. You'll transition from the theatrical sounds of A1 to A2 which suddenly takes things in an unexpectedly funky direction, and by B1 you're enjoying some surprise pop rock. This ability to keep listeners guessing will prove to be one of Akimoto's greatest strengths, and you never know exactly what you're going to get with each of her albums.

- A1. On A Slow Boat To China
- A2. Sing Sing Sing
- A3. It's A Sin To Tell A Lie
- A4. It's Always You
- A5. Come Rain Or Come Shine
- B1. Alexander's Ragtime Band
- B2. Speak Low
- B3. Lullabye In Ragtime ~Good Night Sleep Tight~ The Five Pennies
- B4. The Boy Next Door
- B5. Tennessee Waltz

Artist: Hiroshi Sato
Release: June 21, 1982
Label: Alfa

Awakening

Hiroshi Sato moved to the US in 1979 after growing discontent with the music industry in Japan and the quality of his own creations. While there he ran across the LINN LM-1 drum machine, a device which allowed him to make the exact type of sound he was seeking. This reignited his creative spark, and along with the vocal talent of Wendy Matthews the fantastic album Awakening was born. Like some of his previous records, Awakening manages to combine many genres which probably shouldn't work together but absolutely do. The unique electronic sounds Sato created blend beautifully with Matthews' signing, sending you through a journey with tracks that can range from surreal to solemn. An absolute must listen for fans of the electronic side of City Pop; Awakening truly feels like Sato reborn.

- A1. Awakening (覚醒)
- A2. You're My Baby
- A3. Blue And Moody Music
- A4. Only A Love Affair
- A5. Love And Peace
- B1. From Me To You
- B2. I Can't Wait
- B3. It Isn't Easy
- B4. Awakening
- B5. Say Goodbye

Artist: Narumin & Etsu
Release: June 25, 1982
Label: Philips

Thru Traffic

Thru Traffic is the sole album by Narumin & Etsu, a duo consisting of Hiroshi Narumi and Etsuko Yamakawa. Both of these artists can be heard as vocalists for Love Trip by Takako Mamiya, among many other appearances throughout City Pop. The album is a real hidden gem loaded up with all those elements that fans of the style are bound to love, owed in large part to its wide array of songs which incorporate many genres. Whether that's your usual summertime jam in Summer Touches You, the sensual ballad A3 or the splendidly smooth September Valentine, Thru Traffic has you covered. The duo's vocals work excellently together, and this paired with some consistently excellent instrumentals make every song a delight, especially if you're a fan of those slower tracks. Thru Traffic begs to be enjoyed as one of 1982's sleeper hits.

- A1. Summer Touches You
- A2. Up And Down
- A3. 心のままに
- A4. ストレンジ・ワイン
- A5. September Vallentine
- B1. 月に寄りそって
- B2. Cloudy
- B3. Spell
- B4. ラスト・メッセージ

Coconuts House

Coconuts House is the debut album from Meiko Nakahara, an artist who emerged right when City Pop was really heating up and departed as the party was winding down in the early 1990s. The album has a standout flavor compared to others from the same year, taking a lot of inspiration from differing styles such as Latin, which up to this point was still a style City Pop artists rarely explored. This Latin influence is most prominent in songs such as the party starters A1 and A5, and you can also catch other classic City Pop influences like soul and funk throughout the entire record. The slow stylings of A4 give Nakahara a perfect avenue to show off her singing skills, and the instrumentals in B2 and B4 really hit. Coconuts House is a highly diverse debut for Nakahara with tracks that all work so well together.

Artist: Meiko Nakahara
Release: July 1, 1982
Label: Eastworld

A1. 今夜だけ Dance Dance Dance
A2. Sunset Freeway
A3. バカンス
A4. 涙のスロー・ダンス
A5. 恋はサンバにのせて・・・
B1. タイムリミット
B2. Gemini
B3. ほんのちょっぴりOld Man
B4. City Night
B5. Come Back To Me

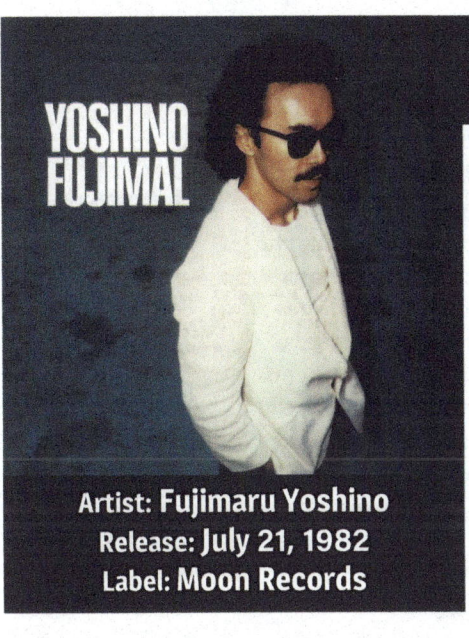

Yoshino Fujimal

The debut album by Fujimaru Yoshino, an artist who had previously helmed his eponymous Fujimaru Band but was now finally ready for a solo outing. Yoshino Fujimal is an excellent pop rock trip equipped with a star-studded lineup of backing vocalists. EPO, Haruko Kuwana and Makoto Matsushita all show up, and its a real delight to hear their voices. The album is also divided into a 'Day Time' and 'Night Time' side, with both sides suiting their theming well. Tracks such as the mighty groovy Who Are You? get the party with some stunning instrumentals, and Midnight Plus 1 will have you dancing in your seat. The night side favors smoother songs like Girl's In Love With Me, and the awfully cool Not What I'm Looking For. Yoshino Fujimal is an extremely well-rounded debut with some memorable tunes to enjoy.

Artist: Fujimaru Yoshino
Release: July 21, 1982
Label: Moon Records

A1. Who Are You?
A2. Midnight Plus 1
A3. One Shot Lady
A4. Free Way 5 To South
B1. Girl's In Love With Me
B2. Shang-Hide Night
B3. Not What I'm Looking For
B4. Pretender

246:3AM

The debut album from Junichi Inagaki, an artist who got his start in the City Pop boom and who continued to release music long past its prime years. The unique name 246:3AM is derived from Japan's highway called Route 246, and the time of 3 AM, which sounds like a fun combination to me. Like some other albums from the era, it blends soft rock with pop to create a sound that's got just enough of an edge, while still being chill enough to just vibe to. Inagaki's singing is great throughout, although he especially shines when accompanied by a backing vocalist or two. You can hear this best in Regret, the album's most popular song. The chorus has a fantastic flow to it, and the multiple singers gives it a feeling of emotional impact, but you'll still be bobbing your head along the whole time.

Artist: Junichi Inagaki
Release: July 21, 1982
Label: Express

A1. ジンで朝まで
A2. Bahama Airport
A3. 海鳴りに誘われて
A4. 蒼い追憶
A5. 月曜日にはバラを
B1. 246:3AM
B2. Regret
B3. Hearts
B4. 日暮山

色彩感覚 (Sense of Color)

Tomoko Aran followed up her debut album with Sense of Color, a noticeably more 'normal' record compared to Nervous Breakdown, which often experimented with trippy instrumental effects. Sense of Color plays it much safer in comparison, feeling more like those classic vocal jazz albums which were quite common early in City Pop's history. The track More Expression provides a classic start to the album, while Disharmony fits the usual City Pop image with a nice duet and some awesome guitar play. Swing Easy likewise brings to mind the kind of music you'd likely hear in a jazz club, and Blue Note is a five-minute-long treat with great instrumentals throughout its runtime. Sense of Color is a surprising shakeup for Aran, ironically because of how safe it feels at times, but that's not necessarily a bad thing.

Artist: Tomoko Aran
Release: July 25, 1982
Label: Warner Bros. Records

- A1. More Expression
- A2. Disharmony
- A3. Probationer
- A4. Love Is The Moment
- A5. Monochrome
- B1. Swing Easy
- B2. Guilty Night
- B3. The Married Man
- B4. Blue Note
- B5. Nostalgia

Fly By Sunset

The second and sadly final album by Ken Tamura takes the approach set up by his previous work Light Ace and greatly improves upon it. Tamura composed every song on the album, along with writing lyrics for quite a few of them, and he was also assisted on the A-side by one of City Pop's premier arrangers in Shigeru Suzuki. Long-Distance Call establishes the album's global feeling with its mostly English chorus; a trait shared with A Little Bit Easier. The track greatly benefits from the inclusion of a female backing vocalist, although it seems her identity is unknown. Make It Or Break It continues Tamura's trend of having some country influence present, and the bass in this one is really kicking. Tamura seems to have more or less retired from music after this, only making very rare appearances writing for albums throughout the years.

Artist: Ken Tamura
Release: 1982
Label: CBS/Sony

- A1. Long-Distance Call
- A2. A Little Bit Easier
- A3. 踊りなよ
- A4. 冷たい夏
- A5. Foot Steps
- B1. ふたりなら
- B2. ジーナ
- B3. Make It Or Break It
- B4. 渚のストローハット
- B5. 愛に時間を

Warm Front

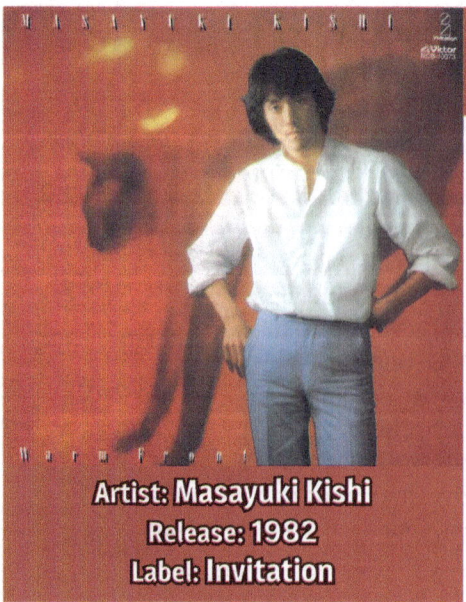

Warm Front is the debut album by Masayuki Kishi, an artist who only released two albums of his own, although he did later collaborate for an anime soundtrack with Takahashi Youichi. His style is a welcome addition to the niche that people such as Masamichi Sugi were becoming well associated with, that being a more pop rock centric approach to City Pop. Kishi separates himself from Sugi by being a little softer with his songs overall though, so expect lots of nice slow mood setters. Some personal favorites include A3 which has a really nice flow throughout its chorus, and you can really hear the passion (and radical guitar play) in Babe. Another good one is Ordinary Girl which will have you swaying to Kishi's lovely singing and its delicate instrumentals. Warm Front is a pop rock hidden gem, and fans of this style will definitely enjoy it.

Artist: Masayuki Kishi
Release: 1982
Label: Invitation

- A1. メッセージ
- A2. Say Good By
- A3. カリフォルニアブルー
- A4. ガールフレンド
- A5. Ordinary Girl
- A6. See You Again
- B1. City Tripper
- B2. Babe
- B3. Silly Boy
- B4. さりげなくAlone
- B5. 真夜中のWhisper

Amore

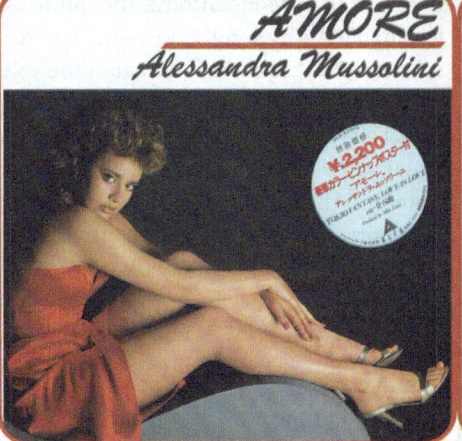

Left: A close up shot of Alessandra which was included as a physical picture in the album.
Center: The cover of Amore is elegant and classy, fitting well with her Italian roots, even if her particular roots are rather controversial.
Right: Another picture of Alessandra from the album. You got about three different photos of her from buying this album.

Artist:
Alessandra Mussolini

Release:
August 21, 1982

Label:
Alfa

Track List:

A1. Tokyo Fantasy

A2. Carta Vincente

A3. 甘い記憶 (Fond Memory)

A4. Insieme Insieme

B1. Love is Love

B2. E Stasera Mi Manchi

B3. Tears

B4. L'Ultima Notte D'Amore

Amore is the one and only album released by Alessandra Mussolini, a name which might ring a bell if you were paying attention in your high school history classes. That's because Alessandra is in fact the granddaughter of Benito Mussolini, the fascist leader of Italy during World War 2. Beyond just her notorious lineage Alessandra is a remarkably interesting figure who has somehow been an actress, musician, and even a model for the European Playboy magazine. Later on in life she made the logical shift to politics, and ever since 1992 she has been involved in various branches of the Italian and European governments, including serving as a member of Parliament. So how did Alessandra, who didn't actually speak Japanese at all, end up creating an album which only ever released in Japan? It seems that many details surrounding this story have never been told in full, but it began when Alessandra and her mother were on a trip to Japan. At some point her mother was asked by a talent agent if Alessandra would be willing to sing for an advertisement, to which her mom responded "of course." However, there was a slight issue; Alessandra did not know how to sing. It's unclear how the drastic leap was made from singing for an advertisement to creating a full album, but Amore somehow came into being regardless. The album is a fascinating hodgepodge of three different languages as she sings in Japanese, English, and Italian, and she surprisingly does a pretty good job considering her lack of experience with Japanese. There's a charm to the imperfection of her singing and the odd pronunciation of some words, but that just serves to make it a more interesting listening experience. Tracks such as Tokyo Fantasy and Fond Memory fit right in with other City Pop songs of the time period thanks to their blending of musical styles, and you can even hear some electronic sound in E Stasera Mi Manchi. A sizeable number of the songs are of course sung in her native Italian, which certainly must've given the album a uniquely international feeling. While English titles and lyrics show up extremely commonly throughout the history of City Pop, but Italian is a much rarer occurrence. Amore is a pretty decent album considering its bizarre circumstances, and it also happens to be quite the collector's item. Amore has never been reprinted since 1982 or released on formats other than vinyl, so expect to pay up for a copy of this one. It seems that even all these years later Alessandra still remembers Amore, and as recently as 2021 she was heard singing a part of Tokyo Fantasy on an Italian TV show. Lots of weird things happened in the 1980s, but Amore stands out as being particularly unusual.

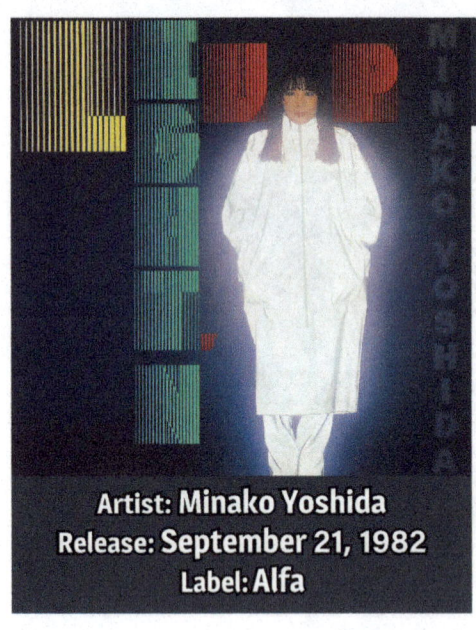

Light'n Up

Light'n Up continues with the precedent that Yoshida seemed to establish in Monochrome, including a track list which featured lengthy songs and a quality over quantity approach. Likewise, Yoshida was once again the sole mastermind behind each and every song, composing and writing lyrics for all eight of them. The eponymous Light'n Up is somehow equal parts a jazzy ballad and disco extravaganza at the same time, and the lyrics beautifully describe the sensation of losing yourself in the thrill of nocturnal city life. Another great track is Night Lights on My Cheeks, which similarly details the mystique of the city as full of colors and people constantly moving. Fitting with its iridescent theming, Light'n Up shines brightly among Yoshida's catalogue, although it'd be her last album until 1986's Bells.

Artist: Minako Yoshida
Release: September 21, 1982
Label: Alfa

- A1. Light'n Up
- A2. 頬に夜の灯
- A3. Love Shower
- A4. 風
- B1. Morning Prayer
- B2. 斜陽 (Reflection)
- B3. 時の向こう
- B4. Alcoholler

Cliché

Cliché is the third and final entry in Taeko Ohnuki's 'European trilogy'. The title itself has a somewhat ironic meaning, as Ohnuki explained that making French styled music was in a way becoming her own cliché, and the album was even recorded over in Paris. The cover is also much more colorful than her past few releases, an intentional choice by Ohnuki who was hoping to distance herself from being perceived as "cold." The album is another creative step forward for Ohnuki and feels even more experimental than Romantique due to its heavy synth sound, something which Ryuichi Sakamoto of Yellow Magic Orchestra contributed to quite a lot. This combined with the European inspired music makes Cliché a peculiar blend of old and new, and a unique musical journey to go through.

Artist: Taeko Ohnuki
Release: September 21, 1982
Label: RCA

- A1. 黒のクレール
- A2. 色彩都市
- A3. ピーターラビットとわたし
- A4. Labyrinth
- A5. 風の道
- B1. 光の力
- B2. つむじかぜ
- B3. 憶ひ出
- B4. 夏色の服
- B5. 黒のクレール (Reprise)

Seventh Avenue South

Seventh Avenue South by Yoshitaka Minami immediately establishes its tone just from the cover alone. It features the painting Nighthawks by Edward Hopper, a famous piece depicting some late-night diner patrons seemingly trapped in a space with no exit. The album likewise fits this nocturnal mood, being perfectly suited to being played well past sunset. Minami managed to pull off some of his best genre blending to date, using styles like jazz, pop, and rock, alongside more of those global (and especially Latin) inspirations to create something which truly suited his unique strengths. Scotch And Rain is just as cool as you'd think, and tracks like Moonlight Whisper or Down Beat lean more towards that classic Minami style pop rock. The instrumentals throughout the album are consistently fantastic, making Seventh Avenue South one of Minami's best releases to date.

Artist: Yoshitaka Minami
Release: September 22, 1982
Label: CBS/Sony

- A1. Cool
- A2. Scotch and Rain
- A3. Moonlight Whisper
- A4. The Girls In Their Summer Dresses
- A5. Observatory
- B1. Down Beat
- B2. Home Town
- B3. Harbor
- B4. Une Femme Qui Sifflent
- B5. Sketch
- B6. Chat Noir (黒猫)

Again

Again is the debut album from Kengo Kurozumi, although he had been releasing singles since 1976. Kurozimi is an artist who is less known overall compared to some of his fellows nowadays but still gave us some real City Pop wonders. The mood for the album is light and cool with just the right amount of energy, the exact kind of vibe that will transport you back to the eighties for a few moments. Some of the standouts include Pastel Love with its phenomenal chorus and guitar play, as well as the miniature disco party going down in Rainy 246. Then there's Sexy Magic, which a big winner for fans of songs with slightly imperfect English lyrics which still get the message across regardless. It's easy to draw comparisons to Tatsuro Yamashita here (their voices even sound kind of similar), but that's more so a compliment.

Artist: Kengo Kurozumi
Release: October 21, 1982
Label: TDK Records

- A1. My Sweet Lady
- A2. Lusia
- A3. Pastel Love
- A4. 黄昏にダンス
- A5. Dear My Love
- B1. Rainy 2•4•6
- B2. Sexy Magic
- B3. セピア シーズン
- B4. Endless Way
- B5. Losing You

Le Plein Soleil

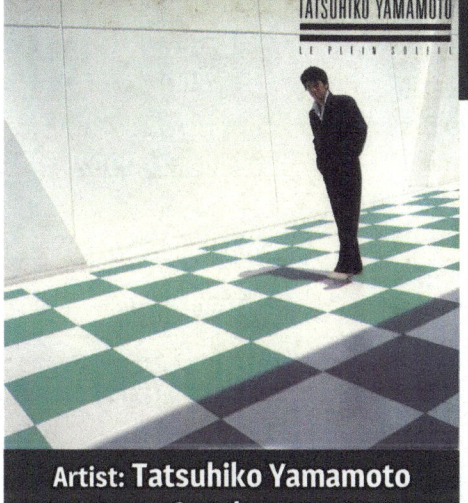

Tatsuhiko Yamamoto's second album for 1982 initially seems to be toned down compared to the very rock heavy I Love You So, as its first song is just a nice piano number akin to some of his early songs. This is quickly revealed to be a ruse when the next song begins playing, as the album might be even more rad than I Love You So. Catherine kicks us off with another gloriously romantic pop rock piece, but the tempo doesn't slow down going into Without Your Love. Jamaican Dream has that tropical flavor you'd expect, whereas Pacific Blue starts off light and only gets more and more frantic. Yamamoto gets in touch with his roots in the piano heavy Lady, and Last Good-Bye is another engaging pop rock creation. Le Plein Soleil and I Love You So both have a lot to offer, and if you enjoy one you're bound to like the other.

Artist: Tatsuhiko Yamamoto
Release: October 21, 1982
Label: Eastworld

- A1. Tayo Ga Ippai
- A2. Catherine
- A3. Without Your Love
- A4. Jamaican Dream
- A5. Pacific Blue
- B1. Sayonara Wa Iwanai
- B2. Last Good-Bye
- B3. Lady
- B4. Welcome To My Party
- B5. Ku-Gatsu No Photograph

Midnight Cruisin'

Kingo Hamada's fourth album arrived in 1982 to take us on a musical joyride, one which would establish him as a titan within the intersection of City Pop and adult-oriented rock. Beyond just those two styles Midnight Cruisin' has traces of just about everything including jazz and funk, making it a perfect example of the kind of musical synthesis artists were becoming more experienced with in the eighties. The album has major hits like A1 with its jazzy undertones, the fun and ever cool Midnight Cruisin', as well as its most popular song A4/Dolphin in Town. Expect to hear the word 'dolphin' very often here, Hamada wasn't kidding when he said the dolphins were in town. Possibly Hamada's most beloved and popular album, Midnight Cruisin' is a City Pop staple and highlight for the entire genre.

Artist: Kingo Hamada
Release: October 21, 1982
Label: Moon Records

- A1. 抱かれに来た女
- A2. 横顔のタクシー・ドライバー
- A3. So, I Love You
- A4. 街のドルフィン
- A5. ほのかなイリュージョン
- B1. Midnight Cruisin'
- B2. せめてからりと晴れてくれ
- B3. シャワールームのある風景
- B4. 真夜中のテニス・コート

Heaven Beach

Left: A cute summertime picture of Anri from the album. Center: The cover of Heaven Beach is seemingly a totally normal shot of Anri at a hotel, although the subject in the center of the frame is actually just a brown paper bag.
Right: Anri walking from an American store on the back of Heaven Beach. What could she have bought?

After releasing her debut album Apricot Jam in 1978, and then Feeling' in 1979, Anri took a short hiatus before Peacock of Sorrow hit the scene in 1981, a record which felt quite unlike her previous efforts due to its New Wave influences. It wasn't until 1982's Heaven Beach when Anri's style and musical identity would truly be solidified and became closely entwined with City Pop, particularly when it came to its ever-reliable summer and/or beach theming. This was largely owed to the contributions from another City Pop icon who was really making a name for himself; Toshiki Kadomatsu. Kadomatsu contributed three songs to the album with Second Affair, Summer Whisper and Fly By Day, all of which ended up being Heaven Beach's most popular tunes. Anri and Kadomatsu would continue to work alongside each other for many years to come, with Kadomatsu often providing Anri with songs and even working as her producer. The star power didn't stop there either, as Satsuya Iwasawa and Fuyumi Iwasawa of Bread & Butter also lent a track each, those being Honesty Man and With Our Backs Against The Summer. With some of City Pop's summertime savants on her side Heaven Beach was just about guaranteed to turn out well, and the difference between it and Anri's earlier records are night and day. The album kicks off with the instantly recognizable guitar play in Second Affair, a pop track about those pesky feelings of love emerging, although there's doubt about the other person feeling the same way. Heaven Beach is also home to one of Anri's biggest hits of all time in Last Summer Whisper, a song which completely changes your mood to mellow within its first second. Its lyrics about heartbreak and yearning for those happier times to return, combined with its absolutely excellent instrumentals, make it a timeless track that can be enjoyed over and over again. Anri composed Lonely Driving which keeps up the theme of romance that didn't quite work out, and the lyrically beautiful Resolution appropriately serves to wrap up this somber beginning for the album. The tone begins to pick up with the groovy sounds of Fly By Day and its ever-intoxicating City Pop mixture of rock, jazz and pop. Flash Back Memories keeps those good vibes going, and Honesty Man's English chorus always garners a smile. Our trip to the beach nears its end with Memorial Story and its lyrics about a fading summer, before the titular Heaven Beach concludes the vacation and even ends on the sounds of seagulls and crashing waves. Heaven Beach is one of City Pop's all-time classics, further cementing the genre's association with summer and giving Anri a winning formula which she would utilize throughout the entire decade.

Artist:
Anri

Release:
November 21, 1982

Label:
For Life Records

Track List:

A1. 二番目のaffair (Second Affair)

A2. Last Summer Whisper

A3. Lonely Driving

A4. Resolution

A5. Fly By Day

B1. Flash Back Memories

B2. Honesty Man

B3. Memorial Story

B4. 夏に背を向けて (With Our Backs Against The Summer)

B5. Heaven Beach

Love Trip

Left: This picture of Mamiya with her cute little hat on is one of the very few pictures we have of her.
Center: The cover of Love Trip makes a striking impression thanks to its angular room design, and Mamiya on that chair has become an iconic City Pop visual.
Right: The single release for Love Trip and One More Night which got a surprise re-release in 2021.

Artist:
Takako Mamiya

Release:
November 25, 1982

Label:
Kitty Records

Track List:

A1. Love Trip

A2. チャイニーズ・レストラン (Chinese Restaurant)

A3. 真夜中のジョーク (Midnight Joke)

A4. 哀しみは夜の向こう (Sorrow Is Beyond The Night)

A5. All Or Nothing

B1. 渚でダンス (Dancing On The Beach)

B2. One More Night

B3. モーニング・フライト (Morning Flight)

B4. たそがれは銀箔の… (Twilight is A Silver Foil…)

B5. What A Broken Heart Can Do

One of the single most mysterious figures in City Pop's history is Takako Mamiya, an artist who dropped one of the style's most iconic albums of all time and was never heard from again. Very little is known about her activities before or after Love Trip released, although she was briefly a backing vocalist for the group PAO around 1979. To make matters more complicated it's very possible that Takako Mamiya wasn't even her real name, as pseudonyms are quite common in the Japanese music scene, thus making attempts at finding her via that name a fool's errand. Mamiya had some help with her first album as a large group of composers were brought on, with a few notables being Akira Inoue and Takao Kisugi, and it's thanks to this wide range of composers that the album feels so diverse. Love Trip is also somewhat in line with other City Pop albums from the time, emphasizing a blending of genres and often espousing contemporary themes which appealed to a modern audience. You'll be jumping around from tranquil jazzy numbers to the energetic pop the genre is often associated with, and the album especially starts to kick up its energy for the B-side. Despite this those who listen to the album often feel a certain overarching sense of strange melancholy throughout it, a factor which greatly contributes to its mystique. Perhaps it's the frequent lyrics about loneliness and the past, or just something inherent about the way Mamiya sings, but you may find some repressed emotions creeping up on you if you're not careful. The subject matter of these songs is as City Pop as you can get, with Mamiya detailing scenes of a Chinese restaurant where she met a former lover and the vivid description of a lonesome late-night drive heard in Midnight Joke, the album's most popular song. Although it is an incredibly beloved album now, Love Trip didn't receive the same glowing praise when it was first released in 1982. The Oricon charts have no records for the album, meaning it was likely a big commercial flop. Following this Mamiya seems to have utterly vanished from music, never being credited on a release ever again. Love Trip managed to achieve a cult following years down the line and many speculated on her whereabouts before the truth was finally revealed on the Korean YouTube channel Minken. In a video interview with Shiina Kazuo, the former director of Kitty Records, he explained that Mamiya did in fact retire after Love Trip sold poorly and got married not long after. Hopefully, Mamiya found happiness in her private life, and maybe she is aware of how many people came to genuinely love the music that she gave us.

Moonlight Island

Artist: Haruko Kuwana
Release: November 25, 1982
Label: Japan Record

Moonlight Island was Haruko Kuwana's album for 1982, although it may end up feeling more like a blast from the past for some. The first four songs are all covers of seventies songs from City Pop's forefathers, including Haruomi Hosono, Eiichi Ohtaki and Tatsuro Yamashita. You can hear creative new renditions of classics like Hosono's Choo Choo Choo Gagoto, and the endlessly coverable Down Town by Sugar Babe. Kuwana's cover of Down Town is especially unique because it has been fully translated into English and given a funky spin, making for a refreshing twist on this masterpiece. The B-side carries its weight as well, featuring a diverse set of tracks that includes Eiichi Ohtaki's B3 or When We Meet in A Dream. Moonlight Island feels both classic and contemporary and hearing fresh takes on these songs will bring a smile to your face.

- A1. ほうろう
- A2. Choo Choo ガタゴト
- A3. ウララカ
- A4. Down Town
- A5. あの頃のまま
- B1. I Love You
- B2. ムーンライト・サーファー
- B3. 夢で逢えたら
- B4. 夜の海
- B5. Yoru No Umi (Pt. 2)

The 20th Anniversary

Artist: Naomi Akimoto
Release: December 16, 1982
Label: Invitation

I'm not sure what it's the 20th anniversary of exactly, but it's definitely full of more jazz-centric City Pop to enjoy. Although jazz is at the forefront here like with her previous albums, there's a spectrum of styles that are mixed in, especially synth-pop and rock. The opening Enjoy Yourself sets the tone well by starting off with some typical cheery jazz notes before quickly changing things up with some jamming guitar, and the album keeps you guessing from then on. You can also hear one of Akimoto's most popular tracks here with Bewitched, a synth-heavy track that really demonstrates her superb singing and the surprisingly effective combo of electronic music and jazz. Some more noteworthy tunes are Sweet Surrender with its memorable instrumentals, while Why Ain't You A Bachelor plays it more straight compared to the album's other songs.

- A1. Enjoy Yourself
- A2. Silent Communication
- A3. Bewitched
- A4. Sweet Surrender
- A5. Misty Like The Wind
- B1. Beginning
- B2. Why Ain't You A Bachelor?
- B3. Joyful Dixieland
- B4. Russian Roulette
- B5. No One Ever Loved You So

Shakin' It Up

Artist: Kaoru Hirose
Release: December 16, 1982
Label: Air Records

Are you ready to shake it up? Shakin' It Up is the sole album by Kaoru Hirose, another mysterious artist who seemed to vanish after this album came out. While the woman herself is an unknown quantity her music making skills are undeniable. Every song on the album features her lyrics, and quite a few were also composed by her. Shakin' It Up fits nicely into the category of soul-centric City Pop, with many of its tracks also being ballads with a funky side. Rila is a Hirose creation which shows off her talents well, as it includes some entrancingly cool instrumentals which pair well with her singing. Another memorable song is the titular Shakin' It Up which has a great sort of lowkey groove to it, and the whole B-side deserves praise as well for songs such as Waving Dream and the fast-paced Round Midnight.

- A1. Cosmic Space City
- A2. Rila
- A3. Shakin' It Up
- A4. To You
- A5. It's So You
- B1. Information Love
- B2. Lovin' Doll
- B3. Waving Dream
- B4. Passing Away
- B5. Round Midnight

Cinderella Until 2:00 ~Friday Magic~

Artist: Meiko Nakahara
Release: December 21, 1982
Label: Eastworld

Meiko Nakahara's second album is one of her most beloved by fans of City Pop, plus its lengthy name is pretty fun to say. The opening track Fantasy is a marvelous example of what City Pop is all about, and it's cemented itself as a favorite for many. Featuring an exciting introduction and romantic lyrics that make you want to dance along, Fantasy is a nostalgic trip you'll return to again and again. The titular Friday Magic is another terrific tune, and that distorted 'disco voice' throughout adds to its eighties charm. Like its predecessor Coconuts House the album gets a lot of mileage out of Latin inspirations, which you can enjoy in tracks A3 and B2, but it's also quite heavy on funk. Then there's Nakahara's singing, which is delightful whether she's performing one of the album's slower tunes, or any of its many pop jams.

- A1. Fantasy
- A2. ジゴロ
- A3. ココナッツの片思い
- A4. パールのマニキュア
- A5. Go Away
- B1. Friday Magic
- B2. 恋の余韻
- B3. ステキなじゃじゃ馬ならし
- B4. ダイヤルまわして…
- B5. 2時までのシンデレラ

Mata Ashita (See You Tomorrow)

Artist: Kazuhito Murata
Release: 1982
Label: Moon Records

Mata Ashita is the debut album by Kazuhito Murata, a figure who would provide us with many albums that met somewhere in between City Pop and pop-rock. The album was made with an extremely fine group of arrangers, as both Tatsuro Yamashita and Shigeru Suzuki lent their talents. Getting help from even one of these men would've been a huge boon, but Yamashita also acted as something of a mentor for Murata. He would often visit Yamashita to learn about music production while he was recording For You, an experience which certainly served the fledgling artist well. Murata composed the whole album himself, which gives it a consistent feeling. It's easy to get lost in the pop rock realm he crafted, as all the tracks featured are lots of fun, making Mata Ashita an album you can't really go wrong with.

- A1. 電話しても
- A2. Whisky Boy
- A3. 想いは風に
- A4. Lady September
- A5. Marias
- B1. Greyhound Boogie
- B2. 波まかせ風まかせ
- B3. Be With You
- B4. 終らない夏
- B5. 波まかせ風まかせ ~Reprise~

黄昏(Twilight) ~Postcard Fantasy~

Artist: Junko Ohashi
Release: 1982
Label: Philips

Junko Ohashi's Postcard Fantasy may have actually been a musical postcard from the United States, as the entire album was recorded in Los Angeles. As such just about the whole band was American and included talent such as Leon Ndugu Chancler, who was the drummer for some song called Billie Jean by some guy named Michael Jackson. The album is otherwise classic Ohashi and still carries that funky and sometimes slightly crazy energy she's known for. A2 or Lady of Venice absolutely rocks out with its guitar play, and A3 frantic instrumentals will accelerate your heart rate. Night of The Lighted City and Looking For Love offer a reprieve before the tempo picks back up throughout the B-side, and the passionate I'm Just A Woman rounds us out. Postcard Fantasy is Ohashi at her finest, and its American flavor makes the album stand out.

- A1. ポストカード・ファンタジィ
- A2. ヴェニスの女
- A3. ベリッシマ
- A4. Night Of The Lighted City
- A5. Looking For Love ～シンデレラ・ナイト～
- B1. Dancing Town
- B2. 愛の踊り場
- B3. シェリー
- B4. 黄昏
- B5. I'm Just A Woman

1983, City Pop Alive

City Pop's glory days aren't slowing down, and 1983 is another year that's in contention for being the genre's pinnacle. Yasuhiro Abe and Yurie Kokubu launched their musical careers here, as did the band S. Kiyotaka and Omega Tribe. This band would become one of the golden age's most prolific groups, but also one of its most tumultuous, as they would spend the decade going through several variations with two different lead singers. 1983 is absolutely stacked with many of City Pop's most quintessential records, some of which even came from newer artists. Piper blessed us with the unforgettable Summer Breeze, an album which decided to largely forego vocals in favor of expressing its seaside atmosphere through its clever usage of sound. Tomoko Aran's Fuyū-Kūkan delivered the ultimate hybrid between City Pop and synth-pop, while Yurie Kokubu made a strong first impression with the awesome Relief 72 Hours. The freshly formed S. Kiyotaka and Omega Tribe were set up for success thanks to their partnership with songwriting genius Tetsuji Hayashi, and their debut album Aqua City absolutely showed what they were capable of. Anri earned a number one single with Cat's Eye and released both Bi・Ki・Ni and Timely!!, two of City Pop's most cherished records which have only grown in popularity. The "king" Tatsuro Yamashita unknowingly made his most popular song ever with Christmas Eve, but the tunes don't stop there, as seemingly everyone was on their A-game this year. The City Pop style was truly alive in 1983, and many artists created their best work here.

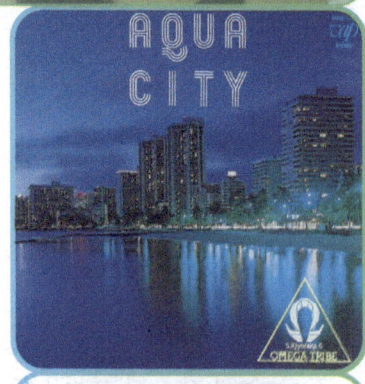

Anri

Few artists in City Pop's history are as universally beloved as Anri, but even fewer had such a lasting impact on how the style is perceived. When one imagines the typical idea of a City Pop song there's a high likelihood they're just thinking about a classic Anri track, particularly one from her golden run of early 1980s albums. Anri's first couple of projects, like her debut album Apricot Jam from 1978, were more akin to Kayōkyoku as opposed to City Pop and only saw modest commercial success, but her approach to music began to drastically change with 1982's Heaven Beach. This was the first time Anri worked alongside Toshiki Kadomatsu, an artist whose smooth genre blending tracks and lyrics about romantic summertime flings worked magnificently with Anri's singing. This partnership resulted in years of consistently excellent City Pop albums, notably 1983's Timely!!, which is often in the conversation for being the style's best of all time. Their collaborative albums Timely!!, Bi・Ki・Ni, Heaven Beach and Coool are all City Pop staples which perfectly demonstrate exactly what the genre is all about; good times, fun in the sun, late-night drives, and the occasional heartbreak. The two eventually went their separate ways for 1986's Mystique, as Anri didn't want to be fully reliant on him and instead sought to be more creatively independent. Anri gradually began improving her songwriting skills until 1987's Summer Farewells, the first album which she produced and wrote the majority of the compositions for. This has been the standard for Anri since, who continued making music way beyond the City Pop years and has adapted quite well to modern musical sensibilities, while continuously experimenting with new styles. Unlike some of City Pop's other icons, who might be known for a famous song or two, Anri has entire albums filled with mega-hits which continue to lure in new fans every single day.

Top: A semi-recent picture of Anri, which is featured on her self-titled album from 2018. Bottom: A younger Anri as seen on the album Feelin from way back in 1979.

AB's

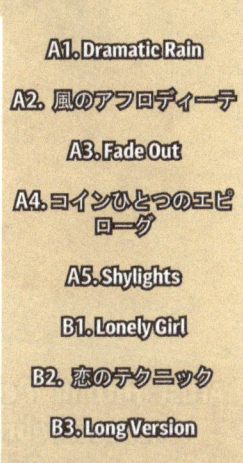

Artist: AB's
Release: January 21, 1983
Label: Moon Records

The debut album for the band AB's, a newly formed group that consisted of some recognizable names like Makoto Matsushita and Fujimaru Yoshino. The band's name was derived from most of its members having an AB blood type, and according to their website because "AB's line up first." As you'd expect from these artists AB's is an incredibly creative first venture which takes inspiration from many genres, ranging from adult-oriented rock to disco and beyond, but it all consistently rocks. The mesmerizing vocals in Deja Vu get the album going, and you may be surprised to learn a song called Dee-Dee-Phone kicks ass. Django, Fill The Sail and Asian Moon all benefit greatly from having multiple vocalists, and In The City Night is the exact kind of jam you'd want to hear on a late evening in 1983. An excellent first album from AB's, and the first of many.

- A1. Deja Vu
- A2. Dee-Dee-Phone
- A3. Django
- A4. Fill The Sail
- B1. Asian Moon
- B2. In The City Night
- B3. Girl
- B4. Just You

Shylights

Artist: Junichi Inagaki
Release: February 1, 1983
Label: Express

Junichi Inagaki's second album Shylights delivered his first big hit in Dramatic Rain, which was originally released as a single. Composed by Kyohei Tsutsumi and featuring lyrics from Yasushi Akimoto, this fun pop track fit Inagaki's voice perfectly, and it secured a respectable spot at number 8 on the charts. The lyricist Akimoto cleaned up when it came to the royalties from the song, and he bought a BMW with them which he naturally named Dramatic Rain. While that was the album's mega hit there's many more adult-oriented rock delights to experience, such as the album's namesake in Shylights which is smooth and romantic. While not as successful as Dramatic Rain, Long Version is another very popular song from this album and provides a ballad with a bit of soft rock injected. Another good album from Inagaki, who had more in store for 1983.

- A1. Dramatic Rain
- A2. 風のアフロディーテ
- A3. Fade Out
- A4. コインひとつのエピローグ
- A5. Shylights
- B1. Lonely Girl
- B2. 恋のテクニック
- B3. Long Version
- B4. Long After Mid-night

Play Room ～ 戯れ

Artist: Nina Atsuko
Release: February 21, 1983
Label: Teichiku Records

Play Room is the debut album by Nina Atsuko, but not actually her first album, as she had previously released City under the alias Eri Hayakawa. As you may expect from the incredibly diverse sounds that make up City Pop, Play Room features a wide range of styles, although the album gets most of its mileage from jazz. You can also spot bits of Latin inspiration, rock, soul and more throughout its track list, all of which are guaranteed to keep you on your toes. A2 feels like you've stepped into a synth-heavy disco, and the funk instrumentals in Lair are killer. The album also knows when to reel it back with tracks like A4 and the powerful A5. The B-side holds up as well, with Man or Boy being a frantic start to the side, while B2 and Let Me Kiss will have you moving and grooving. A stellar re-debut for Nina, Play Room is one to check out.

- A1. Communication (ワン・ノート・サンバ)
- A2. マッチ売りの少女 (ジャニー・ギター)
- A3. Lair (キサス・キサス・キサス)
- A4. Mr. ボージャングルス
- A5. 明日に架ける橋 (Bridge Over Troubled Water)
- B1. Man Or Boy (イパネマの娘)
- B2. 艶しい関係 (ベサメ・ムーチョ)
- B3. Let Me Kiss (ウェイブ)
- B4. 戯び (おいしい水)
- B5. 幻の手 (幸福せの黄色いリボン)

Reincarnation

Artist: Yumi Matsutoya
Release: February 21, 1983
Label: Express

From the ever-productive Yumi Matsutoya comes Reincarnation, a real highlight from her already incredibly impressive catalogue. This album gave us a number of excellent songs, such as the eponymous Reincarnation which has fast-paced vocals, and a healthy dosage of rock instrumentals. The saxophone playing from Jake H. Concepcion in A2 goes crazy as per usual, and Night Walker paints a beautifully sad picture of loneliness in the neon landscape of the city. Esper has a unique start with it's very difficult to understand distorted English speech at the beginning, and B2 keeps the rock trend going with its guitar action. B3 has those stunning lyrics you'd expect from her, and Matsutoya's melancholic singing might just get to you. Reincarnation offers the listener those expectedly excellent tracks, and a few curveballs.

- A1. Reincarnation
- A2. オールマイティー
- A3. Night Walker
- A4. 星空の誘惑
- A5. 川景色
- B1. Esper
- B2. 心のまま
- B3. ずっとそばに
- B4. ハートはもうつぶやかない
- B5. 経る時

Next Door

Artist: Hitomi "Penny" Tohyama
Release: February 1983
Label: Columbia

Penny kept busy throughout 1983 and gave us two excellent albums, starting off with Next Door in February. We kick off with a beyond funky start in Exotic Yokogao, a track which is perfectly suited for dancing along to. The distorted background voice really adds to that eighties charm, making this a must listen for fans of disco. You can also notice how much Penny's Japanese has improved from listening to Good-Bye, since it's easy to forget that's not her native language at this point. The groove doesn't stop on the B-side either as Love Is The Competition keeps the party going, and it's hard to resist singing and vibing a little to this one. We're also treated to a moving ballad in Get My Love before closing out with Our Lovely Days, which is guaranteed to bring up some nostalgic feelings.

- A1. Exotic Yokogao
- A2. Take Off Your Sunglass
- A3. Teardrops Romance
- A4. Good-Bye
- A5. Kiss The Yesterday
- B1. Love Is The Competition
- B2. High-Heel Dancer
- B3. Mystery Drive
- B4. Get My Love
- B5. Our Lovely Days

Hold Me Tight

Artist: Yasuhiro Abe
Release: March 1, 1983
Label: Express

The debut album by Yasuhiro Abe, another consistent addition to the City Pop family who had previously worked alongside Mariya Takeuchi and EPO, the latter of whom appears on this album for the chorus. Abe's style fits right in with other artists from the time, and feels somewhat reminiscent of Masamichi Sugi, which makes a lot of sense when you learn he was a member of Sugi's Red Stripes band. You can look forward to tunes that really embrace a sort of cool pop philosophy such as We Got It! and the very fun Cafe Flamingo, but the album has its share of heartbreakers too. A4 especially shows off Abe's wonderful singing voice which pairs excellently with a chorus, as does Season. More songs await on the B-side like Bad Boy before the lengthy and moving Manhattan rounds out Abe's first of many albums.

- A1. We Got It!
- A2. Season
- A3. I Love You
- A4. 裸足のバレリーナ
- A5. Hold Me Tight
- B1. Cafe Flamingo
- B2. Single Room
- B3. Bad Boy
- B4. Funny Lady
- B5. Manhattan

In Motion

Artist: Minako Yoshida
Release: March 25, 1983
Label: Alfa

In Motion is Minako Yoshida's own take on a live album, based on performances from September of 1982. You can enjoy many of her most popular songs released from Twilight Zone to Light'N Up, although many of them have little twists and altered arrangements to make them feel fresh. Being performed live also means there's less flourishes added after the recording process, which provides a fantastic opportunity to hear a more 'natural' side of these iconic tracks. Noticeably absent from the album are any sounds from the audience such as applause, an intentional choice by Yoshida who deemed it to be "unnecessary." Perhaps she's just not one for indulging in such self-gratification, letting the music speak for itself. This would be her last album for another three years, as it wasn't until 1986 when her self-published record Bells was released.

- A1. Uptown
- A2. Cat
- A3. Let's Do It
- A4. Lovin' You
- A5. The Sea
- B1. Tornado
- B2. Alcoholler
- B3. Monster Stomp
- B4. Town

Vitamin E.P.O

Artist: EPO
Release: April 5, 1983
Label: Dear Heart

It's not as helpful as Vitamin C, but the delightful music in Vitamin E.P.O probably has some sort of benefits. The name of the album was inspired by a health-conscious trend going on in Japan around the time, so maybe some of those hip joggers enjoyed listening to this on their Walkman. One song in particular, B1 or 'U, fufu, fufu' was quite the success and gave EPO her first top ten hit, which was also featured in many commercials throughout the years. The chorus has a very universal appeal as EPO sings "U, fufu, fu," which doesn't really mean anything and thus transcends language. Another stellar track from the album is Pay Day, an ode to that oh so glorious moment in time when your bank account isn't totally in shambles. Another excellent release, Vitamin E.P.O stands out as a high point for her entire discography.

- A1. Vitamin E・P・O
- A2. 土曜の夜はパラダイス
- A3. 無言のジェラシー
- A4. Would You Dance With Me?
- A5. あなたを奪えない
- B1. う, ふ, ふ, ふ
- B2. Pay Day
- B3. かなしいともだち
- B4. 五分遅れで見かけた人へ
- B5. Bye Bye Baby
- B6. う, ふ, ふ, ふ, Part II

ひとかけらの夏 (Fragment of Summer)

Artist: Kazuhito Murata
Release: 1983
Label: Moon Records

Fragment of Summer is Kazuhito Murata's second album, and this one was made in conjunction with a certain City Pop king. Tatsuro Yamashita took up the mantle of producer and worked extensively with Murata for this record, and the two often had late night jam sessions which lasted until the morning hours. The resulting product was a refined pop rock experience which felt right at home in the easygoing eighties. Songs such as Summer Dream provide a lighter mood to drift away to, whereas A3 really bumps up the energy. So Long, Mrs. ended up as one of the album's most popular songs and works as a great sample slice for Murata's music. The album was originally meant to end on the ballad Love Has Just Begun, but Yamashita suggested that a cheerful ending was more so Murata's style, thus the brief and lighthearted B5 closed it out.

- A1. 一本の音楽
- A2. Summer Dream
- A3. 台風ドライブ
- A4. So Long, Mrs.
- A5. Catching The Sun
- B1. Travelin' Band
- B2. やさしさにGood-bye
- B3. 幻影
- B4. Love Has Just Begun
- B5. ニコニコ・ワイン

111

Summer Breeze

Left: The three main members of Piper Keiji Yamamoto, Takashi Shima, and Ya Ido jamming out, although this album is pretty light on the vocals.
Center: The cover of Summer Breeze is a perfect symbol of City Pop's fixation with the beach and summer.
Right: The colorful track list and credits from a recent release of the album.

Two years after their first album I'm Not In Love was released the members of Piper returned with Summer Breeze, although the band was barely recognizable from its 1981 incarnation. More than half of Piper's original members had left the band at this point, most notably vocalist George Hikita who departed over some disagreements about the change in direction Piper was taking for Summer Breeze. Luckily Hikita eventually returned as the lyricist for their album Gentle Breeze later that same year, while Ya Ido joined to fill the gaps left by the retired members, thus establishing Piper's permanent trio of Yamamoto, Shima, and Ido. So, what about the upcoming Summer Breeze was so conceptually different that it caused Hikita to temporarily leave the band? As the name suggests, the album was designed from the ground up to evoke those summer vibes, something City Pop has been well associated with since the start, but the band hoped to accomplish this with minimal usage of vocals. This approach was inspired by the electronic pioneers of Yellow Magic Orchestra, as well as Tatsuro Yamashita's mastery over the style, two influences which came together to make the ultimate easy-listening delight. We begin with the always welcome cliche of waves crashing into the shore, followed by radio static eventually which tunes right into the positive sounds of Shine On. The track manages a perfect balance between energetic and chill, setting the tone for the rest of the album quite well. Then the titular Summer Breeze gives us one of the more lyrically inclined songs, naturally including quite a few English phrases, but it still keeps that relaxing mood up. Things heat up some in Hot Sand which perfectly utilizes tropical drumming, subtle electronic sounds and the ocean's natural cascades to replicate a beach adventure at home. Sadly, it seems our vacation has taken a sour turn as Gentle Shower expresses a vow to never fall in love again, which is then followed up by Twilight, a song that encapsulates a feeling of loneliness just a little too well. That dour mood doesn't last forever though since the B-side begins with Samba Night's groove and the unique electronic journey through Starlight Love. The song's distorted vocals give the song a hypnotic and almost inebriating sound, as if you've had a couple too many beers tonight. Night Shore treats us to another incredible show of musical talent from Piper, then Angel Smile and Moonlight Beach fill roles as some of the album's more 'normal' City Pop bops with some incredibly fun vocals. Summer Breeze is a wonderfully designed album by Piper which nails the cool vibe of City Pop in a way that few other artists were able to replicate.

Artist: Piper
Release: May 1, 1983
Label: Yupiteru Records
Track List:
- A1. Shine On
- A2. Summer Breeze
- A3. Hot Sand
- A4. Gentle Shower
- A5. Twilight
- B1. Samba Night
- B2. Starlight Love
- B3. Night Shore
- B4. Angel Smile
- B5. Moonlight Beach

On The City Shore

Artist: Toshiki Kadomatsu
Release: May 21, 1983
Label: Air Records

1983 was a huge year for Kadomatsu, especially since this was when he produced Timely!! for Anri, one of the all-time classics of City Pop. For his own ventures though we were treated to On The City Shore, and along with it more examples of what made him the master of beachside pop. Off Shore gets the vacation started with an expectedly fun track, and Summer Emotions fills the mandatory 'song about the summer and romance' checkbox. The chorus for Take You To The Sky High is golden, and its instrumental session midway through is hype every time. Take Me Far Away has both jazz and funk in spades, and the fun keeps going throughout Anklet and Dreamin' Walkin'. Let Me Say... and Say...Good Night sort of function as pieces of the same song, closing us out with a moving ballad and quick instrumental track as we say goodbye to the city shore.

- A1. Off Shore
- A2. Summer Emotions
- A3. Ryoko!!
- A4. Beach's Widow
- A5. Take You To The Sky High
- B1. Take Me Far Away
- B2. Anklet
- B3. Dreamin' Walkin'
- B4. Let Me Say...
- B5. Say... Good Night

Seaside Lovers

Artist: Various
Release: May 21, 1983
Label: CBS/Sony

Seaside Lovers – Memories In Beach House is another collaborative effort from a trio of influential artists in the Sound Image Series, this time with Masataka Matsutoya, Akira Inoue and Hiroshi Sato. Similarly to the series past collaborations the songs were made independently with each musician providing a few tracks, and the result is another memorable summertime journey. The tracks within take inspiration from a wide range of styles, but there's a general underlying electronic theme which makes them both surreal and calming with a lively pop injection. Lovers Paradise would pair nicely with a colorful drink, and Lilika Shinzato's vocals really put you at ease. Melting Blue is likewise hypnotic, and its subdued vocals really help transport you to a mini vacation. There's lots of excellent music relax to here in Seaside Lovers, another very welcome addition to 1983.

- A1. Lovers Paradise
- A2. Melting Blue
- A3. Sun Bathing
- A4. Sunset Afternoon
- A5. X's And O's
- B1. Wind, Wave And Wineglass
- B2. Coconuts Island
- B3. Evening Shadows
- B4. Blue Memories

Mistress

Artist: Beers
Release: May 25, 1983
Label: Bourbon Records

Mistress is the only album by the duo Beers, which consisted of Yoko Hashimoto and Megumi Saitoh, and it's a real hidden gem. The pair's voices work splendidly together as they explore a variety of styles, including those cool pop tracks, smooth and jazzy numbers, and emotional ballads. The opening track and A3 both have a nice light groove going on, and the saxophone play from Jake H. Concepcion is lovely as always. Those who enjoy those slow mood setters will love A2, A5 as well as A4, which really show off this duo's harmonious singing. The instrumentals found in B1 are tight, and B4 is a track which is sure to inject some optimism into your day thanks to how fun it is. We're treated to a beautiful farewell in B5, closing out this lone album from an incredibly talented duo which really deserves a try.

- A1. 壊れたワイパー
- A2. 蒼い朝 Day Break Rain
- A3. ランダムに・・・
- A4. Hold Me
- A5. 愛の鍵
- B1. 夜明けの舟
- B2. 片隅のアベニュー
- B3. ラッキー・ストライク・マン
- B4. クィーン・オブ・ハート
- B5. ためらいの午後

Fuyü-Kükan

Left: The back of Fuyü-Kükan features a fun reel of pictures featuring Tomoko Aran, and some water, since water is all over the place in City Pop.
Center: The beautifully colorful background of Fuyü-Kükan was actually created using a computer, which is quite impressive for 1983.
Right: Another image of Aran from inside the album.

In the leadup to 1983 Tomoko Aran had released two albums with fairly different philosophies. Her debut album Nervous Breakdown was a very experimental synth-pop creation featuring some unconventional sounds which helped Aran stand out among the crowd. Then in 1982 she released Sense of Color, a much more typical (but still good) album compared to her first foray. It seemed that from these two experiences Aran, along with composers Masatoshi Nishimura and Masanori Sasaji, found a sort of synthesis, combining the unique charm of Nervous Breakdown with the wider appeal of Sense of Color to create Fuyü-Kükan. The name translates to "Floating Space" in Japanese, an apt descriptor for this otherworldly City Pop classic which has it all. There's a little of everything you'd associate with City Pop here, notably the synth-pop sound Aran was introduced with, but it's also packaged with rock, funk, soul and many more stylistic inspirations. This is well displayed in the introductory Body To Body, a song which is equal parts energetic pop tune, fun love song and also a total rock out session with some electronic flourishes for good measure. The album gets a little funkier in Lonely Night, which has some wonderfully entertaining English phrases throughout, and its interesting usage of what could best be called electronic jazz leaves an impression. I'm In Love is one of the album's many big hits, but it especially grew in popularity during City Pop's revival period. Aran's beautiful singing and instrumentals make it feel like a truly nostalgic, romantic song from your younger days, even for those who have never heard it before. Fuyü-Kükan keeps you on your toes with the fast-paced digital world of Je le m'ama before we arrive at the main attraction in Midnight Pretenders. It's Aran's most well-known song for a good reason, as it's a delicate pop track which gets fantastic usage out of backing vocals which complement its romantic lyrics. Midnight Pretenders was also heavily sampled in The Weeknd's song Out Of Time from 2022, as in the two tracks have virtually the same instrumentals, giving this retro Japanese tune a modern retooling. The fun doesn't stop there either as Summer Tapestry arrives to inject some groove into your life, and we're treated to another oddball in HANNYA which swaps from high to low pitched vocal distortions which make it one of the album's most creative tracks. Baby, Don't You Cry Anymore then is a beautiful ballad with a rock twist which concludes our trip through Aran's unique dimension. An all-time City Pop classic, Fuyü-Kükan is practically required listening for synth-pop enjoyers thanks to its many unique and memorable songs.

Artist:
Tomoko Aran

Release:
May 28, 1983

Label:
Warner Bros. Records

Track List:

A1. Body To Body

A2. Lonely Night

A3. I'm In Love

A4. ジ・レ・ン・マ (Je le m'ama.)

A5. Midnight Pretenders

B1. ひと夏のタペストリー (Summer Tapestry)

B2. HANNYA

B3. しゃくなYesterday (Shaku Na Yesterday)

B4. Baby, Don't You Cry Anymore

Bi · Ki · Ni

Left: The back of Bi · Ki · Ni includes a message from Anri; "Come back to this beach when summer comes."
Center: The cover of Bi · Ki · Ni shows off a joyful Anri really rocking that hat.
Right: Another shot of Anri from the album, who truly was the star visual for this album.

Artist:
Anri

Release:
June 5, 1983

Label:
For Life Records

Track List:

A1. Good Bye Boogie Dance

A2. Dancin' Blue

A3. September Walkin'

A4. Lady Sunshine

A5. Yes I'm In Love

B1. Surf City

B2. Just Be Yourself

B3. Beach Boy In My Heart

B4. Summer Focus

B5. Affection

1982's Heaven Beach was a big win for Anri, whose collaborative efforts with Toshiki Kadomatsu were proving to be quite fruitful. Naturally, this momentum was kept up with Bi · Ki · Ni, an album which followed in Heaven Beach's footsteps as an exciting summertime celebration jam packed with fun and memorable tracks. This time around Kadomatsu's involvement was evident in the design of the album itself, as it was split into two distinct sides based on City Pop's most common topics. The A-side was known as the 'Disco Side' and featured songs which were all composed by and included lyrics from Kadomatsu, effectively making this his creative domain. The B-side was then known as the 'Sea Side' and was crafted by Anri alongside Takeshi Kobayashi, who had previously composed the tracks Resolution and Flash Back Memories on Heaven Beach. The album kicks off with its most recognizable song, the Anri classic Good Bye Boogie Dance. This track ironically starts Bi · Ki · Ni with a farewell as despite its upbeat opening and instrumentals which make it perfect for some a light boogie session, the song actually revolves around one last dance with a person they'll likely never see again. This bittersweet dichotomy is kind of a City Pop staple, as many other popular songs from the genre such as Midnight Door/Stay With Me initially seem to be fun pop tunes, but they present a rather saddening tale. This is contrasted by Dancin' Blue which essentially presents the opposite situation, this time the dance taking place is born out of frustration with the other person's antics and a desire for independence. The mood becomes just a bit more melancholic with September Walkin's description of a fading summer, although this doesn't last long as Lady Sunshine ushers in the heat's return along with a seasonal romance. Yes I'm In Love then closes out the Disco Side with a romantic ballad as things come full circle, with the song detailing a reignited love which will hopefully last forever. The record then flips over to the B-side, but those themes of summer romance don't go away. Just Be Yourself provides us with another heartbreaker about the anticipation of a farewell phone call which never seems to arrive, then we get to enjoy Beach Boy In My Heart, a delicate tune which transitions nicely into the instrumental treat Summer Focus Summer Focus which is a real instrumental treat. We're given one last romp with Affection, a song which both says goodbye to a lover as well as the album's listener. Bi · Ki · Ni is another excellent collaboration between Anri, Kadomatsu and Kobayashi, although sometimes slightly overshadowed by her next album, the extraordinarily popular Timely!!

Melodies

Left: The single release for Christmas Eve and White Christmas, which is so popular there's been over 30 different releases for it.
Center: The cover of Melodies is simple but colorful, and reflects his new musical philosophy well.
Right: Yamashita as seen on the back of the record.

Tatsuro Yamashita was doing better than ever after his albums Ride on Time and For You were both major successes, although there was some concern that this would be his commercial peak. Yamashita had turned 30 in 1983, a milestone where it sadly became more difficult to secure big hits, especially in the fast-paced music world of the 1980s. Another issue on the horizon was the future of his struggling label Moon Records, which Yamashita was acting as the executive director for. The staff involved all agreed that they had around half a decade to get the ailing label back on course, something Yamashita likely could have done by commercializing his music even further. However, Yamashita rejected this idea, and in fact went down the opposite course by making music which ignored the trends of the day, much like how he did back in Sugar Babe. This time he also intended to inject even more of himself into the music by writing lyrics for almost every song. This was something which Yamashita admitted wasn't his strong suit, and most of his earlier albums utilized lyricists like Minako Yoshida. Some of the personal themes he incorporated into his lyrics included the alienation felt by city dwellers, a City Pop classic, as well as masculine concepts such as roguishness. The resulting Melodies was an album with a distinct flavor from his previous releases, while still keeping much of that Yamashita philosophy, especially in regards to the lyrics. Yamashita's approach of putting as much of himself into the music as possible is clear in the opening Jody, where every single instrument except the saxophone was played by Yamashita himself. One song in particular stands out among the rest though, that being Yamashita's most popular song ever in Christmas Eve. When the single first came out in December of 1983 it wasn't a groundbreaking success, peaking at number 44 on the Oricon charts, but this all changed towards the end of the decade. The song became massively popular, reaching the coveted number one position in 1989, and ultimately claiming the throne of the bestselling single throughout the 1980s. This acclaim has continued for decades, as Christmas Eve has held a spot in the Oricon's top one hundred most popular songs for nearly forty years, which was worthy of a Guinness World Record. As one of the most reliable songs seemingly ever, Christmas in Japan just isn't complete without hearing this uplifting tune at least once. There is a tinge of irony to be found in this situation, as Melodies was in some ways considered the beginning of Tatsuro Yamashita's decline. Little did anybody know that this same album included a song which would stand the test of time like very few ever could.

Artist:
Tatsuro Yamashita

Release:
June 8, 1983

Label:
Moon Records

Track List:

A1. 悲しみのJody (She Was Crying)

A2. 高気圧ガール (High Pressure Girl)

A3. 夜翔 (Night-Fly)

A4. Guess I'm Dumb

A5. ひととき (Moment)

B1. メリー・ゴー・ラウンド (Merry Go Round)

B2. Blue Midnight

B3. あしおと (Footsteps)

B4. 黙想 (Meditation)

B5. クリスマス・イブ (Christmas Eve)

"J"

Artist: Jake H. Concepcion
Release: July 5, 1983
Label: Dear Heart

Jake H. Concepcion has a reputation as one of the most prolific saxophone players in City Pop's history, and Japanese music in general, but he has a few albums to his name as well. "J" feels like the closest to City Pop within his discography and consists mostly of jazzy covers of Western songs, all of which are sung in English by Mr. Concepcion. The most famous song here is Pure Imagination by Anthony Newley and Leslie Bricusse, which you'll likely know thanks to its appearance in the film Willy Wonka & The Chocolate Factory. It's given a funky and jazzy overhaul here and is one of the album's highlights, but Without You is another bombastic performance from Jake and the crew. That Old Black Magic allows keyboard player Hiroshi Sato to flex his skills, and Tonight The Night closes the album out in style.

- A1. (Jei)
- A2. The Old Music Master
- A3. Hong Kong Blues
- A4. Pure Imagination
- A5. Without You
- B1. That Old Black Magic
- B2. Girl Talk
- B3. Tonight The Night
- B4. J

Quiet Skies

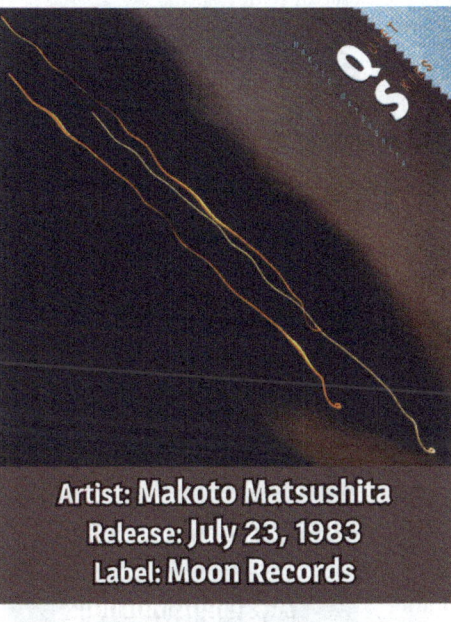

Artist: Makoto Matsushita
Release: July 23, 1983
Label: Moon Records

Makoto Matsushita's third album was surprisingly his last for 35 years, as he didn't release another until 2019's Visions. Always an innovator, Quiet Skies proved to be Matsushita's most experimental album yet, even more so than the creative Pressures and The Pleasures. Every track is given proper time to simmer, as all of them are a minimum of five minutes long, with Sight Of The Dawn being an impressive ten minutes in length. Each song feels like a journey into a parallel world, and it's easy to get totally lost in the fascinating fusion of styles here. If you liked some of the soothing tunes found in First Light then Quiet Skies has that in spades, making it a perfect album for some late-night relaxation. Despite this being Matsushita's last album for a long time he stayed involved as a musician, composer and arranger for the rest of City Pop's golden years and beyond.

- A1. Sight Of The Dawn
- A2. Views From Fire Mountain
- A3. Lucky Guy
- B1. Going Home
- B2. The Feather Heart
- B3. Cage Of Dreams

J.I

Artist: Junichi Inagaki
Release: September 1, 1983
Label: Express

J.I released later on in 1983 after his earlier album Shylights, and it too included a big hit. A3 or Summer Horn has beautiful singing from Inagaki which sort of blurs the line between a ballad and a pop song, finding that perfect balance. Its lyrics are also classic City Pop, detailing feelings evoked from the nostalgic sound of a certain car's horn, which was heard quite often during a summertime fling. It's a track that's likely to bring up some memories you'd maybe rather forget, especially from those more innocent days. Creating this track was no easy feat either, as the crew spent an entire week recording just this song, and more than one hundred takes were necessary to get it right. Other great tracks include Maria, which has a super memorable chorus, and the energetic but still balanced B4 also impresses.

- A1. Maria
- A2. 夏の何力
- A3. 夏のクラクション
- A4. 男と女
- A5. Everybody's Valentine -想い焦がれて-
- B1. 蒼い雨
- B2. 言い出せなくて
- B3. 一人のままで -There's No Shoulder-
- B4. エスケイプ
- B5. 生まれる前にあなたと…

Aqua City

Left: The members of Omega Tribe alongside frontman Kiyotaka Sugiyama, as seen on a CD release for the album.
Center: The cover of Aqua City is pretty on point with its title, and definitely contributed to City Pop's association with water.
Right: The single release for Summer Suspicion and Sea Dog On The Shore.

Throughout the history of City Pop there are many excellent bands such as Piper to be enjoyed, but the style is generally more associated with those prominent solo artists. One band which managed to distinguish itself is Omega Tribe, a group that would go through various iterations with different lead singers, although its most recognizable form is likely this one helmed by Kiyotaka Sugiyama. The band was in good hands from the moment they were signed to a label, since Tetsuji Hayashi was brought on to compose their debut single Summer Suspicion, a track that's as City Pop as it gets. The song offers up some pop rock instrumentals and high energy vocals, although its lyrics detail some trouble in paradise as a summer fling heads in the wrong direction. Combine that archetypal subject matter with some English phrases sprinkled in, and you have a recipe for an early eighties hit. Summer Suspicion took some time to gather momentum, but it eventually managed to breach into the top 10 singles, cementing itself as one of the band's headlining tracks. In fact, when this iteration of the group broke up in 1985 their farewell concerts had Summer Suspicion as the last song performed, showing just how important it was to the band and its fans alike. Aqua City was then released as their first record a few months later and was a major success, easily cracking into the top five albums and selling well over 100,000 copies. Those who enjoyed Summer Suspicion would've felt right at home with Aqua City's offerings, as the whole album is built off those similar enduring themes of romance, summer, and life in the city. Tetsuji Hayashi provided most of the album's songs, but Kiyotaka Sugiyama also displayed his skill and composed several tracks such as Paddling to You, a perfect little beach time number. Midnight Down Town is another Omega Tribe classic with some bass work which gets the song off to a funky start, and the whole song is drenched in that urban flavor the genre is so well known for. Light Morning stays true to its name with S. Kiyotaka's delicate singing, while Transit In Summer's awesome chorus and instrumentals make it quite memorable. It's easy to melt away into the sounds of Trade Wind, which really feels like you're drifting off on a sailboat and lends itself well to the album's aquatic theming. We reach a fitting conclusion with Alone Again as we must say goodbye to that short-lived summer love, and as Aqua City comes to a close, we're left with the sounds of crashing waves. Aqua City is an excellent debut album from S. Kiyotaka & Omega Tribe which fits the bill for City Pop perfectly and houses many excellent songs that are very emblematic of the style.

Artist:
S. Kiyotaka & Omega Tribe

Release:
September 21, 1983

Label:
Vap

Track List:

A1. Summer Suspicion

A2. Paddling To You

A3. Midnight Down Town

A4. Light Morning

A5. Umikaze Tsushin

B1. Transit In Summer

B2. Trade Wind

B3. Sexy Halation

B4. Alone Again

Point Zero

Artist: Junko Ohashi
Release: September 21, 1983
Label: Philips

Junko Ohashi provided us with another distinctly American flavored bop of an album in Point Zero, plus the fact that it was recorded in New York is advertised on the record's hype sticker. Despite being one of Ohashi's lesser-known albums it includes quite a few hidden gems and Ohashi personally considers it to be her 'treasure'. The album kicks off with the appropriately titled Dancin', a song that's guaranteed to have you tapping your feet along to the disco universe it creates. In Your Lovin' is a delight, and we're treated to one of Ohashi's classic slow ballads with Firefly. Sadly, after this release Ohashi went on a lengthy hiatus, and her next album wasn't released until 1988. As it turns out Ohashi became so enamored with the New York lifestyle she took a break from recording music to spend more time there.

- A1. Dancin'
- A2. In Your Lovin'
- A3. Can't Get Enough
- A4. Firefly
- B1. Caught In A Shower
- B2. Sensual Night
- B3. Perfect Melody
- B4. Sugao No Mamade

Relief 72 Hours

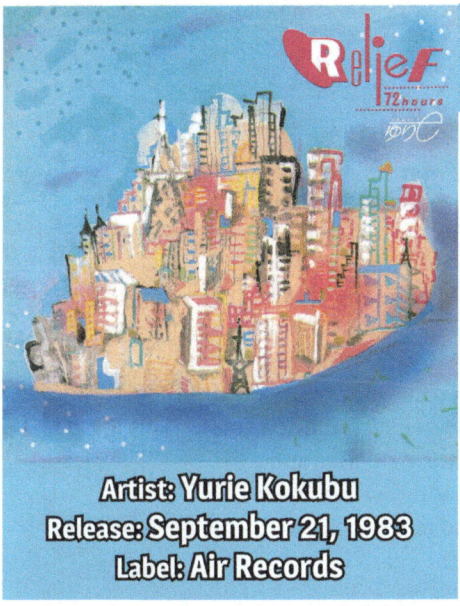

Artist: Yurie Kokubu
Release: September 21, 1983
Label: Air Records

1983 gave us the debut album from Yurie Kokubu, an artist who had quite an impact on City Pop and can be heard singing on albums such as Timely!!, After 5 Clash and more. Relief 72 Hours seemed destined for greatness as it was produced by the mastermind behind hits like Stay With Me, Tetsuji Hayashi, who was also involved with composing many of the album's tracks. Unsurprisingly its most popular song Just A Joke was made with some of that Hayashi magic and has an instantly recognizable opening, a beyond catchy chorus and funky instrumentals that will have you dancing along every time. Just a Joke is a City Pop staple, but it's just one of Relief 72 Hours plentiful jams. The entire album is thoroughly enjoyable with some highlights being A1 which brings the energy right from the start, while Dancing Tonight offers another highly groovy tune to get down to.

- A1. スノッブな夜へ
- A2. 恋の横顔
- A3. Weekend Love
- A4. Love Song
- A5. とばしてTaxi Man
- B1. 回転扉
- B2. Dancing Tonight
- B3. パーティーにひとり
- B4. Just A Joke
- B5. Last Woman

Rosé

Artist: Mari Iijima
Release: September 21, 1983
Label: Victor

The debut album from Mari Iijima, an artist who first got her start as a voice actor with roles such as Lynn Minmay in Macross before making the leap towards a career in music. The lyrics and compositions for the whole album were Iijima's work, and the result was an interesting mixture of old and new. Iijima utilized the talents of Ryuichi Sakamoto of Yellow Magic Orchestra to help give it an electronic sound, while her singing is reminiscent of an older Kayōkyoku style. Iijima's singing range allows her to create a pleasant and light atmosphere in songs like Blueberry Jam and Love Sick, and you can really hear the passion in Shine Love. Songs can range from the bubbly pop you'd expect from such a pink looking album to surprisingly surreal, and B3 gets really funky with it. An incredibly solid first album from Iijima who had decades of music to make.

- A1. Blueberry Jam
- A2. まりン
- A3. My Best Friend
- A4. Love Sick
- A5. Secret Time
- B1. きっと言える
- B2. Shine Love
- B3. ガラスのこびん
- B4. ひまわり
- B5. ひみつの扉
- B6. おでこにKiss

Can I Sing?

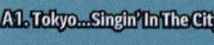

City Pop's original master of fusion is back with Can I Sing, an album with some new twists to look forward to. It's heavier on the electronic sound compared to his previous albums, although his classic influences like jazz still take the spotlight here. This new experimentation with electronic stylings appears right from the start with Tokyo…Singin' In The City, a track defined by its digitally distorted vocals and keyboard play. Can I Sing also gives Takanaka's underrated singing skills more prominence than usual, which you can enjoy hearing in Straight From Your Heart and Santigo Bay Rendez-vous, among other songs. A few standout songs are Funk 'N' Roll Train which is as lively as the name suggests, while Cry Baby Cry exudes a wonderful stoic coolness. You can never go wrong with the superb Takanaka action that Can I Sing houses.

Artist: Masayoshi Takanaka
Release: October 5, 1983
Label: Kitty Records

- A1. Tokyo…Singin' In The City
- A2. 我ら星の子
- A3. Sail On Fire
- A4. Straight From Your Heart
- A5. Jumping Take Off
- B1. Santigo Bay Rendez-Vous
- B2. Funk 'N' Roll Train
- B3. Cry Baby Cry
- B4. Noon
- B5. Can I Sing…For You

Sexy Robot

Penny's second album for 1983 would ultimately become her most popular ever, which is no surprise considering it's a City Pop masterpiece. Sexy Robot manages to perfectly fuse those styles synonymous with the 1980s like synth-pop, disco, rock, and many more into a real musical treat. The eponymous Sexy Robot is cool and lowkey, setting the tone for the album well. Wanna Kiss is the album's most popular track as well as Penny's biggest hit, and it earns its spot in City Pop history as an endlessly listenable tune. A track which really exemplifies the eighties night life is Tuxedo Connection, which is naturally completed with some English phrases thrown in here and there. The album is also home to Cathy, a more low-key track which is another one of Penny's most popular. Sexy Robot about requires a listen and is easily one of the year's best records.

Artist: Hitomi "Penny" Tohyama
Release: October 21, 1983
Label: Columbia

- A1. Sexy Robot
- A2. Wanna Kiss
- A3. Tuxedo Connection
- A4. Let's Talk In Bed
- A5. We Are In The Dark
- B1. Behind You
- B2. Try To Say
- B3. Cathy
- B4. Slow Love
- B5. Be Mine

Signifie

With her 'European trilogy' concluded Taeko Ohnuki moved on to the next advancement in her style with Signifie. While some of those European influences still remain, the album is more experimental in nature, getting heavy usage out of a synth sound graciously provided by Ryuichi Sakamoto on keyboard. While the music is a little out of the ordinary and sometimes psychedelic, it doesn't quite venture into utterly bizarre territory, making it a wonderful time for those willing to step out of their comfort zone. Ohnuki's gentle voice is incredibly well suited to this style of music, allowing the unique instrumentals to shine while her vocals work comfortably alongside them. Despite its experimental nature Signifie was a huge hit for Ohnuki, managing to hit number six on the Oricon charts and becoming her bestselling record yet.

Artist: Taeko Ohnuki
Release: October 21, 1983
Label: Dear Heart

- A1. 夏に恋する女たち
- A2. 幻惑
- A3. Signe
- A4. Patio
- A5. ルクレツィア
- B1. テディ・ベア
- B2. Recipe
- B3. アーニャ
- B4. Siesta
- B5. エル・トゥルマニエ

Gentle Breeze

Artist: Piper
Release: October 25, 1983
Label: Yupiteru Records

Several months after Piper gave us the premium summer listening experience Summer Breeze they returned with Gentle Breeze. Gentle Breeze contrasts its sibling by being more of a 'typical' City Pop album with spotlight put on the lyrics and thus feels more like their debut I'm Not In Love. It's also less consistently themed compared to Summer Breeze but is still fabulous either way. Despite what the album's serene cover suggests many of the songs are fun and full of life, with I've Got A Feeling immediately getting the party started, and Ride on Seaside has groove to spare. The album becomes truer to its name around the midway point with Highway Of The Sun, the hypnotic sounds of Show Me and the relaxing Breezing. While Gentle Breeze is less known compared to Summer Breeze it's still a worthy addition to 1983's amazing lineup.

- A1. I've Got A Feeling
- A2. Ride On Seaside
- A3. New York, Paris, London, Tokyo
- A4. Highway Of The Sun
- A5. Show Me
- B1. Breezing
- B2. Bamboo Island
- B3. Time & Tide
- B4. Funny Bird
- B5. Moon Child

Noriki

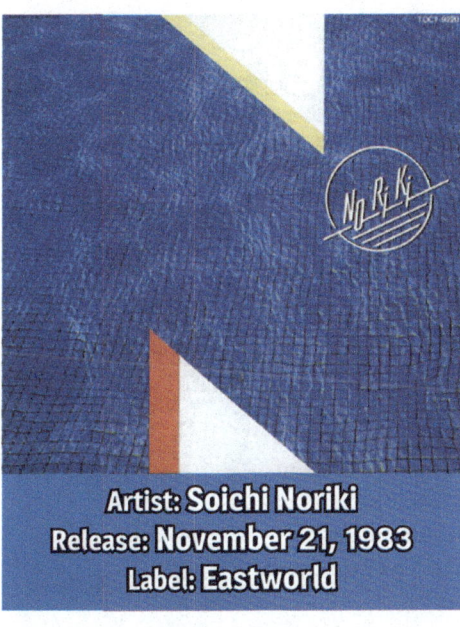

Artist: Soichi Noriki
Release: November 21, 1983
Label: Eastworld

Soichi Noriki's self-titled debut album introduces us to another of City Pop's most talented fusion artists. You can catch him performing on renowned albums like Toshiki Kadomatsu's Gold Digger ~With True Love~ and Momoko Kikuchi's Tropic of Capricorn, but he also makes a very strong showing here. Noriki is a record that's quite heavy on the jazz and funk, but there's also a considerable number of electronic instruments at play here. Similarly to other similar fusion albums it's light on the vocals, but you can enjoy Yurie Kokubu who's the singer on A1 and B3. Those two tracks are naturally some of the album's best, and both are successful at creating a relaxing and subtly cool atmosphere. Cozy's Melody is another great song with some phenomenal guitar work, but the album is a treat from start to finish.

- A1. You Need Me
- A2. Anyway
- A3. Black Duck
- A4. Cozy's Melody
- B1. Rag Box
- B2. Ballade
- B3. Do What You Do
- B4. Go Over The Hill

Voyager

Artist: Yumi Matsutoya
Release: December 1, 1983
Label: Express

Yumi Matsutoya's Voyager has some of the most stunning visuals of any City Pop cover, creatively mixing the aquatic and urban imagery the genre was strongly associated with. The album is perhaps less experimental compared to last year's Reincarnation, but those looking for more of a 'classic' Matsutoya album will certainly get their fill here. The opening track has a jazzy flavor and lyrics about a woman's attempts to have some fun with her girlfriends after a breakup, but their cheerful moods contrast with her own. Some other good tunes include A5 with its moving vocals, and the smooth Typhoon. Voyager's most noteworthy track is B5, The Girl Who Leapt Through Time, which was used as the theme song for a 1983 movie of the same name. The rhythm Matsutoya gets into while singing the chorus gives it a real impact and closes out the album well.

- A1. ガールフレンズ
- A2. 結婚ルーレット
- A3. ダンデライオン～遅咲きのたんぽぽ
- A4. 青い船で
- A5. 不思議な体験
- B1. ハートブレイク
- B2. Typhoon
- B3. Tropic Of Capricorn
- B4. 私を忘れる頃
- B5. 時をかける少女

Full Moon

Artist: Junko Yagami
Release: December 5, 1983
Label: Discomate

Junko Yagami was on the grind in 1983, releasing three albums throughout the year, although she was saving the best for last with Full Moon in December. The album is among her most beloved by fans of City Pop, especially thanks to the inclusion of Twilight Bay City, one of City Pop's golden children and a staple of playlists everywhere. Its funky instrumentals instantly transport you back to the eighties and fills your soul with the nostalgic feelings City Pop is so associated with and features timeless subject matter of failed romance. The song definitely earns its spot in City Pop's hall of fame, but the album has a lot more to love, such as the playfully romantic Follow Me, a catchy tune with a magnificently designed chorus. Naturally is similarly great and likewise has an addictive chorus which really exemplifies Yagami's talent as a songwriter.

- A1. Follow Me
- A2. Naturally
- A3. 黄昏のBay City
- A4. 陽だまりのあなた
- A5. 抱きしめてあげる
- B1. 綿雪&銀紙星
- B2. No!
- B3. ハートブレイクホテルで朝食を
- B4. Full Moon
- B5. Two Notes Samba

Green Water

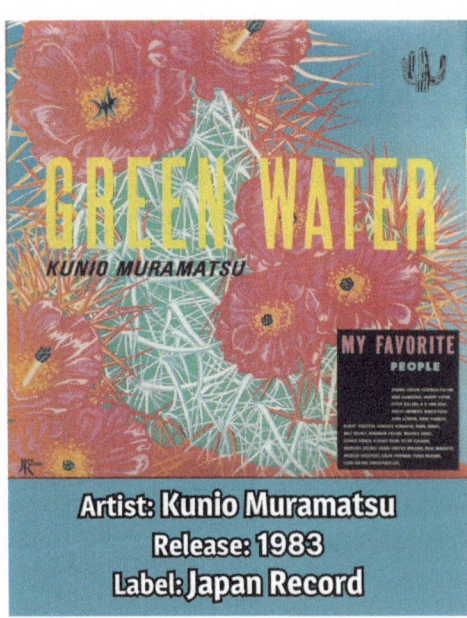

Artist: Kunio Muramatsu
Release: 1983
Label: Japan Record

The first solo album by Kunio Muramatsu, a name you have encountered previously in this book, as he was originally a member of Sugar Babe alongside Tatsuro Yamashita and Taeko Ohnuki. Muramatsu had been active in the music world since Sugar Babe disbanded, notably performing on A Long Vacation and other projects alongside Eiichi Ohtaki, but he was ready to take the next step for his career in 1983. Green Water is similar to other pop rock albums which City Pop was closely related to, such as Masamichi Sugi's albums, but there's some twists here as well. The Party and A2 are model fun pop tracks to get things started, while A4 and B1 are similarly energetic. A3's calming vocals and hypnotic instrumentals make it easy to get lost in, and one of the album's most memorable. Pop rock devotees might want to look into Green Water, and the rest of Muramatsu's work.

- A1. The Party
- A2. 僕のガールズ
- A3. フェアリー
- A4. ジェラシー
- B1. 天国色の夢 (Heaven Color's Dream)
- B2. アフターケア
- B3. うたたね
- B4. KATHARINA
- B5. Midnight Desire

Painted Woman

Artist: Masaki Matsubara
Release: 1983
Label: Canyon, Agharta

Masaki Matsubara had been a very well-established guitarist and member of the City Pop family for almost a decade, and he had previously released two solo albums. Painted Woman is perhaps his most well-known amongst fans of the style since it fits in so well with other albums from the era. This is owed to its distinctly Western style with exclusively English vocals and influences from disco and jazz, resulting in an album quite unlike what you'd expect. Songs like Make It With Me and Shining Star feel like some real disco deep cuts, and Matsubara's instrumental skills are on full display with Tequila Toast and S.O.S. (Society of Soul). Those who enjoy 1983's extremely popular subgenre of tropical or summer themed songs will enjoy Sunset Lullaby and Pacific Coast HWY, and it's impressive to see what Matsubara is capable of when given the reigns.

- A1. Make It With Me
- A2. Night Scanners
- A3. Shining Star
- A4. Silly Crush
- A5. Tequila Toast
- B1. S.O.S. (Society Of Soul)
- B2. Painted Woman
- B3. Sunset Lullaby
- B4. Pacific Coast Highway
- B5. Sky High

Timely!!

Left: A 1984 calendar featuring Anri which was included with the first 50,000 copies of Timely!!
Center: The beach-bound Anri seen on the cover of Timely!! is one of City Pop's most recognizable images.
Right: The inside of Timely!! is full of nice pictures which are reminiscent of a nostalgic photo album.

Artist:
Anri

Release:
December 5, 1983

Label:
For Life Records

Track List:

A1. Cat's Eye (New Take)

A2. Windy Summer

A3. Stay By Me

A4. A Hope From Sad Street

A5. You Are Not Alone

B1. 悲しみがとまらない (I Can't Stop The Loneliness)

B2. Shyness Boy

B3. Lost Love In The Rain

B4. Driving My Love

B5. Good-Night For You

Bonus: Remember Summer Days

One of City Pop's greatest years was also home to one of its greatest albums; Timely!! by Anri. A shining headliner for the whole genre, Timely!! is the perfect way to introduce prospective listeners to what City Pop is all about. It encompasses all of the traits the style is associated with, including a diverse range of musical influences, some perfectly cheesy English lyrics and contrasting themes of summer-time fun, urban romance and solitary melancholy. Like her past few releases Timely!! was helmed by Toshiki Kadomatsu as its producer, who worked overtime to squeeze multiple of City Pop's most iconic songs into one album, but back in 1983 its biggest hit was crafted by Yuichiro Oda and Miura Yoshiko. Cat's Eye was made as the opening theme for an anime of the same name, and it seized the number one single ranking for several weeks. The version here is slightly revised from the original, hence the (New Take) part of the title, but either way it works as an exciting start to the album with a memorable chorus. From here we enter peak City Pop as designed by Kadomatsu, Anri, and Tetsuji Hayashi who shared songwriting duties, starting with the delightfully joyful Windy Summer. This breezy track heralds the glorious emergence of the summer before Stay By Me tells a classic tale about love in the city, although these good times soon dissipate. A Hope From Sad Street is one of the more underrated songs from Timely!!, and its depiction of a street filled with bittersweet memories is really brought to life thanks to the backing vocals by Yoshihiko Shiraishi and newcomer Yurie Kokubu. Sorrow only builds as You Are Not Alone and I Can't Stop The Loneliness offer conflicting scenarios about solitude in difficult times. While the prior songs affirm support for others after being heartbroken, the latter continues to lament in solitude while those painful feelings refuse to go away. Despite its sad lyrics I Can't Stop The Loneliness has rather cheery instrumentals, something which oddly seems to translate into success for City Pop songs, as this is one of Anri's biggest hits of all time. Fortune seems to turn around in the spectacularly fun Shyness Boy, another jewel from the album with a perfect chorus. Another popular genre cliche of driving around with a romantic interest is covered in Driving My Love, but as the city settles down so does Timely!! with its final track, the moving Good-Night For You. However, in later releases the bonus track Remember Summer Days was included, a perfect ode to all the fun memories that come with the summertime, bringing the album full circle. Timely!! is a City Pop masterpiece which deserves its reputation and acclaim as one of the genre's most popular records.

1984, Making Waves

1984 is another one of City Pop's most revered years which is home to many beloved albums, noteworthy debuts, and even a few changes in musical identity. Toshiki Kadomatsu departed from the reliable summertime themes of his previous albums and instead made After 5 Clash, an album which truly put the "city" in City Pop by spotlighting the enthralling urban life. Tatsuro Yamashita took on the unique challenge of creating a soundtrack album for an upcoming movie, Big Wave, while his wife Mariya Takeuchi returned after a years-long hiatus. Her new album Variety truly displayed the songwriting talent she developed during her break, but she also made what might just be the most cherished City Pop song of all time with Plastic Love this year. Plastic Love would help reignite interest in the genre decades later, particularly in the Western world. where City Pop was largely unknown. The year also saw the idol Momoko Kikuchi make her debut with Ocean Side, an album that fit in perfectly with the style thanks to Tetsuji Hayashi's involvement. Other artists didn't stray far from what worked, such as S. Kiyotaka and Omega Tribe who released River's Island and Never Ending Summer, while Anri's album Coool served as a worthy follow-up to the iconic Timely!! Of course, it wouldn't be City Pop if there wasn't at least a little weird stuff going on, and in 1984's case we have records from actor Jackie Chan and American wrestler Terry Funk to look forward to. 1984 is another year that's in the conversation for being City Pop's absolute pinnacle, and it's stuffed with late night parties, romance, and some ocean side fun.

Tatsuro Yamashita

Akin to how Michael Jackson is known as the King of Pop, or Elvis Presley the King of Rock and Roll, Tatsuro Yamashita also holds a crown as the King of City Pop. Yamashita could be considered the style's single most important and influential figure due to his early presence as one of City Pop's progenitors as well as his consistent output of constantly evolving music. In his youth Yamashita was fascinated by the soft rock and soul heard from Western artists such as The Beach Boys, an interest which naturally inspired the innovative and meticulously produced music he would be making as an adult. As a member of the band Sugar Babe, he was one of the first artists to advance the folk-oriented sounds of 1970s New Music towards a more upbeat Americanized style, one which was especially attractive to young urbanites and became what we now think of as City Pop. Following Sugar Babe's breakup Yamashita continued crafting music in his signature style via albums like Spacy and Moonglow, but his big hit finally came with Ride On Time, a phenomenally successful, extremely catchy single that brought him mainstream attention and a wider following. Throughout the 1980s he wooed audiences and topped the charts with his 'resort style' music heard in For You, an album which matched the optimistic tone of the decade, or his cherished track Christmas Eve, one of Japan's most consistently popular holiday songs. Perhaps what's most impressive about Yamashita is his mastery over all aspects of the music making process, often working diligently as a writer, producer, and performer on multiple instruments for his albums and truly embodying the concept of a singer-songwriter. Even as City Pop drifted away from the public's interest in the 1990s Yamashita held on to a loyal fanbase which has only continued to grow, and with the modern revival of interest in City Pop many new listeners have flocked to the man who started it all.

Tatsuro Yamashita is a uniquely talented figure in City Pop who was basically a one-man band. He was a master of every aspect of music creation from songwriting to performing.

Music Tech of The Times

The 1980s were a fascinating decade for music which introduced us to many of the most iconic songs, albums and artists of all time, but it was also an era of rapid technological advancement which completely upended the way music was consumed and created. Perhaps the most iconic invention of the decade was the Sony Walkman, a little cassette tape playing gizmo that released in 1979 and became the de-facto music listening apparatus for many. The Walkman stood out because it allowed people to take their music with them wherever they went, and this newfound freedom meant you were no longer limited to jamming out at home or in your car, now you could actually explore the bustling city while listening to music about that same bustling city. Its portability and the privacy of headphones aligned perfectly with the more individualistic attitude of the 1980s, something which was complemented by personalized mixtapes and the general youth appeal that City Pop had. While now it's quite normal to have various artists on one playlist, back then it was quite exciting being able to have Tatsuro Yamashita, Toshiki Kadomatsu, Anri and Momoko Kikuchi all serenading you on one tape. Around the same time the compact disc or CD emerged as a game-changer for how music was distributed. The first commercially available CD player was released in 1982 and throughout the decade CDs slowly began replacing vinyl records as the preferred format for music. The (at the time) futuristic digital storage on a CD offered a number of advantages compared to its analog brethren, such as higher sound quality, no surface noise or pops, a much smaller size and the ability to hold more music despite being more compact than vinyl records. As CD players became more affordable and widespread record companies began prioritizing CD releases, sometimes even offering bonus tracks that weren't available on vinyl to lure in customers. City Pop artists were similarly quick to capitalize on the benefits of this new format, with records like Eiichi Ohtaki's A Long Vacation achieving remarkable financial success on CD. This meant that City Pop was among the first genres to be popular on CD, but also one of the last genres to be generally associated with analog formats like cassette tapes, as by the 1990s the vinyl record was getting steadily phased out. By the end of the 1980s record labels had begun significantly reducing vinyl production, and for much of the 1990s and early 2000s vinyl records became something of a relic, the sort of artifact you'd find somewhere in your grandparent's house collecting dust. The tides have certainly turned in the past decade or so, as the popularity of vinyl records has come back in a big way, leading to many re-releases of classic City Pop albums on their original format. The 1980s even shook up the way music was made as we saw the rise of computers, digital synthesizers, drum machines and samplers, tools that fundamentally altered how music was produced. Synthesizers like the Yamaha DX7 allowed musicians to create futuristic sounds that fit the decade's aesthetic perfectly and helped establish genres like synth-pop, which in turn heavily influenced City Pop's own sound. Unfortunately, as the 1990s rolled around that same level of intense advancement in musical tech slowed down, partially due to the stagnation the Japanese economy underwent in the following decade, leaving the nineties without a symbol like the Walkman or a major CD-level leap forward. The Walkman and CDs were both major milestones in music history and their effects on how we consume music are still strongly felt today with how portable and personalized our smartphones are.

Top: The original TPS-L2 Walkman model was a brilliantly designed piece of technology with few gimmicks. Its release also perfectly coincided with health-conscious trends of the eighties, so joggers could now enjoy their runs with a musical companion. Center: The Compact Disc or CD was the way nearly everybody in the 1990s and early 2000s experienced albums. That was until those pesky iPods and music streaming services came along and made them largely obsolete. Right now, CDs are in that awkward stage where they aren't old enough to be retro, but maybe in a decade or two they'll see a resurgence like vinyl records did. Bottom: Vinyl records have made a major comeback lately, and many City Pop icons have gotten in on the action. Tatsuro Yamashita has re-released many of his classic albums on vinyl, giving a new generation a chance to enjoy these classics as intended.

What Can I Do?

Artist: Keiko "Myrah" Tohyama
Release: January 21, 1984
Label: Express

Talent seemingly runs in the Tohyama family, as Keiko is actually the sister of City Pop darling Hitomi "Penny" Tohyama. Keiko or "Myrah'" had a much less extensive career compared to her sister's, as she only released this one album, but it's still a splendid listen. What Can I Do? is filled with moving vocal performances from Myrah and is especially enjoyable for fans of slow jams. Tracks such as Drop On By and Water nail that classy, old-school vocal performance atmosphere, but the album also has many songs that fit in with the rosy image of City Pop. Suteki Na Inspiration feels like a quick trip back to the 1980s, while Love Collection adds some funk to your life. Myrah's appearances in music are fairly rare past this album, but you can hear her as a backing vocalist for a few of Yukihiro Takahashi's albums alongside her sister Penny.

A1. What Can I Do?
A2. My Guy / Cafe Sign
A3. Night Step
A4. Suteki Na Inspiration
A5. Drop On By
B1. Love Collection
B2. Water
B3. Woman
B4. Omoide Ni Shinaide

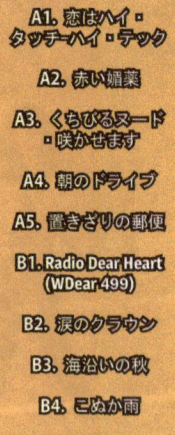

Hi·Touch - Hi·Tech

Artist: EPO
Release: February 21, 1984
Label: Dear Heart

EPO's Hi Touch - Hi Tech from 1984 has a noticeable shift towards more electronic influences, and the title of the album reflects this. Whereas Vitamin EPO was named as such in reference to health conscious trends in Japan, this album derives its name from reactions to advancements in technology. The title was meant to espouse a message about finding balance between technology and the natural existence of mankind, which is also evident in the music. EPO crafted a great sound when introducing electronic stylings to her unique view on City Pop, which can best be heard on tracks such as A2, A3 and B3. Old and new continue to collide in B4, another unique cover of a Sugar Babe song which is given a moving makeover here. Hi Touch - Hi Tech is another solid album from EPO, especially for those who enjoy a light electronic fare.

A1. 恋はハイ・タッチハイ・テック
A2. 赤い媚薬
A3. くちびるヌード・咲かせます
A4. 朝のドライブ
A5. 置きざりの郵便
B1. Radio Dear Heart (WDear 499)
B2. 涙のクラウン
B3. 海沿いの秋
B4. こめか雨
B5. ラスト・ワルツ

Poison 21

Artist: Naomi Akimoto
Release: February 21, 1984
Label: Invitation

The venomous Poison 21 had Naomi Akimoto incorporating even more synth-pop into her music while minimizing the jazz which dominated her first albums, and it was made alongside other synth superstars. Akimoto split lyrical duties with Tomoko Aran who wrote about half of the album's tracks, and you can enjoy hearing Hiroshi Sato as a composer and performer. The album gets off to an energetic start with Tonite, and The Way You Love Me's chorus feels designed to repeat in your head. Akimoto's singing has a perfect flow in Tricky, and the mixture of rock and a surreal atmosphere for Lion In My Pocket and Auto Charger are quite effective. Poison 21 is a real highlight of synth-pop and City Pop's eternal friendship with plenty of electronic songs to fall in love with, plus the duo of Tomoko Aran and Naomi Akimoto working together is a real treat.

A1. Tonite
A2. Missing You
A3. The Way You Love Me
A4. My Love Can Only Grow
A5. Lake Dimension
B1. Tricky
B2. Lion In My Pocket
B3. Telepathy
B4. Auto Charger (Shut Off)
B5. Amazon

Love Me

Artist: Jackie Chan
Release: February 22, 1984
Label: Elektra

First of all, yes, film star Jackie Chan has released quite a few albums throughout the years, but what's possibly even more surprising is how many City Pop artists were involved in making Love Me. Most of the tracks were composed by Tsugutoshi Goto, who is credited on many prominent City Pop releases, and there's a cover of Toshiki Kadomatsu's song Wait For Me. You can also hear Shigeru Suzuki playing guitar on two tracks and Yurie Kokubu on backing vocals for B4, making for an unexpectedly stacked roster. The album has a mix of pop and soul tunes sung in both Japanese and English by Jackie Chan, who's honestly a better singer than you'd maybe expect. The instrumentals are solid throughout, with Movie Star and Wait For Me being especially good, but the album is mostly just a fun piece of City Pop/Jackie Chan trivia.

- A1. Movie Star
- A2. ジャッキーの伝説
- A3. マリアンヌ
- A4. もう一度聞かせて
- B1. Love Me
- B2. 4月になれば
- B3. Hello Happy Song
- B4. Wait For Me

Gentle A Man

Artist: Hideki Saijo
Release: March 5, 1984
Label: RCA

Hideki Saijo's musical career dated all the way back to 1972, way before most City Pop artists had gotten started, but 1984's Gentle A Man fits with the genre better than his previous releases. This is partially due to another industry veteran composing many of the album's tracks, that being Tsugutoshi Goto who had been involved with City Pop since the very beginning. His compositions include A2, A3 and A5, three diverse tracks which all have creative and beautiful instrumentals. B1 was composed by Toshiki Kadomatsu and is instantly recognizable as such just from the opening alone. Saijo's singing shines brightest when he is performing slow and romantic tunes like A5 and B3, which are some of the album's best, but all of the tracks in Gentle A Man are well made and very welcome additions to the genre.

- A1. センチメンタル・モーテル
- A2. Onesided Night
- A3. 彼女は不機嫌
- A4. Do You Know
- A5. 帰港
- B1. Through The Night
- B2. かぎりなき夏
- B3. Love・Together
- B4. Winter Blue
- B5. ポートレート

EACH TIME

Each Time

Artist: Eiichi Ohtaki
Release: March 21, 1984
Label: Niagara Records

Each Time is the final Eiichi Ohtaki album released while he was still alive, as all of his records from the 2010s and onwards are posthumous. The album is conceptually quite similar to his earlier musical sensation A Long Vacation, with Takashi Matsumoto returning as its lyricist. You can look forward to more of Ohtaki's signature fun vision for pop rock and Matsumoto's lyrical ability in one of 1984's best. Ohtaki also sought to debunk a long-held belief in the industry that an album needs hit singles to be a success, and as such he just didn't release any singles from Each Time. It seems that Ohtaki proved himself right, since the album was so good it actually managed to surpass the highly impressive sales numbers of A Long Vacation and became his only album to achieve the number one ranking.

- A1. 魔法の瞳
- A2. 夏のペーパーバック
- A3. 木の葉のスケッチ
- A4. 恋のナックルボール
- A5. 銀色のジェット
- B1. 1969年のドラッグレース
- B2. ガラス壜の中の船
- B3. ペパーミント・ブルー
- B4. レイクサイド ストーリー

127

River's Island

Artist: S. Kiyotaka & Omega Tribe
Release: March 21, 1984
Label: Vap

The tribe is back for their second album, River's Island, which has a lot in common with their previous Aqua City due to Tetsuji Hayashi's continued involvement. As such you can expect many more romantic and youthful tunes which radiate that eighties flair. The titular River's Island is a City Pop delight, masterfully combining a feeling of cool solitude with celebratory joy, and Asphalt Lady's fantastic chorus about a run-in with a real bombshell always hits. Kimi No Heart Wa Marine Blue was a highly successful single back in 1984, and its heartbreaking tale of regret and yearning for a former partner is still a real tearjerker. Other notable songs include Do It Again which really gets the boogie going, and Silent Romance finishes the album with another moving story of sorrow and romance gone wrong.

- A1. River's Island
- A2. Asphalt Lady
- A3. Do It Again
- A4. Saturday's Generation
- B1. Kimi No Heart Wa Marine Blue
- B2. Saigo No Night Flight
- B3. Because
- B4. Rainy Harbor Light
- B5. Silent Romance

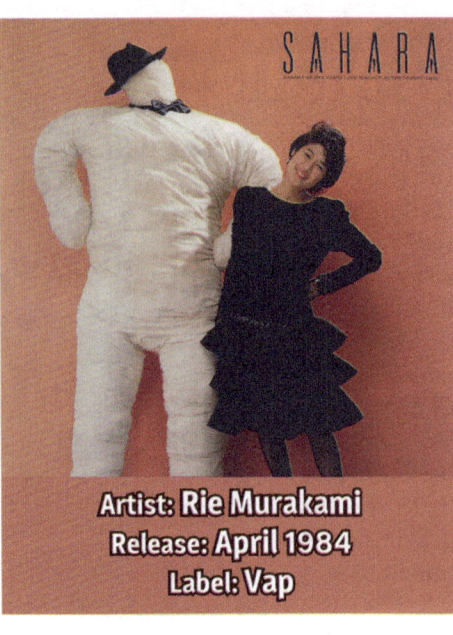

Sahara

Artist: Rie Murakami
Release: April 1984
Label: Vap

The sole album by Rie Murakami is a quite beloved entry in City Pop history, although there's sadly little information available about the artist herself. Sahara is one of only two albums that Murakami was ever credited on, with the other being Chi Chi from 1982, but the paper trail seems to go cold afterwards. Murakami did leave quite a legacy with this sole album though, as it's a very fun and varied record with some very memorable compositions. The album was made with a diverse group of songwriters, including a few Westerners. During its runtime you can enjoy the whimsical synth sounds of Fall In Love, the eponymous Sahara and sensitive tunes like I Won't Last A Day Without You. While Murakami's jovial singing is a big draw the instrumentals really make Sahara stand out as one of 1984's most creative releases.

- A1. Fall In Love
- A2. Sahara
- A3. Every Song I Sing
- A4. I Won't Last A Day Without You
- A5. T.N.T.
- B1. Eternally (Instrumental) ~ Smile
- B2. Say Cheese
- B3. I'm The One For You
- B4. If I Ever Lose This Heaven
- B5. Take Me Home

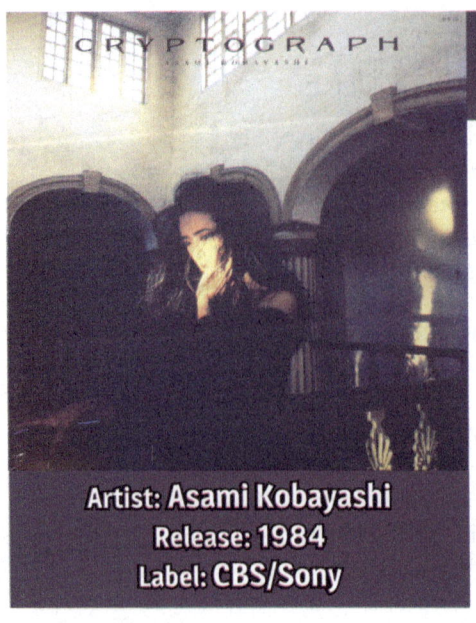

Cryptograph

Artist: Asami Kobayashi
Release: 1984
Label: CBS/Sony

Cryptograph was Asami Kobayashi's first album in nearly ten years, with her last release being the album Pastel Love from 1975, right when City Pop was getting started. Kobayashi spent most of that time working as an actress, but her return to music was bolstered by one of the industry's goliaths. Yumi Matsutoya produced the album while also providing some lyrics and compositions, all of which helped to give Cryptograph a level of quality not seen in most comeback records. The album also takes inspiration from some global sources since many of the tracks were composed by Westerners, with A1 and B4 both being from Italian songwriters. Kobayashi's own classy singing voice ties the whole album together, pairing very well with its disco and sometimes even new age influences.

- A1. Tsukikage No Paranoia
- A2. Binetsu
- A3. Typhoon
- A4. Grand-Prix No Natsu
- A5. Transit
- B1. Sugar Shuffle
- B2. Koi Nante Kantan
- B3. Anemone
- B4. Amaoto Wa Chopin No Shirabe
- B5. Lolita Go Home

After 5 Clash

Left: The back of After 5 Clash forms a complete image with the front, giving you a full view of that big ol' high heel.
Center: The cover of After 5 Clash takes the city part of City Pop to a new level.
Right: Another high heel seen in the album, making for quite the interesting visual alongside City Pop's two favorite colors; pink and blue.

Artist:
Toshiki Kadomatsu

Release:
April 21, 1984

Label:
Air Records

Track List:

A1. If You...

A2. Midnight Girl

A3. Airport Lady

A4. Maybe It's Love Affair

A5. Will You Wait For Me

B1. Step Into The Light

B1. 2. After 5 Crash

B2. Never Touch Again

B3. I Need You

B4. Heart Dancing
(あいらびゅ音頭)

Since 1981 Toshiki Kadomatsu had created three stellar albums which all revolved around a general summertime/resort/vacation motif, and he played major roles in Anri's thematically similar albums. It seemed that a stylistic shake up was in order, and in this case, he'd be leaving the beach and returning to the metropolitan world that City Pop derives its name from. After 5 Clash (sometimes referred to as After 5 Crash) takes Kadomatsu's music in a more urban-centric direction with a heavy emphasis on influences such as disco, funk and soul, all genres that are heavily associated with partying and the nightlife. You can also find lots and lots of English lyrics, and themes of steamy romance are prevalent all throughout. The end result was an album that feels like it was crafted to be a definitive example of what City Pop is about, and all of those wonderful eighties tropes are here. If You...sets the mood with a funky track that immediately differentiates this album from Kadomatsu's previous work. There's something very infectious about how Kadomatsu speeds up when singing certain verses, and his words line up perfectly to the song's beat, making it very fun to groove along to. Love abounds in this album, and most of the A-side is dedicated to tunes about romance, no matter the outcome. Midnight Girl is a gorgeous slower song with perfect backing vocals provided by Yoshihiko Shiraishi and Yurie Kokubu, while Airport Lady explores a seemingly one-sided attraction. The bass in this one is really kicking, and the catchy chorus will probably pop up in your head every now and then. You'd be forgiven for thinking Maybe It's Love Affair is about a party or something fun, since despite its sad subject about the end of a relationship the instrumentals are super catchy and positive sounding. Will You Wait For Me is a wonderful romantic ballad with an electronic rock segment, which is awesome and just feels so emblematic of the eighties. The party kicks back up on the B-side with Step Into The Light, a synth heavy disco track with some mostly understandable English lyrics sung in a rap style. It's as delightfully cheesy as it sounds, and its follow-up piece After 5 Crash just keeps the good vibes going. It's a song about the city's denizens letting loose after 5 PM strikes, at which point they're free to party all night, and a similar energy is captured in Never Touch Again. The party starts to settle down with the delicate loving emotions expressed in I Need You, but we've got one last burst of energy in Heart Dancing with its unique mixture of styles, as we exit with the sounds of cheering, clapping and fireworks. After 5 Clash was a very welcome change of pace for Kadomatsu, and it's an ideal representation of what made City Pop so fun.

Variety

Left: The back of Variety includes a photo of Takeuchi's pup Goofy, who is given special thanks in this album.
Center: The graceful cover of Variety keeps things simple but elegant with a monochrome picture of Takeuchi.
Right: The very lowkey single release for Plastic Love and its club mix, a song which became inseparable from City Pop.

Mariya Takeuchi made her glorious return to music in 1984 after spending a few years enjoying her married life with Tatsuro Yamashita, who also worked as Variety's producer. Variety was originally planned to feature songs by several different composers, akin to Takeuchi's previous records, but she actually spent the past few years perfecting her songwriting skills. Tatsuro Yamashita was incredibly impressed by the songs written during her hiatus, and so Variety was made to be Takeuchi's first album featuring tracks exclusively written by her, lyrics and all. This gives Variety a feeling of consistency and unity some of her earlier albums lacked, but the title is also quite appropriate as there's a very diverse range of styles utilized here. It also seems that Takeuchi's holy matrimony was quite the source of inspiration since most of Variety's tracks revolve around romance in some way. Again is an uplifting start to the album, but the main draw is A2 or Plastic Love, a song that's in contention for being City Pop's greatest ever. The song's gorgeous lyrics explore someone coping with a breakup by filling her life with shallow romance and disco dances. These meaningless relationships and songs are both described as being plastic, much like all the other disposable items we fill our modern lives with. In some ways Plastic Love is a critique on the same extravagant subject matter other City Pop artists celebrated, implying that such a life of indulgence may actually be quite hollow. Takeuchi sings every syllable with a subtle emphasis, giving the song an incredible flow and impact that combines nicely with the captivating instrumentals. Plastic Love would later become one of the primary forces behind City Pop's resurgence in interest during the 2010s, but that story is reserved for later on. While Plastic Love is naturally the biggest draw here, there's many more songs in Variety to enjoy, and the romantic themes just keep going. Let's Get Married is an adorably wholesome track, and one can only imagine where the newlywed Takeuchi drew inspiration from, while Broken Heart highlights her impressive English singing skills. There's some rock and roll to be had in Night at The Ampitheater, while Let Me Sing On The Mersey Beat leans more towards pop rock. Variety was a great success for the returning Takeuchi, achieving the number one spot on Japan's Oricon charts, but fans of her music would once again be kept waiting. It would be yet another three years before her next album Request was released, an understandable gap considering that same year Mariya Takeuchi and Tatsuro Yamashita welcomed their daughter Minako Yamashita into the world.

Artist:
Mariya Takeuchi

Release:
April 25, 1984

Label:
Moon Records

Track List:

A1. もう一度 (Again)

A2. プラスティック・ラブ (Plastic Love)

A3. 本気でオンリーユー (Let's Get Married)

A4. One Night Stand

A5. Broken Heart

B1. アンフィシアターの夜 (Night at The Amphitheater)

B2. とどかぬ想い (Unfulfilled Love)

B3. マージービートで唄わせて (Let Me Sing On The Mersey Beat)

B4. 水とあなたと太陽と (With Water, You, and The Sun)

B5. ふたりはステディ (Going Steady)

B6. シェットランドに頬をうずめて (Cheek To Cheek In Shetland)

Sunshine Kiz

Artist: Piper
Release: May 10, 1984
Label: Yupiteru Records

The summer's back, and so are the members of Piper for another hot, hot record. Sunshine Kiz is more similar to their Gentle Breeze album from the previous winter, as opposed to the mostly instrumental experience that Summer Breeze provided. Despite this many of the distinctive stylings and influences found in Summer Breeze are well represented here. Those who liked all of the electronic tricks and techniques Piper had been using will also enjoy this album, as they can be heard in songs like the namesake Sunshine Kiz, Seaside Runner and Velvet Eyes. Hidin' In Your Shelter is a unique one for Piper, but the combination of rocking instrumentals and the breathy backing vocals makes for a fun time. While not as beloved as some of Piper's other works Sunshine Kiz still delivers on the fun atmosphere the band is known for.

A1. Sunshine Kiz
A2. Seaside Runner
A3. Velvet Eyes
A4. Hidin' In Your Shelter
A5. Natsu Wa Dokokae
B1. Boku No Love Song
B2. Futari No Summer Time
B3. Silver Sun
B4. Fuiuchi No Manazashi
B5. Daydream Believer

Visitors

Artist: Motoharu Sano
Release: May 21, 1984
Label: Epic

Motoharu Sano continues the City Pop tradition of integrating multiple different styles into one, although Visitors really stands out. This is thanks to Sano's injection of rap into the mix, something you definitely don't see in City Pop that often. You can hear Sano perform some light rapping on A1, A5, B3 and B4, but this is often mixed in with his other favorite influences including electronic and funk. Most of the other songs are more traditional pop rock, albeit with their own twists thrown in, but every song has a strong identity. The experiment here surprisingly works excellently, and Sano's rapping gives Visitors a sound unlike basically any other City Pop album to date. Sadly, this idea was rather short lived, at least within the realm of City Pop, as rap never really mingled with the style in the same way synth-pop did.

A1. Complication Shakedown
A2. Tonight
A3. Wild On The Street
A4. Sunday Morning Blue
B1. Visitors
B2. Shame
B3. Come Shining
B4. New Age

More Relax

Artist: Tomoko Aran
Release: May 28, 1984
Label: Warner Bros. Records

Tomoko Aran followed up on the synth-pop/City Pop crossover masterpiece Fuyū-Kūkan with More Relax, an album with a personality quite unlike its predecessor. It was made in conjunction with members of the Casiopea, a jazz fusion band whose activities stretch from 1979 to the present day. Every track was composed by a band member, with Aran being the album's main lyricist, and the results are phenomenal. The synth sound heard in Fuyū-Kūkan is still very prominent, but it has been toned down overall to make room for other genres like funk which have been beautifully blended, as you'd expect from a fusion band like Casiopea. Tracks like Slow Nights serve up some name-appropriate chill sounds, but there's plenty of exciting disco influenced tunes such as A5 and B3. More Relax has a lot to love, and the team-up between these artists really works.

A1. Drive To Love (愛の海へ)
A2. Slow Nights
A3. Relax
A4. I Can't Say Good-bye
A5. E ☆ SPY (エ・ス・パ・イ)
B1. Waterless Pool (水のないプール)
B2. もう一度 South Wind
B3. 裸足のサロメ
B4. 13月の奇跡
B5. Privacy

Big Wave

Left: The credits and track list of Big Wave, which features a dude surfing. All of these images do, actually.
Center: The cover of Big Wave, which proudly announced that it includes music from the movie of the same name.
Right: Another gnarly surfer bro seen on a picture inside the album.

Tatsuro Yamashita was no stranger to making music for commercials, with his biggest hit Ride On Time even originating from one, but he was about to venture into new turf. He was tasked with creating a soundtrack for a feature length film called Big Wave, a documentary primarily about west coast surfers, but subjects like paragliding and dirt bike racing are also explored. Yamashita was quite busy at the time working on his wife Mariya Takeuchi's return album Variety, among other things, so many of Big Wave's songs were repurposed from other sources. Notably the B-side mostly consists of covers of Beach Boys songs, and many A-side tracks were reworked English renditions of songs from his albums Melodies and For You. Extra attention was placed on Yamashita's English pronunciation this time around, since despite spending his life listening to Western songs, he still wasn't satisfied with his English singing. To help remedy this Yamashita had the album's lyricist Alan O'Day coach him, although some accounts make this seem like more of a self-inflicted bootcamp. The album's producer Ryuzo Kosugi recalled that O'Day seemed to be going really hard on Yamashita, a sentiment which O'Day agreed with. While O'Day was perfectly okay with toning it down Yamashita insisted that the training sessions should be thorough. Thanks to their hard work and combined grueling efforts Yamashita's skills with English singing improved considerably, which served him well for the creation of this album and many more to come. While the album's tracks might come from a variety of sources there's no denying how well it suits the film's subject matter, as it's a full-on summertime extravaganza. The Theme From Big Wave's lyrics were based on Yamashita's view of surfing as a solitary activity, a concept which Alan O'Day interpreted into his own words. Jody and Your Eyes are both English renditions of some previously made songs, and the highly memorable Magic Ways is a song Yamashita wrote a few years ago but never put to use. Luckily it was given another shot at life here as it's one of the album's highlights and a favorite among Yamashita's fans. The B-side is loaded with covers of songs from The Beach Boys, and they unsurprisingly suit the rest of the album perfectly. This leaves Only With You and both parts of I Love You as original songs created just for this album (Part 1 coming after Part 2 is not a mistake in the book by the way), but the consistent theming of the songs chosen made it all come together naturally. The film Big Wave didn't really make waves at the box office and is now largely forgotten, but this excellent soundtrack by Yamashita gives it a place in City Pop history as a fun oddity.

Artist:
Tatsuro Yamashita

Release:
June 20, 1984

Label:
Moon Records

Track List:

A1. The Theme From Big Wave

A2. Jody

A3. Only With You

A4. Magic Ways

A5. Your Eyes

A6. I Love You (Part 2)

B1. Girls On The Beach

B2. Please Let Me Wonder

B3. Darlin'

B4. Guess I'm Dumb

B5. This Could Be The Night

B5. I Love You (Part 1)

Coool

Artist: Anri
Release: June 21, 1984
Label: For Life Records

It's cool, baby! The dynamic duo of Anri and Toshiki Kadomatsu united once again for Coool, and it's unsurprising to learn that it's another City Pop grand slam. The album kicks of with the super groovy sounds of Bring Me To The Dancenight, a track which is loaded with a healthy dosage of mostly sensible English phrases, and Gone With The Sadness, which is dedicated to a much-needed escape from the city. Surprise of Summer has a very nice tropical sounding opening you'll recognize in an instant, and it's unmistakable as a Kadomatsu creation. The track's romantic lyrics and great instrumentals helped to make this track one of the album's most popular. Other great tunes are I Can't Ever Change Your Love For Me and Flashin' Light, but the whole album is expectedly fantastic.

- A1. Bring Me To The Dancenight
- A2. Gone With The Sadness
- A3. Kimamani Reflection (New Version)
- A4. I Can't Ever Change Your Love For Me
- A5. Silly City Girl
- A6. Morning Highway
- B1. Surprise Of Summer
- B2. Flashin' Night
- B3. Mercury Lamp
- B4. He's My Music
- B5. Maui

Gravy

Artist: Yasuko Agawa
Release: June 21, 1984
Label: Invitation

Yasuko Agawa is a jazz artist who had been releasing albums regularly since 1978, but 1984's Gravy has become quite desirable among fans of various genres. Gravy is an album that heavily features American composers and performers, giving it an authentic jazz-funk sound, but it also appeals to soul and pop enthusiasts. Songs like the eponymous Gravy have a retro vibe which harkens back to jazz's early days, while L.A. Night fits in well with City Pop's urban sound. You can get some disco action in with The Music (Is The Way I Live), while Meant To Be really gives Agawa's singing a chance to shine. The energy keeps up for the B-side with some of the album's more lighthearted tunes like Dance Mary Dance and Meant To Be before we close out on another moving performance in Who You Are.

- A1. Gravy
- A2. L.A. Night
- A3. The Music (Is The Way I Live)
- A4. Catch It 'Fore It Falls
- B1. Meant To Be
- B2. Red Lights
- B3. Dance Mary Dance
- B4. Who You Are

Magical

Artist: Junko Ohashi
Release: July 1, 1984
Label: Philips

Junko Ohashi's Magical is more so a compilation album featuring many of her best tracks, but there's a few previously unreleased songs here as well. Some of these were used for commercials like the introductory Isn't It Magic, which definitely has a 'cosmetic advertisement' sort of vibe, but is still a beautiful song regardless. Then there's A Love Affair which is pure Ohashi and Ken Sato magic, the exact kind of exciting track she's so well associated with, but the album is loaded with some of their most classic tracks. Iconic songs like Telephone Number, I Love You So and many more can be found here, making this a perfect starting point to get into Ohashi's music. The album's cover also serves as a haunting reminder of more innocent days, back when the Twin Towers in New York City were still standing.

- A1. Isn't It Magic
- A2. Perfume
- A3. A Love Affair
- A4. I Love You So
- A5. Lost Love
- A6. Tasogare
- B1. Telephone Number
- B2. Sherry
- B3. Another Day, Another Love
- B4. Dancin'
- B5. In Your Lovin'
- B6. Sugao No Mamade

Ocean Side

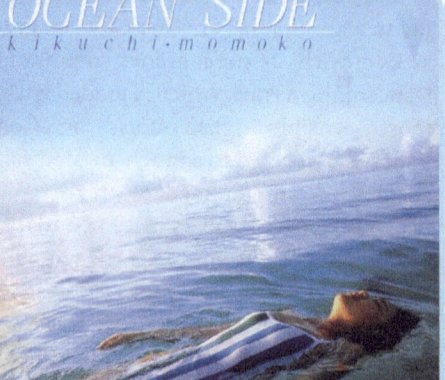

Left: The single release for Summer Eyes and Stardust Requiem. Some of Momoko Kikuchi's early singles featured a little peach can design somewhere, since Momoko is Japanese for "peach child." Center: The aquatic visuals of Ocean Side feel right at home with its City Pop fellows. Right: A nice underwater shot of some fishies to really complete the ocean aesthetic of the album.

Ocean Side is the debut album from Momoko Kikuchi, an incredibly gifted young idol with a City Pop flair. Kikuchi was scouted by a talent agent at only 15 years old but quickly established herself in the world of show business, starring in movies, appearing on magazine covers, and of course making music. However Kikuchi's music would differ greatly from other idols of the time, who usually went for a bubblier pop sound, since she got help from one of City Pop's very best. Tetsuji Hayashi was responsible for composing her first singles, and all of the tracks found in Ocean Side, which gives her songs that special Hayashi sound akin to his other ultra-successful work. Lyrical duty was then split between Junko Sato, Kumiko Aoki and Yasushi Akimoto, who went on to produce for AKB48, the second highest selling Japanese music group of all time. For good measure S. Kiyotaka & Omega Tribe were brought on as backing vocalists, completing one of the most stacked debut records in the genre's history. Those who are familiar with Hayashi's other productions know to expect another banger brimming with funk and soul, but Kikuchi's characteristic singing voice is the real star here. Her voice is soft and delicate, pairing perfectly with the extremely cool sounding music to create something unparalleled within City Pop. The titular Ocean Side is an awesome start to the album which gets stuck in your head due to the prominent bass throughout, and the voices from the all-male Omega Tribe provide a nice contrast to Kikuchi's feminine voice. Shadow Surfer is a fun track involving some unrequited attraction at the beach, but the album's most popular is Blind Curve, another romantic tune with a fantastically singable chorus. The funky instrumentals work especially well alongside Kikuchi's own performance here, showing how ordinarily opposing concepts of cute and cool can complement each other quite well. City Pop's unspoken summer quota is met with Summer Eyes, and Futari No Night Dive gives us a beautiful performance from Kikuchi with some especially moving lyrics. The B-side is then home to Evening Break, a track which explores another City Pop classic, driving around with a love interest. We then close out with So Many Dreams and I Will, with the latter being a lengthy seven-minute-long performance where you can enjoy more of Kikuchi's distinctive voice. Ocean Side wasn't just a success for the rising talent, it was a homerun, claiming the number one ranking and cementing Kikuchi's place in the music industry. Her career was only just beginning though, and her time in the spotlight was far from over.

Artist:
Momoko Kikuchi

Release:
September 10, 1984

Label:
Vap

Track List:

A1. Ocean Side

A2. Shadow Surfer

A3. Blind Curve

A4. Summer Eyes

A5. Futari No Night Dive

B1. Seishun no Ijiwaru

B2. Evening Break

B3. So Many Dreams

B4. I Will

Summer Time Romance～From KIKI

Artist: Toshiki Kadomatsu
Release: August 5, 1984
Label: Air Records

The first compilation album from Toshiki Kadomatsu put together hit songs from his first three records, now with a radio twist. The collection is presented by DJ Kamasami Kong, and KIKI is actually a real radio station from Hawaii which he was a host for. This isn't just a gimmick though, as the entire compilation is designed with this radio presentation in mind. Kong actually does a brief intro for each and every song, sometimes talking about who it's dedicated to or suggesting the listener call in and make a song request, making it feel very realistic. This eighties radio style pairs so perfectly with Kadomatsu's summer and resort themed music, and it's a great way to enjoy many of his early tracks. Kamasami Kong would later lend his fabulous voice to other similarly themed City Pop compilation albums, with some being as recent as 2023.

- A1. Off Shore
- A2. Summer Emotions
- A3. Office Lady
- A4. Ryoko!!
- A5. Window On The Shore (Beach's Widow)
- A6. It's Hard To Say Good-Bye
- A7. Prelude
- B1. Friday To Sunday
- B2. Step Into The Light
- B3. Do You Wanna Dance
- B4. Space Scraper
- B5. Take You To The Sky High
- B6. Let Me Say...

Chocolate Lips

Artist: Chocolate Lips
Release: November 21, 1984
Label: Carnival

Chocolate Lips is the sole album from the group of the same name, although their makeup was rather unconventional for a Japanese band. The members consisted of Miho Fujiwara, a vocalist who was also in the band Pazz, as well as James W. Norwood and Jimmie L. Weaver, two Black American artists. This team up gave rise to some fantastically funky music which incorporated many of the genres that made the 1980s so memorable, all while serving up healthy servings of soul, jazz and disco. Fujiwara's high-pitched voice is a surprisingly good match for this style of music and really adds to the unique charm of Chocolate Lips, who manage to keep the energy up for the album's whole runtime. James Norwood and Jimmie Weaver also give excellent performances on the bass and saxophone respectively, although they unfortunately don't seem to show up on another City Pop record.

- A1. Sexy Eyes
- A2. Day Dreamin'
- A3. Tell Me Why
- A4. Foolish Girl
- A5. Weekend Lover
- B1. Milk & Honey
- B2. Midnight Step
- B3. Feel So Good
- B4. In Time

Dream Hunter

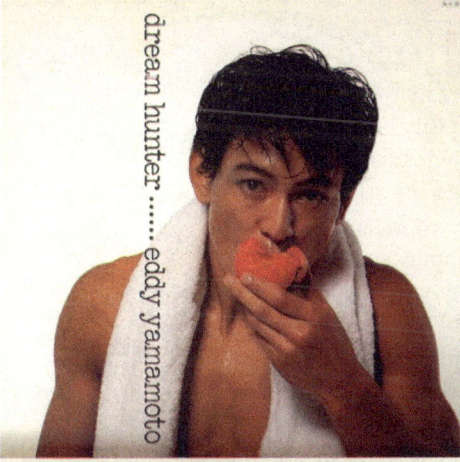

Artist: Eddy Yamamoto
Release: November 21, 1984
Label: CBS/Sony

Eddy Yamamoto's Dream Hunter is one of only two albums that he released during his short tenure in music, although he actually made his debut with some singles in 1980 and 1981. Dream Hunter itself is a fairly niche album which never even got a release on CD, but it is very prized among fans of the intersection between synth-pop and City Pop. The A-side is made up of compositions from Western artists, except for Masatoshi Nishimura who co-wrote Just You, but the big highlight here is a cover of Just The Way You Are by Billy Joel. Yamamoto puts an electronic and hypnotic spin on this seventies classic, but the preceding tracks are also great. Take It To The Top and Just You are both a ton of fun, and that energy definitely keeps up for the B-side with the funky sounds of Baby I'm In Love and Song For You.

- A1. Let Me In Your Life
- A2. Take It To The Top
- A3. Just You
- A4. Just The Way You Are
- B1. Baby I'm In Love
- B2. More And More
- B3. Making Love
- B4. Song For You
- B5. Dream Hunter

No Side

In Japan games of rugby are concluded by the referee shouting "no side," as in no side has currently the ball, which is where the album gets its name from. A2 is also centered around rugby as Matsutoya sings about a player's failure to secure a win, as well as her own attempts to understand the player's mindset. Then there's Downtown Boy which was made as something of a response to Billy Joel's song Uptown Girl. Uptown Girl describes an average guy's perspective on his attraction to a high-class woman, while Downtown Boy is the opposite, and it's cute listening to the songs one after the other. Another interesting tune is B1 which stars a woman trying to use magic to win back a former boyfriend, although unfortunately it seems rituals involving shredding his old shirts aren't working out for her.

Artist: Yumi Matsutoya
Release: December 1, 1984
Label: Express

A1. Salaam Mousson Salaam Afrique
A2. ノーサイド
A3. Downtown Boy
A4. Blizzard
A5. 一緒に暮らそう
B1. 破れた恋の繕し方教えます
B2. 午前4時の電話
B3. 木枯らしのダイアリー
B4. Shangrilaをめざせ
B5. ノーサイド・夏-空耳のホイッスル

Never Ending Summer

The tribe closed out 1984 with an album dedicated to City Pop's eternal love, the summer. Of course, you can also expect their exemplary mix of genres here with a strong emphasis on rock and soul. Never Ending Summer gets things going with Misty Night Cruising, a heart pumping tune about a romantic drive with some bass that really bumps. Eastern Railroad has funk and jazz to spare, while Twilight Bay City is a lighter pop song with lyrics fitting of the City Pop moniker. They weren't kidding when they advertised this summer as never ending, since the final four tracks all flow into each other, but each song gradually slows down the pace. While the first volume of this song is your usual pop rock Omega Tribe fare, the fourth is a sentimental ballad which ends the album strongly. A terrific end to their activities in 1984, although 1985 will prove to be this incarnation's last.

Artist: S. Kiyotaka & Omega Tribe
Release: December 21, 1984
Label: Vap

A1. Misty Night Cruising
A2. Eastern Railroad
A3. Twilight Bay City
A4. Riverside Hotel
A5. Stay The Night Forever
B1. Never Ending Summer I
B2. Never Ending Summer II
B3. Never Ending Summer III
B4. Never Ending Summer IV ~ Prolog

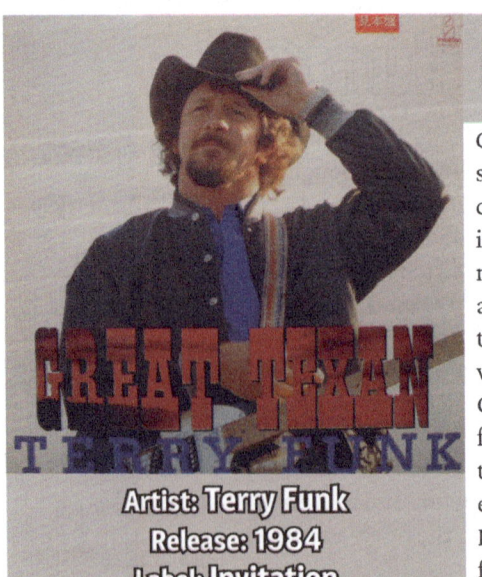

Great Texan

Great Texan is another really weird piece of City Pop history starring Terry Funk, a legendary American wrestler with a career that spanned decades. Despite being a wrestler based in the USA, Great Texan was only ever released in Japan and nearly everyone involved in the band was Japanese. The album is half funny little oddity starring a guy who can't sing that well, but it's also half weirdly good City Pop. The songs within are surprisingly catchy and varied, utilizing many of City Pop's biggest sources of inspiration including rock and funk, which is quite appropriate to the man's name. You get to enjoy memorable tracks like the opening Great Texan, an energetic pop introduction to Terry's grandeur, the hilarious Barbra Streisand's Nose, and many more. Terry Funk did unfortunately pass away in 2023 at 79 years old, but his career in wrestling (and City Pop) is historic.

Artist: Terry Funk
Release: 1984
Label: Invitation

A1. Great Texan
A2. Touch Your Heart
A3. We Like To Rock
A4. Change Your Mind
B1. Barbra Streisand's Nose
B2. Roppongi
B3. We Hate School
B4. Great Texan (Theme From Terry Funk)

1985, The Magical Midway

It has now been about ten years since City Pop materialized, and in that time we've met some extraordinarily talented artists and got to experience some of the absolute best of the genre. 1985 isn't quite as stacked as some of the previous years, but there's still tons of amazing music and interesting developments to explore. Junko Yagami stunned Japan with Communication, her most 'City Pop-like' album yet with a heavy emphasis on disco and synth-pop. Synth-pop was seemingly the talk of the town this year, as seen with artists like Anri and Taeko Ohnuki incorporating electronic music into their albums Wave and Copine respectively. Toshiki Kadomatsu continued his exploration of urban nightlife through Gold Digger ~With True Love~, an album which was even more intense than After 5 Clash from last year. While the big stars were hard at work a couple of hidden gems also appeared, like Aru Takamura whose deep voice gave her a unique selling point. Kyosuke Kusunoki gave us the very underrated record Just Tonight, while Michiru Kojima also made a strong first impression with Best Friend. 1985 was sadly also a year of farewells for some artists. Rajie, who had been involved with City Pop since nearly the beginning, left us with her final album Espresso this year, as did the band Piper who departed with Lovers Logic. However, the biggest surprise by far was the breakup of S. Kiyotaka & Omega Tribe, who were at the height of their popularity. The band gave us two more wonderful albums before lead singer Kiyotaka Sugiyama decided to go solo, leaving the group's future in a precarious state.

Momoko Kikuchi

Top: Momoko Kikuchi as she appeared back in the 1980s when she was one of Japan's most popular idols.
Bottom: A more recent picture of Kikuchi, another City Pop artist who seemingly never aged.

Momoko Kikuchi is an unconventional figure in the history of City Pop whose fame extended beyond her music and reached other forms of entertainment such as movies and television, all while being one of Japan's most popular idols in the mid-1980s. Kikuchi was scouted by a talent agency at a young age and quickly found success by starring in commercials, landing a leading role in the film Hole In You Pants and even being featured on the cover of the magazine Momoco, which was named after her. Then in 1984 Kikuchi made her debut as a singer with three singles and the album Ocean Side, all of which were composed by Tetsuji Hayashi, the man responsible for several of City Pop's most renowned tunes. Hayashi's exciting and funky compositions combined with Kikuchi's incredibly soft voice to form a dream which offered something totally different from the music of other idols. Ocean Side ranked number one on Japan's weekly Oricon charts, but the real measure of her fame was in 1985 when she became the youngest artist to ever perform in Tokyo's Budokan arena and even drew a bigger crowd than The Beatles. Kikuchi's popularity stayed strong as she continued her idol activities and released iconic records like Adventure, but she naturally sought a change after so many years in entertainment. In an effort to shed her innocent image she formed the band RA MU, a somewhat experimental group which unfortunately did not garner a major audience. Following this Kikuchi released the solo album Miroir in 1991 and mostly stuck to acting afterwards, but she has lived quite the fulfilling life since. Kikuchi has had two children, acquired a Master's degree, worked as an activist for kids with disabilities and even participated in the torch relay for the 2020 Tokyo Olympics. Forty years later her beautifully soft singing voice and brilliantly written tunes still hit just right and have now lured in fans from multiple generations.

City Pop's Unsung Heroes

As discussed previously City Pop is a unique genre in terms of how intricately connected many of its stars were, so much so that you could almost think of them as being part of a musical family. While this phenomenon is most evident with the style's big stars, like Tatsuro Yamashita and Mariya Takeuchi, there's also a substantial number of musicians who were more quietly shaping City Pop through their myriad appearances on albums. Many of these less celebrated artists were involved since the genre's inception, such as Ken Sato, who is perhaps most well known for being Junko Ohashi's husband and main composer. Sato was among the first to really nail down the magic formula for what City Pop was going to sound like, doing so way before almost anybody else caught on. In the 1980s his clientele included some goliaths such as Anri, but his most illustrious creation is Junko Ohashi's track Telephone Number, a treasure of a song which is among City Pop's most well-known. Telephone Number is actually the musical half-sibling of Miki Matsubara's genre-defining song Stay With Me, as both tracks feature lyrics by Yoshiko Miura, a brilliant lyricist who can be spotted on an extensive list of albums for idols and City Pop artists. Miura's lyrics often explored some of City Pop's most enduring subjects like the complications of romance in the modern age, themes which feel just as applicable nowadays as they were back in the 1980s. When recording time came along there was usually a shortlist of extremely talented specialists to call up, and if you needed some saxophone action then Jake H. Concepcion was the guy for the job. His countless appearances earned him the title "King of Sax", and when you listen to his performances it becomes clear why he earned that crown. Jake shows up on an almost unbelievable number of albums, including some of the all-time best like Timely!! and Adventure. If you can think of a good City Pop album there's a high chance Jake showed up on it, but a few other instruments had dedicated 'go-to' guys. Trombonist Eiji Arai was there from day one playing on foundational records like Caramel Mama and Cobalt Hour, and if you needed a bassist then Tsugutoshi Goto was your man, but he could also compose and arrange a few tracks while he was at it. City Pop also had a number of iconic guitarists including Masaki Matsubara, Yuji Toriyama, and Chuei Yoshikawa. Matsubara was a highly accomplished musician who rocked out on many albums, but he also released several of his own like Painted Woman in 1983, whereas Yoshikawa was more known for his excellent acoustic guitar playing. Then there were percussionists Motoya Hamaguchi, Nobu Saito and Pecker (whose real name is Hashida Masahito, and yes Pecker is a funny moniker), a trio of industry veterans who added serious depth to any project they were involved in. Coincidentally two of the genre's most prestigious keyboardists both had Sato as their last name, Jun Sato and Hiroshi Sato, although they're not related (Sato is just a common last name in Japan). Both men were highly valued for their own specific talents, with Jun Sato being a very skilled arranger, while Hiroshi Sato was a major innovator for electronic sound in City Pop who released beloved records such as Awakening. City Pop has an unending list of consistent performers, songwriters and arrangers who put in countless hours of work to make the genre what it was, not to mention all the behind-the-scenes people like the studio engineers and producers who also deserve credit. Sadly, many of the musicians mentioned here have passed away, but their innumerable contributions to Japanese music and City Pop's history are eternal.

Top: Yoshiko Miura is a lyricist who did a lot for City Pop and contributed to some of the style's most renowned tunes, but even many diehard fans of the genre haven't seen a picture of her before. It's always nice being able to put a face to a name, especially for somebody as impactful as Miura.
Center: Masaki Matsubara was one of City Pop's guitar playing greats, but the genre was quite blessed with an elite array of guitarists to select from like Shigeru Suzuki and Makoto Matsushita.
Bottom: Motoya Hamaguchi (right) alongside Minako Yoshida, two of City Pop's founding artists. The close ties all of these artists have is one of City Pop's strongest selling points, and you can really tell how much they all enjoyed working together.

Communication

Artist: Junko Yagami
Release: February 10, 1985
Label: Moon Records

Junko Yagami's Communication launched over a year after her last album Full Moon, partially due to her record label Discomate dissolving. Luckily, she was picked up by Moon Records, the same label Tatsuro Yamashita belonged to, since Communication is certainly a candidate for the best City Pop album of the year. All of the genres that influenced Full Moon are cranked up while Yagami introduces even more boogie and synth-pop to give Communication an inimitably eighties sound. Tracks such as Imagination and the titular Communication give us the fun vibe City Pop is known for, then A4 is a nostalgic romp with some of Yagami's best vocal work (and the track's excitement for the year 2000 make it feel very retro, in a good way). Communication is a meticulously crafted album from Yagami that reflects City Pop at its creative zenith, and it's one of her most celebrated works.

A1. Imagination
A2. チーター
A3. Communication
A4. 1984 (西暦2000年に向けて)
A5. Miss D.J.
B1. カシミヤのほほえみ
B2. ジョハナスバーグ
B3. どんな手段使っても
B4. Believing
B5. Reaching Out

Bitter And Sweet

Artist: Akina Nakamori
Release: April 3, 1985
Label: Reprise Records

Akina Nakamori's Bitter And Sweet brought in a new cast of City Pop composers and arrangers to fill out its track list, although the star of the show this time around was Toshiki Kadomatsu who worked as an advisor on the project and wrote a handful of songs. You can also hear tracks from EPO and Minako Yoshida, but the arrangement and lyrical credits are also full of familiar names. Bitter And Sweet is a quite varied album which rarely sticks to one particular style or mood for long as you'll be bouncing from the high-energy EPO track A2 to the moody A3 and then you're at a synth-pop symphony in A4. Toshiki Kadomatsu's two songs Unsteady Love and So Long take advantage of his talent with fun pop songs and cool romantic tunes, while Minako Yoshida's April Stars gives the album a fitting finale.

A1. 飾りじゃないのよ涙は
A2. ロマンティックな夜だわ
A3. 予感
A4. 月夜のヴィーナス
A5. Babylon
B1. Unsteady Love
B2. Dreaming
B3. 恋人のいる時間
B4. So Long
B5. April Stars

Aru First

Artist: Aru Takamura
Release: May 21, 1985
Label: Invitation

Aru First is in fact the first album by Aru Takamura, an artist who had a short career with two records coming out between 1985 and 1986. Takamura immediately makes an impression with her deep and powerful voice that's quite unlike other female City Pop artists, instead being more reminiscent of some Western vocalists. All of the accompanying songs are unmistakably City Pop though, and they're also quite varied thanks to the substantial number of composers brought on, including Tatsuro Yamashita for A1 and Kazuhito Murata for A5 and B2. With such a moving voice you'd expect the album to mostly consist of slower ballads, but Aru First is instead filled with fun dance worthy delights to revitalize your spirit. The album is one of 1985's greatest hidden gems with a spectacular vocalist and many memorable tracks to love.

A1. Last Step
A2. 恋は最高 (I'm In Love)
A3. 恋のやりとり
A4. ハートブレイク・サマービーチ
A5. パーティーが終った後で
B1. 今夜だけワンス・アゲイン
B2. ブレーキを踏んで怒って
B3. Let's Your Love Grow (ほどけたハート)
B4. Say That You Love Me
B5. 恋はデリケート

Gold Digger ~With True Love~

Gold Digger ~With True Love~ continued Kadomatsu's exploration of an urban-centric sound, as well as the themes you'd associate with a lifestyle full of partying and romance. The album's lyrics are also a bit more overtly sexual compared to After 5 Clash's, with tracks like A3 and A4 getting especially raunchy, and even the cover suggests a late-night fling gone awry. This emphasis on an adult tone further carried over into the music itself which was designed with dancing in mind. Kadomatsu along with co-producer Michael H. Brauer were able to create an authentic American disco vibe here, further complemented by integrating even more synth-pop. The album succeeds at encapsulating a certain image of Tokyo's nightlife in the 1980s, one where you could dance, drink and date in excess, a cool idea regardless of how realistic that actually was.

Artist: Toshiki Kadomatsu
Release: May 21, 1985
Label: Air Records

A1. I Can't Stop The Night
A2. Springin' Night
A3. Move Your Hips All Night Long
A4. Secret Lover
A5. Melody For You
B1. Tokyo Tower
B2. Prajñā (Violence In The Subway)
B3. Mermaid Princess
B4. It's Too Late
B5. No End Summer

This Boy

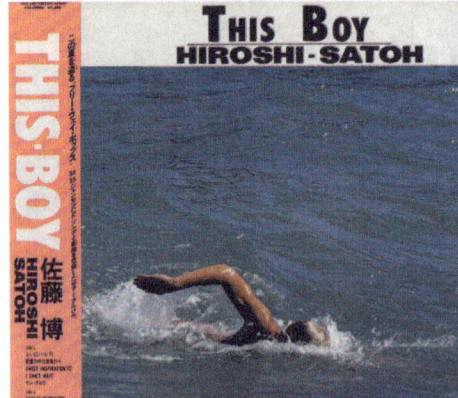

Which boy? This Boy! Hiroshi Sato's latest is mostly a compilation album consisting of songs from Awakening and Sailing Blaster, but there's also a few remixes and tracks previously released as singles. Some of the original songs here include the pop rock inspired A2 and the captivating electronic realm of B3, then there's B6 which serves as a memorable finale. The other songs included in this compilation were great choices, especially I Can't Wait which returns from Awakening and Love Is Happening from Sailing Blaster. Throughout This Boy you'll get to hear Sato's mastery over electronic music, but the styles utilized here are incredibly varied. It all comes together and makes This Boy a great first album for prospective fans of Sato's music, but it's also a perfect sampler for the electronic focused side of City Pop.

Artist: Hiroshi Sato
Release: May 25, 1985
Label: Alfa

A1. Shiny Lady
A2. Kioku No Naka No Mirai Kara
A3. Sweet Inspiration '85
A4. I Can't Wait
A5. Sun Glow
B1. Love Is Happening
B2. Always
B3. Gemini
B4. Say Goodbye
B5. Angelina
B6. This Boy

Just Tonight

1985 unsurprisingly had a handful of 'one album wonders', like Kyosuke Kusunoki with Just Tonight, but he was also previously a member of the bands Camel Land and The Wood. Kusunoki's music is a very nice addition to the adult-oriented rock side of City Pop and comes easily recommended to fans of artists such as Makoto Matsushita, or those who are down with that particular brand of coolness only this genre can provide. Soul and disco are at the forefront here with songs that are both grooving and moving such as Sugar Dance and For Our Love, and roughly half of the tracks are sung in English while the others are in Japanese, an impressive showing of Kusunoki's singing chops. The paper trail on Kusunoki's activities does go somewhat cold beyond this release, but it is a greatly appreciated and underrated addition to the City Pop legacy.

Artist: Kyosuke Kusunoki
Release: June 5, 1985
Label: King Records

A1. Sugar Dance
A2. Get Down
A3. For Our Love
A4. Just Tonight
B1. 渚にて～Close To You
B2. Love Devotion
B3. Come To Me Again
B4. 夜を忘れて
B5. 地図なき未来 (ゆくて)

Copine.

Although Taeko Ohnuki was past her European trilogy of albums those global influences hadn't gone far, as evidenced by 1985's Copine. Some of these worldly traits include the album's name which comes from a French word for 'friend', and the opening track Les Aventures De Tintin gets its title from the Belgian comic The Adventures of Tintin. Then there's track A2 which was made with a heavy Italian inspiration, and most of the album was recorded in New York City. Copine seems to have taken a little bit from every corner of the Earth, which is well reflected in the album's diverse songs. Ohnuki continues to deliver more quality synth-pop tracks here, especially with A1 which seamlessly blends electronic and rock, but there's also some more classic feeling songs here like A3 which has some beautiful singing, and B3 which emphasizes jazz.

Artist: Taeko Ohnuki
Release: June 21, 1985
Label: Dear Heart

A1. Les Aventures De Tintin
A2. ベジタブル
A3. 春の嵐
A4. Siena
A5. Amico, Sei Felice?
B1. Out Of Africa
B2. Leave Me Alone
B3. Jaques-Henri Lartigue
B4. しあわせな男達へ
B5. 野辺

Espresso

Rajie released her final album Espresso this year, closing out her journey as one of synth-pop and City Pop's earliest pioneers. Espresso serves as a fitting finale which really does feel like the culmination of a whole career, and it may also be Rajie's most experimental yet. Every song here was written by a different composer and often a different lyricist which makes Espresso highly varied. There are quite a few songs that feel like classic Rajie with a nice mix of pop and electronic, including A1, A2 and B3, but most of the album consists of creative tracks that feel more akin to New Wave. Following this Rajie would rarely appear as a backing vocalist but didn't cross paths with her fellow City Pop artists much. Rajie has a special place in the history of the genre with seven great albums to try, especially for fans of synth-pop and electronic music.

Artist: Rajie
Release: June 21, 1985
Label: Eastworld

A1. Kanashimi No Elephant
A2. Mangekyo
A3. Espresso
A4. Mizu No Kioku
B1. Magic Flower
B2. Misshitsu
B3. Yumeiro Densetsu
B4. Hikari To Kage
B5. Gozen Goji No Mermaid

Wave

Anri's Wave may seem like just the latest in her summer themed discography, but it manages to carve out a distinctive identity for itself. Wave is an album that's noticeably heavier on the synth-pop sound, and many of its tracks feel more experimental in nature while still being recognizable as City Pop. The album makes a strong impression from its first track with the bonkers City Fiction, a track filled with distorted voices, killer guitar, and crazy English lyrics. The fast-paced fun continues with A2 and the incredibly cool songs Into The Body and Take It, while Lover's Night is an adorably romantic tune. You can really light up the disco floor with 16 Beat and B5, and the album closes out on a high note with Oversea Call. Wave is another excellent addition to Anri's catalogue with quite a few creative twists along the way.

Artist: Anri
Release: June 21, 1985
Label: For Life Records

A1. City Fiction
A2. 夜明けのSoldier
A3. Into The Body
A4. Long Island Beach
A5. Wave
B1. Take it
B2. Lover's Night
B3. 16 Beat
B4. Oversea Call
B5. 瞳は永遠の香り

Another Summer

Artist: S. Kiyotaka & Omega Tribe
Release: July 1, 1985
Label: Vap

The summer of 1985 is here, and fittingly so are the members of Omega Tribe with Another Summer. Not much has changed for the band stylistically, so anybody who has enjoyed their past work knows what to expect here, but it does contain some of their biggest hits. Dear Breeze is a definitive Omega Tribe track with an opening and lyrics that illicit nostalgia, but A3 reigns as their most popular song of all time. Ironically, the track was something of a rush job that Tetsuji Hayashi and lyricist Chinfa Kang wrote in just two days to fulfill a deadline for a TV commercial. The band was then recalled from touring to record the track, who took another day to complete it. The final result was one of City Pop's poster children, a classic ode to both summer and romance which showed that sometimes perfection actually can be rushed.

- A1. Route 134
- A2. Dear Breeze
- A3. Futari No Natsu Monogatari ~Never Ending Summer~
- A4. Toi Hitomi
- B1. Scramble Cross
- B2. Mayonaka No Screen Board
- B3. Ai No Shinkiro
- B4. You're A Lady, I'm A Man
- B5. The End Of The River

Twilight Made...

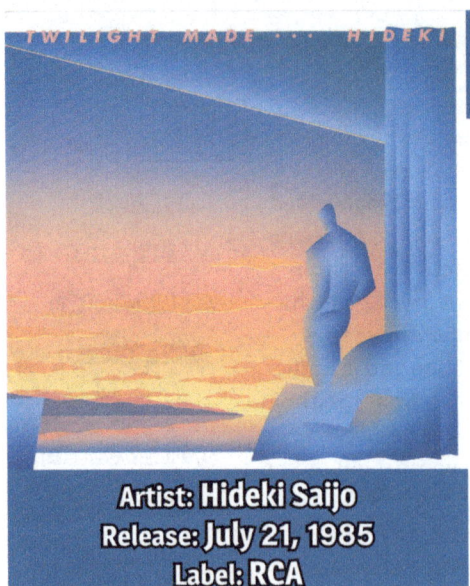

Artist: Hideki Saijo
Release: July 21, 1985
Label: RCA

Hideki Saijo doubled down on City Pop with Twilight Made, an album created with even more of the genre's stars. Toshiki Kadomatsu returned from Gentle A Man to compose around half of the album's tracks, and this time Fujimaru Yoshino was brought on to make a few songs. We also get to hear Minako Yoshida's lyrics alongside Kadomatsu's compositions, a real City Pop dream combo which hadn't happened until now, and Yoshida also provides backing vocals on some tracks. Another old school City Pop artist here is Akira Okamoto, who previously went by Issei Okamoto, and he composed the slower paced B1 and B5. With such a talented team behind it Twilight Made turned out excellently, and there's something here for everybody, especially if you're into Kadomatsu's energetic approach topped off with some smooth and moving tunes.

- A1. Sweet Surrender
- A2. Beat Street
- A3. Halation
- A4. ワインカラーの衝撃
- A5. Platinumの雨
- B1. リアル・タイム
- B2. オリーブのウェンズディ
- B3. Beautiful Rhapsody
- B4. Television
- B5. レイク・サイド

Best Friend

Artist: Michiru Kojima
Release: September 5, 1985
Label: For Life Records

Michiru Kojima's debut album may seem like just another addition to the constantly expanding City Pop genre, but it was made with two of the industry's finest. Best Friend was entirely composed by Tetsuji Hayashi, who gave it that inimitable pop sound, while the illustrious Takashi Matsumoto did the lyrics. Thanks to this prominent duo the album has all the attributes of eighties City Pop, including its usage of genres like soul and jazz, while Matsumoto has us covered with classic topics such as romance blooming in the summer. The artist herself deserves praise as well since her singing works perfectly with these tracks and evokes the youthful energy City Pop is known for. Kojima continued to make music until 1992, after which she pursued a career in acting, but she has since returned with the album Sing For You in 2021.

- A1. オーシャン・ブルー
- A2. 学園祭
- A3. 週末のイエスタディ
- A4. Best Friend
- A5. 蜃気楼
- B1. セプテンバー物語
- B2. プリテンド
- B3. テレフォン
- B4. 逢えるかもしれない

Tropic of Capricorn

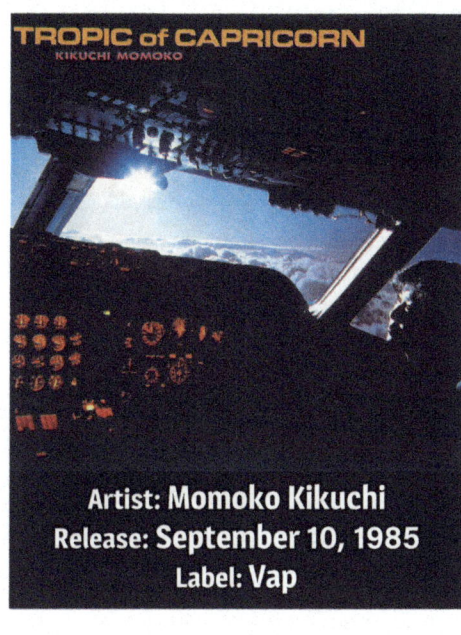

Artist: Momoko Kikuchi
Release: September 10, 1985
Label: Vap

Momoko Kikuchi followed up on the massive success of Ocean Side with Tropic of Capricorn, although not much changed for this release. Tetsuji Hayashi once again composed every song, so the same brilliant songwriting from Ocean Side is still present here, although the members of Omega Tribe sadly didn't return, likely since they were a few months away from disbanding. You can enjoy the combination of Kikuchi's unique voice with Hayashi's genre defining music, making it an easy recommendation for fans of Ocean Side. The album is a wonderful time from start to finish, but its most noteworthy track is definitely Graduation, a beautifully nostalgic tune which managed to become a number one charting hit for Kikuchi. Tropic of Capricorn just barely missed the number one spot, instead reaching a second-place peak, which is still pretty good.

- A1. Graduation
- A2. Calendar Ni Initial
- A3. Koi No Projection
- A4. Manatsu No Sequence
- A5. Dear Children
- B1. Boy Friend
- B2. Southern Cross Dreaming
- B3. Alfa Flight
- B4. Ai No Surf Break
- B5. Minami Kaikisen

Door of The Heart

Artist: Maiko Okamoto
Release: October 21, 1985
Label: Victor

Maiko Okamoto is an artist who had a brief career in music and only released two albums, but both were very high-quality works made with contributions from City Pop bigshots. Door of The Heart was exclusively written by Etsuko Yamakawa, a musician who can frequently be heard on the chorus for many City Pop albums, but she also occasionally arranges and composes music. Most of the album's lyrics were then done by Yu Aku, one of Japan's most prolific lyricists with hundreds of songs to his name. The beautiful but melancholic opening in A1 might lead you to believe it's a downer of an album, but Yamakawa instead gave Door of The Heart a bright and cheerful sound, even when the tracks do delve into more solemn subject matter. It's very recommended for those looking for something on the lighter side as Okamoto's adorable singing is sure to brighten your day.

- A1. ハートの扉
- A2. 桜吹雪クライマックス
- A3. ロマンスしたい
- A4. Love Is Easy
- A5. 愛って林檎ですか
- B1. 恋にエトセトラ
- B2. ファンレター
- B3. もしもし
- B4. Snow Bird
- B5. ロマンチックがもの足りない

Purple Rose

Artist: Mariko Tone
Release: October 25, 1985
Label: Bourbon Records

Purple Rose is the second album by Mariko Tone, an artist who appealed to the always popular intersection between Synth-pop and City Pop. Tone was well equipped for this venture though, as you can enjoy performances from musicians like Fujimaru Yoshino and Masataka Matsutoya here. The album starts with a fun dance track in Broken Eyes, a song which Tone said is a real stress reliever. Talk To Me is ironically on the other end of the extreme as the English lyrics and album's tight production schedule made her cry the night before recording it. The slower pace of A5 was initially somewhat uncomfortable for Tone, who was used to fast-paced tunes, but eventually she found the change of pace quite relaxing. A similar moment of growth happened with It's A Lonely Love, the first song Tone wrote lyrics for which totally uprooted her doubts about her skills as a lyricist.

- A1. Broken Eyes
- A2. Talk To Me
- A3. Wishes
- A4. 少しだけ…
- A5. カレンダー
- B1. 海が見たい
- B2. It's A Lonely Love
- B3. 都会のゆううつ
- B4. 摩天楼物語
- B5. You

Lovers Logic

Artist: Piper
Release: October 25, 1985
Label: Moon Records

Piper released their final original album Lovers Logic in 1985, although this one didn't focus on the summer in the same way their previous work did. Lovers Logic is instead a diverse production which really exemplifies Piper's ability to mix styles and use sound in interesting ways, which is fitting considering that was one of their main draws. The band and most of its members ceased their activities after the release of Lovers Logic, although you can catch vocalist Keisuke Yamamoto on a few projects. Piper would finally reunite for a live show in 2001, but their true renaissance came in the 2010s. The renewed interest in City Pop during that decade brought a lot of attention to Piper, leading to many of their albums being put on CD and available digitally for the first time. The band has since kept up their activities with frequent live shows.

A1. Starlight Ballet
A2. I Love You
A3. Trade Wind
A4. New York-Review
A5. Keep On Loving You
B1. ACT-III
B2. Please Please
B3. Photograph
B4. Go Back
B5. Daylight Blue

Da・Di・Da

Artist: Yumi Matsutoya
Release: November 30, 1985
Label: Express

Yumi Matustoya's albums are typically named after a particular song housed within, while some titles have a deeper meaning which isn't immediately obvious. Da・Di・Da's name comes from neither of these and is instead just based on a funny sound Matsutoya made one time. Otherwise Da・Di・Da is another album from Matsutoya which very much falls within her wheelhouse, as in there's many songs about romance, breakups, and the wintertime. The album takes off with the surprisingly rock heavy A1, a song about the pain associated with the end of a relationship, while A2 is a more comedic song with a romantic Christmas theming. Another track which feels very appropriate to call City Pop is Babylon, which has Matsutoya beautifully comparing the modern day city to the titular ancient civilization.

A1. もう愛は始まらない
A2. 人のストリート
A3. Babylon
A4. Sugar Town はさよならの町
B1. メトロポリスの片隅で
B2. 月夜のロケット花火
B3. シンデレラ・エクスプレス
B4. 青春のリグレット
B5. たとえあなたが去って行っても

First Finale

Artist: S. Kiyotaka & Omega Tribe
Release: December 11, 1985
Label: Vap

First Finale is the very appropriately named last studio album from this incarnation of Omega Tribe, since just two weeks after this record was released Kiyotaka Sugiyama left the band. This was the end result of creative disagreements which had been brewing between the production crew and bandmates all year, but Tetsuji Hayashi managed to convince them to make one last album for their fans. First Finale is a fitting goodbye for one of City Pop's most legendary bands with some excellent songs, and it closes out this chapter of their history on a high note. The album reached number 1 on the charts and ended up being Japan's 9th bestselling album of the year. Following this Kiyotaka Sugiyama, Tetsuji Hayashi and the remaining band members all went their separate ways and pursued their own projects, including the next incarnation of Omega Tribe.

A1. Garasu No Palm Tree
A2. Yunagi Tsushin
A3. November Blue
A4. Remember The Brightness
A5. Kiri No Down Town
B1. Platonic Dancer
B2. Nidome No Eve
B3. Kimi Wa In The Rain
B4. First Finale

1986, End Of The Golden Age

The 1980s were now halfway over, and while City Pop was still maintaining its presence as one of Japan's most popular genres the winds of change were blowing. The music world was rapidly shifting away from the long-established method of recording on analog tapes and towards the digital future, a development which some artists really struggled with. Tatsuro Yamashita found this transition especially challenging due to his familiarity with analog recording, leading to a lengthy and frustrating production process for his next record, Pocket Music. Meanwhile, one of City Pop's biggest bands had finalized their divorce after Omega Tribe's lead singer Kiyotaka Sugiyama split to pursue a solo career. Luckily for Omega Tribe's fans catastrophe was avoided when they found a new vocalist in Carlos Toshiki and then regrouped as 1986 Omega Tribe. Anri then continued her own artistic journey and released two albums, Trouble In Paradise and Mystique, both of which were fairly different from her classic albums like Timely!! Momoko Kikuchi's collaborations with Tetsuji Hayashi continued to impress as she released Adventure, one of City Pop's most cherished albums and a go-to example of what the genre is all about. The year was also blessed with some stellar debuts, such as Kaoru Akimoto who debuted with Cologne, another incredibly beloved album which included the iconic City Pop track Dress Down. 1986 is another fantastic year for the genre, although it can also be considered the end of the 'golden age' of City Pop as the number of relevant debuts and releases of acclaimed albums does begin slowing down.

Omega Tribe

Top: The members of S. Kiyotaka & Omega Tribe, with Kiyotaka Sugiyama on the far left. Bottom: The band's incarnation as 1986 Omega Tribe, now starring Carlos Toshiki (second from the right) as their lead singer.

Omega Tribe is one of City Pop's most iconic bands, but also one of its most complicated, as their roster and even name never stayed settled for very long. The band's original form manifested in 1983 with S. Kiyotaka & Omega Tribe, a group led by vocalist Kiyotaka Sugiyama and produced by Koichi Fujita, with compositions from Tetsuji Hayashi. Their debut album Aqua City perfectly captured the traits City Pop was so associated with, such as urban or aquatic theming and mixing of genres like pop, rock and electronic. Omega Tribe topped the charts and became one of Japan's most popular acts, but after releasing several popular albums Sugiyama left the band at the height of their fame. Rather than disband entirely the remaining members of Omega Tribe and producer Fujita carried on as 1986 Omega Tribe, now with newcomer Carlos Toshiki as their vocalist. Despite the shakeup Omega Tribe remained popular with songs like You Are 1000% and Super Chance being huge hits, although after just two years the group morphed again into Carlos Toshiki & Omega Tribe when bandmate Mitsuya Kurokawa departed. History repeated itself in 1991 when Carlos Toshiki left to go solo, although future attempts to keep Omega Tribe going were comparatively more awkward. By the 1990s the City Pop sound they were so associated with was considered old news and the sales of their records dipped. The group DOME featured some of the original band members, but they only released one album, whereas their spiritual successor band Weather Side fared somewhat better with three albums. In the 21st century the renewed interest in City Pop has reignited the love for Omega Tribe's amazing music, which has a sort of unified appeal despite the band's many forms. Since then, lead singers Kiyotaka Sugiyama and Carlos Toshiki have even performed with their old bandmates live once again, truly bringing this epic tale full circle.

Ta Ta Ya My Love ~ARU 2nd.~

Artist: Aru Takamura
Release: January 21, 1986
Label: Invitation

Aru Takamura's second and last album gives us some more chances to enjoy her uniquely beautiful singing, but it also shakes things up by integrating more synth-pop. Many of the tracks here were composed by Masatoshi Nishimura, the man responsible for writing most of Tomoko Aran's synth-pop masterpiece Fuyü-Kükan, so fans of that album are sure to enjoy this one. Throughout this final journey with Takamura, you'll hear funky tunes akin to the tracks from her first album, albeit now with some electronic spin, as well as the classic slower jazzy songs like A2 and B2. B3 and B5 are some of the best examples of Takamura's deep voice being put to great use, and it's a shame we didn't get to hear more of it. Takamura unfortunately passed in 2014 due to cervical cancer, but she left us with two amazing albums to love and appreciate.

- A1. I'm In Love
- A2. 最後のTenderness
- A3. 皆既月食
- A4. Beat Goes On
- B1. Ta Ta Ya My Love
- B2. Appeal To You
- B3. Inside
- B4. ½ × Love
- B5. Good Luck Again

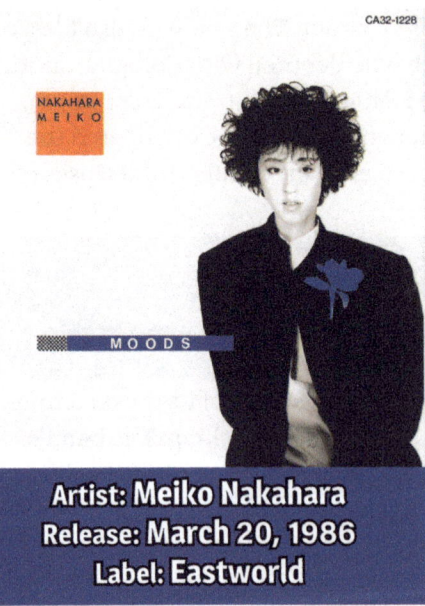

Moods

Artist: Meiko Nakahara
Release: March 20, 1986
Label: Eastworld

Meiko Nakahara's latest album Moods has a wealth of new tracks for you to experience, all of which have a fresh flavor. The enticing sounds of Gimme, Gimme Motions set the stage before the atmospheric A2 and So Shine wow you with their instrumentals. Moods was a very well-chosen name for this album considering how moving its tracks are, like We Were In L.A. which rounds out the A-side, and Lonely Woman, which has an excellent vocal performance from Nakahara. You can also hear one of her most popular songs here in Russian Roulette, a very catchy tune which was also used as opening song for the sci-fi anime series Dirty Pair. Luckily for fans of Nakahara's earlier albums we do get another Latin-inspired jam to end things on with Salsa In N.Y, a memorable ode to city life with an elegant ending.

- A1. Gimme, Gimme Motions
- A2. Bird Of Paradise = 極楽鳥のテーマ
- A3. So Shine
- A4. We Were In L.A.
- B1. Number 1
- B2. Broken Piano = こわれたピアノ
- B3. Lonely Woman
- B4. Russian Roulette (LP Version) = ロ・ロ・ロ・ロシアン・ルーレット
- B5. Salsa In N.Y. = New Yorkでサルサ

Cologne

Artist: Kaoru Akimoto
Release: March 21, 1986
Label: Invitation

Cologne may be Kaoru Akimoto's only solo album, but that's probably fine since she achieved perfection on the first try. The album is a masterpiece that wonderfully represents City Pop as a genre in its prime, especially with its ultra popular track Dress Down. The song has become one of City Pop's representative tunes due to its recognizable opening, funky instrumentals and Akimoto's cool delivery which warps you to a night in eighties Tokyo. Cologne is no one trick pony though; it's packed with memorable songs including the lively A2 which flows directly into Dress Down, the moving B3, and B2, a fun song which is another of the album's best. Akimoto's involvement in City Pop was somewhat limited past Cologne's release, but she does later appear as a vocalist in the band Shambara alongside Yurie Kokubu.

- A1. Beginning
- A2. ナルシスト
- A3. Dress Down
- A4. Two Call
- A5. 夜が終わる時
- B1. 嘆きのPuzzle
- B2. 我がままなハイヒール
- B3. 今日はひとりきり
- B4. Love Letter
- B5. 月夜

Pocket Music

Left: A depiction of Yamashita by Kyozo Hayashi, whose clay artwork gave Pocket Music an unconventional look.
Center: Pocket Music's cover is colorful and cute while also being totally different from any of Yamashita's past albums.
Right: The various shades of blue for the albums imagery is another example of City Pop's love for the color.

Artist:
Tatsuro Yamashita

Release:
April 23, 1986

Label:
Moon Records

Track List:

A1. 土曜日の恋人 (Saturday Lover)

A2. ポケット・ミュージック (Pocket Music)

A3. Mermaid

A4. 十字路 (Crossroads)

A5. メロディ、君の為に (Melody For You)

B1. The War Song

B2. シャンプー (Shampoo)

B3. どんな手段使っても (By Whatever Means Necessary)

B4. Lady Blue

B5. 風の回廊 (コリドー) (Wind Corridor)

The music industry was rapidly evolving in the 1980s, especially when it came to advancements in recording technology. Artists and studios were gradually moving away from recording on analog tapes and instead switching to digital equipment, a change which often affected the music itself. The audio compression from analog recordings gave the music a more natural and full sound compared to the digital method, which was still undergoing some growing pains, and sometimes felt sterile or even harsh on the ears. This wasn't much of an issue for artists that were heavily using synthesizers or other electronic methods to make their music, but Tatsuro Yamashita faced some problems. The "gutsy" natural sound Yamashita spent his career perfecting was difficult to achieve on digital recordings and those analog methods he was comfortable with were quickly getting phased out. Yamashita even considered trying to stockpile as much analog equipment as possible, but this was a losing battle against time. Yamashita ultimately decided to buckle down and embrace the future by recording Pocket Music digitally, although this production would be one of his most challenging yet. The album was originally intended for a 1985 release but was pushed back due to a combination of dissatisfaction with the music's quality, technological hurdles and busy schedules. The computers and other devices used were a massive time sink that constantly needed to be replaced or upgraded and forced the production to undergo three major equipment overhauls. Even the human element was rather unreliable, as many of the artists Yamashita recorded with were becoming quite popular themselves and weren't as readily available for sessions, thus Yamashita had to fill in the gaps with his own instrumental performances. Pocket Music did finally release in April of 1986, but Yamashita referred to it as a "prototype" for his work with digital recordings which he would continue to improve going forward. Despite the transition complicating the album's production Pocket Music still feels like Yamashita at his very best, and it's just as bright and warm as his previous work. The album found harmony between Yamashita's style, which takes heavy inspiration from the works of the past, and the encroaching digital future which made him adopt some new methodology. This is demonstrated from the very first track, Saturday Lover, which was written to be reminiscent of music from the 1960s, or songs including A2 and A4 which present a powerful new side to Yamashita's singing. Although it was quite a struggle to put together, Pocket Music still turned out to be a fantastic addition to Yamashita's history.

Love Life

The debut album from Cindy, an artist who had previously appeared on albums alongside Hiroshi Sato and Yumi Matsutoya. Love Life feels more like a Western album due to its many American composers and stylistic influences, especially all of those 1980s favorites like disco. Cindy herself even lived in the United States for some time, so her English singing is phenomenal and works especially well with all of the album's romantic tunes like Inside Of Your Love and You & I. One particularly famous artist also played a role in Love Life, that being Stevie Wonder who composed Think Your Love Away and played keyboards for that track as well as Try Your Luck Again. Both tracks are highlights which are light on instruments other than Stevie Wonder's keyboard playing, but the entire album is a remarkably good first project from Cindy.

Artist: Cindy
Release: April 25, 1986
Label: Kitty Records

A1. One Track Mind
A2. Garden Of Love
A3. Inside Of Your Love
A4. Skin Deep
A5. Spread The Love
B1. Think Your Love Away
B2. Try Your Luck Again
B3. You And I
B4. Something In The Air

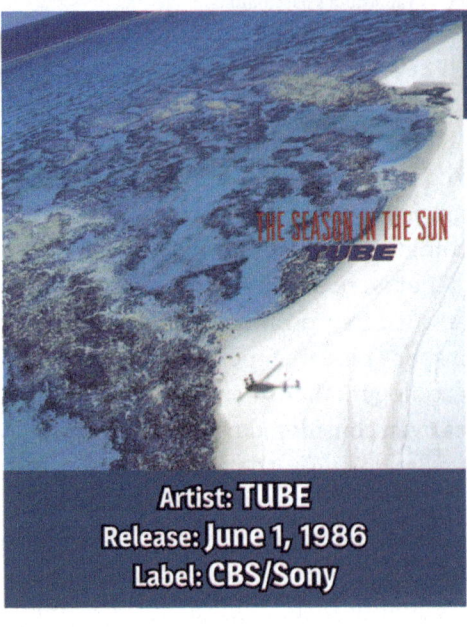

The Season In The Sun

The Season In The Sun is one of the many summer/vacation themed albums from TUBE, a band which has remarkably kept the exact same four members since 1985. It's easy to draw comparisons to Omega Tribe, another band with a similar theming and adult-oriented rock style, but TUBE never really garnered the same level of attention when City Pop became a hot topic again. Fans of pop rock or AOR have a lot to look forward to with TUBE, since they've released dozens of albums stuffed with uplifting and lighthearted tracks like A3, which is one of their most popular tunes. Unlike some other posers the members of TUBE were really committed to this seaside aesthetic, even in the 1990s and 2000s when a lot of other City Pop era artists had moved on. Their musical style has obviously evolved and changed over the years, but there's a lasting consistency to TUBE that's quite charming.

Artist: TUBE
Release: June 1, 1986
Label: CBS/Sony

A1. Weekend-NATU-通信
A2. 夏の住所はOn The Beach
A3. シーズン・イン・ザ・サン
A4. あの娘に急上昇
A5. わたせなかったI Need You
B1. 内海（うつみ）Seaside
B2. Right On!
B3. サザン・パシフィック
B4. Have A Nice Trip
B5. Tears

Mystique

With a new year came a new approach for Anri's music as she was now ditching the typical beach aesthetic and instead pursuing an "Oriental Summer" theming. This was also her first album since Heaven Beach which didn't involve Toshiki Kadomatsu in some way, a choice Anri intentionally made to avoid being creatively dependent on him. Anri also took on more songwriting duties for Mystique, composing four of the album's tracks while the others were done by Yuichiro Oda, Hiroshi Sato and Ichiro Hada. Mystique is maybe less memorable than last year's Wave, which played around with electronic sound quite heavily, but there's still some exceptional songs here. Sentimental Express is a great pop track written by Anri, as is the moving All Of You. Mystique is one of Anri's less popular albums from the era, but it's still a good time.

Artist: Anri
Release: June 5, 1986
Label: For Life Records

A1. Red Moon Calling
A2. Sentimental Express
A3. Honeymoon Shuttle
A4. Mystery Zone
A5. All Of You
B1. Morning Squall
B2. Southern Comfort
B3. Pride And Tears
B4. Whisper In Paradise
B5. Easy Break

Touch And Go

Artist: Toshiki Kadomatsu
Release: June 11, 1986
Label: Air Records

Toshiki Kadomatsu's Touch And Go scales back the adult overtones found throughout Gold Digger ~With True Love~ and instead prioritizes being a fun time with an international flair. Most of the tracks were recorded in New York or Los Angeles and came with some distinctly American twists. You can often hear American backing vocalists performing alongside Kadomatsu while the B-side has some songs with rap segments performed by Rodney Stone. Kadomatsu's propensity for danceable tracks is alive and well here, especially with Lucky Lady Feel So Good and Take It Away, and his heartwarming ballads are just as moving. One song that might be very special for fans of early City Pop is 1975, which shouts out some of the genre's pioneers like Sugar Babe, Yumi Arai, Tin Pan Alley and many more, showing Kadomatsu's admiration for his predecessors.

- A1. Overture ~ Take Off Melody
- A2. Lucky Lady Feel So Good
- A3. Take It Away
- A4. August Rain ~ It's Our Pure Hearts ~
- B1. Pile Driver
- B2. 1975
- B3. Good-Bye Love
- B4. The Best Of Love

Adventure

Artist: Momoko Kikuchi
Release: June 25, 1986
Label: Vap

Momoko Kikuchi and Tetsuji Hayashi teamed up once again for 1986's Adventure, a record which is absolutely in the conversation for being one of City Pop's best of all time. The album houses a number of the style's most beloved tunes, including the brilliantly written track Adventure which adds in just the right amounts of rock and synth-pop, as well as the chill sound of Mystical Composer. Many of the songs here have an ethereal quality due to Kikuchi's soft singing and the hypnotic instrumentals, traits which make Adventure feel quite nostalgic. You might just catch a case of Déjà vu imagining the bright lights of 1980s Tokyo while listening to Night Cruising, Good Friend, or many of the other incredible songs here. Adventure is practically required listening for fans of City Pop that really captures the genre's unique appeal.

- A1. Overture
- A2. Adventure
- A3. Autumn Wind Story
- A4. Nami ni Naritai
- A5. Night Cruising
- B1. Ame no Realize
- B2. Akai Inazuma
- B3. Good Friend
- B4. Mystical Composer
- B5. Tomorrow

Summer Breeze

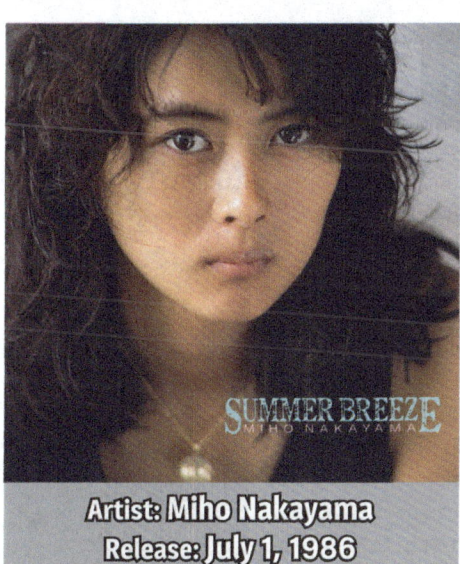

Artist: Miho Nakayama
Release: July 1, 1986
Label: King Records

Miho Nakayama made her debut in 1985 with the albums 「C」 and After School, which were more akin to the Kayōkyoku that Japanese idols were well associated with, but that started to change with Summer Breeze. This is largely thanks to the inclusion of a few esteemed City Pop composers, namely Daisuke Inoue who previously worked on Anri's Coool, as well as the always welcome Toshiki Kadomatsu. Their compositions gave Summer Breeze a fun tone with an emphasis on styles that are easy to dance along with, such as disco. The album was also home to one of Nakayama's most popular tracks, You're My Only Shinin' Star, which only got a single release in 1988 due to popular demand. The emotional single scored the number one spot on the weekly singles chart, which is especially impressive when you learn Kadomatsu wrote its lyrics in an hour.

- A1. Tropic Mystery
- A2. クローズ・アップ
- A3. Leave Me Alone
- A4. ひと夏のアクトレス
- A5. Ocean In The Rain
- B1. サインはハングルーズ
- B2. Rising Love
- B3. わがまま
- B4. 瞳のかげり
- B5. You're My Only Shinin' Star

Beyond...

Kiyotaka Sugiyama made his solo debut with Beyond... after leaving Omega Tribe, but it seems there were no hard feelings since the band's producer Koichi Fujita worked as an executive producer here as well. The majority of the album's tracks were composed by Sugiyama himself and are unsurprisingly very reminiscent of the music he was making with Omega Tribe, so you can expect all of the City Pop fixtures like synth-pop and soul here. Sugiyama's talent for writing energetic songs hasn't faded whatsoever, and the romantic ballads are quite plentiful here as well. Of particular note is B3, his debut single which peaked at number 4 on the Oricon charts, although the version on the album is slightly different. Beyond... was a major success for the now solo Sugiyama and scored the number one ranking, beating 1986 Omega Tribe's Navigator which got second place.

Artist: Kiyotaka Sugiyama
Release: July 2, 1986
Label: Embark, Vap

- A1. Ocean
- A2. What Rain Can Do To Love
- A3. Position oの憂鬱
- A4. One More Night
- A5. Alone
- A6. Illusionを消した夜
- B1. You Don't Know Me
- B2. Long Time Ago
- B3. さよならのオーシャン
- B4. Reflexive Love
- B5. Miss Dreamer

This Guy

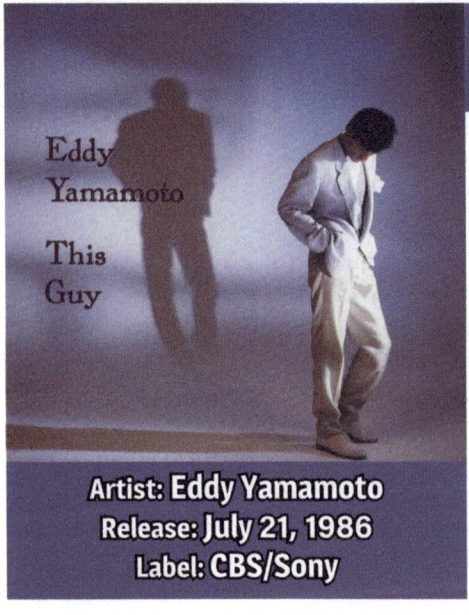

Which guy? This Guy! Eddy Yamamoto's final album follows in the footsteps of its predecessor Dream Hunter by loading up on danceable disco tunes, beautiful ballads and synth-pop symphonies. The album also exclusively features English lyrics sung by Yamamoto which are sometimes bolstered by appearances from Cindy as a backing vocalist, who can be heard on tracks A2, A4, A5 and B1. The diversity of genres and top-notch instrumentals are some of the album's greatest strengths and they're especially excellent on tracks such as Flight Of Fancy, Should We Carry On and We Can Stop The Hurtin'. This Guy was a worthy final album for Yamamoto, whose appearances in music afterwards are quite sparse. He never released any singles beyond this point either, but both Dream Hunter and This Guy are appreciated additions to City Pop's legacy.

Artist: Eddy Yamamoto
Release: July 21, 1986
Label: CBS/Sony

- A1. Moanin'
- A2. Flight Of Fancy
- A3. Mona Lisa
- A4. My Cherie Amour
- A5. Should We Carry On
- B1. We Can Stop The Hurtin'
- B2. Last Tango In Paris
- B3. My Ever Changing Moods
- B4. This Guy Is In Love With You

Urban Blue

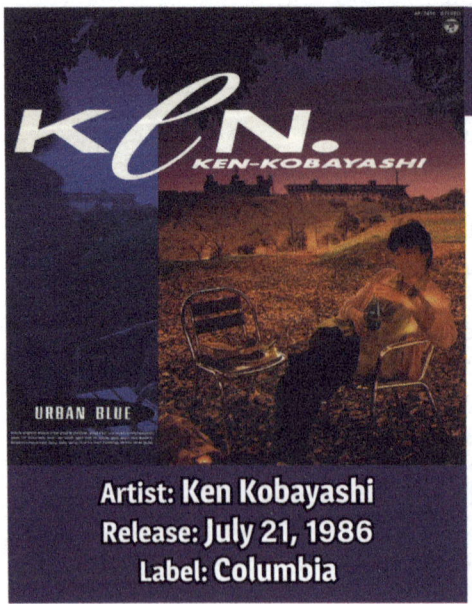

Another one of those mysterious artists that make the genre so interesting made his debut in 1986; Ken Kobayashi. We don't know very much about Kobayashi beyond the two records and one mini album he released, but they're all worthwhile additions to City Pop history. Urban Blue was almost entirely composed by Kobayashi himself, except for the instrumental A1 which was written by Tadashi Namba, and the album fits in nicely with other albums from the mid-1980s. You can look forward to a lot of lighthearted pop tracks, but there's also some groovy songs like B2 and B4, and of course you can't go wrong with some emotional ballads. Kobayashi later released Sizzle in 1987 and Warm Breeze in 1988, then seemingly vanished afterwards. A niche artist in City Pop, but one whose brief discography is worth exploring.

Artist: Ken Kobayashi
Release: July 21, 1986
Label: Columbia

- A1. Urban Blue (Instrumental)
- A2. 君の瞳のブルー
- A3. ラベルの無いカセット
- A4. Walking Alone
- A5. Mistake
- B1. 熱帯夜急行
- B2. Count Down
- B3. 恋のジグソーパズル
- B4. Lady My Love
- B5. Never Say Good-Bye

Navigator

Left: The members for this iteration of Omega Tribe, now starring Carlos Toshiki as lead vocalist.
Center: The cover of Navigator sticks with the aquatic imagery Omega Tribe was so well known for.
Right: The single release for You Are 1000%, their incredibly successful debut track, and Your Graduation.

Artist:
1986 Omega Tribe

Release:
July 23, 1986

Label:
Vap

Track List:

A1. Blue Reef

A2. You Belong To Him

A3. Aquarium In Tears

A4. Navigator

A5. Night Child

B1. 君は1000% (You Are 1000%)

B2. 21 Candles

B3. Older Girl

B4. North Shore

The future of Omega Tribe was left in a precarious position after lead vocalist Kiyotaka Sugiyama planned to split from the group, and to make matters worse Tetsuji Hayashi would no longer be lending them his songwriting talents. Despite these setbacks producer Koichi Fujita was intent on keeping his project alive, and he was already scouting for a new vocalist before Sugiyama left. That's when he heard a demo tape from Carlos Toshiki, a Japanese man raised in Brazil whose light and sweet singing voice seemed like a perfect fit for the role. Fujita also scouted Mitsuya Kurokawa who previously toured with Momoko Kikuchi and kept the band's two remaining original members Shinji Takashima and Toshitsugu Nishihara, thus creating 1986 Omega Tribe. The inspiration for the reformed band's first single came about when Fujita and Toshiki were on a Hawaii trip together and started discussing the Japanese and Portuguese languages. Carlos explained that the Japanese word for 1000, "sen", sounded like the Portuguese word for 100, "cem", and the combination of those words followed by the rhyming "percent" caught Fujita's attention. You Are 1000% was composed by Tsunehiro Izumi with lyrics by Masako Arikawa, who was a lyricist for many of Omega Tribe's songs from their last incarnation, and it came to life as an uplifting romantic ballad with an addictive chorus. Toshiki was quite proud to have You Are 1000% as his first original song, and it also performed extremely well, achieving a peak spot of number 3 on the Japanese Oricon charts while selling over 350,000 copies. Their first album Navigator released two months later and diverged just enough from Omega Tribe's past records, while still appealing to their core audience's fondness for adult-oriented rock and the general summertime vibe the band was designed around. Navigator also sets itself apart by emphasizing an electronic sound in songs like You Belong To Him, and the disco influences are cranked up to match. Carlos Toshiki proved that he was the right choice since his soft singing fits these songs about love and aquatic adventures fantastically, and you can especially appreciate his voice in Aquarium In Tears and North Shore. The group also showed that they could thrive without the songwriting skills of the now absent Kiyotaka Sugiyama and Tetsuji Hayashi, since the tracks were all composed by bandmates Takashima and Nishihara, as well as Tsunehiro Izumi and producer Fujita. 1986 Omega Tribe made quite the statement with Navigator, which peaked at second place on the Oricon charts and ensured the band's future for the next few years with Carlos Toshiki headlining as their vocalist.

Shake It Paradise

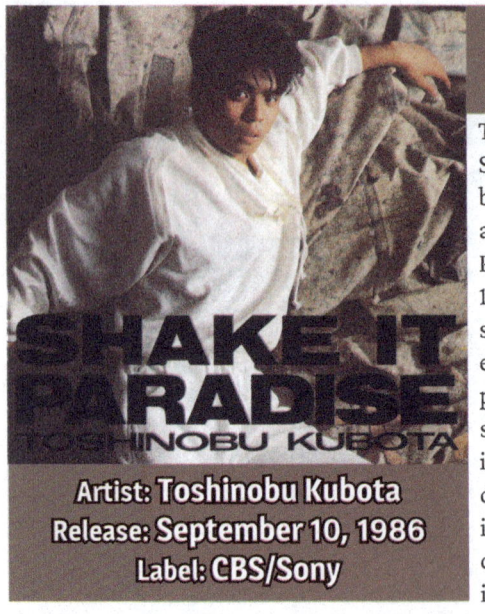

Artist: Toshinobu Kubota
Release: September 10, 1986
Label: CBS/Sony

Toshinobu Kubota really got things moving and groovin' with Shake It Paradise, a debut album which was heavily inspired by his love for genres such as soul and R&B. Kubota was also among the first to heavily incorporate an R&B sound into City Pop, something which would become more popular as the 1980s progressed. Shake It Paradise is home to some awesome songs which feel much more refined than what you'd expect from a debut record, especially with its many exciting pop and disco tunes like A1, A3 and B1. Kubota also flexes his serenading skills with Missing, a sweet and soft ballad which is still among his most popular tracks. Shake It Paradise did decently for a debut album, although it didn't quite break into the weekly top 10 it did settle at a solid 11th place and closed out the year at 33rd, a promising start to Kubota's influential career.

- A1. 流星のサドル
- A2. Olympic は火の車
- A3. Shake It Paradise
- A4. Missing
- A5. 失意のダウンタウン
- B1. To The Party
- B2. もうひとりの君を残して
- B3. Somebody's Sorrow
- B4. Dedicate (To M.E.)
- B5. Inside カーニバル

It's Friday

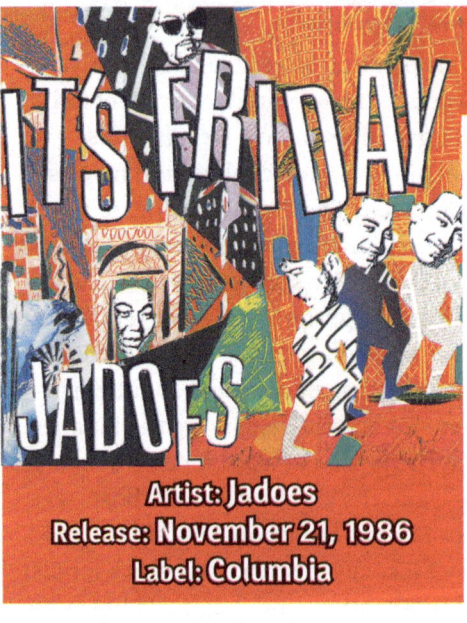

Artist: Jadoes
Release: November 21, 1986
Label: Columbia

It's Friday is the debut album by Jadoes, a band that initially found more success as a comedy group, but they never gave up on their musical aspirations. In order to jumpstart this process, they learned Toshiki Kadomatsu's address and left him a demo tape (this would get you arrested nowadays), a bold tactic which was emblematic of Jadoes' unconventional way of doing things. Kadomatsu was understandably quite surprised by their approach, but he liked what he heard and agreed to produce Jadoes' first album and worked with the band for years. Despite his involvement almost every song was composed by the band members themselves, and their creativity really shines here. No genre is safe from Jadoes as you'll hear bits of everything from hip-hop to jazz to disco and synth-pop, and they get especially funky with tracks like A2 and Friday Night.

- A1. Ikasuman
- A2. 夏のDU・BI DA・BA
- A3. Step By Step
- A4. Windy Moon
- B1. Friday Night
- B2. Cool
- B3. Silent Night
- B4. I Wanna Hold You Tonight
- B5. In The Moon

Mona Lisa

Artist: Akemi Ishii
Release: November 21, 1986
Label: CBS/Sony

Akemi Ishii's debut album is filled with tracks by composers from all over the globe, although a few stand out among the rest. A2 or Oh What A Night For Love was written by the legendary Dolly Parton and gave the album a nice lowkey track, while its most popular song Cha Cha Cha has a super simple but addictive chorus and was a number one hit back in the day. Mona Lisa's most recognizable song for Westerners is easily Ishii's cover of B1, Take My Breath Away, a track which is best known for its appearance in the movie Top Gun. Its inclusion here is kind of surprising considering that film and Mona Lisa both came out in 1986, but it's still neat to see this unexpected crossover between City Pop and Top Gun. Ishii released a handful of other synth-pop albums until 1990, which is when her final record Brazilian Night came out.

- A1. O La La
- A2. インスピレーションの夜
- A3. Cha Cha Cha
- A4. You Make Me Happy
- B1. 死んでもいい =Take My Breath Away
- B2. ジュ・テーム～悲しみの見える窓～
- B3. 恋は不滅
- B4. 流されて
- B5. 愛は嵐

Trouble In Paradise

Artist: Anri
Release: November 21, 1986
Label: For Life Records

Several months after Mystique was released Anri returned with Trouble In Paradise, an album that was fully recorded in London and utilized many talented composers. The recently debuted Toshinobu Kubota wrote the in-your-face Time Out alongside Ichiro Hada, plus there's a handful of songs from the always excellent Hiroshi Sato. Trouble In Paradise keeps up Anri's experimentation with synth-pop, among other genres, with one standout example being The Torch which heavily emphasizes electronic sound. Then there's Fallen Angel which gets some R&B into the mix, a genre which was slowly making its way into more City Pop albums. Trouble In Paradise is another one of Anri's underrated post-Timely!! records which shows her wide stylistic range and willingness to try new things.

A1. The Pages Of Your History
A2. Time Out
A3. Imitation Lover
A4. The Torch
A5. A Slowboat To Heart
B1. Trouble In Paradise
B2. Precious Time
B3. Fallen Angel
B4. Christmas Calendar
B5. Curtain Call

Crimson

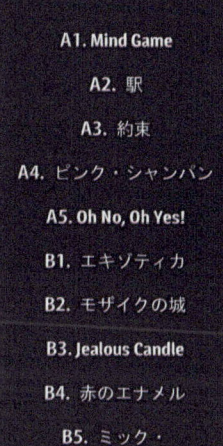

Artist: Akina Nakamori
Release: December 24, 1986
Label: Reprise Records

Akina Nakamori's Crimson is one of the year's most popular records, one which might feel unusually familiar to fans of Mariya Takeuchi. That's because she was the composer and lyricist for half of the albums tracks, and her musical brilliance was utilized well here. The other half were then composed by Akiko Kobayashi, an accomplished artist in her own right who released a number of albums. The goal in using female composers was to create a "feminine warmth and grace" for Crimson, a concept the team certainly achieved. Nakamori's powerful voice is well-suited to the many ballads here, especially Takeuchi's Oh No, Oh Yes! which she later self-covered on 1987's Request. Synth-pop faithfuls also have something to sink their teeth into with tracks like B2 and B3, but you'll definitely find a song or two that suits your taste here.

A1. Mind Game
A2. 駅
A3. 約束
A4. ピンク・シャンパン
A5. Oh No, Oh Yes!
B1. エキゾティカ
B2. モザイクの城
B3. Jealous Candle
B4. 赤のエナメル
B5. ミック・ジャガーに微笑みを

Bells

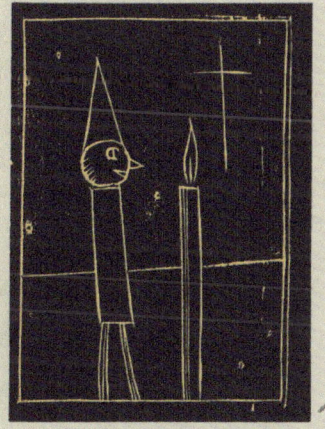

Artist: Minako Yoshida
Release: 1986
Label: Edition Gaspard

Bells was Minako Yoshida's first studio album since Light'N Up in 1982, but by this point Yoshida had left her record label Alfa and was instead doing freelance work helping artists like Toshiki Kadomatsu and Mari Iijima. Although she wasn't currently working as a main artist Yoshida would still record music just for the fun of it, including the song Christmas Tree which she had previously performed live. Yoshida was eventually convinced to make something out of these recordings; a self-published CD which was limited to only 3000 copies. The music within emphasized soul, one of the most common elements in her work, but it's probably closest to being a Gospel/Christmas album. Yoshida gives some exceptionally moving performances here, making Bells worth looking into despite it being a niche part of her lengthy musical career.

1. Wind
2. Christmas Tree
3. Pavement Of Light
4. Shadows Are The Thoughts (Of The Radiance)
5. Thanks To You
6. Dreaming

1987, Calm Before The Storm

1987 might be the end of City Pop's golden age, as many of the style's most revered albums have already come out by now, but there's still much fun to be had. Possibly the most exciting development for longtime fans of the genre was Mariya Takeuchi's return after a three year hiatus. Request was fully composed by Takeuchi herself, just like her previous album Variety, and she once again proved her talent as a songwriter with this wonderful record. Fellow City Pop veteran Anri had also been honing her compositional craft for Summer Farewells, while Toshiki Kadomatsu took an unexpected turn and released Sea Is A Lady, his first instrumental album. Both Summer Farewells and Sea Is A Lady felt like explorations of classic coastal City Pop concepts, albeit presented in very different forms, but a few records really gave listeners a throwback. Taeko Ohnuki got the gang back together for A Slice Of Life, while Shigeru Suzuki brought in many of the genre's original icons for Sunset Hills Hotel. This year is also when we got Yurie Kokubu's Steps, her first album since 1983, as well as some new artists to enjoy such as the sisterly duo Milk and the rather unique sounding Midori Hara. The year is full of underrated debuts, new ideas and old reliables, but it's also one of the last 'normal' years in City Pop's history. The excellent Japanese economy which inspired so many of City Pop's liberating themes was now in a bubble, one where the value of stocks and land was unsustainably increasing by the day. It wouldn't be long now before that bubble popped and ended the City Pop party, but that'll be a problem for the 1990s to deal with.

Mariya Takeuchi

Thousands of City Pop fans began their fascination with this fifty year old genre by only knowing of one artist and one of her songs; Mariya Takeuchi and Plastic Love. The song became a surprise hit on YouTube in the 2010s and introduced many to a seemingly forgotten world of incredible music with a nostalgic eighties charm, while her adorable smile imprinted a striking and joyful visual into our minds. Takeuchi and her music became synonymous with City Pop in the Western world, but in her native Japan she's always been an enduring and influential figure. Takeuchi released her debut album Beginning in 1978, then in 1979 while working on her album University Street she met Tatsuro Yamashita, her future husband and another one of City Pop's biggest names. The two formed a musical power couple and frequently worked on each other's projects. with Yamashita often working as a producer and performer on Takeuchi's albums. That is until Takeuchi took a hiatus for the birth of their daughter, but this time away actually bolstered her songwriting prowess. Before becoming a mother Takeuchi typically outsourced her music from other artists, but when she did return for 1984's Variety she was now crafting all of the compositions and lyrics for her albums, such as the ones heard in Plastic Love. Takeuchi's release schedule would continue to be sparse past this point, but her fans always patiently awaited the next Takeuchi album, even if there was the occasional eight year gap they had to endure. Throughout her career Takeuchi has maintained a reputation for creating beautiful and exceptionally elegant music which doesn't chase trends but still achieves fantastic commercial success. It's quite possible that for many Westerners City Pop would have still been a niche and largely forgotten blip in musical history if not for Takeuchi, but beyond just the ultra-popular Plastic Love she has decades of other unforgettable tracks to discover and fall in love with.

Top: A cute retro picture of Mariya Takeuchi back in the 1980s. Bottom: A photo of Takeuchi nowadays, an icon of Japanese music with a historic career.

Crystal Night

Artist: 1986 Omega Tribe
Release: February 4, 1987
Label: Vap

Crystal Night was the second album released by this iteration of Omega Tribe, but also their last. That was quick! Not long after this album's release guitarist Mitsuya Kurokawa left the group, which was then renamed to Carlos Toshiki and Omega Tribe to give Carlos more exposure. The album housed many more hits from this short-lived version of Omega Tribe, most notably their number one ranking single Super Chance. Akin to their previous success with You Are 1000% the track is an upbeat pop rock number which suits Carlos's soft voice perfectly, but songs like the titular Crystal Night and Phoenix are also musical delights. Thanks to its memorable songs the album did secure the number one ranking for Omega Tribe, surpassing their debut album Navigator which capped out at second place.

- A1. Counterlight
- A2. Lady Free
- A3. Phoenix
- A4. Indian Summer
- A5. I'll Never Forget You
- B1. Crystal Night
- B2. Ipanema Rain
- B3. Super Chance
- B4. For Each Other

Sunset Hills Hotel

Artist: Sunset Hills Hotel
Release: February 21, 1987
Label: Interface

The first of three albums in the Imagination File series brought together an entourage of City Pop veterans, including many of those old favorites. Shigeru Suzuki worked as the main arranger and conductor for the project, but we also have appearances from Yoshitaka Minami, Ginji Ito, Taeko Ohnuki, Masataka Matsutoya and many more. The album's tracks were all composed by different artists, but it's unified by a focus on genre fusion and theming that will feel quite familiar to City Pop fans with titles like West Beach Drive and Night Flight. These tunes are incredibly smooth and generally relaxing, so it's always a fine choice when you need some winding down at the end of the day. Even though City Pop was losing steam at this point it's great to see that collaborative spirit still alive and well, just like the good old days when the genre was young.

- A1. Night Flight
- A2. Cafe On The Wave
- A3. Sweet Reservation
- A4. 6:30 P.M. Breeze
- A5. West Beach Drive
- B1. Transit Airport
- B2. Purple Rose Good-Bye
- B3. On The Second Honeymoon
- B4. Long Distance Call
- B5. Her Sunset Smile

Groovin'

Artist: Toshinobu Kubota
Release: April 22, 1987
Label: CBS/Sony

Toshinobu Kubota's second album Groovin' gives us plenty more R&B inspired tracks from this (at the time) new artist we can get down to. Groovin' hosts many diverse tracks which appeal to fans of styles ranging from synth-pop to ballads, with some especially recommended energetic songs being the fast-paced Randy Candy and Lady Suicide. The record's most popular song is Track 2, a funky synth-pop tune with a romantic side which was definitely the centerpiece for some memorable nights in late-eighties Japan. Another highlight is Track 9 which has some classic City Pop subject matter about a random encounter in the city and a great flow to it. Groovin' performed far better than Kubota's debut album Shake It Paradise and sold over a million units while earning third place ranking on Japan's weekly Oricon charts, a major jump from his previous album's 11th place.

1. Psychic Beat
2. 北風と太陽
3. Place
4. Randy Candy
5. Lady Suicide
6. 一途な夜、無傷な朝
7. ダイヤモンドの犬たち
8. 薄情 Love Machine
9. 永遠の翼
10. Visions
11. 八番目の虹の

Summer Farewells

Artist: Anri
Release: May 2, 1987
Label: For Life Records

Anri truly found her footing with Summer Farewells, the first of her albums which she produced. It also included more of her own compositions than any of Anri's past records, with seven of its tracks being composed by her, while the others were done by future Omega Tribe member Joey McCoy. Just by listening to the album you can tell that Anri's skills as a songwriter have truly matured now, as tracks like Dance With Nostalgia make you feel at home with the kind of fun, light-hearted track City Pop is associated with, while B2 highlights her penchant for moving ballads. The album fits in better with beloved albums like Timely!! as opposed to Anri's more experimental mid-eighties records, but it's by no means a rehash of her prior efforts. Summer Farewells is a significant release in Anri's history which proved she had the talent and skills to stand on her own.

- A1. Dance With Nostalgia
- A2. Café 25
- A3. ボーイフレンド
- A4. 浮気な彼のために
- A5. シャネルでグッドバイ
- B1. Moon In The Rain
- B2. さよなら シングル・デイズ
- B3. 霧雨に消えてゆく
- B4. Happy Endでふられたい
- B5. ホノルル・バースデイ・イヴ

Escape From Dimension

Artist: Momoko Kikuchi
Release: May 27, 1987
Label: Vap

Escape From Dimension is one of Momoko Kikuchi's less popular albums, but it should win some kind of award for having a really sick name. Tetsuji Hayashi was once again the album's sole composer, as he was for Kikuchi's previous three records, so that same level of quality is present here. Escape From Dimension does set itself apart from its sibling albums by prioritizing an electronic sound which is best heard in tracks such as the blood-pumping Dreamin' Rider and B3. Some of these songs put a new spin on the chill and sometimes surreal atmosphere heard in some of Adventure's tracks, especially with Ivory Coast and Last Runner, but these synth stylings also perfectly replicate that urban excitement the genre is known for in Yokohama City of Lights. While not as cherished as some of Kikuchi's other albums Escape From Dimension still has a lot to offer.

- A1. Starlight Movement
- A2. Dreamin' Rider
- A3. Yokohama City of Lights
- A4. Say Yes!
- A5. Ivory Coast
- B1. Non Stop The Rain
- B2. Last Runner
- B3. 夜明けのバスターミナル
- B4. Sundial

MiDo

Artist: Midori Hara
Release: June 21, 1987
Label: Triad

The debut album from Midori Hara, a later addition to City Pop's history with a very particular singing voice. It's difficult to describe without hearing it for yourself, but her high pitched voice and way of enunciating is rather unlike any other artist. You'll often see it being referred to as an acquired taste, and although her characteristic singing may not appeal to everyone there's no denying the quality of her compositions. The majority of the album was written by Hara and featured some very refined and diverse tracks, ranging from the cool serenity of A2 to the whimsical A3. Another excellent song here is B1 which features a crossover of funk, pop and jazz, then B4 closes the album out strongly with its hypnotic atmosphere. MiDo is an incredibly solid work and Midori Hara really showed what she was capable of here.

- A1. Ta・Ra・N・Te・Ra たいむすりっぷ！
- A2. すべてが冬の色
- A3. 月曜日の憂鬱
- A4. 御乱心春色変化
- A5. うつろふ時間の中で
- B1. おもちゃの○△□
- B2. 気持ち半分魔女気分
- B3. Good Night
- B4. 好きといふ気持ち

Free Drink

They had me at 'Free Drink', but throwing some Jadoes action into the mix makes this even better. Toshiki Kadomatsu continued acting as a producer for Jadoes and as such their music is quite reminiscent of his own work, so expect lots of groovy tunes you can boogie down to. Stardust Night is definitely the album's main draw as it's Jadoes most popular track by far, a classic City Pop tune with an optimistic cool factor and perfectly timed chorus. Some of the album's other fantastic tracks include the lighthearted Summer Lady and The Girl That Kills Me which is a real testament to Jadoes creative vision. Free Drink also has a nice selection of mood setters on the B-side such as Give Me Your Love Again and The Time Takes You Away to keep things balanced in this awesome album from Jadoes.

Artist: Jadoes
Release: July 1, 1987
Label: Columbia

- A1. Summer Lady (Album Version)
- A2. Stardust Night
- A3. Hot Melody
- A4. The Girl That Kills Me
- B1. 6月のフォトグラフ
- B2. Shining You
- B3. Give Me Your Love Again
- B4. The Time Takes You Away (時は雨の彼方に……)
- B5. Woman, I Want You

Sea Is A Lady

Toshiki Kadomatsu surprised us yet again with Sea Is A Lady, an instrumental album that still captures the urban and seaside vibes he's closely tied to. The album is split up into a Cute Side which harkens back to his earlier summer-centric music with tracks like the bright A2, as well as a Sexy Side which is reminiscent of his more recent work that explored city life. Kadomatsu's ability to perfectly create a scene with music is quite stunning and you can distinctly visualize a summer day winding down in A5 or a late-night drive in B4. Sea Is A Lady is one of the year's most memorable albums and provides some fantastic listening material for fans of Kadomatsu's work and instrumental jams. Thirty years later he would remake it as Sea Is A Lady 2017, an album dedicated to both the late bassist Tomohito Aoki and Hiroshi Sato.

Artist: Toshiki Kadomatsu
Release: July 1, 1987
Label: Air Records

- A1. Way To The Shore "Eri"
- A2. Sea Line "Rie"
- A3. Night Sight Of Port Island "Midori" (Night Flight Of DC-10)
- A4. Sea Song "Naomi"
- A5. Sunset Of Micro Beach "Satoko"
- B1. Oshi-Tao-Shitai "Kaori Aso" (Memories Of Dusseldorf)
- B2. 52nd Street "Akiko"
- B3. The Bass Battle "Chako"
- B4. Midsummer Drivin' "Reiko"
- B5. Lovin' You "Sawako"
- B6. Sea Song (Reprise)

Request

Following the release of her 1984 album Variety Mariya Takeuchi took a three year long hiatus to focus on raising her daughter, although she did still provide compositions for other artists. A few of those songs were self-covered and given new life in Request, such as Oh No, Oh Yes! which was originally made for Akina Nakamori. Although Request doesn't have a genre-defining smash hit like Plastic Love, it is one of Takeuchi's most high quality albums with a number of beloved tunes like A5 and B4. Every song is a testament to Takeuchi's skills as a songwriter and lyricist, made perfect by her husband Tatsuro Yamashita playing a majority of the instruments heard throughout. Takeuchi's release schedule would continue to be rather sparse from here on, with her next album Quiet Life not manifesting until 1992, but loyal fans always looked forward to her music.

Artist: Mariya Takeuchi
Release: August 12, 1987
Label: Moon Records

- A1. 恋の嵐
- A2. Oh No, Oh Yes!
- A3. けんかをやめて
- A4. 消息
- A5. 元気を出して
- B1. 駅
- B2. テコのテーマ
- B3. 色・ホワイトブレンド
- B4. 夢の続き
- B5. 時空の旅人

A Slice Of Life

Artist: Taeko Ohnuki
Release: October 5, 1987
Label: Dear Heart, Midi Inc.

Taeko Ohnuki's A Slice Of Life was a very welcome reunion for many members of City Pop's original clique. You can spot Ohnuki's longtime Yellow Magic Orchestra collaborators Haruomi Hosono and Yukihiro Takahashi here, as well as mainstays like EPO and Ray Ohara. Although the synth-pop sound Ohnuki has gradually mastered and become known for is still quite present here A Slice Of Life does take a more traditional approach with its instrument usage. Many songs simply use a classic bass, guitar and drums setup played by some of the industry's brightest, so fans of this high-quality streamlined approach have something to look forward to. A few songs on the B-side take things even further by only utilizing Ohnuki's vocals and keyboards, resulting in some truly beautiful music that really lets her voice take center stage.

- A1. あなたに似た人
- A2. もういちどトゥイスト
- A3. 人魚と水夫
- A4. スナップショット
- A5. 恋人たちの時刻
- B1. 五番目の季節
- B2. Hymns
- B3. 木立の中の日々
- B4. ぼくの叔父さん
- B5. 彼と彼女のソネット

Masahito Arai

Artist: Masahito Arai
Release: October 21, 1987
Label: Humming Bird

This may be Masahito Arai's eponymous solo debut album, but he had been making music with various bands such as Pal since the 1970s. It becomes very clear while listening to the album that this isn't Arai's first outing, since his music feels like a very polished and welcome throwback to the smooth adult-oriented rock side of City Pop. A1 immediately starts the album with a definitive City Pop tune that's lighthearted and full of English lyrics, but Arai also flexes his skills with smooth tracks through A2 and A4. It's an excellent album from this lesser known artist, who later released two more similar albums, 1988's Fuzzy and 1989's Necessary. Then in 1994 Arai got involved in Omega Tribe's tangled web by becoming the lead vocalist of Brand New Omega Tribe, a spinoff project which was largely disconnected from the original band.

- A1. Kimi Wa Ima...
- A2. Yume Ni Reserve
- A3. Moon Lady
- A4. Morning Subway
- A5. Yasashisa No Nakae
- B1. Rolling Heart
- B2. Fuyu No Photograph
- B3. Dance, Dance, Dance
- B4. Labrea
- B5. Love

Steps

Artist: Yurie Kokubu
Release: October 21, 1987
Label: Air Records

Yurie Kokubu finally gave us another album with Steps, which came out four years after her debut with Relief 72 Hours. Whereas that album was made by utilizing many different composers Steps was exclusively written by Hitoshi Haba, a relative newcomer to the industry. Haba really put in work for this album though, as also wrote lyrics alongside Kokubu and performed as a backing vocalist. Steps gets things going with the frantic fun of I've Got You Inside Out, an unforgettable showcase of Kokubu's mighty vocals which then transitions into the exceptionally smooth I Wanna Be With You. Then you'll get taken on a galactic journey in Cosmic Love, delight in the uplifting groove of Just Go Up and enjoy all the other splendid tunes on the slower paced B-side. Steps is another iconic City Pop album from Kokubu which includes many of her most popular tracks.

- A1. I Got You Inside Out
- A2. I Wanna Be With You
- A3. Cosmic Love
- A4. Just Go Up
- A5. Take A Little Bit Of My Love
- B1. Counting Down The Days
- B2. In Your Eyes
- B3. Margarita
- B4. You Are Love For Me

Quarterback

Artist: Masanori Ikeda
Release: October 21, 1987
Label: Eastworld

Masanori Ikeda's debut record was made with some pretty impressive names, especially for fans of a little band called Omega Tribe. Some of the album's composers include Tetsuji Hayashi and Kiyotaka Sugiyama, while Koichi Fujita acted as the album's producer, just as he was doing for Omega Tribe. Unsurprisingly those who enjoy Omega Tribe or Kiyotaka Sugiyama's music will probably enjoy Quarterback's somewhat similar tunes. Two of the album's most popular tracks are Night Of Summer Side, the only song here composed by the group Nobody, as well as Shadow Dancer, a Hayashi contribution. Ikeda's time in music was relatively short as he only released albums from 1987 to 1990, although he did ultimately settle into the acting profession which he has been involved in for nearly forty years.

A1. Night Of Summer Side
A2. Beat Of Clash
A3. All Or Nothing
A4. Shadow Dancer
A5. Room Ocean View
B1. Quarterback
B2. Burning Eyes
B3. River Side ジレンマ
B4. Let Me Love

Kana

Artist: Kanako Wada
Release: December 25, 1987
Label: Air Records

Kanako Wada's bringing the boogie with Kana, her second album, although it is probably her most well-known among City Pop aficionados. Kana was composed by several artists who have been involved in the genre since its early days including Daisuke Inoue, Yuji Toriyama and Ken Sato, one of the best to ever do it. Synth-pop fanatics have a lot to sink their teeth into with Kana, as most of the record's tracks are full of that electronic energy. One of the album's most renowned tracks include A2, a passionate jam with impactful lyrics about romance and the unsettling feeling of the seasons rapidly coming and going. Sunday Brunch is another popular track with fantastic instrumentals, an impactful performance from Wada and simple but effective lyrics. Kana is an excellent album from Wada, who retired from the industry in 1991.

A1. Party Town 〜 What Can I Do For You 〜
A2. 悲しいハートは燃えている
A3. 誕生日はマイナス1
A4. 不確かなI Love You
A5. 鳥のように
B1. Sunday Brunch
B2. 冬の水族館
B3. 哀しみのヴァージン・ロード 〜 Never Fall In Love 〜
B4. Musicに肩よせて
B5. C.クローデルの罪

Milk

Artist: Milk
Release: 1987
Label: J&L Records

The sole self-titled album by Milk, a duo consisting of sisters Ritsuko and Rie Miyajima. Although they're not exactly household names in City Pop land they crafted a knockout album stuffed with influences like synth-pop, funk and disco. Almost all of the tracks here were composed by the pair and you can really appreciate their skill at crafting funky tunes with For A Week Story, but there's also some hypnotic songs thrown in like A4 and Parting. Another gem from the album is B1, a track which has both of them performing as vocalists. The girls don't team up for every song, but both are skilled vocalists in their own right and make each song memorable. Although they never released another album the sisters have stayed active in the industry, with Rie composing songs for the Pokémon series and Ritsuko writing many tracks for the idol group AKB48.

A1. For A Week Story
A2. Wake Up
A3. Last Dance
A4. 白い雨
B1. サヨナラはValentinday
B2. Parting
B3. 視線（まなざし）に I Feel So Love
B4. You're The One
B5. "Thank You" For You

1988 & 1989, Goodbye Showa

As the decade drew to a close Japan's asset bubble situation only accelerated and stock prices were reaching somewhat concerning highs, so now was a good time to enjoy some City Pop tunes and not think too hard about the possibility of this all going kaput. Sadly, a reminder of time's unstoppable march arrived in January of 1989 as Emperor Hirohito died at the age of 87, thus heralding the end of the Showa Era which began all the way back in 1926. Although the Emperor had been a ceremonial figure with no true power since Japan's defeat in World War 2, he still represented a fascinating and complicated era of Japanese history defined by seemingly conflicting concepts. Imperialism, democracy, war, peace, economic hardship and prosperity were all part of the Showa story, and that story had turned over to a new chapter as Emperor Akihito took the throne; the Heisei Era. City Pop is largely associated with the Showa era, and the transition to Heisei could be seen as the beginning of the end for the style's popularity, but still some classics in these exciting but uncertain years. Tatsuro Yamashita reflected on his experience as a parent and former child for The Boy In Me, his most introspective work yet, while Momoko Kikuchi took a major gamble with her new rock band RA MU. The short-lived group Shambara featured Yurie Kokubu and Kaoru Akimoto, who both worked to make an incredibly memorable album, while the legendary Miki Matsubara released her final album Wink, which was perhaps another omen that City Pop's time was running out. Welcome to the Heisei Era, and the beginning of City Pop's twilight years.

Tetsuji Hayashi

Tetsuji Hayashi isn't a name that every fan of City Pop will be familiar with, but few songwriters influenced the sound and perception of the style like he did. Many of the genre's most celebrated songs and albums involved Hayashi, and we even have him to thank for what might be City Pop's crown jewel. Early in his career Hayashi contributed to the style's development by composing for Junko Ohashi, one of the first artists who could comfortably fall under the City Pop descriptor due to her frequent mixing of Western genres like disco and jazz, but the real slam dunk for Hayashi came in 1979. His song Midnight Door/Stay With Me was sung by Miki Matsubara and turned out to be a highly successful and scarily catchy tune which served as something of a template for a City Pop hit. The English phrases and Western musical influences heard in Stay With Me were highly appealing to Japanese audiences at the time, although Hayashi probably wasn't expecting his music to end up beloved by a new generation 30 years later too. Mixing genres like synth-pop, disco and soul were a part of Hayashi's playbook from then on, and he was soon collaborating with many of the style's icons. Mariya Takeuchi, Anri, EPO and Yurie Kokubu all performed his songs, but the artists he worked most closely with were S. Kiyotaka & Omega Tribe and Momoko Kikuchi. Hayashi wrote every song heard on Momoko Kikuchi's iconic albums like Adventure and Ocean Side, giving her a very unique sound compared to other idols from the period. Then there was S. Kiyotaka & Omega Tribe, whose summer-centric pop rock records were stuffed with Hayashi's compositions. Both were also among Japan's most popular musical acts at the time, consistently achieving top rankings for their singles and albums. Hayashi's myriad tunes are some of City Pop's greatest of all time and it's hard to imagine the genre without his tracks for Miki Matsubara, Momoko Kikuchi and many more.

Many City Pop fans haven't seen Tetsuji Hayashi's face before, but he's responsible for many of the style's most popular tracks. There's a high likelihood your favorite City Pop tune is just one of his many creations.

Before The Daylight

Artist: Toshiki Kadomatsu
Release: February 5, 1988
Label: BMG Victor Inc., Om

This album's full title is actually Before The Daylight ~Is The Most Darkness Moment In A Day, a grammatically questionable and very long (but cool) name. After the instrumental Sea Is A Lady Kadomatsu returned to familiar territory with more of his danceable party tracks which appealed to night life enthusiasts, akin to what we heard in Gold Digger ~With True Love~. The album does distinguish itself by adding in funkier R&B, a trend that was becoming more popular as the decade dwindled. A1 creates an exciting atmosphere before A2 and A3 set up a sensual mood, then there's plenty of fun to be had on the B-side with tracks like B2. Before The Daylight is another very good release from Kadomatsu but is generally less memorable than some of his more popular party time albums.

- A1. I Can Give You My Love
- A2. Lost My Heart In The Dark
- A3. Thinking Of You
- A4. Get Your Feelin'
- B1. Can't You See
- B2. Remember You
- B3. Lady In The Night
- B4. I'd Like To Be Your Fantasy

Catch The Nite

Artist: Miho Nakayama
Release: February 10, 1988
Label: King Records

Miho Nakayama collaborated with Toshiki Kadomatsu once again for 1988's Catch The Nite, now in a much greater capacity. Kadomatsu served as the album's producer and primary composer, although you can also hear tracks from Hiroshi Sato and Hideki Fujisawa from Jadoes. Catch The Nite was designed for listeners to play the album all the way through, something which was easily accomplished by including many of the year's best tracks. All of City Pop's notable influences are abundant here such as disco, funk, synth-pop and jazz, making it feel like a genuine celebration of the genre's history up to this point. The album impressively managed to rank number one for its vinyl, CD and cassette releases, showing that this style still had many devoted fans. An outstanding album from the end of City Pop's glory days and one of the year's highlights.

- A1. Overture
- A2. Misty Love
- A3. Triangle Love Affair
- A4. Sherry
- A5. スノー・ホワイトの街
- B1. Catch Me
- B2. Just My Lover
- B3. Far Away From Summer Days
- B4. Get Your Love Tonight
- B5. 花瓶

The Actress In The Mirror

Artist: Meiko Nakahara
Release: March 5, 1988
Label: Eastworld

As the bubble economy rages on, we've got some more Meiko Nakahara to delight in, and The Actress In The Mirror has a broad selection of tracks. One of her most popular tunes can be found here right from the start with Dance In The Memories, a track which allows you to easily immerse yourself in the nostalgia City Pop is strongly associated with. The song mostly consists of repeated "I just dance in the sweet memories" verse, but thanks to its great flow the song never really gets old. What's Going On adds a super funky tune you can groove to with a very memorable bass segment, then there's the exciting A5 which was used as one of the opening themes for the anime Kimagure Orange Road. Killer instrumentals and classic City Pop themes await on the B-side with Paradise Island and Caribbean Night, among other tracks which make this one of Nakahara's best albums.

- A1. Dance In The Memories
- A2. What's Going On
- A3. Don't Be Silly
- A4. Infinite Love
- A5. 鏡の中のアクトレス
- B1. Paradise Island
- B2. Caribbean Night
- B3. ビーチ・バーからの手紙
- B4. Casanova
- B5. In Your Eyes

Down Town Mystery ("Night Time" Version)

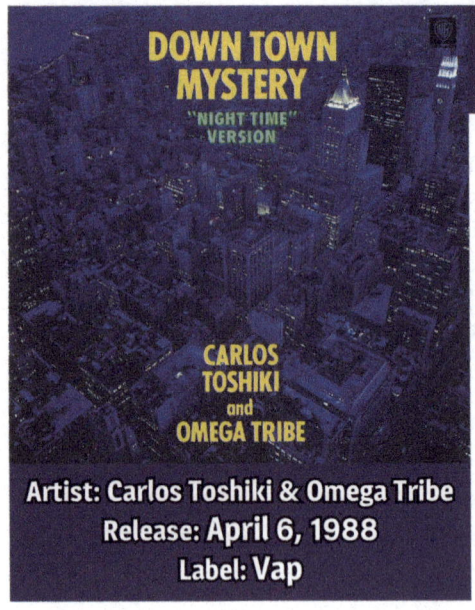

Artist: Carlos Toshiki & Omega Tribe
Release: April 6, 1988
Label: Vap

After Mitsuya Kurokawa left Omega Tribe due to health complications the band was renamed to give lead vocalist Carlos Toshiki more prominence and to do away with the '1986' in their previous title. They were also now joined by Joey McCoy, a Black artist who had previously worked with Anri on Summer Farewells. Fortunately for Omega Tribe's fans the band's general style hasn't changed up much to coincide with the new name, so all of those funk, soul and synth-pop stylings are still thriving here. Memorable tunes like Call Back Again and Mantero Island await, as does Down Town Mystery, the source of the album's interesting name. The version found here is called the "Night Time" version, whereas the single release was the "Daylight" version. Both are essentially the same song, just mixed by different people to give each one a slightly different sound and vibe.

- A1. Emmy Angel
- A2. Call Back Again
- A3. Sky Surfer
- A4. Dream
- A5. Slow Boat To Moonlight
- B1. Down Town Mystery
- B2. Matenro Island
- B3. Stay Girl Stay Pure
- B4. The Last Love Song

Radio Days

Artist: Masayuki Suzuki
Release: April 21, 1988
Label: Epic

The second album by Masayuki Suzuki sets itself apart from his debut record Mother Of Pearl by getting more City Pop icons involved, including the king himself. Tatsuro Yamashita was the producer and composer for the album's first three tracks, as well as for the finale in B5, while his wife Mariya Takeuchi was the lyricist for A2 and A3, naturally making these some of the album's best. Takeuchi's lyrics and Yamashita's funky compositions were a match made in heaven for Suzuki's extremely cool voice, which just feels naturally suited to this kind of music. You can also spot a couple of songs by Hiroshi Sato here like B2 and B3 which both demonstrate Sato's mastery over genre mixing, but Suzuki's own compositions are fantastic as well. Suzuki has continued to stay active in music since the 1980s, with his most recent album Snazzy releasing in 2024.

- A1. "おやすみロージー" Introduction
- A2. Guilty
- A3. Misty Mauve
- A4. Wild Beat
- A5. 微笑みを待ちながら
- A6. 雨に願いを
- B1. Dry・Dry
- B2. For Your Love
- B3. Tandem Run
- B4. 河の彼方
- B5. おやすみロージー (Angel Babyへのオマージュ)

Boogie Woogie Mainland

Artist: Anri
Release: May 21, 1988
Label: For Life Records

After writing the majority of the songs in her last album Summer Farewells Anri is back with Boogie Woogie Mainland, the first album which was entirely composed by her. Although we're pretty late into City Pop's lifespan by now Anri is still keeping all of the influences the style is closely associated with intact, including disco, synth-pop and unsurprisingly boogie. This makes Boogie Woogie Mainland feel more closely related to some of Anri's classics like Timely!! and can be easily recommended to fans of those albums. A1 starts the album off with the exact sort of boogie-centric tune you're hoping for before A3 and D.J I Love You turn it all around with some lyrical heartbreakers. For a one-two punch of summer-themed tracks about romance look no further than the deceptively cheery B4 and B5, the album's most popular track.

- A1. Boogie Woogie Mainland
- A2. Please ! Make Me Cry
- A3. 愛してるなんてとても言えない
- A4. D.J. I Love You
- A5. 私だけのJoker
- B1. Goodbye Future
- B2. Mercy! Mercy!
- B3. Edge Of Heaven
- B4. 最後のサーフホリデー
- B5. Summer Candles

Style

Artist: Keiko Kimura
Release: May 21, 1988
Label: Interface

The debut album from Keiko Kimura, an artist who released a handful of solo albums between 1988 and 1991, but she's also a member of the short lived Bossa nova duo Quelqu'un with Haruo Kubota. Quite a few of City Pop's godfathers worked on this album, most notably Shigeru Suzuki who produced it and composed most of the album's tracks. We also have appearances from Takashi Matsumoto as a lyricist for some tracks, plus compositions from Masamichi Sugi, Kazuhiko Kato and Asami Kado, who have all been there from the start. Style harkens back to City Pop's early days when chill tracks with pop undertones were one of its main draws, and in some ways, it feels more like a seventies album. Kimura's singing range perfectly suits these kinds of songs, whether that's the relaxing A2 or the groovy A3 she gives a fantastic performance on this underrated album.

- A1. Good Morning
- A2. Take Me To The Spring
- A3. Don't Call Me On The Phone
- A4. Sinjirarenation
- A5. City Of Water
- B1. Love Me to Coltrane Music
- B2. Do You Remember Me
- B3. Black Manicure
- B4. Good Bye Eggman
- B5. Charade '88

Wink

Artist: Miki Matsubara
Release: May 21, 1988
Label: Victor

Wink would prove to be the final album Miki Matsubara released in her lifetime, but she gave us something special for this last endeavor. A motley crew of songwriters were on board for this project, many of whom we're well acquainted with by now. Songs by City Pop veterans like Masamichi Sugi and Kazuhito Murata can be heard here, and we even get one more track from Tetsuji Hayashi who wrote Matsubara's debut song Stay With Me nearly a decade ago. As such Wink turned out to be a diverse but still very polished album with a focus on energetic pop tracks that are easy to dance to. Even the more melancholic tunes have a funky side to them, but you can also catch songs that are heavy on pop rock. Matsubara got married afterwards and mostly did songwriting work throughout the 1990s before tragically passing away in 2004 due to cancer.

- A1. B・S・T
- A2. 女神の右手
- A3. ハートの鍵貸します
- A4. In The Room
- A5. Sorry
- B1. カフェ・イ・アルテ
- B2. "Be"-Rock
- B3. メロディアス
- B4. 路上のパラダイス
- B5. 雨の中の女

Aqua

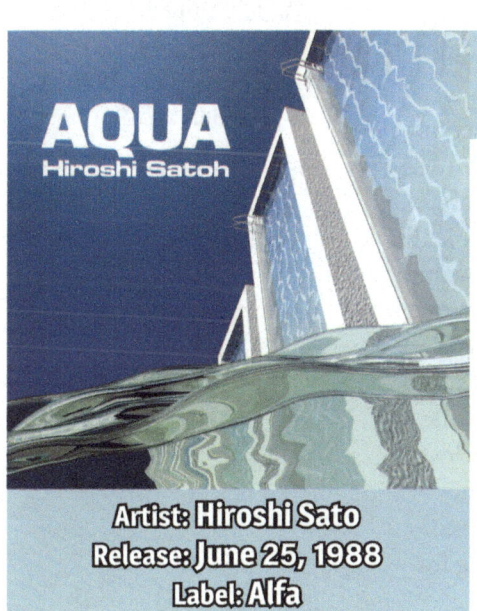

Artist: Hiroshi Sato
Release: June 25, 1988
Label: Alfa

Hiroshi Sato's Aqua has a cover that just screams City Pop with towering vertical swimming pools that resemble buildings, but the music is just as creative. Sato has cranked the funk and disco up to the max for this album while still giving every song a serene coolness that brings you right back to the 1980s. The opening Aqua lures you in with some truly hypnotic keyboard work until Seat For Two arrives and really sets the tone for the rest of the album as a fun, uplifting and at times calming experience. A couple of wonderful tracks for the instrumental enthusiasts are Transfusion and Can't Buy Me Love, then some beautiful duets await in Where It All Began and For Your Love. Sato bids us farewell with another showcase of his underrated singing skills in I Sing For You, thus concluding another fantastic record from one of City Pop's masters of style mixing.

- A1. Aqua
- A2. Seat For Two
- A3. Love Is The Answer
- A4. Transfusion
- A5. Where It All Began
- B1. For Your Love
- B2. My Friend
- B3. Picnic
- B4. Can't Buy Me Love
- B5. I Sing For You

僕の中の少年 (The Boy In Me)

Left: Yamashita as seen on the back of The Boy In Me with a contemplative expression.
Center: The ethereal cover of The Boy In Me presents this album as being a more introspective work from Yamashita.
Right: The single release for Get Back In Love and First Luck.

The creation of 1986's Pocket Music was a tale of man versus machine as Tatsuro Yamashita was forced to grapple with advancements in recording technology upending his music making process, but his next album would be an introspective project that reflected Yamashita's life at the time. The album's name, The Boy In Me, was first thought of after the birth of Yamashita's daughter back in 1984, an event which naturally had an unprecedented effect on his life perspective. The theme of his own youth passing by and being inherited by his child was especially present in songs like the titular B4, although some saw his now distant juvenescence as a negative. Yamashita's plan was to make this album more conceptual to show off his talent as an artist, but the staff at his record label wanted a return to the classic 'resort music' he had become famous with in albums like For You, a creative conflict which Yamashita attributed to being past his prime. While he was only 34 years old Yamashita still resigned himself to believing he could only have a hit song if it was an age-appropriate sentimental ballad, which he sought to do by releasing Get Back In Love as a single. The label was hesitant since catchy pop tunes typically did better as singles, but Yamashita's intuition was proven right when Get Back In Love became his first top ten hit in years. The track's success helped to boost Yamashita's confidence, but he also viewed its inclusion in the album as a determining factor for The Boy In Me's financial success. Its beautiful lyrics and potent chorus made it one of the album's most memorable songs, but many of its other tracks had unconventional origin stories as well. A1 or New Tokyo Rhapsody was inspired by the people depicted in early Showa era movies and comparisons between Yamashita's life and theirs, and its lyrics about the lights of the city and summer ending are some of the album's most stereotypically City Pop feeling. The abstract lyrics for Luminescence came together when Yamashita spotted the constellation Orion while walking his dog late at night, despite the time of year being totally wrong for Orion to make an appearance, while B3 draws from Yamashita's own experience singing hymns at his Catholic kindergarten. B3 was also originally meant to be reminiscent of a song Yamashita recorded off the radio while in the United States, although he never actually knew the songs name and even lost the tape, making it a true mystery as to what song it actually was. The conflicting concepts of youth, experience, fame and decline all worked together to create The Boy In Me, an album which once again achieved the number one weekly ranking for Yamashita.

Artist:
Tatsuro Yamashita

Release:
October 19, 1988

Label:
Moon Records

Track List:

A1. 新・東京ラプソディー (New Tokyo Rhapsody)

A2. Get Back In Love

A3. The Girl In White

A4. Sea Song "Naomi"

A5. 踊ろよ、フィッシュ (Dance, Fish)

B1. Luminescence

B2. Marmalade Goodbye

B3. 蒼氓 (Blue Sky)

B4. 僕の中の少年 (The Boy In Me)

Thanks Giving

Left: The single for Love Is A Work Of The Heart and Water Silk Road made a very strong impression with its Sci-fi art by Yasufumi Fujii.
Center: The cover of Thanks Giving lures you in with the majestic serenity of an island at night.
Right: A picture of Momoko Kikuchi from inside the album, who avoided having her face on any of RA MU's singles or the cover of Thanks Giving.

Artist:
RA MU

Release:
September 14, 1988

Label:
Vap

Track List:

A1. Rainy Night Lady

A2. Carnaval

A3. 夏と秋のGood-Luck
(Summer and Autumn Good Luck)

A4. Two Years After

A5. 少年は天使を殺す
(The Boy Kills The Angel)

B1. One And Only

B2. Tokyo野蛮人

B3. 片想い同盟

B4. Late Night Heartache

B5. Love Talk

Momoko Kikuchi had been on top of the entertainment industry ever since her debut back in 1984, achieving numerous number one charting singles and albums while also appearing in TV shows and movies for most of her teenage life. Fame is a fickle friend however, as while she maintained widespread popularity the sales for her music began gradually slipping as she became an adult. This coincided with Kikuchi's growing desire to break away from her image as an idol who relied on music written by others and instead take her career in a new direction, one where she was more directly involved. In February of 1988 Kikuchi surprisingly announced the upcoming debut single by RA MU, a new band which starred herself as the lead vocalist. RA MU was introduced as a rock group, although they also took influence from various styles like R&B and funk while keeping Kikuchi's trademark soft singing to create something quite different from her solo work. Initial reception to the announcement and their first single were both mixed, partially due to Kikuchi's sudden distancing from her idol image, but also because RA MU's style just wasn't very appealing to a wider demographic. A common complaint was that Kikuchi's voice didn't suit the music, but their R&B inspired sound was also an acquired taste that hadn't yet gone mainstream in Japan. The band saw middling success with their first three singles, all of which at least ranked in the Oricon chart's weekly top ten, however these weren't very impressive numbers considering Kikuchi's star-power. Some even believed RA MU was meant to be a "comic band" releasing music as a joke, which obviously wasn't true, but it did show the disconnect between the band's vision and how they were perceived. Their debut album Thanks Giving did finally come out in September of 1988 and received a lukewarm reception, peaking at fifth place on the charts. The struggling band finally dissolved in 1989 so Kikuchi could continue advancing her acting career, leaving RA MU as an odd piece of musical history. As interest in City Pop was eventually revitalized more people began to look back on RA MU and found out just how underrated this short-lived band truly was. Thanks Giving and RA MU's handful of singles are all incredibly well-made tracks that appeal to fans of City Pop and also reflect just how creative the group really was. The R&B heard throughout pairs very well with all the other eighties styles that made City Pop so fun, so don't be surprised if you end up grooving to tracks like A5 and B2 or singing along with Rainy Night Lady. RA MU sadly didn't get the recognition they deserved back in 1988, but they managed to eventually find their audience in the 21st century.

Artist: Miho Nakayama
Release: July 11, 1988
Label: King Records

Mind Game

Just a few months after the killer album Catch The Nite released Miho Nakayama was back at it again with Mind Game. While her previous album was largely composed by Toshiki Kadomatsu Mind Game instead brought on a greater variety of songwriters, including the likes of Cindy and Toshinobu Kubota on the B-side. Their influence gives that side's tracks a unique hip-hop spin, something which was steadily becoming more popular as the nineties drew ever closer. Cindy provided a beautiful ballad in I Know which stands out among the album's fast paced tunes, two of which Toshinobu Kubota wrote with Velvet Hammer and Take It Easy. The A-side also has its own excellent selection of tunes like Strange Parade and Why Not? with its memorable saxophone segments, but Mind Game is a fun experience all around.

A1. Into The Crowd
A2. Strange Parade
A3. Why Not?
A4. Cat Walk
A5. Moonlight Sexy Dance
A6. In The Morning
B1. Mind Game
B2. I Know
B3. Velvet Hammer
B4. Take It Easy
B5. Long Distance To Heaven
B6. Husky Town

Artist: Toshinobu Kubota
Release: September 30, 1988
Label: CBS/Sony

Such A Funky Thang!

Such A Funky Thang! has one of the year's most memorable titles and covers, especially when you realize the 'A' consists of two dinosaurs fighting each other. Kubota's music has since been influenced by New Jack Swing, an R&B sub-genre with an emphasis on rhythm that heavily utilized synthesizers and sound samplers. Some prominent New Jack Swing artists included Bobby Brown and Janet Jackson, and although the genre died down in the 1990s it has had a modern resurgence via artists like Bruno Mars. Such A Funky Thang! is a thick album with thirteen R&B inspired tunes to check out including the lighthearted Dance If You Want It and Indigo Waltz, another of Kubota's signature slow jams. Apparently the third time was the charm for Kubota as Such A Funky Thang! was his first album to reach number one on the weekly rankings.

1. Dance If You Want It
2. High Roller
3. Love Reborn
4. Yo Bro!
5. Merry Merry Miracle
6. Such A Funky Thang! 〜隕石が落ちた日〜
7. Gone, Gone, Gone
8. すべての山に登れ
9. Boxer
10. Indigo Waltz
11. Drunkard Terry
12. 覚えていた夢
13. Such A Funky Thang! -Reprise-

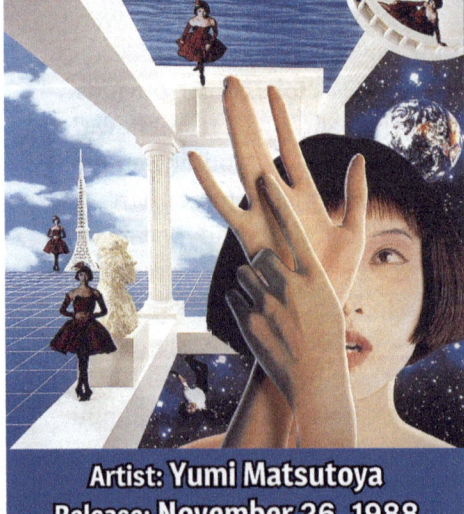

Artist: Yumi Matsutoya
Release: November 26, 1988
Label: Express

Delight Slight Light Kiss

Yumi Matsutoya's Delight Slight Light Kiss has a real tongue-twister of a title, but it was a major financial success even by her own lofty standards. It was the fastest Japanese album to reach over a million units sold and it was also the first of Matsutoya's records to close out the year with the overall number one ranking. Both loyal fans and those discovering Matsutoya for the first time must've loved this album as it delivers on the romantic pop songs she's so well-known for. There are cutesy tracks like A5 which details a date at somebody's hometown as well as the tragic tales heard in A3, a song about a joint birthday and farewell party. Of course, the album keeps things inspirational via B1, a track about a lover's spat which is left on a happy ending, while B4 explores a dedicated romance as a woman drives through a snowstorm to be with her special somebody.

A1. リフレインが叫んでる
A2. Nobody Else
A3. ふってあげる
A4. 誕生日おめでとう
A5. Home Town へようこそ
B1. とこしえに Good Night (夜明けの色)
B2. 恋は No-Return
B3. 幸せはあなたへの復讐
B4. 吹雪の中を
B5. September Blue Moon

Candee

Artist: Candee
Release: December 25, 1988
Label: Taurus

The sole album by the titular artist Candee, who is sometimes credited under her real name Nozomi Takao. It features a diverse roster of composers, notably a few members of Casiopea, as well as Kenjiro Sakiya and a few Western artists. Candee really struts her vocal talents in this album which has a heavy soul flavor, especially for songs such as A5 and B1, but other influences like disco are prominent too. Although she never released another album Candee continued to work as a backing vocalist for Tatsuro Yamashita, who kept her as a mainstay for his live performances from 1991 onwards. She sadly passed away in 1998 because of complications involving acute hepatitis, a loss which greatly affected Tatsuro Yamashita, who was so distressed by her death he even contemplated putting an end to his concerts.

- A1. For You
- A2. あなたがいるから ～Your Love Keeps Gettin' Better
- A3. Baby Tonight
- A4. Break Out
- A5. Just Lovin' You
- B1. Heaven's Where We Are
- B2. Here For You
- B3. I'm Glad
- B4. Water Front Express
- B5. Family

Dark Crystal

Artist: Minako Yoshida
Release: April 10, 1989
Label: Sohbi

Minako Yoshida finally returned in 1989 with Dark Crystal, her first 'normal' studio album since 1982's Light'n Up. When offered a contract with the Sohbi label Yoshida signed on without even really knowing what kind of record she wanted to make, instead opting to just figure it out as she went along, a real testament to her easygoing personality. Yoshida quickly got back into the groove of being a producer and had full control over the album's direction, although during this time she faced a terrible tragedy. Yoshida's husband Aki Ikuta, a fellow musician who worked on some of her albums, had passed away in 1988, a loss which greatly affected the music of Dark Crystal. Yoshida would later reflect that her mental state gave the album "a rigid and machinelike quality," but fans of her older music are still likely to enjoy Dark Crystal's lengthy tracks and powerful atmosphere.

1. Starbow
2. Gifted
3. Tang Tang
4. Crystal
5. Heat Wave
6. Nosferatu
7. 凪
8. December Rain

Shambara

Artist: Shambara
Release: July 20, 1989
Label: Polydor, Gargoyle

The sole album by the eponymous Shambara, a short-lived band which starred some City Pop greats. The group featured a killer vocal duo consisting of Yurie Kokubu and Kaoru Akimoto, with Akimoto being an especially welcome member considering her limited appearances in City Pop. Tetsuo Sakurai and Akira Jimbo of Casiopea were also involved and their expertise in genre fusion was well used in Shambara. The album has all sorts of styles that it plays around with, especially City Pop's close companions like rock, electronic and soul. The opening On The Earth really shows how guitarist Nozomi Furukawa can rock out, and you'll be blown away by the wild vocals on track 2. That energy keeps up throughout the whole album with many memorable tunes like Solid Dance and Delicious Lover, so you can never go wrong giving Shambara a listen.

1. On The Earth
2. 恋の瞬間 ～Can't Stop My Love
3. Take Me Higher
4. Solid Dance
5. Lovin' You
6. Delicious Lover
7. Monochrome
8. Aquariumの都会
9. Hurry Up To You
10. In The Universe

Hide 'n' Seek

Artist: Miho Nakayama
Release: September 5, 1989
Label: King Records

The Showa era may be over now, but that doesn't mean we can't get some of the period's icons together for another fun musical romp starring Miho Nakayama. You can enjoy some R&B influence in the first four tracks, all of which were composed by Cindy, who was just a year away from releasing her magnum opus Angel Touch. Cindy's presence here is especially appreciated considering her relatively sparse appearances, but Nakayama herself also composed a few tracks like the incredibly moving Endless My First Love. Then there's B1 and B2 from Anri, two fun pop tracks which inject you with some intoxicating energy and really demonstrates how far she's come as a songwriter and. The final track is a renewed version of a Toshiki Kadomatsu classic, You're My Only Shinin' Star from his debut album Sea Breeze, which is given a beautiful cover to finish up Hide'n' Seek.

A1. Party Down
A2. Hide 'N' Seek
A3. Destiny
A4. Naked Cruising
A5. Endless My First Love
B1. Virgin Eyes (Edit Version)
B2. Stardust Lovers
B3. Island Blue
B4. Split Love
B5. You're My Only Shinin' Star

Time The Motion

Artist: Kahoru Kohiruimaki
Release: November 11, 1989
Label: TDK Records, Paisley Park

Kahoru Kohiruimaki's Time The Motion surprisingly features a few songs from an internationally beloved music legend. The late Prince was the composer and producer for the tracks Mind Bells and Bliss, plus the album was even co-published under his Paisley Park label. Fans of Prince's music will feel right at home with these songs, as his signature style of soul and funk with a dash of electronic sound is shown off well here. While those two tracks are the album's most interesting there's a bunch of other exciting pop tunes to enjoy, like the energetic Wild Generation or Dreamer, a song which is constantly shaking things up to keep you listening. Synth-pop superfans might be into track 8 and the eponymous Time The Motion, but the album has enough variety to satisfy a wide audience.

1. Wild Generation
2. Dreamer (Long Version)
3. いい子を抱いて眠り名よ
4. In The Rain
5. Mind Bells
6. Bliss
7. Everything's All Right
8. アスファルトの帰り道
9. Time The Motion
10. リバーサイドパーク
11. Silent Blue

Love Wars

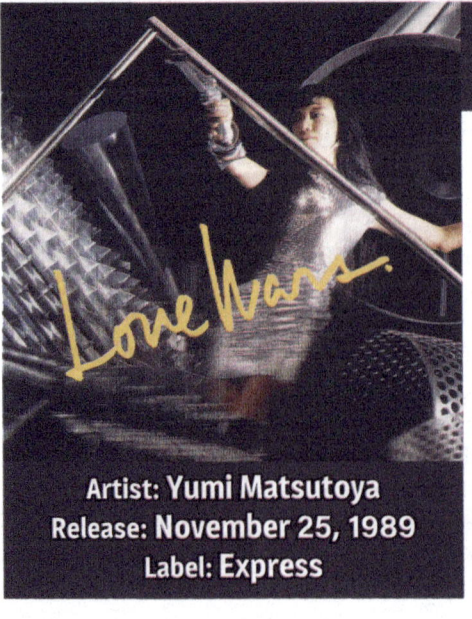

Artist: Yumi Matsutoya
Release: November 25, 1989
Label: Express

Love Wars was released amidst the peak of Yumi Matsutoya's popularity, which happened to coincide with the pinnacle of the Japanese bubble economy. As another glimpse into the capitalist wonderland of 1980s Japan the album was intensely promoted with ads on television and radio, and you could even spot posters in train stations, so the general public was definitely aware of this upcoming release. Among the album's musical offerings are Wanderers, a personal favorite of Yumi Matsutoya's which describes a romantic motorcycle ride, and A4, the exact kind of emotional ballad that made Matsutoya such a titan in the music world. We close out on another beautifully romantic tune, Anniversary, one of her most popular tracks. Love Wars was a stunning success for Matsutoya and achieved the number one ranking for the entire year.

A1. Valentine's Radio
A2. Wanderers
A3. Love Wars
A4. 心ほどいて
A5. Up Town は灯ともし頃
B1. トランキライザー
B2. ホームワーク
B3. 届かないセレナーデ
B4. Good-bye Goes By
B5. Anniversary

1990 & 1991, The Lost Decade

All good things must end eventually, and in City Pop's case the genre essentially met its demise at the turn of the decade. The Japanese economic bubble finally popped and totally collapsed the value of stocks and other assets, bringing Japan into the stagnant 1990s, otherwise known as the Lost Decade. This in turn put an end to the life of leisure City Pop was synonymous with, and City Pop itself soon followed, as many of the genre's artists moved on from the style or just retired after 1991. This makes 1991 this a good place to mark as the unofficial 'end' of the genre, or at least when its mainstream popularity declined substantially. It's not all bad though, as these final two years were full of great albums which blurred the line between eighties and nineties music. Cindy released her beloved album Angel Touch, a flash of City Pop brilliance in the new decade, while Carlos Toshiki & Omega Tribe left us with Natsuko, their final album as a band before Carlos went solo. Other genre mainstays like Anri and Taeko Ohnuki just kept making their fantastic music and continued to experiment with new approaches, while Tatsuro Yamashita gave us another exceptionally high-quality album with Artisan. Toshiki Kadomatsu created the instrumental delight Legacy Of You and All Is Vanity, but we also have releases from familiar names such as Junko Ohashi, Yumi Matsutoya and Yurie Kokubu to look forward to. Sadly, 1991 was a year of farewells for some of the most acclaimed City Pop artists, namely Momoko Kikuchi and Meiko Nakahara, who both released their final original albums this year. It's time to say goodbye to City Pop, at least for a few decades.

Haruomi Hosono

Haruomi Hosono's impact on Japanese music (including City Pop) is so far-reaching it's actually difficult to comprehend. A truly brilliant artist, we may never see another musician with such a diverse skillset ever again.

Now that we're at the very end of the City Pop journey it feels appropriate to discuss one of the men who started it all, Haruomi Hosono. It's not an overstatement to say that Hosono is among the most influential musicians of the 20th century, especially considering his work uniquely extends far beyond just one genre. Hosono was a pioneer of folk rock in Japan and was quite noteworthy for combining rock music with Japanese lyrics, which was a surprisingly contentious topic among purists, who believed it was only rock music if it was sung in English. His debut album, the fantastic Hosono House from 1973, continued to buck trends as it was unlike anything else in the market at the time. Hosono's unconventional blending of genres from across the world became a defining trait of his works, but his various bands were also impactful in their own unique ways. The psychedelic rock group Apryl Fool preceded his solo debut by more than a decade, and the New Music band Happy End pushed a distinctly Western sound into the Japanese music industry. Then there was Tin Pan Alley, the members of which all contributed to City Pop's development enormously through performances, arrangements and compositions on some of the genre's greatest albums. His work with electronic music in Yellow Magic Orchestra was also pivotal for expanding the popularity of synth-pop in Japan, another foundational piece of the City Pop formula which many artists began to specialize in. Beyond his innovations which directly affected City Pop, Hosono continued to make music of all kinds ranging from the highly experimental to the traditional, and his creativity hasn't slowed down even a little despite being over seventy years old. Haruomi Hosono's legacy in Japanese music is unprecedented, and it's very possible that without him City Pop wouldn't have become the genre we know and love today.

City Pop's Decline

The music industry and consumer interest can be quite volatile, as you never know when a genre or style is here to stay or if it's merely a passing trend, but City Pop's downfall is directly tied to the climate it was created in. City Pop had a killer run in the mainstream, especially in the 1980s when the Japanese economy was really hot and the music matched the optimistic tone of the decade, but that economic bubble had to burst at some point. City Pop essentially met its end in 1990 when the Japanese stock market crashed, the value of the yen weakened drastically and property values in Tokyo plummeted. This was the beginning of The Lost Decades, a period of economic stagnation which has lasted far beyond the 1990s and continues to haunt Japan even today. The economic struggles Japanese people faced in the 1990s were sadly antithetical to City Pop, a genre with fun and often luxurious themes which thrived in the bubble economy of the 1980s. A Japanese salaryman with an imploding stock portfolio who might lose his job probably wasn't in the mood for an album about tropical vacations, all-night parties, or any other now retroactively idealistic and unaffordable concepts. Those themes suddenly came across as painful reminders of better times, as opposed to the nostalgic reflection of positivity we view them as now, although those same concepts were probably getting kind of tiresome anyways. Regardless of the economic situation, many of City Pop's artists had been singing about thematically similar things for a while now, so consumers probably weren't getting their minds blown by the latest single exploring the paradox of urban loneliness, or an album cover featuring a guy on the beach. Some artists were much more guilty of treading old ground than others, and the genre obviously covered a wide range of topics, but it was difficult to shake that image when most of City Pop's hit tracks revolved around a handful of similar ideas. City Pop also began losing ground to new styles which had more youth appeal, most notably J-pop, the modern form of Japanese pop music which is still enormously popular in its native land and abroad. By the 1990s City Pop had existed for around fifteen years and held on to its mainstream popularity for a solid decade, more than enough time for a new generation to emerge with totally different taste, as well as a different outlook on life. The more cynical attitude of 1990s Japan was the perfect environment for artists and consumers who were drawn to edgier themes, and genres such as rock or hip-hop were perfect outlets for Japan's new teenagers and young adults. Bands like B'z, L'Arc-en-Ciel and Zard were massively popular in the 1990s and 2000s thanks to their seamless blending of modern pop and rock, the exact kind of sounds that decade's consumers were looking for. The music was safe enough to be commercially viable, as those bands are still among Japan's most successful music acts of all time, but it had just enough bite to satisfy an audience that was a little more edgy. As for many of City Pop's most prominent artists, they simply moved on with their careers and adapted to modern sensibilities, often fitting in with the developing J-pop genre. Despite their efforts very few of them ever reached or surpassed their sales from the 1980s, while other artists like Meiko Nakahara and Miki Matsubara simply stopped making new music altogether. If the story ended here, it would be a sad, albeit natural conclusion to the story of City Pop. It was a genre rooted in the modernity of a certain time period, one which had simply run its course and became a reminder of better times, although in 1991 it was likely too soon to feel a true sense of nostalgia for those days.

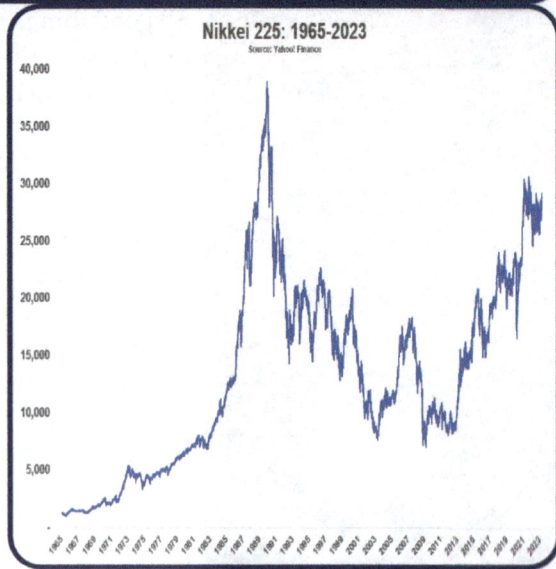

Top: Eek, a graph! This shows the extreme overvaluation of the Japanese Nikkei stock index during the 1980s, and its precipitous collapse in the 1990s. The Japanese stock market has struggled to return to those illustrious 1980s numbers after numerous setbacks like the 2008 financial crisis and the effects Covid had on the global economy. The previous all-time high average of 38,957.44 from 1989 was finally surpassed in 2024, an event which took 35 years.

Bottom: B'z consists of members Koshi Inaba (left) and Takahiro "Tak" Matsumoto (right). They're the most successful music artists in Japanese history, selling more than 100 million records.

Let's Fall In Love Again

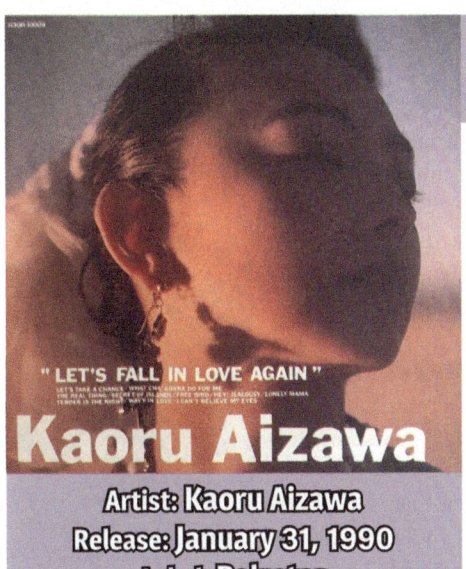

Artist: Kaoru Aizawa
Release: January 31, 1990
Label: Polystar

Kaoru Aizawa was among the final 'one album wonders' to grace City Pop, but she did give us a fantastic showing for this sole project. Let's Fall In Love Again was created with a diverse group of songwriters, including a handful of Westerners, but for City Pop fans the two names that will stick out are Ichiro Hada and Kazuhito Murata. Hada lights the album up by crafting many of its most energetic tracks, such as Free Bird (no relation to the Lynyrd Skynyrd song) which has a crisp electronic sound emblematic of the 1990s era switch to digital audio. You can catch little bits of nearly every genre that often found its way into City Pop like synth-pop and soul during the album's runtime, but its many ballads like Tender Is The Night are especially noteworthy. Little information exists about Aizawa's activities after this album, as she doesn't appear to be credited on any work past this release.

1. Let's Take A Chance
2. What Cha' Gonna Do For Me
3. The Real Thing
4. Secret Of Islands
5. Free Bird
6. Hey! Jealousy
7. Lonely Mama
8. Tender Is The Night
9. Wavy In Love
10. I Can't Believe My Eyes

Self Portrait

Artist: Junichi Inagaki
Release: April 4, 1990
Label: Fun House

Junichi Inagaki was keeping the City Pop spirit going even this late in the genre's lifespan, and the music within Self Portrait doesn't feel far removed from his past work. That obviously means to expect more of Inagaki's signature pop tunes such as Shine On Me, a nice light opening for the album. Ballads which really tug at your heartstrings were always Inagaki's strongest suit, and there's plenty of those to enjoy here. Track 2 or 1969 Unrequited Love is one such ballad, a track which layers nostalgia upon nostalgia as Inagaki reflects on a girl he was in love with way back in 1969, but those feelings still remained even twenty years later. Akin to City Pop's other artists Inagaki adjusted his formula slightly with future releases to fit in better with the trends of the nineties, but you could always expect a moving performance from him.

1. Shine On Me
2. 1969の片想い
3. 夏が消えてゆく
4. いちばん近い他人
5. 心からオネスティー
6. この空
7. 恋するカレン
8. Yes, She Can
9. The Love Is Too Late

Pagoda

Artist: Junko Ohashi
Release: April 21, 1990
Label: Epic

Pagoda was the final album Junko Ohashi released while being signed to the Epic label, although it was made during a period when amateur bands were extremely popular, leaving more established solo artists like Ohashi in a somewhat unfavorable environment. Ohashi worked extra hard to make Pagoda as good as it could be and give the world more of the excellent pop music she was known for. The styles Ohashi was so associated with like funk and soul are still thriving here while her vocals sound extra clean thanks to it originally being a CD only release, although in 2024 Pagoda was put on vinyl for the first time. Junko Ohashi continued to release music throughout the 1990s and into the 2000s, with her final album Terra 3 coming out in 2019. She sadly passed away due to cancer in 2023, but she'll always be remembered as one of City Pop's first and most brilliant stars.

1. 時のバザール
2. Tokyo Calling
3. 微笑みの向こう側
4. 朝焼けに消えて
5. Snow Fall
6. The Power Of City
7. バラードにして
8. 彼女のApril Morning
9. You Can Love Someone

New Moon

Artist: Taeko Ohnuki
Release: June 21, 1990
Label: Midi Inc.

It's time for one more album with Taeko Ohnuki, New Moon, a fantastic capstone for her artistic development throughout the City Pop years. The album has traces of DNA from every era of her music, ranging from her early masterpieces to the to the more stylistically traditional music heard in A Slice of Life. The synth-pop she became so acclaimed for is also alive and well, but it's less prominent overall compared to some of her past work. New Moon's instrumentals are absolutely gorgeous, and the songs have an overall classy and soothing vibe, which is only complemented by Ohnuki's wonderful singing. Fans of Ohnuki's music have a lot to enjoy in New Moon, regardless of which era of hers is your favorite. Ohnuki stayed very active in the following decades and frequently released new music, but her past albums also became extremely popular when City Pop was rediscovered.

1. 泳ぐ人
2. Call My Heart
3. We Are One Circle
4. 楽園をはなれて
5. 風の吹く街 -Hello New Days-
6. My Bravery
7. 花咲くころに
8. 水の上の一日 -A Day On The Water-
9. Little Hope
10. 地球ファミリーのテーマ -The Wind Of My Heart-
11. 花・ひらく夢

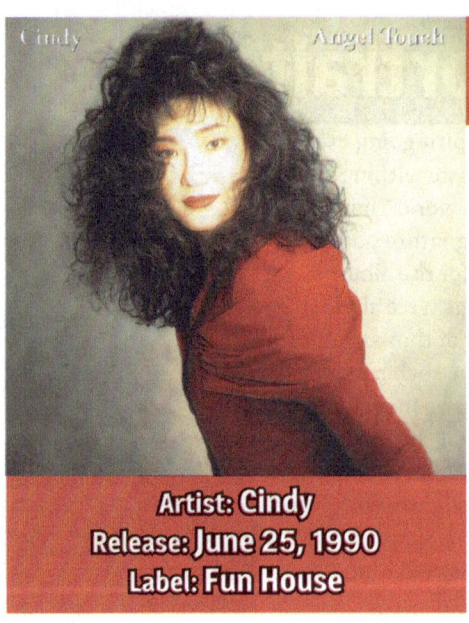

Angel Touch

Artist: Cindy
Release: June 25, 1990
Label: Fun House

Cindy returned four years after her debut album Love Life with Angel Touch, which might just be the most beloved record from City Pop's twilight years. Her talent with romantic and soulful ballads has only improved since Love Life and the album uniquely utilizes elements of R&B, which you can hear in track 2 and Candle Light. Track 7 or Believing In Ourselves is Cindy's most popular song, a gem of a tune that reminds you of what makes City Pop so special. The instrumentals act as a perfect companion to Cindy's stunning singing, which especially shines during the chorus. The final track Must Be Lucky concludes the album just right with its abundant record scratches and a groove that feels caught between the eighties and nineties in the best way possible, although that also applies to Angel Touch as a whole.

1. Surprise
2. せつなくて
3. Destiny
4. When Tomorrow Comes
5. 天使の気持ち
6. Special Ever Happened
7. 私達を信じていて
8. Candle Light
9. Fall In Love
10. When Tomorrow Comes (Reprise)
11. Must Be Lucky 〜愛の国へ〜

Legacy Of You

Artist: Toshiki Kadomatsu
Release: July 25, 1990
Label: Om

The instrumental experiment Toshiki Kadomatsu concocted with 1987's Sea Is A Lady was succeeded by Legacy Of You, another all-instrumental fusion joyride. The album shares a similar theme as Sea Is A Lady with an emphasis on music that evokes a cool beachside atmosphere, or the hipper urban side of City Pop that Kadomatsu was also quite familiar with. Kadomatsu also really capitalized on the CD's vastly increased storage space, as most of the tracks are over six minutes long, with some like Premonition of Summer being nearly ten minutes. Fortunately, Legacy Of You combines quality and quantity as each track is a memorable demonstration of Kadomatsu's eternal talent at setting a certain mood. Some highlights include track 5 with its incredible guitar play and the frantic fun of track 11, but every song here is a winner in its own right.

1. Premonition Of Summer (Kiyomi) - Suma (Midori)
2. 飛翔 (Sayuri)
3. At Canal St Club (Misako)
4. 流氷 (Yuriko)
5. Mystical Night Love (Chisato's Dream)
6. Tsugaru (Keiko)
7. Stress By ストレス (Chisato M.)
8. Twilight River (Yukari)
9. Daylight Of Alamoana (Yuko)
10. NH-CA's Struttin' (Crossing At Airport) (Sanae)
11. Parasail (at Ramada Beach) (Reiko)
12. Sato

Natsuko

Artist: Carlos Toshiki & Omega Tribe
Release: July 25, 1990
Label: Warner Bros. Records

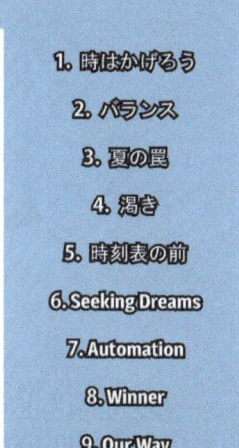

After almost half a decade of Omega Tribe being led by Carlos Toshiki the band once again split up, right at the tail-end of City Pop's history. Creative differences and Carlos's desire for a solo career were responsible for the split, but luckily Natsuko was a fond farewell for this version of the band with many songs from Carlos, as well as bandmates Joey McCoy and Toshitsugu Nishihara, but there's also a surprise appearance here from Yumi Matsutoya. The first track on the album was one of her compositions and it was also the only time the two musical forces crossed paths, making it a special treat for City Pop fans. Natsuko is an underrated album full of the cool urban tunes Omega Tribe became so famous for, but it's also one of their more experimental albums with tracks that feel out of left field and represent a band giving it their all for one last production.

1. 時はかげろう
2. バランス
3. 夏の罠
4. 渇き
5. 時刻表の前
6. Seeking Dreams
7. Automation
8. Winner
9. Our Way
10. 君に逢えない月曜日

Silent Moon

Artist: Yurie Kokubu
Release: September 21, 1990
Label: Air Records

Yurie Kokubu is here to give us another memorable melting pot of an album in Silent Moon. It's also an all-star production from the end of City Pop's lifespan, as you can catch Kaoru Akimoto and even Minako Yoshida as lyricists. The record utilizes City Pop ingredients ranging from classics such as soul, to newer influences like R&B to make for some fun and memorable tunes. You can boogie down to more classically City Pop songs like track 5 and Moment Of Summer or enjoy its plentiful moving ballads like I Love You. After this Kokubu continued to release albums throughout the 1990s and into the 2000s, and in 1996 she began writing Christian music. Since then her music has mostly been gospel focused, and she's done work turning hymns into songs that are more digestible for a Japanese audience.

1. Silent Moon
2. One More Chance
3. Saturday Nite
4. 遠い夜明け
5. 私にだけForever
6. I Love You
7. It's A Destiny
8. Moment Of Summer
9. It's A Party
10. It's Hard To Say Good-Bye ～さよならは愛の言葉～
11. Whisperin'
12. I Love You (English Version)

Gazer

Artist: Minako Yoshida
Release: October 25, 1990
Label: Sohbi

Minako Yoshida's previous project Dark Crystal had a very "hard" sound due to it being largely created using computers, but she wanted her next record Gazer to be comparatively softer. Gazer still has many intense tracks, but you can certainly hear the lighter approach she was taking in songs such as Starlet and track 5, which has a nice funky edge to it. As you'd expect from Yoshida all of the tracks here are quite long and really suck you into the experience she designed. Gazer is another one of Yoshida's nineties albums which isn't as well-known, but it's still recommended for fans of her past work. Yoshida went on another hiatus after Gazer before returning in 1995 for Extreme Beauty, and every few years after that we were blessed with another one of her soulful creations. City Pop owes a lot to Minako Yoshida for being one of the style's foundational artists with an approach unlike anybody else's.

1. Warning
2. Gazer
3. 友達
4. Starlet
5. 愛してる?
6. Silencer
7. 時間をみつめて
8. 午後の恋人
9. Corona

L'arc~en~ciel

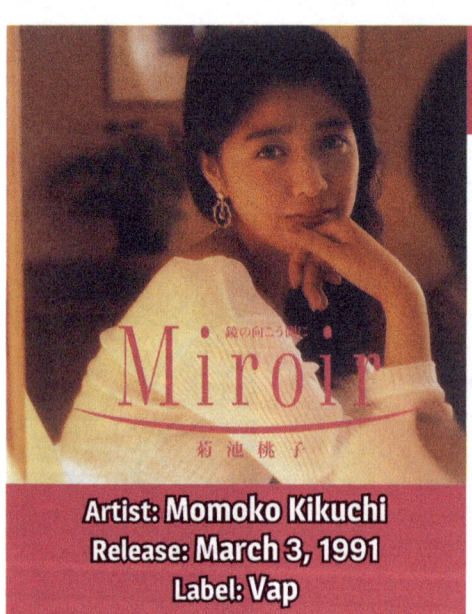

Artist: Keiko Utsumi
Release: January 25, 1991
Label: Polydor

Keiko Utsumi's L'arc~en~ciel was created with help from a couple of City Pop veterans including Masayuki Kishi and Fujimaru Yoshino who both composed some songs, as well as Shigeru Suzuki who gave us a real throwback by arranging half of the album's tracks. The other half was then arranged by the late Hiroshi Shinkawa, another important figure in City Pop's history who contributed to numerous albums. L'arc~en~ciel still has a lot of that eighties City Pop DNA mixed in, something very evident through tracks like 2, 8 and 9 which all have that disco/synth-pop blend the decade was so associated with. Utsumi's performances on these energetic pop tunes are great, but many of the album's more soulful songs are also quite moving, especially track 5 which is one of the main draws here.

1. 空に虹が浮かんでも
2. ランチ・タイム物語（ストーリー）
3. 抱きしめて～シュールな恋
4. 春の花束（ブーケ）
5. オーロラの見える時～ワン・サイド・ラヴ
6. 去年の恋人
7. 寒い夜
8. イリュージョンの都会（まち）
9. プリファレンス
10. 風が通り過ぎた午後

Miroir

Artist: Momoko Kikuchi
Release: March 3, 1991
Label: Vap

Miroir was surprisingly Momoko Kikuchi's last album until 2014 as she instead pivoted her career to focus on acting. It also stands out as being the first of her albums which wasn't fully composed by Tetsuji Hayashi and instead used a variety of songwriters such as Etsuko Yamakawa. Naturally that Hayashi sound Kikuchi was so associated with has largely faded in favor of a more typical pop style. The instrumentals here are especially beautiful and pair very nicely with Kikuchi's soft singing, making it a worthwhile album for those who dig her unique voice. Although she ceased recording new music Kikuchi did continue to act in movies and TV shows and appearing as a regular guest on talk shows. Since then, Kikuchi has lived a fulfilling life as a mother, acquired a Master's Degree and worked as an advocate for disabled children.

1. ガール・フレンド
2. 今日は100度目のケンカ
3. ドリーム・ボードが出る夜に
4. 窓
5. 愛・未来
6. 恋人たちの地平線
7. きっと待ってる
8. ハロー・ミスター・マンデイ
9. 恋をして……
10. 五月の雨
11. 鏡

Fire & Snow

Artist: EPO
Release: March 9, 1991
Label: Virgin

EPO's Fire & Snow was a unique attempt at breaking away from the City Pop sound she had been developing since the beginning of her career. The album instead focuses on electronic house music, which is more subdued than the energetic synth-pop these artists became so familiar with. Fire & Snow also received an international release in July of the same year which has different tracklist and order, seemingly to try and capitalize on the popularity of house music in foreign markets. EPO's career in music afterwards was similar to many of her City Pop peers, who also modulated their style to be more like modern J-pop. While that's pretty normal for City Pop artists EPO broke the mold by also becoming a licensed hypnotherapist, so if you've got any lingering trauma that needs dealing with maybe book a session with her sometime.

1. Overture
2. 恋のひとひら
3. 素足
4. When 2 R In Love
5. You Are My Fantasy
6. Love Lost Forever
7. 星になれなかった涙
8. Sa Sa
9. Why
10. So Long
11. 赤い川

Artist: Anri
Release: June 1, 1991
Label: For Life Records

Neutral

1991 may have been the year when City Pop 'ended', but it was business as usual for Anri, who released an interesting fusion of natural theming with dance-centric tracks in Neutral. Many of the songs here get great usage out of sound effects that pull you into environments like the serene jungle, but many more entrance you with funky instrumentals that are caught between the end of the 1980s and start of the 1990s. It's that fascinating middle ground where the musical identity of one decade is slowly leaving while another is developing, ironically paralleling the same situation that City Pop was born into. Anri stayed very active after Neutral and kept up a steady release schedule well into the 21st century, maintaining a position as one of the most relevant City Pop figures well past the genre's prime.

1. Back To The Basic
2. プライベート Sold Out
3. イヤリング ~Tears Of Two~
4. Rap Up Africa
5. Voice Of My Heart
6. Oasis
7. Sweet Emotions
8. 9月のHometownから
9. 愛はCommunication
10. St. Imagination
11. 嘘ならやさしく

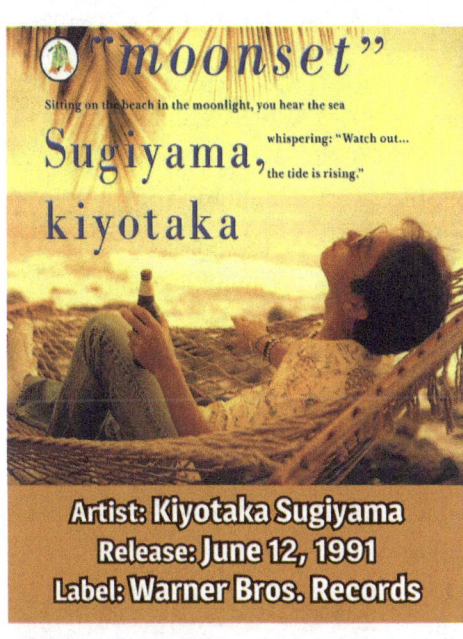

Artist: Kiyotaka Sugiyama
Release: June 12, 1991
Label: Warner Bros. Records

Moonset

Are you ready for one more beach side romp with Kiyotaka Sugiyama? Luckily this is far from his last summertime themed album, since Sugiyama was rather committed to the City Pop vibe and aesthetic when many of his fellow artists were moving past it. Moonset is just one example of Sugiyama keeping the vibe alive in the 1990s, so if you enjoyed some of his prior chill pop rock experiences you'll probably like the tunes here. Some highlights are track 2 with its cool instrumentals and track 3, an impactful ballad. Later on there's Yellow Ribbon, which is sure to lighten your mood, then the titular Moonset wraps things up on a high note. Sugiyama was one of the most consistent artists after City Pop's downfall and usually released an album every year or so. He has also performed live with the members of his former band Omega Tribe, as if the 1980s never left us.

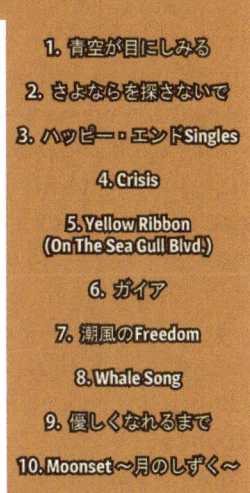

1. 青空が目にしみる
2. さよならを探さないで
3. ハッピー・エンドSingles
4. Crisis
5. Yellow Ribbon (On The Sea Gull Blvd.)
6. ガイア
7. 潮風のFreedom
8. Whale Song
9. 優しくなれるまで
10. Moonset~月のしずく~

Artist: Toshiki Kadomatsu
Release: July 3, 1991
Label: Om

All Is Vanity

The dramatic cover of All Is Vanity might seem to imply a major shift in Kadomatsu's style as the new decade gets going, but it's still quite like the City Pop he had been making for years now. The classically Kadomatsu elements are all here, especially his favorite topics like romance and ocean related hijinks, so you may be surprised by how well it fits in with his earlier albums. The rest of the 90s were a mixed bag for Kadomatsu fans, as he announced a hiatus from singing in 1993 and mainly worked as a producer for other artists. Kadomatsu did finally return in 1999 and has kept up a steady release and live performance schedule ever since. In the 2010s Kadomatsu's music became much more akin to his City Pop classics and he even remade some classic albums such as Sea Breeze. In 2025 he released Forgotten Shores, an excellent example of how good modern City Pop can be.

1. 夜離(よが)れ ~You're Leaving My Heart
2. 夏回帰 ~Summer Days
3. 海 ~The Sea
4. この駅から… ~Station
5. ただ一度だけ ~If Only Once
6. All Is Vanity
7. Up Town Girl
8. Distance
9. 彷徨 ~Stray At Night
10. What Is Woman

Artisan

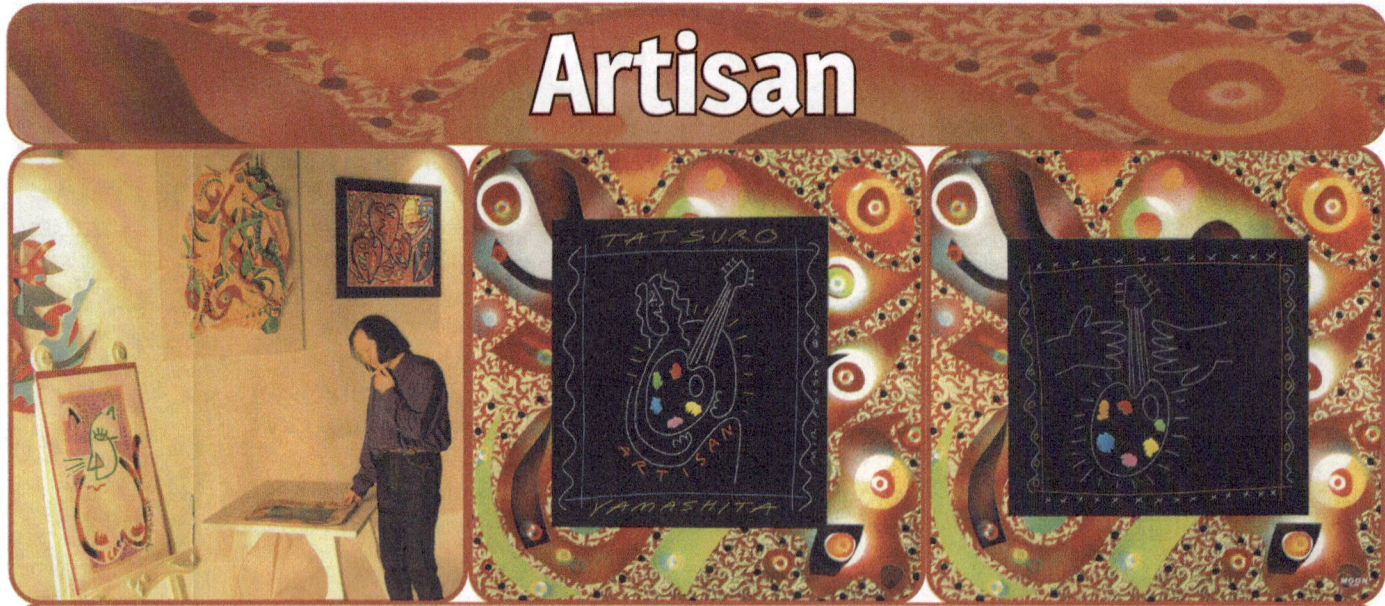

Left: Tatsuro Yamashita gazing upon some artwork, like he's some sort of artisan or something. Center: The unconventional art from Andre Miripolsky continues Yamashita's trend of having radically different covers for all of his albums. The same artist was also commissioned for his 1989 live album Joy. Right: Some imagery of the cute guitar/palette hybrid seen on the cover.

After releasing the more conceptually experimental albums Pocket Music and The Boy In Me Tatsuro Yamashita sought to make another one of his classic singer-songwriter albums in Artisan. The title of Artisan, or somebody who physically crafts things with their hands, was chosen to intentionally differentiate Yamashita from the many other musicians who had taken to calling themselves 'artists' during this time, a trend which he seemingly found to be slightly pompous. Yamashita stood true to the album's title and forged it almost by himself, as he was the composer and lyricist for almost every song while also playing the majority of the instruments, while a few tracks such as 4 and 6 are entirely Yamashita's performances. The album's opening track Child of Atom is also one of its most interesting as it was dedicated to the late Osamu Tezuka, a foundational figure in Japanese manga who created series such as Astro Boy. Artisan was nearly complete when Yamashita heard about Tezuka's passing, but he managed to grind it out and finished the song extremely close to the album's deadline. The eternal City Pop theme of youth returned in track 2 or Goodbye Summer Days, a song inspired by some of Yamashita's past memories of a poolside date being interrupted by bad weather. Goodbye Summer Days also tied back to the themes of maturation heard in The Boy In Me, as the track was written when Yamashita's daughter was about to become an elementary schooler, a huge milestone for any parent. You would think with a song with a name like Tokyo's A Lonely Town would be another brainchild of 1980s City Pop, but the song was actually a cover of the song New York's A Lonely Town by The Trade Winds, an American band that was active during the 1960s. Yamashita was heavily inspired by American music from the 1950s and 60s, so hearing a cover of one of those songs here just feels right, plus the lyrics are largely the same as the original with just a few alterations to make it more appropriate to the Tokyo setting. Artisan is an album that feels like the accumulation of Yamashita's total life experience and his interest in music from all over the world, while it's also a fitting 'finale' to City Pop's time in the spotlight. It combines many of the styles Yamashita and his fellow City Pop musicians were so influenced by while also taking full advantage of the digital tools he previously struggled with while creating Pocket Music. Following this Yamashita's release schedule slowed down substantially, but his music continued to maintain a certain level of popularity, so much so that Yamashita has continued to reign as the most successful solo male artist in Japanese music history. Hail to the king!

Artist:
Tatsuro Yamashita

Release:
June 18, 1991

Label:
Moon Records

Track List:

1. アトムの子
(Child of Atom)

2. さよなら夏の日
(Goodbye, Summer Days)

3. ターナーの汽罐車
(Turner's Steam Locomotive)

4. 片想い
(Unrequited Love)

5. Tokyo's A Lonely Town

6. 飛遊人 —Human—
(Flying Tourists —Human—)

7. Splendor

8. Mighty Smile
(魔法の微笑み)

9. "Queen Of Hype" Blues

10. Endless Game

11. Groovin'

Self Jam

Self Jam
Hiroshi Sato

Artist: Hiroshi Sato
Release: July 21, 1991
Label: Alfa

Hiroshi Sato's Self Jam is one of the more obscure releases in his discography, but even in his least popular albums Sato never disappoints. Self Jam will feel familiar to those who have listened to his previous albums, as it's filled with the synth-pop he had been mastering since the 1970s. A handful of the album's best include track 2, an impressive display of Sato's range, and the chill journey of track 6. While most of the songs here are Sato's compositions, we do have a delightful cover of the hit Beatles song Come Together which puts a fun spin on this classic track. Hiroshi Sato sadly passed away in 2012 due to an aneurysm, but his contributions to Japanese music and especially City Pop were monumental. He will especially be remembered as a pioneer of electronic music, a genre blending mastermind and one of the style's most illustrious keyboardists.

1. Self Jam Beat
2. 君の風が動いた
3. Sign Of My Life
4. Come Together
5. Just An Angel
6. 水彩の蒼影
7. Passenger
8. I Pray For You
9. 星の国
10. 地球

State Of Amber

Artist: Junko Yagami
Release: July 21, 1991
Label: NEC Avenue

Junko Yagami closed out the City Pop years with State of Amber, an album which put heavy emphasis on synth-pop and R&B, two influences which several of her contemporaries were also taking a liking to. In the 1990s Yagami and her husband John J. Stanley moved to the United States to raise a family, although she still regularly released albums and traveled to Japan for concerts. The September 11 terrorist attacks in 2001 had a traumatic impact on Yagami and caused her to develop a fear of flying and being away from her children, leaving 1997's So Amazing as her final album for 15 years. It would ultimately be the devastating 2011 Tohoku Earthquake which inspired Yagami to not live in fear anymore and instead resume her activities as a singer. She has since released numerous albums and performs for concerts regularly.

1. Prologue
2. Cosmopolitan
3. Quiet Storm
4. Lonely Heart
5. Seasons Change 〜帰らざる季節〜
6. State Of Amber
7. Living In Brazil
8. Love Shot
9. Touch The Sun 〜太陽に向かう島〜
10. Stairway To Heaven
11. Talk Radio
12. Epilogue

Don't Be Afraid

Cindy "Don't be afraid"

Artist: Cindy
Release: August 25, 1991
Label: Fun House

Cindy's third and final album amplifies the 90s R&B sound that was developing in last year's Angel Touch to make something that feels quite distant from City Pop but is still very enjoyable for fans of her previous records. Many of the tracks were unsurprisingly written by Western composers which gives them an authentic American sound, plus you can even enjoy a cover of the Rolling Stones song Satisfaction. Don't Be Afraid's fast paced and funky tunes like Tell Me Why and So Long Goodbye pair nicely with its plentiful moving ballads, which Cindy excels with as you'd expect. Cindy was less active in music for the rest of the 1990s, but she did write some songs for Miho Nakayama and other artists before sadly passing away due to cancer in 2001. The three albums she gave us are all fantastic pieces of City Pop history and her presence is greatly missed.

1. Tell Me Why
2. So Long, Goodbye
3. In The Rain
4. Rose Color
5. Live So Fast
6. Barely Friends
7. Little Love
8. 愛がさびしい時〜ドント・ビー・アフレイド
9. Satisfaction

On The Planet

Meiko Nakahara's final album happened to release in 1991, the same year when several other genre icons like Momoko Kikuchi moved on to other things. Fortunately, Nakahara did close out her career with quite an album as On The Planet packs in all of the styles her music took inspiration from. The ever reliable Latin influence which Nakahara differentiated herself with is still thriving in tracks 2 and 8, but On The Planet still provides ways to get your electronic groove on. Everlasting Love and Special Feeling 102 are some of the album's smoothest and most romantic tunes, and for a more blood-pumping time you can turn on ABCD! or Imitation Lover. While it is a great last album from Nakahara, she did leave show business and essentially vanish not long after its release, leaving an enduring mystery for her fans.

Artist: Meiko Nakahara
Release: October 30, 1991
Label: Eastworld

1. サバンナの夢
2. To The Storm -嵐の中へ-
3. Everlasting Love
4. Miami Dream -Don't Be Shy-
5. ABCD!
6. Special Feeling 102
7. Fairly Tale
8. サンバ・セニョリータ
9. Imitation Lover
10. Fortune -銀の月夜のハネムーン-

Dawn Purple

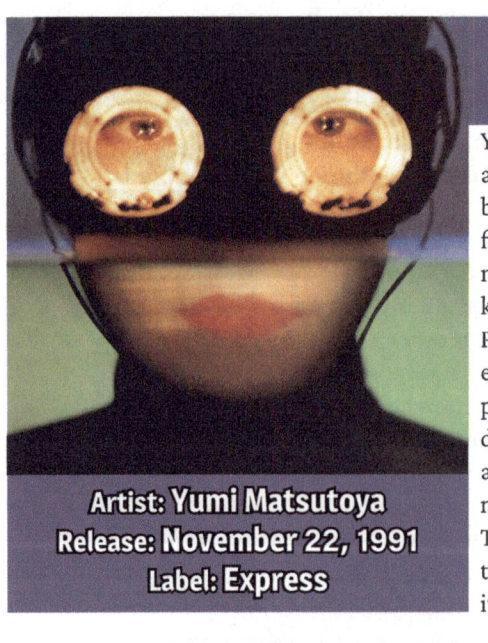

Yumi Matsutoya's Dawn Purple fits in nicely with her other albums that have unusual name origins, but this one might be the oddest yet. Purple was chosen as it's apparently the first color babies see while developing in the womb, although most sources say that it's actually the color red, so who knows. It was also referencing the 1991 eruption of Mount Pinatubo in the Philippines, one of the deadliest volcanic eruptions of the 20th century, as there was reportedly a dark purple sky following the event. While Matsutoya's popularity did decline slightly after the bubble years she still held strong as one of Japan's most popular artists, creating dozens of number one ranking albums and selling over 42 million units. This makes her by far the most successful City Pop artist of all time, a suitable achievement considering she was there when it all started.

Artist: Yumi Matsutoya
Release: November 22, 1991
Label: Express

1. Happy Birthday To You ～ヴィーナスの誕生
2. 情熱に届かない ～Don't Let Me Go
3. 遠雷
4. Dawn Purple
5. インカの花嫁
6. 千一夜物語
7. 誰かがあなたを探してる
8. タイム リミット
9. サンド キャッスル
10. 9月の蝉しぐれ

Emotional - 右側のハートたちへ

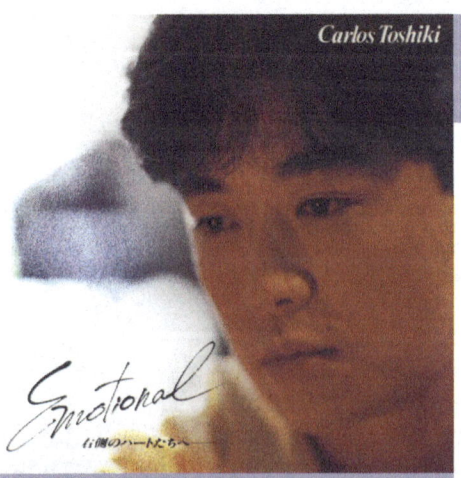

Carlos Toshiki has repeated history by splitting from Omega Tribe in favor of a solo career, just as Kiyotaka Sugiyama did. The journey that Carlos undertook was more complicated than Sugiyama's though, as he made three solo albums before rebranding to Toshiki Takahashi and releasing the album Shake It Down in 1995. After suffering from a disc herniation Carlos returned to his native Brazil without any intentions of making more music and instead inherited his parent's restaurant. The story takes an unexpected turn after this point as Carlos went back to university, specialized in biotechnology and began working for a company that produced a heat-resistant garlic seed which was able to grow more easily in Brazil. In more recent times Carlos has even returned to performing live alongside the band B-EDGE, which included a handful of his former bandmates from the 1980s.

Artist: Carlos Toshiki
Release: December 21, 1991
Label: Warner Music Japan

1. 夜明けまで Borderless
2. Never Rains On Saturday
3. Believe Me
4. Brazil Nights
5. Sophisticated Lady
6. 孤独な天使
7. November Beach
8. Sonho de Um Menino
9. 右側のハート

What Happened After?

It would be inaccurate to say that City Pop simply ended after 1991, since no musical style ever truly vanishes, but its popularity and prevalence did fade substantially. As mentioned previously many of the genre's stars did well adapting to changing musical sensibilities. Most started making music akin to J-Pop or kept modeling their music after some of City Pop's progenitors like adult-oriented rock and soul. While some City Pop artists kept up a steady release schedule after 1991, others slowed down their output substantially. The husband and wife duo of Tatsuro Yamashita and Mariya Takeuchi were far less active in the nineties, with Takeuchi only releasing 1992's Quiet Life, while Yamashita's fans had to wait until 1998 for Cozy. Others were more active, notably Anri who found one of the best balances between a consistent schedule and changing up her music to fit with what a nineties audience was interested in. While Yumi Mastutoya held on to immense popularity she was no longer the untouchable industry titan she had been in the late 1980s. Newer artists supplanted her as the hottest topics in music, and by the mid-90s even she seemed quite nostalgic for the good old days. In 1996 she hosted Yumi Arai The Concert With Old Friends, a throwback to her early career where she performed several of her original hit songs alongside some iconic musicians. Many of City Pop's veterans like Shigeru Suzuki, Jake H. Concepcion and her husband Masataka Matsutoya all appeared here, giving longtime fans of her music a real treat. Then there were the few who asked "if it ain't broke, why fix it?" like Kiyotaka Sugiyama, who was always there to offer a fine CD full of pop rock ballads with a tropical flavor in those trying times. It became rarer and rarer to find music which really matched City Pop's vibe in the 1990s, especially from newer artists, but if you look hard enough, you'll find them. Naoko Gushima made her debut in 1996 with Miss. G, an album which felt a lot like a throwback to those cool 1970s classics. Gushima's music used a concoction of soul, pop and funk which was very reminiscent of City Pop, something which is especially noticeable with her popular track Candy, a song which is incredibly easy to mistake for an early 1980s tune. Then in 2003 the group Ryusenkei released their album City Music, an unmistakable love letter to the sort of music which was so popular twenty years ago. The album felt exactly like a modern attempt at the genre which had defined the previous generation, as you can enjoy plenty of City Pop's familiar inspirations like jazz and soul throughout, but the song titles and lyrics were truly brilliant. Songs like Tokyo Coaster and Airport '80 showed a deep admiration for the genre, while also being perhaps just a little tongue-in-cheek about City Pop's tropes. The album was even made available on the genre-appropriate vinyl in extremely limited quantities, an especially cool idea considering this was in 2004, and at the time vinyl records were absolutely not a hot commodity. Ryusenkei continued releasing albums throughout the 2000s, including their iconic record Tokyo Sniper from 2006, another perfect throwback to the golden age of City Pop. Its tracks are stuffed with lyrics about driving along the bustling city and dancing the night away, subjects which probably felt like overdone cliches by the end of the 1980s, but those same themes were now quite enticing to a 2000s audience. While the 1990s and 2000s were lacking in artists whose music could really be called City Pop, it was clear that the long dormant genre did have a charm which many music fans gravitated towards. Few could have expected that City Pop would see a massive resurgence in popularity, but even fewer would've guessed how many of these new fans wouldn't even be Japanese.

Top: Yumi Arai The Concert With Old Friends is available on CD for anyone to enjoy this nostalgic piece of history. The backing band for this concert is full of names you'd see on the credits list for a 1970s City Pop album, which is very fitting.
Center: Naoko Gushima's Miss G and other albums helped fill the City Pop drought of the 1990s, but we wouldn't see a real revival of the style until the following decades.
Bottom: Ryusenkei's Tokyo Sniper from 2006 was one of the first albums to revisit the tropes of City Pop in the modern day. The band went dormant after 2009's Natural Woman, but they returned in 2020 and have released four new albums since.

The Rediscovery

City Pop was largely a thing of the past in the 1990s and 2000s, but the style's many records were still desirable to a certain niche. One of the first upticks in interest for City Pop came about thanks to music enthusiasts known as "crate diggers" who delighted in scouring through old records to find whatever suited their taste. Collectors like DJ Chintam were especially fond of tunes from the seventies and eighties which had a Western flavor, such as the work from Tatsuro Yamashita, among others. The various albums and songs these crate diggers scoured would then be used for live DJ performances or put into playlists with similar music and shared online. Thanks to the Internet these songs were able to be more easily accessed by listeners from across the globe, and throughout the 2000s and especially 2010s City Pop slowly caught people's attention via YouTube and other websites. The first international communities that formed around City Pop's revival were naturally small, and many of them centered around remixing pre-existing songs into new subgenres such as Vaporwave and Future Funk. In the latter half of the 2010s these remixes started gaining traction online, with one of the most popular being Night Tempo's 2016 remix of Mariya Takeuchi's classic song Plastic Love. Night Tempo's remix was faster and more energetic than the original tune, greatly contrasting the original's somber atmosphere, but still capturing the essence of what made it such a well-designed song. The remix's remastered version from 2020 currently sits at nearly eight million views, but it was just one of many uploads and remixes which introduced people to the world of City Pop. Perhaps as a side-effect of Night Tempo's remix the original Plastic Love also became extraordinarily popular, and much of City Pop's renewed interest can be traced back to an upload of the song from a user known as Plastic Lover. Their upload of the track stood out thanks to its enticing thumbnail; a black and white photo of Mariya Takeuchi. This picture was originally taken by Alan Levenson and used for the single release of her song Sweetest Music, not Plastic Love, but the mismatch worked in attracting viewership either way. The monochrome picture of Takeuchi turning around and smiling was like an irresistible invitation to join her in the 1980s for a while, playing in to the nostalgia that's so inherent to City Pop. The combination of the excellent song and alluring visuals made this upload of Plastic Love increase in popularity exponentially and it eventually reached over sixty million views, although it has since been removed from the platform. YouTube users seemingly couldn't escape Takeuchi's smile, but the viewership on Plastic Love also trickled down to other City Pop tracks. YouTube's algorithm then suggested more videos to users that were similar to other City Pop videos they've already watched, and soon enough their feeds were flooded with these oddly nostalgic songs. The long-forgotten genre of City Pop surprisingly became a global phenomenon with millions of new listeners, and the trend continued to gain traction with other viral events like Miki Matsubara's Midnight Door/Stay With Me exploding in popularity in 2020. The genre's various artists and record labels have also unsurprisingly enjoyed the genre's newfound profitability, leading to many albums being put on digital platforms like Spotify for the first time ever. Fans of physical media were also delighted when these retro albums were reprinted in their original vinyl format for the first time in decades, and compilation albums like the Pacific Breeze series have been fantastic samplers for some of the genre's slickest tunes. The nostalgic songs of City Pop continue to fascinate listeners half a century later, but its story of decline and rebirth is as unforgettable as the music itself.

Top: South Korean DJ Night Tempo is one of the most prolific Future Funk artists, a subgenre which remixes City Pop tunes and often makes them even more energetic than before. In recent years he has even done official remixes of these classic tracks in his Showa Groove series.
Center: This monochrome photo of Mariya Takeuchi taken by Alan Levenson is the definitive City Pop image, one which captured the hearts of so many unsuspecting YouTube users and introduced millions to the genre.
Bottom: The Pacific Breeze series of compilation records made by Light In The Attic Records feature some splendid song choices from many of the artists covered in this book. The record labels who own the rights to these songs were initially quite confused about why an American company wanted to license obscure seventies and eighties tunes, which is funny considering how popular City Pop eventually became overseas.

References

" 「EPOインタビュー」." 昭和40. Creta Publishing, 2019. 64-67.

" 「MUSICIAN FILE 大貫妙子徹底研究」." Music Steady, Vol. 3, No. 4. 1983. 68-95.

" 「MUSICIAN FILE 杉真理徹底研究」." Music Steady Vol. 3 No. 2. Steady Publishing, 1983. 115-146.

" 「THE STORY OF REMARKABLE "FILE1 佐野元春徹底研究"」." Music Steady Special Edition Vol. 5. Steady Publishing, 1985. 13-56.

" 「大滝詠一 Talks About Niagara Complete Edition」." Record Collectors Special Edition. 2014.

" 「待ってくれた大滝」." New Friends, Old Friends. Asahi Shimbun, 1985.

" 【インタビュー】当山ひとみ、これまでのキャリアを振り返る ." 21 February 2019. barks.jp.

Arcand, Rob and Sam Goldner. "The Guide to Getting Into City Pop, Tokyo's Lush 80s Nightlife Soundtrack." 2019 24 January. Vice.com.

Bassil, Ryan. "An 80s Japanese Track Is the Best Pop Song in the World." 13 June 2018. Vice.com.

BER Staff. "The Japanese Economic Miracle." 26 January 2023. econreview.studentorg.berkeley.edu.

"Beyond the Needle: History of Vinyl Records." n.d. victrola.com.

Blistein, Jon. "City Pop: Why Does the Soundtrack to Tokyo's Tech Boom Still Resonate?" 2 May 2019. Rolling Stone.

Cabitt, Rachel. "The Technicolor Influence of Kayōkyoku Records." 30 October 2024. theartofcoverart.substack.com.

Chandonnet, Henry. "45 years ago, the Walkman changed how we listen to music." 24 December 2024. fastcompany.com.

Daily Shincho Editorial Department. "山下達郎はなぜ「ルージュの伝言」でコーラスをつとめたのか." 15 November 2016. Daily Shincho.

Dwyer, Ciaran. "The amazing history of Yellow Magic Orchestra: Unpacking Japan's most influential electronic music band." 18 April 2022. mixmag.asia.

Entertainment, Oricon. Album Chart-Book Complete Edition: 1970-2005. 2006.

Grey, Aaron. "History of Synth Pop." 8 December 2022. playalonerecords.com.

Hagiwara, Kenta and Manabu Yuasa. "Special Feature "Niagara Triangle Vol.2." Record Collectors Vol.31, No. 4. Music Magazine, Inc, n.d. 70-85.

"Hiroshi Sato Interview Conducted by P-Thugg of Chromeo." 15 October 2022. synthhistory.com.

"http://junko-ohashi.com/disco_album.html." n.d. Junko Ohashi Official Site. 10 December 2023.

http://www.masamichi-sugi.net/biography/index.html. n.d.

https://web.archive.org/web/20081226082219/http://www18.ocn.ne.jp/~hbr/JP1_e.htm. 26 December 2008.

https://www.ameba.jp/profile/general/sonicelove/. n.d.

Impoco, Jim. "Life After the Bubble: How Japan Lost a Decade." 18 October 2008. The New York Times.

Kadomatsu, Toshiki. 角松敏生81-01……Thousand day of yesterdays. Shinko Music, n.d.

KonichiValue Japan. "City Pop: Why is Gen Z Obsessed with 40-Year-Old Japanese Songs?" 25 November 2023. YouTube Video.

—. "Japan's Bubble-Burst: The Party That Wasn't Supposed to End." 11 January 2023. YouTube Video.

Kubota, Taihei. "さまざまな音楽ジャンルを丁寧に教えてくれる誌上講座が開講！ 皆さん、急いでご着席ください!!" 22 March 2007. bounce.com.

—. "第4回――オメガトライブ." 24 June 2009. tower.jp.

Kurimoto, Hitoshi. "シティポップ（再）入門：寺尾聰『Reflections』"奇跡の年"に生まれた名実ともにシティポップの頂点." 7 November 2021. realsound.jp.

Malm, William P. "Japanese music." n.d. www.britannica.com.

Matsunaga, Kiyomi. " 「吉田美奈子"インタヴュー ～都市の光と影を鮮やかに歌い続ける吉田美奈子23年間のあゆみ～"." Record Collectors February Special Issue. 2012. 94-103.

Michael Saba. "Japanese City Pop and the Rise of Future Funk." 13 September 2019. YouTube Video.

Mower, Kelly. "Omega Tribe is a Japanese act from the 80s that has Changed Faces and Forms a Number of Times." 10 May 2019. otaquest.com.

Nielsen, Barry. "The Lost Decade: Lessons From Japan's Real Estate Crisis." 31 August 2024. Harvard Business Review.

Ohnuki, Taeko. "ROMANTIQUE (Liner Notes)." RCA/BMG JAPAN, 2006.
—. "Sunshower (Booklet)." PANAM/CROWN, 2007.

Onuki, Shunji. "Vinyl production finds groove in Japan, thanks to social media." 13 November 2022. asia.nikkei.com.

Paugam, Van. "Interview with the City Pop Godfather: Tetsuji Hayashi." n.d. vanpaugam.com.
—. "The Tragic End & Lasting Appeal of Miki Matsubara." n.d. vanpaugam.com.
—. "What Happened to Takako Mamiya? [Mystery Solved]." n.d. vanpaugam.com.

Piper. "Summer Breeze (Liner Notes)." Yupiteru Records, 1983.

Ponder, Stacie. "No Skips: Takako Mamiya - LOVE TRIP (1982)." 25 August 2023. stacieponder.rocks.

Pope, Vittorio. "Amore, the Japanese record by Alessandra Mussolini." 13 April 2007. orrorea33giri.com.

Sakura Stardust. "This CityPop Artist has been Missing 30 years." 8 January 2022. YouTube Video.
—. "This CityPop Idol Quit to Start a ROCK BAND." 20 April 2024. YouTube Video.

Salazar, J. (2021). Memory Vague: A History Of City Pop [Thesis]. UNIVERSITY OF MASSACHUSETTS AMHERST.

"Sanremo a Live non è la D'Urso: in studio Alessandra Mussolini canta la sua canzone in giapponese." 8 March 2021. today.it.

Sexton, Paul. "'Sukiyaki': Kyu Sakamoto Charms The World." 15 June 2025. www.udiscovermusic.com.

Shibuya, Yoichi. "「インタビュー 吉田美奈子×山下達郎」." CUT April 1995 Special Issue. 1995. 84-91.

Shinchosha Publishing. "『僕の音楽キャリア全部話します』." 2016. 88-89.

SLOW BURN RECORDS TEAM. "A Comprehensive Introduction to Vinyl Records." 29 June 2023. slowburnrecords.com.

Starnes, Sadie Rebecca. "Hosono Haruomi." July 2019. brooklynrail.org.

Takeuchi, Mariya. " Portrait 40th Anniversary Remastered Edition (Liner Notes)." Ariola Japan, 2019.
—. "Miss M (Booklet)." Ariola Japan/Sony Music Labels Inc., 2012.

Tao. "The Shōwa era and how it changed Japan." 27 April 2022. gogonihon.com.

The Editors of Encyclopaedia Britannica. "Pete Seeger." 27 May 1999. Encyclopaedia Britannica.

Wolf, Thomas P. "Hirohito." 2023. www.ebsco.com.

Yamashita, Tatsuro. "Big Wave 30th Anniversary Edition (Commentary)." MOON/WARNER MUSIC JAPAN, 2014.
—. "CIRCUS TOWN (Booklet)." RCA/BMG FUNHOUSE, 2002.
—. "Go Ahead! (Booklet)." RCA/BMG FUNHOUSE, 2002.
—. "It's a Poppin' Time (Booklet)." RCA/BMG FUNHOUSE, 2002.
—. "MOONGLOW (Booklet)." RCA/BMG FUNHOUSE, 2002.
—. "Pocket Music ('91 REMIX) (Insert)." MOON/MMG, 1991.
—. "Spacy (Booklet)." RCA/BMG FUNHOUSE, 2002.

Yuasa, Manabu. "「対談 伊藤銀次×大滝詠一」." Record Collectors, Vol. 25, No. 4. 2006. 54-61.
—. "「特集 シュガー・ベイブ」." Record Collectors, Vol. 24, No. 1. 2006. 42-47.

Zhang, Cat. "Talking to the Anonymous YouTuber and the Photographer Who Helped Mariya Takeuchi's "Plastic Love" Go Viral." 18 May 2021. Pitchfork.com.
—. "The Endless Life Cycle of Japanese City Pop." 24 February 2021. Pitchfork.com.

"山下達郎「クリスマス・イブ」ギネス認定！３０年連続オリコンチャートイン." 25 March 2016. sanspo.com.

Made in the USA
Coppell, TX
05 March 2026

72849100R00109